Unfinished Symphony

Unfinished Symphony

George M. Stirling

Memory Lane

First published in Great Britain by Memory Lane

ISBN 978-1-908515-02-5

Printed and bound by Good News Books Ltd, Ongar, Essex, England.

'Hope is a symphony flowing like a quiet river through every man's life.'

Nai Soon

FOR TWO GHOSTS AND A MEMORY

FOREWORD

An Oriental poppy bloomed in our garden on a dull November day during Remembrance Week. Just one bloom. For some time I had thought of getting my father's book published. It had been tucked away by him for many years. After he died, I found it. We had always swapped plants and seeds, and the Oriental poppy was one such plant. The sight of that one bloom was a wake-up call for me. I felt I was being told what to do. Now at long last, my father's book is published.

The cover of the book has been designed by Leah Foden, great granddaughter of the author.

The back cover photograph shows the author with his three months old great granddaughter Leah, taken fifteen years ago.

Moyna Foden

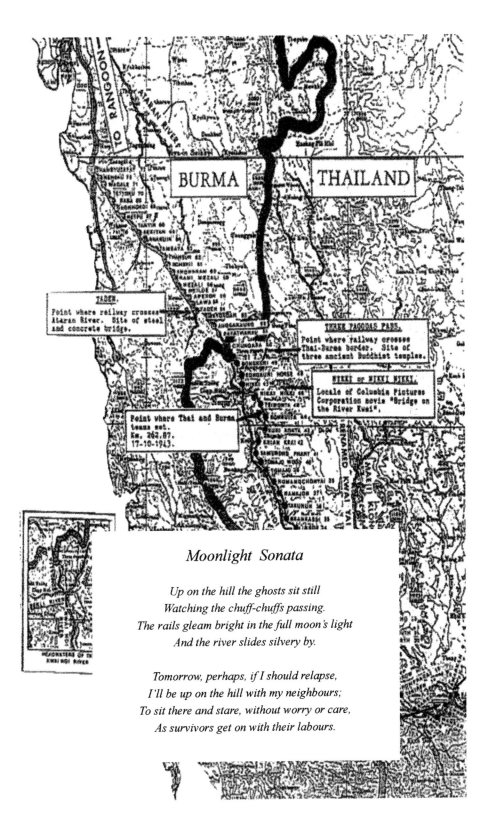

BURMA   THAILAND

TADEN.
Point where railway crosses
Ataran River. Site of steel
and concrete bridge.

THREE PAGODAS PASS.
Point where railway crosses
Thai-Burma border. Site of
three ancient Buddhist temples.

NYKE or NIKKI NYKI.
Locale of Columbia Pictures
Corporation movie "Bridge on
the River Kwai".

Point where Thai and Burma
teams met.
Km. 262.87.
17-10-1943.

Moonlight Sonata

Up on the hill the ghosts sit still
Watching the chuff-chuffs passing.
The rails gleam bright in the full moon's light
And the river slides silvery by.

Tomorrow, perhaps, if I should relapse,
I'll be up on the hill with my neighbours;
To sit there and stare, without worry or care,
As survivors get on with their labours.

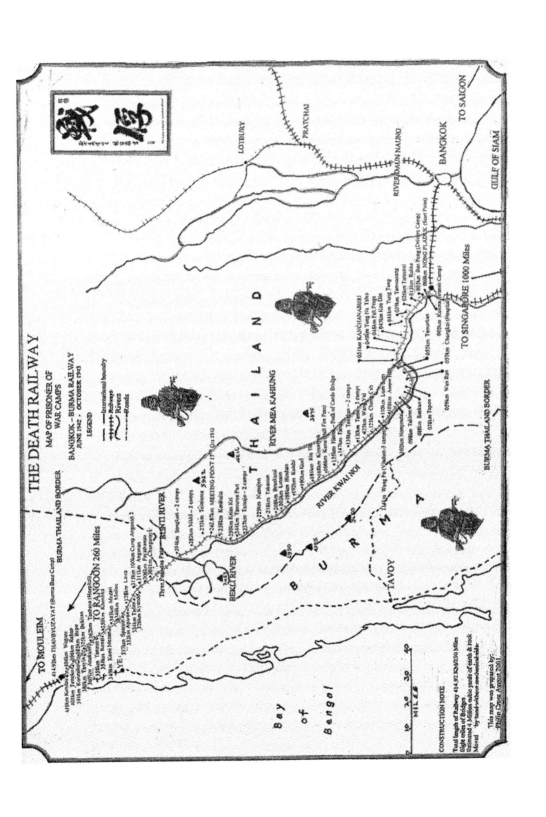

THE DEATH RAILWAY

MAP OF PRISONER OF
WAR CAMPS

BANGKOK – BURMA RAILWAY
JUNE 1942 – OCTOBER 1943

LEGEND

+–+–+ International boundry
       Railway
       Rivers
- - - - Roads

CONSTRUCTION NOTE

Total length of Railway 414.92 KM/250 Miles
Eight miles of Bridges
Estimated 14.1 Million cubic yards of earth & rock
Moved   by hand without mechanical aide

This map was prepared by:
Philip CDees August 2001

TO MOULEIN

BURMA THAILAND BORDER

TO RANGOON 260 Miles

KHWAE RIVER

RUNTI RIVER

Three Pagodas Pass

RIVER KWAI NOI

RIVER MEA KAHUNG

B U R M A

TAVOY

T H A I L A N D

Bay
of
Bengal

MILES
0 10 20 30 40

KANCHANABURI

TO SINGAPORE 1000 Miles

BURMA THAILAND BORDER

BANGKOK

RIVER DAUN NAUNG

LOTBURY

PRATCHAI

TO SAIGON

GULF OF SIAM

NONG PLADEK (Start Point)

CONTENTS

Chapter One: The Japs Take Over 1

Chapter Two: Blood on the Sand 13

Chapter Three: Nai Soon 23

Chapter Four: The Sikhs Get One 39

Chapter Five: Smithy Yearns For a Coconut 49

Chapter Six: Advice in the Afternoon 61

Chapter Seven: The Quick and the Dead 71

Chapter Eight: Jim Sing Drinks a Toast 89

Chapter Nine: Little Flower 99

Chapter Ten: Fukanda: Child of Old Japan 115

Chapter Eleven: 'On Active Service' 125

Chapter Twelve: General Salute Goes to a Tea Party 133

Chapter Thirteen: God Looks Over My Shoulder 145

Chapter Fourteen: Youth in Shoddy Raiment 159

Chapter Fifteen: Moonlight on Changi Creek 171

Chapter Sixteen: Dowdy Tuans 185

Chapter Seventeen: Hail, Jonathan 195

Chapter Eighteen: The Flag Is Waved 209

Chapter Nineteen: Nice People… and Not So Nice People 233

Chapter Twenty: The Calling Hills 235

Chapter Twenty One: 'Old Soldiers Never Die' 249

Chapter Twenty Two: The Monkeys Laugh 263

Chapter Twenty Three: Farewell, Jonathan 277

Chapter Twenty Four: 'Black Joe's Blood is Red' 289

Chapter Twenty Five: Too Many Memories 305

Chapter Twenty Six: Tomorrow Is Never 319

Chapter One

The Japs Take Over

In the evening the doves returned to the flame tree. They came back quietly and without rapture, as if feeling the way. Subdued and not sure of themselves, they poised tentatively on the topmost twig waiting for something to happen. When it didn't, they settled down and began to coo, ignoring the branch that dangled like a broken arm, where a shell from the last barrage had burst. They ignored, too, the gash in the earth below their tree, where the two men had crouched secure in the belief that for the last time the earth would shield them from the fury of the Jap.

Make-believe flame throwers, the splotches of blood glistened in the evening sun, while the doves cooed in sublime indifference and made plans for their future. For them there was no yesterday - only today and tomorrow…

Over the Lion City, and in an ever-spreading arc to the west, the smoke hung in billowing clouds and spirals of greasy black – oil! – while from a dozen other points more plebeian fires hung out their crêpe in mourning for Singapore.

Ever since the great quiet had fallen like a blanket over the valley, I had been sitting beneath the flame tree trying to adjust myself to the new chapter that was opening in my life. One moment there had been noise and strife, and the not improbable chance of death thrown in for good measure. Then, like a door closing to shut out all sound, the quietness had come.

As quickly as that…

Momentarily the door opened to let in the accentuated crash of mortar as the Indian troops across the road, unable yet to believe that there was no longer need for that sort of thing, sent an erratic bomb *whooshing* over to where the Japs were waiting to close in. When the Indians, unnerved perhaps by the noise they were making – noise which for the first time they had really heard – had ceased to torment the air, the silence was complete… as impenetrable as a prison cell, but

1

more pregnant with menace than the noise that had preceded it.

Sitting on an ammo box beneath the flame tree, I lived again that last few minutes of battle as the Japs ripped holes in the velvet carpet of the tennis court, into the raised bank of which Sommers and I had burrowed, with more success than the two who had looked for added protection from the tree that spread above their trench and, as they thought, protected it.

As a negation of the hopes, their blood now lay splashed petal-like beneath the flame tree that had betrayed them; their packs lay twisted like disembowelled animals, spewing their contents onto the stained grass with a pathetic indifference that was echoed by the doves overhead.

On the lip of the blood-stained trench lay a shining mess tin with a jagged hole in its centre. That morning I have given it to Jackson, one of the two who had been in the trench and, looking through the hole, I could see again Jackson's back and the mess the shrapnel had made. 'Is he dead?' I wondered, and left it at that, knowing I was not particularly interested in the answer.

If Jackson was dead his worries were over while mine were just beginning. And that mess tin, it probably would have been useful to me in the new life that was coming in with the dying day. Pity I hadn't kept it for all the benefit Jackson got from it, now lying peacefully and probably dead beneath the flame tree.

Despite my apparent indifference to Jackson's fate, my imagination kept coming back to him, finding it difficult to accept his eclipse at the last moment of the drama that gave Singapore to the Japs and made me a prisoner. His companion in the trench had no place in my speculation; he had died as I helped lift him out of the grave he had dug. That probably accounted for my disinterest in him: once you're dead you no longer rate consideration. At least that had been my experience during the long trek down Malaya.

Pondering that, I wondered whether I would have shrugged Jackson off too, had he been dead. Apparently he wasn't, so he was still entitled to some consideration such as my giving him the mess tin such a short while ago. Now it, like him, was damaged beyond repair.

Then I thought, repentant: Damn the mess tin! Anyone would think it was of more important than Jackson with whom I had only a fleeting relationship. On that reflection I knew my indifference was artificial; it was Jackson I was interested in, not the mess tin through which I kept seeing his back where the shrapnel had clawed into it. I also saw in retrospect the shell with his name on it leave the Jap gun as the curtain was closing to end an era in which Singapore had played but a minor role even though it had been billed as the star attraction in the drama that had just ended.

2

But where was the gun? For some indefinable reason I found it necessary to pinpoint its exact location. On Syme Road where Trek Ling's decrepit fish shop had squatted before the Jap airmen removed it and its assorted stinks from the neighbourhood.

No; that would be too far west and Jackson would not have received his parting salutation from the Japs and my mess tin... Damn the mess tin! I would erase it from my mind. Concentrate on locating the gun that fired the last shot. Bukit Tima roundabout? That was it! So sure was I, and so pleased, I could almost see the gun and count the figures squatting about it, smoking and chattering like a gaggle of debutants at a ball now their mission was complete and Jackson had got a ticket for his repatriation – whatever that meant in the circumstances.

After clearing the village, the Japs would have come tearing out of the rubber pulling the gun. With their usual alacrity and perception they would quickly choose the most advantageous location and open fire. To accomplish what? Hit a flame tree a mile away and blow the backs out of the two men who crouched in its shade while the clock ticked out the last minute before the curtain came down on the drama that was fortress Singapore...

'Damn that tree!' I thought, suddenly resentful; not about the unfortunate Jackson but about Singapore and what its eclipse could mean for my future.

Unlike the doves, I was painfully aware of the new power that reigned in the island and of the blood that made crazy patterns beneath the tree from which they saluted the new twilight that was about to break over Singapore. For them where was no yesterday; only today and tomorrow.

For me, too, there was no yesterday: I had had that. And if the tomorrows came, I did not know if I wanted them...

In me there was the bitterness of defeat and the sense of being let down. I was an ill-used pawn and I felt sore. I wished the battle, such as it had been, had not ended so suddenly – and so tamely. It would have been more digestible had the end come as Sommers and I had planned it. Confident in the belief that the Army would fight to the last in the defence of the city, we had buckled an extra bayonet to our hips. Short Gurkha bayonets they were, and sharp. Nine inches of polished steel. Mine still hung at my bolt with its brightness untarnished and its point, by means of which I had hoped to send so many Japs – relatives of the dead – to worship at Yasukuni, still unblunted.

While the Union Jack over Fort Canning was replaced by the Rising Sun of Japan, and the sun – my sun – chased the shadows out from beneath the flame tree and glistened anew on the blood spots that were a punctuation mark

3

to my reflections, I sat in meditation until a whoosh of flame shooting into the sky and the dull rumbling of an oil tank brought me back to reality.

Above the town, the smoke pillars were trying to unite Japan's new acquisition with the sky but were conversely depleting her war effort by many million gallons of oil.

Watching the smoke, a thought came to me and I gave it utterance: 'You could have saved your bombs. The oil was as good as yours anyway…'

'Just what I was thinking,' came a voice from the other side of the tree. Following it came Sommers' reassuring figure, bedraggled and bleary eyed. 'People do a lot of silly things in war, Mick,' he added as though I didn't know. 'Look at that oil going up. I bet the Japs knew that Singapore would be theirs in a couple of days when they bombed it. Silly buggers! They'll be needing all the oil they can get before this is over…'

'They'll be needing more than oil,' I agreed without conviction, thinking of the rapid advance the Japs had made coming down Malaya, chasing Sommers, me and what was left of the battalion after the flight from Jitra. Now here he was reminding me of episodes I wished to forget.

Leaving that unpleasant reflection, I asked him, coming closer to the cloud that was moving up fast on our now limited horizon:

'What do you think of our chances, John?'

Sommers was inspecting the blood-stained trench reflectively. I waited while he sorted out his answer from among the gory debris.

'Jackson and that other bloke will probably be better off in the long run than we shall, Mick. That's my opinion.'

'Bit decisive,' I retorted, 'but I'll go along with it. Time, the great arbiter, will tell…'

'It's early yet to hazard a guess as to what is going to happen to us as prisoners of war, Mick. To the best of my knowledge, the Japs have not had Europeans as prisoners – certainly not on such a massive scale. I suspect they will react to their new acquisition in one of two ways. Either we shall be given all of the privileges laid down in the Hague Convention or, conversely, the Japs will be so elated by their successes that their normal respect for the British Army will be submerged by their new-found superiority, and we shall suffer accordingly. Frankly, I incline to the latter supposition, Mick.'

'As do I, John. Incidentally, Japan did not sign the Hague Convention. Not that that will matter if they are determined not to abide by it. Come to that, why should they? Today they are lords of the earth – at least this bit of it – and

4

will behave as they choose whether they have signed the Convention or not. After all, it is only another piece of paper and we already know the worth of such mementoes.'

'That's doubly true, Mick, and I suppose there is little we can do about it.'

'No war was ever lost until the last battle, John. Just because we have lost this round, does not mean we have got to sit on our arses and do nothing about it. I'm thinking about the possibility of escape, of getting away from all this chaos. What's your reaction?'

It was not really necessary to put that question to John: I already knew what he would say. But I had to ask him just the same.

'I'm all for it, Mick,' he agreed readily, 'but things are a bit vague at the moment. Why, we don't even know where precisely the Japs are. However, if you think we stand a chance of getting away if we pushed off after dark, I'm willing. Some of the chaps are going to do that, so why shouldn't we…?'

What he said was true. Some of the men were going to attempt a getaway by sea – too obvious a way out that gave little hope for success. The Jap Navy would be on the look-out for any would-be escapees and the chances of a boat remaining undetected were non-existent.

No. If there was a way out, it was not by sea. Our best plan, as I saw it, was to endeavour to get over the Causeway and so into Malaya, a comparatively simple operation provided we knew where the Japs were hiding themselves. They had not yet put in an appearance and I was stymied, not knowing in what force and disposition they were on the island, though I had my own idea about it.

'There's nothing to stop us leaving here, John,' I told Sommers. 'The Japs are apparently feeling self-conscious and not over-anxious to make our acquaintance…'

'For a victorious army, they are certainly keeping well in the background,' he retorted, yawning. 'One would think they'd have been swarming all over the place by now. I know we should if the boot were on the other foot. Perhaps they are giving us a breathing space in which to get used to the idea of no longer being the Great White Tuans of the land… it's about two hours, isn't it?'

'Just about. If you think we stand a chance we'll push off after dark.'

'Suits me, Mick. Got any ideas about how we should proceed? We can't just say 'ta-ta' and walk off into the darkness as though we were going for a pee.' As if to back up his assertion, he strung out against the flame tree, ignoring the blood and what it represented. Sommers was like that: he could cope with most situations matter-of-factly. Cool, that was Sommers; both now and during our close-knit reliance on each other coming down Malaya.

'In my opinion escape by sea is out, John. The Jap navy will have that exit closed tight. I suggest we try the back door. After all, the Japs entered by it and it's still standing open. If we can negotiate the Causeway safely, we'll just head back up Malaya, though I must confess the thought of plodding back through all that rubber and jungle is depressing – and we haven't started yet! There is also the problem of the locals who are not likely to be co-operative now that we no longer are *tuans* but menial POWs.'

'Can't blame the blighters for that, Mick. They've got to play it safe by kow-towing to whoever cracks the whip. At the moment it's not us.' Sommers grinned sardonically. 'The days of the Great White Tuan are over, Mick. The goodwill of the locals will now be extended to their new masters. It was never given to us just because we were British but because we were the masters. You'll see what I mean after the Japs get organised and a few heads start to roll. I may be wrong, of course, but somehow I suspect I am not...'

'I'll go along with that, John. Nevertheless we shall be dependent on the locals for food and water if we do manage to get across the Causeway safely.'

'From there on it's a long way to anywhere, Mick. Thailand, for instance, or possibly Burma.'

'About 700 miles,' I needlessly reminded him. Like me, he had already done the long slog south before the onrushing Japs.

'No need to remind me,' John retorted reflectively. 'My feet are still aching. In the event of us reaching Thailand, if we decide to go that way, the Thais may be a problem as they have thrown in their lot with the Japs, though before international relationships were jumbled they were friendly towards the British, I believe. Obviously the Japs will be pushing on towards Rangoon now they've completed their mopping-up operations here. Personally I believe they won't get there for a lengthy period – if ever they do. Very difficult country to fight your way through.'

'So was Malaya, or at least it should have been,' I retorted irritably. 'Let us hope our lads put up a better show in Burma than we did in Malaya. Otherwise the Japs will be in Rangoon long before we get there if we finally decide to take that route out.'

'If you believe that, Mick, it would be foolhardy to push off without an operational plan. And speaking of plan, we'll need a map of some sort, especially if we do decide to go via Burma. Knowing where you're heading is half the battle when trying to get from A to B in unknown territory.'

'Planning is all very well, John, but all the planning in the world will not safeguard you unless you have a smidgen of luck to go with it. We had that once or twice coming down Malaya, otherwise we would not be standing here speculating about the possibilities of escape when, for all we know, we could become candidates for a firing squad when the Japs decide to come along to claim their prize.'

'If you have any belief in that possibility, Mick, I'm all for pushing off after dark hoping that Lady Luck will guide us safely over the Causeway.'

Somers went back to the flame tree and had another pee as if to relieve the tension.

'That's better,' he said, coming back. 'What do you think, Mick?'

'I haven't had one yet,' I informed him, stringing out against the raised bank of the tennis court. 'I agree; that's better. As to your suggestion that we push off after dark, I'm not in such a tearing hurry to get away. There are a few essentials we shall need before imposing ourselves on Lady Luck.'

'Such as?'

'A compass and, if possible, a couple of revolvers, and that map you mentioned, if we can get it.'

'The officers will have all that gear. I expect it will all be dumped in a heap tomorrow. We'll wait till then…

By now the shadows had lengthened, replacing the sun beneath the flame tree where the short twilight was lingering about the blood-stained trench before venturing out over the pitted tennis court to join the deeper shadows thrown by the big house on the hill.

Settling down beneath the flame tree, John and I let the doves coo us to sleep despite the jollification going on by the campfire the remnants of the battalion had lit. We were not in the mood for a singsong.

The truck came up the road and stopped near a clump of hibiscus, beside which I stood watching John who, in turn, was watching a pile of arms and sundry equipment growing larger by the minute as the men came along in ones and twos to place their weapons on it. Some of the men going through this degrading ritual showed no concern. Others stood by the pile, momentarily undecided.

Watching them and Sommers, I knew what they were thinking: 'I've a damned good mind to smash it against that tree over there, and to hell with orders…' - hadn't I experienced the same rebellious impulse when earlier I stood by the pile of arms waiting to put my rifle into the keeping of the Japs? I had even walked the short distance to the tree, grasping the inverted rifle by the barrel;

then, looking again at the fast-growing heap of weapons, I had thought: 'Cheap heroics, now that the time for heroics is over. What difference will one rifle make? Captain Bell will be getting the wind up if I do that.' This last thought at the vision of the captain on his knees grubbing among the grass for the round I had ejected from my magazine when ordered to unload and place all of my ammunition on the heap that was growing up alongside the weapons.

I remembered the captain's plaintive: 'You should not have done that Stirling,' and my reply, 'I don't suppose the Japs know how many rounds of .303 we've got.' And I hadn't said 'Sir,' and was childishly pleased about that.

Like my liberty, the formality of "siring" was receding further and further into the background of yesterday as the days went past – and this was the second day of our captivity.

Now here were the first of the Japs: two of them in a commandeered British truck – one of the sights I would have to get used to. As they alighted on the road below where Sommers stood up on the bank, I wondered how they would behave, and what they were after. Two three-stars they were. Odd that two lone privates should be the first to venture among us. Probably having a snoop round to see what they could pick up before their officers came along.

At the thought I slid the ring off my finger and dropped it into my pocket, sending my watch in after it. No point in taking chances. A Jap was a Jap, and had no social standing at the moment. This particular watch was not of much value, but it kept good time, and that might be a useful asset.

Or would it? Had time ceased to matter? Was not it standing still, waiting for something to develop? Would not it now be measured by the rising and the setting of the sun, at least for the next six months or so? It would take the British that long to hit back for Singapore. There were the Yanks, too, of course. Pearl Harbor would have upset them – maybe more than Singapore had upset us – and they would be anxious to redress their tarnished pride.

It was reassuring to know that we had not been the only self-centred bigots when the honourable – and despised – Japanese had got annoyed and started their assault on Britain's long-established dominance in the Far East.

But what was going on down on the road?

Leaving their truck alongside which they had been standing, shouting at each other, or so it seemed to me, the two Japs walked across the road and started to climb the bank where John stood watching; then, as another figure intruded itself onto the scene – our platoon sergeant – the Japs altered their line of march and went back to the road.

Along came the sergeant looking unconcerned, but not feeling it. He was

8

just about to forsake the road and so dodge the unwelcome guests, when there came a shout from the Japs as one of them raised an arm shoulder high to waggle his hand, reminiscent of a duck treading water. Not knowing what was expected of him, the sergeant stood undecided until Sommers, who knew the 'come here' sign, shouted:

'They want you, Sergeant. Better find out what they want.'

'Why the hell should I?' the sergeant retorted in his best platoon voice. 'If the buggers want to know something, they can come and ask me; they're only privates.'

'And you are a POW, Sergeant, or have you forgotten?' Sommers reminded him. 'Rank no longer carries any weight.'

'Yeah, I suppose you're right,' the sergeant admitted, glancing at his stripes. 'I reckon I'd be better off without these. The colonel did advise us to watch it.'

To the accompaniment of a great deal of shouting the sergeant approached the two Japs. When one of them grabbed his arm I realised what all the fuss was about.

Tentatively I felt for the watch in my pocket as John drew back so that he was partly screened from the Japs on the road. Listening to their excited chatter as they divested the sergeant of his watch, I realised how difficult it was going to be to heed the advice of our colonel who earlier had said:

'No matter what the degradation the Japanese may inflict on you while we remain prisoners, remember that this day in being compelled to lay down your arms you have suffered the greatest humiliation possible for a British soldier.

'I can only hazard a guess as to how the Japs will treat us, but that there will be many unpleasant incidents is inevitable. Already there have been some in Singapore. Officers and men have been compelled to kneel in the streets and perform other acts of humiliation by the Japanese.

'Naturally you will want to react in the normal manner should any Japanese soldier molest you. Take my advice and do not retaliate. I realise that this will be difficult for you, but retaliation will only make our unhappy situation worse...'

While the sergeant rubbed his cheek where one of the Japs had swiped him because he had not responded quickly enough, the colonel's advice intruded and I was sorry for the sergeant, probably for the first time in our acquaintance; John, too, had profited from the sergeant's discomfiture. As one of the Japs slewed round to give him the 'Come here' sign, he stepped back into cover, leaving the two Japs on the road making hysterical noises. I emulated John, feeling that the colonel had not overstated his warning.

The Japs did not follow us up the bank as I had expected. They climbed back into the lorry and drove off, probably satisfied with their trophy.

John was rubbing his jaw as though it had been he who had been slapped and talking to Captain Bell when I rejoined him. The captain was Officer-in-charge of surrendered arms and apparently he was not relishing his promotion. As I approached I heard John unexpectedly say, for I assumed they were discussing our first incident:

'Stirling and I are thinking about making a break for it, sir. Our intention is to make it over the Causeway and head up Malaya. We are optimistic about our chances of getting to Burma, or possibly somewhere closer to hand, where assistance to get away may be available provided the locals are co-operative…'

'It's a long way to Burma or Thailand, Sommers. At least eight hundred miles, and difficult country, too…'

'We realise that, sir,' I put in, not omitting the 'sir' this time. 'It is essential on that account that we have a compass, and a couple of revolvers, too,' I added, looking at the display laid out at the captain's feet.

'There's plenty of them here,' insinuated John, following my look. At the same time he bent down and negligently picked up a compass which he began to study as though he had never seen one in his life before.

'I'm afraid you can't have any of these,' came the captain's voice like a douche of cold water, and John nearly dropped the compass in astonishment. 'They've been counted.'

'Not by the Japs, surely?' he said, incredulous that such a thing had already happened.

'No,' agreed Captain Bell, 'they haven't shown up yet, except for those two you were telling me about. But we expect them any time now.'

'But surely,' urged John, 'if we took what we want they would not be any the wiser. And,' he added, forestalling the captain's comeback, 'If they are found on us it will be our funeral. Isn't that so, Mick?'

'Of course. We expect to take anything that's coming in the event of the Japs finding us in possession of any of this stuff,' and I waved a hand over the natty looking pistols that not so long ago had graced the hips of Captain Bell and his fellow officers, not to mention a sergeant or two. However, the captain was not impressed by the assurance, or maybe he was thinking of those rounds I had ejected into the grass and which he had been so long in finding.

'I'm sorry,' he said with a finality that was not to be denied, and a formality that was just that, 'but you can't have them. Anyway, there is little possibility

10

of your getting away, and you are better off without them.'

'Isn't that for us to decide?' retorted John, slipping the compass up his sleeve.

'Yes. In the circumstances I suppose it is,' agreed the captain. 'Just the same, I cannot let you have that compass. Put it back...'

Watching John, I could see that he was getting ready to refuse, and to back up his refusal with strong words if necessary. As his throat started to work, I said, 'Let him have it back, John. After all, the Japs will probably find more use for it than we ever did. Come on...'

*****

The house on the hill, Mount Echo, was impressive, fit for a billionaire. It must have been on that account that the officers, forgetting that the war was over and that their temple had come down in the ruins about their ears, decided to have it for their mess. John and I had prior rights to it – at least we felt that way about it for we had been the first to discover its amenities – by right of possession, and were enjoying our first game of billiards as prisoners of war when the eviction order showed up in the person of the R.Q.M.S., who was taking over the house for the officers. Not that we should have minded if we have been allowed to continue with our billiards. There was room for us and the officers, too, but the R.Q. did not think so, so we agreed with him and left – though John did not leave empty-handed as I later found out, and by then it was too late...

Selecting an armful of bedding from the best bedroom, we left the house and went to share the shade beneath a frangipane tree with two gunners who were willing to let us shelter from the sun which, now that it was Japanese, was doing its best to show its disapproval of our continued existence. Unlike us, the gunners were not particularly interested in the heady fragrance of the frangipane, nor in the big house with the billiards table, though, doubtless, they had enjoyed many a game before the Japs altered their mode of passing the time.

Now they lay unheeding and uncomplaining in the shade of the frangipane tree as John and I settled down between their graves to keep them company, but not to stay...

The liquor John had confiscated from the officers' mess waggon tasted clean and smooth on the palate, or possibly it was because we both realised that it probably would be the last we should have for a long time.

How long that was going to be we were not then worried about; also our resentment at being turned out of the big house was momentarily slipping into the limbo of yesterday, which now did not exist, or so I thought.

Mixed with the heady fragrance of the frangipani, the result of John's transgression induced in me a beatific feeling of complete stupefaction as, drowsing and near somnolent, we sat with the gunners and watched the sun throwing the shadows of the big house at us.

Nearer and nearer came the shadows. Inevitably, I thought the bombardment would fall on its target and so bridge the ever-narrowing gap that separated us from the dark stairway leading over the lawn to the ruined gable of the big house where, in all probability, our gunner friends had gone out by the back door. Just before the gap closed I slept, and sleeping, dreamed the most awful dream.

I was standing in the gap of light with one hand pressing against the slant of shadow that was trying to connect with the shadow leaning out from the frangipani tree against which my other hand was shoving in a desperate endeavour to keep the gap from closing. All the while I watched in despair as John and the two gunners fought an Homeric battle for possession of the brandy bottle, which I knew to be empty.

Even in my extremity I realised that was had not been fair to the gunners – or generous. This was the result. John, bottle in hand, was trying to tear himself away from the clutching embrace of the gunners and so escape across the gap.

Chapter Two

Blood on the Sand

As the long column of prisoners moved up the road towards Changi, an ex-British cantonment, I was reminded of a similar scene I had witnessed from the comfort of a cinema seat some time before the Japanese had decided that Asia would be better for a Jap-sponsored Co-Prosperity Sphere and that Singapore rightfully belonged to them. In those days I had marvelled at the spectacle of thousands of Italians trudging across the desert – just as now we were trudging along the road – with here and there a solitary British Tommy to keep them company.

Now we were duplicating the picture but in our case there was a difference: not one guard accompanied the marching column. Nor did I see any Jap troops on the long trek to internment with the exception of two on duty at the cross roads outside the city and these honourable gentlemen were inscrutable in their disinterestedness as we passed by, and might have been two disgruntled Malayans for all the notice they took of us.

By the roadside lay littered the debris of the conflict that had hurricaned for such a short time before blowing itself into a white flag, leaving us stranded and jumbled up with the other litter of war.

A sweet, sickly smell, not unlike decayed frangipani flowers, wafted out from the occasional drain-pipes and wayside ditches. Often in the past this nauseating stink had come to me from some gully or clump of swampy scrub where someone had come to the end of the rainbow and found his pot of gold, empty or otherwise, I did not know…

Singapore, which had received a few scars, mainly from Japan's young eagles, over which a new fungus was quickly spreading like weeds after rain, looked almost empty. From every point floated the victory flags of Japan, put out by a grateful populace anxious to propitiate their new god. Some of the zealots had been over anxious for many of the fried eggs had obviously been cooked in a hurry and were more nearly scrambled than fried.

One old Chinese, in whose shop I had bought silk handkerchiefs a week previously, had been in such a hurry to get his new flag up that he had omitted to pull down the Union Jack which still floated proudly amid a sea of garish and alien emblems of ambition.

As we swung along the streets, those of the populace who had ventured out looked at us with immobile faces and eyes that appeared not to see, and I had the feeling that I was not really there; that I was in the grip of another nightmare and would presently awake to see the pavement abustle with the usual jostling and vociferating crowds who were not usually averse to pause and watch the *tuans* as they marched through the town.

Now the people had not time for us: we had had our little hour. Their sympathy for us was dead, and for a long time would remain so. To them we were bad debtors who were absconding without fulfilling their obligations. And that, I thought, experiencing no resentment at their apparent lack of interest in our fate, was near enough the truth. In allowing the Japs to take over Singapore, inadvertently or otherwise, we had left the Singaporeans to the mercy of their new god.

Should he prove an exacting deity, as no doubt he would, their future might be not all piousness…

*****

At dawn on the third day the fifty thousand-odd British and Colonial troops started to enter the confines of Changi. All that day the straggling columns poured in, and for a fortnight after small bodies of men were still coming out of Singapore.

Changi, the former British military cantonment occupying the greater part of the north-east area of the island, did not fit into my picturisation of what a prisoner of war camp under the Japanese would be like. This pleasant track of land, with its up-to-date barrack blocks and troops' quarters nestling in the hills above the village, made an ideal site for an internment camp.

Out in the Straits the bulk of Paula Ubin and lesser islands showed up darkly against the distant and mist-enveloped Johor, and broke the flat perspective.

Where I had expected the confining influence of barbed wire and an all-round curtailment of personal liberty, there was, in the early days, a complete absence of the former, while the non-appearance of Jap guards in the area allowed us to move about at will for some weeks after coming to Changi. So

14

much so that anyone not knowing the true state of affairs might have mistaken Changi beach for a pleasure resort where thousands of sun-tanned nudes disported themselves from sun up till dusk.

In the interval between the landing of the Japs on the island and our coming, Changi had been deserted, for the garrison had withdrawn before the menace of the enemy thrust for Singapore. The civil population, too, had fled, heaven knows where, and the village lay empty and ransacked – sprawled like an empty corncob athwart the highway. The looters had picked the place clean, some enterprising individual had even gone so far as to break up the watches and clocks in the jeweller's shop into their component parts, and these now lay scattered like blobs of quicksilver about the village streets and on the main road.

In the scramble for billets that ensued as the different regiments poured into the camp, to some of whom it had been home for a number of years previously, I was fortunate in being allotted a small cell-like dwelling, one of a row of six which comprised the kitchen quarters of the erstwhile police station behind which they yawned emptily. Sommers was not so fortunate and had to go with the crowd who were overflowing the barrack blocks, straggling along the hillside.

Our own administration was still in operation, guided from a distance by the dictates of the I.J.A., who evidently were not over curious to see just what sort of a bunch of has-beens they had netted.

The job with first priority was to furnish my billet and to make it as comfortable as circumstances would permit. This I proceeded to do as soon as I was given possession.

Looking over the village I found that there was still meat on its skeleton, and I resolved to make my billet as comfortable as possible, even though I was not contemplating a long stay with my new hosts. My first find was a camp bed in fairly good condition, and with it in my possession I was assured of many a good night's sleep.

The same day two mats from a ransacked shop came to my industrious searching, and these made an admirable covering for the floor. Beneath a pile of rubbish in the same shop, I unearthed a couple of curtains, the smaller of which gave a domesticated look to the little window through which came the smell of the sea, and sometimes the gaze of a too inquisitive neighbour. The large curtain made an ideal sunblind for the door and, though slightly ostentatious in the circumstances, it was a sheer necessity, for it allowed me to leave the door open while still retaining the privacy that was denied to so many others.

At the end of two days' scrounging my billet was completely refurbished, and I was very proud of it – proud and comparatively content.

From a clump of bananas I had unearthed a polished oak table, obviously hidden there by the owner before he evacuated the village or by a looter unable to carry it away. Later, a basket chair, pictures for the walls, including a Kodak enlargement of two children romping hand-in-hand over an English meadow – a subject for future nostalgia, but very pleasant for all that – were added.

Nor was the rehabilitation of my quarters finished with these acquisitions. A lamp, with a plentiful supply of oil, was essential if I were going to spend the evenings in comfort. These I found in a native hut on the beach; also a clock that went when I carried it, losing nothing on that account for time was of little importance. Finally, a collection of books and – Susy Ann. Then last, but by no means least, Fishooks, my cat.

Susy Ann was a caution. Dressed in a purple sarong with a crimson sash tied about her middle, she sat in my basket chair unconcerned and delicately aloof with a smile – a mixture of approbation and faint disillusionment – on her lovely face.

Framed in the raven black of her hair, the perfect oval of her features, milk white with an under-lacing of cream – the cream that forms on the milk before it is turned out of the bottle – was an adornment to any apartment, and added lustre to mine.

But I did not tell her that. She might be a native, admitted, but she was all woman just the same, and I did not want to start housekeeping by spoiling my housekeeper.

Susy Ann was just that, and sometimes, I think, she was grateful for being rescued from the wrecked laundry in which I one day found her sitting in lonely dejection. At least she took it for granted that I should take her into my home for I, too, was alone, and together we might know the blessings of mutual companionship and, perhaps, eventual understanding.

This aloneness of mine was one of the greatest assets of my apartment, which Susy Ann did nothing to disrupt. In the evenings I could sit and read, or write, as the mood took me. Where Sommers and the others across the road had noise and the coming and going of a restless multitude to contend with, I had the quietness and the blessings of a well-ordered household. All due, I might add, to my being in company H.Q. But there it is, obviously, a serpent in every Garden of Eden. There has to be one, for life would be too slipshod an affair without it.

To me one night came the scrawniest kitten I have ever seen. Inside it was the serpent. Catapulting it out of bed to the accompaniment of the most heartrending caterwauling, I found the kitten – a mere morsel of skin and bone – tangled up in a fishing line which sometimes dabbled hopefully in Changi Creek.

In my recollection the line had never held anything more substantial than the smell of fish, but even that was sufficient lure for the hungry waif. Looking for food where there was none, he got a hook firmly embedded in one ear, and a new name – Fishooks.

I think I may safely say that when Fishooks came into my house, peace went out of the window.

Susy Ann did not like cats, and once or twice I came home to find her lying in quiet hysterics on the floor while Fishooks reclined in aloof detachment on the chair. A state of affairs that was most undignified and which, had I possessed less sentiment, would never have arisen.

Usually Fishooks lay at the foot of my bed and did not interfere with my rest. Then, as the tin of milk I had been hoarding against an emergency began to have an effect on his desiccated hide, he took to prowling round in the moonlight, never satisfied and always doing some mischief.

One night he gave me near hysterics – not quiet ones like Susy Ann's – by crawling under my blanket and rubbing against my leg. After a couple of encores of that sort of thing I began to sympathise with my housekeeper and to regret parting with my tin of milk.

Sommers was sceptical of my domestic arrangements when he came to see me. He did not think it right that I should continue to live in splendid isolation with Susy Ann, with whom, he said, my relationship might not be understood in some quarters. But then, John was not an individualist: he liked the noise and companionship of his fellows, and was not averse to mucking in with all and sundry, as I was.

To me Susy Ann was the perfect companion. She did not question my goings out or my comings in. To her I did not have to explain my moods – and they were diverse. She took everything for granted, even the changing of her sash for a more becoming one, for she was a woman, and all women like to look their best when there is a man about – even though he be a prisoner and not his own master.

Pleasant as was the society of Susy Ann, I found it necessary as the days went by to find occupation in some other sphere of existence. Thus far the Japs had left us more or less alone and free to roam about at will when we were not imposed on by our own people who, day by day, were regaining the bumptious officialism that had been temporarily disrupted by the fall of Singapore.

Routine fatigues were becoming the order of the day – necessary or otherwise – so that I was glad when my endeavours to make a fishing net out of scraps I had collected from native dwellings by the sea came to the notice of the R.S.M. He suggested that I become the company fisherman and see what I could do in the way of augmenting our food supply, which was daily getting worse as the rations brought out from Singapore with us melted away.

John, too, was keen on being a fisherman as he had been detailed as a gardener and had no fondness for horticulture.

All day we laboured to make a net out of a collection of holes which we tied together with pieces of string and strips of rag, hoping to emulate the Galilean episode and so keep our comrades from slow starvation. When the holes were eventually tied one to the other our net was so cumbersome that two extra men were needed to operate it. These, we found, could not be spared from the endless round of fatigue. At least the C.M.S. said so, but our patron the R.S.M. had other ideas, or maybe he was getting browned off with the rice which daily was becoming more apparent on the menu – and rice and fish are like peas in a pod – they cling together to their mutual advantage.

Over the way two of my former cronies – Richard Laverton, a go-getter if ever there was one, and Bert Smith, slow but amenable to discipline – were being bored to death cutting grass with table knives.

Company Office – all powerful as it had been before the Japs went on the warpath – said it was necessary to do this to keep the mosquitoes in check. It was also necessary, they said, to do a lot of other silly things, and if you did not do them, you would be put on a whizzer and shown what was what.

We already knew that, of course, but Company Office did not agree with the general interpretation – which was universal. This was one case in which thirty thousand Britons were wrong and had, therefore, to forsake much of their paddling on the beach, and pleasant walks in the shade along the hillside, for the more mundane occupation of carrying out the silly orders falling among us like confetti at a wedding when the bride is a popular debutante, or its equivalent.

Drawn into the vortex of conflicting opinion, Richard and Smithy welcomed the opportunity to become fishermen and free agents, for as potential food providers, we owed allegiance to none but the R.S.M. and our own conscience – and these were very elastic owing to continual stretching.

Fifty yards from my window Changi Creek emptied itself into the sea, and one morning before the tide came rushing up the net was taken down and given its first dip as a component. Approximately 20 feet wide at the mouth, it tapered away to a tail as long as the net was wide, and in this tail we expected to catch our daily bread. Maybe we wouldn't catch sufficient fish for the battalion, but

18

if the sea were kind there should at least be enough for breakfast, and, perhaps, one or two for the R.S.M.

The fish in the Creek were not greenhorns: they had seen a net before. Or perhaps it was our lack of finesse that discouraged them. While the big ones turned tail and headed for the open sea, the little ones, flying fish mostly, took to the air and skimmed over the net in contemptuous flight. A few however, were too slow in their take off – there are always a few laggards in any society – and were caught. Small though they were, they were duly cooked and consumed with a 'Here's hoping' from Laverton. Smithy said nothing. Being a bit of a sentimentalist, he was perhaps sorry for the younglings, but like the well-disciplined worker he was, kept his reflections to himself.

Sweeping the sea, or that part of it we could reach, with dexterity our fishing party landed some of the queerest monsters I have seen. These, of course, were thrown back, or kept for curios until they stank. Afterwards we learned that the more repulsive looking a marine animal, the better it is to eat. But by then it was too late for us to profit from this knowledge.

Fish we caught, not in plenitude maybe, but in sufficient numbers to make the effort worthwhile. And we had fun too. On one occasion Smithy, who for some obscure reason removed his false teeth before venturing into the water, caused a bit of a stir by losing them. He had placed the teeth on a piece of driftwood just above the high-water mark, or so he said, and when he went to collect them, they were missing.

We had left it rather late that evening before returning from the beach. And, as by then the Japs had a machine-gun posted in the village to command the strip of beach from which the prisoners bathed and fished, it was advisable not to loiter there after dusk.

Smithy was broken-hearted by the loss of his dentures, but I pointed out that it was a distinct advantage to remain alive without teeth than remain on the beach looking for them and risk the likelihood of getting a burst or two from the machine-gun in the village.

It was cold comfort to tell Smithy that he would probably not be needing teeth for a long time. Maybe never if our diet was not soon spiced with something more palatable and substantial than jungle stew.

In the last flicker of daylight the hunt for Smithy's teeth went on, and was abandoned only when the moon refused to come out from behind a cloud and co-operate.

Back in my billet Smithy sat sucking his gums and bewailed his loss for an hour. Then abruptly rising off the bed he ran out and down to the breach.

Ten minutes later there was a bang from the direction of the Creek, and shortly after Smithy back biting his gums from which the teeth were still missing and with the doubtful distinction of being the first prisoner to be fired on in Changi.

Luck was with him, however. At dawn he hurried back to the beach, and there was there teeth laying on the sand with the water taking fitful pecks at them.

In the afternoon of a day about a week later two trucks came out from Singapore and stopped by the machine-gun post in the village. Under a heavily armed guard thirty odd Chinese men were taken down to our bathing beach and butchered with Tommy guns. Our Tommy guns. Why the Japs chose this spot for their private massacre was hard to define, unless it was an old Japanese custom to rub out people and leave the bodies lying along the shore for the waves to disport themselves over. Or maybe it was an Oriental way of saying: 'Look out that the same thing does not happen to you.'

Whatever the reason for the wrath of their new sun god, the young Chinese were well and truly dead, and lay asprawl on the sand, while their blood dyed the shells on the beach and tinted the tops of the wavelets with the colours of the setting sun. Some of them lay there until the afternoon of the following day, for the tide refused to be an accessory after the fact and flung them in grotesque heaps further up the beach, instead of taking them down to the sea. Eventually they were buried in the scrub of the little headland that ran out between the Creek and the sea, and peace departed from the beach.

Gone now was the thrill of bathing in the brackish waters of the Straits. The pit containing the murdered Chinese was too close at hand to be shut out and forgotten. It seemed sacrilegious to laugh and run about the sands among with tracery patterns of their blood still lingered. Blood which would not have been spilled had we not failed them and let the Japs come in to make sacrifice to their thirsty sun god.

It was necessary still to continue fishing, but even that was soon to be denied us by a Japanese order prohibiting all personnel from the vicinity of the sea. Before that happened, however, we made a record catch which burst our net asunder and put us out of commission as fishermen just as surely as the Jap order to keep away from the sea.

On the last evening we had trawled up and down the beach and had a dozen small flying fish and a couple of crabs to show four our efforts as the light began to fade as a warning that it was time to go back to our billets. Owing to the insistence of Richard Laverton, who all along had been insistent that one day we should catch so many fish in the net we could not be able to haul it ashore, we decided to make one final effort to prove our ability.

20

Taking the net out for the last time in order to humour him, we dragged it along a ledge beyond which the sea fell away in a dark and sullen-looking chasm. As we progressed, it gradually became more difficult to tow the cumbersome net along behind, but gradually we worked it along the ledge and then turned for the shore to find we were unable to get the net out of the water.

The long tail was a heaving mass of squirming fish which splashed in frantic anxiety to get back to deep water. They were making a good job of it, too, for the rotted cord was giving in a dozen places as we pulled mightily at the ropes to make our catch secure. Fortuitously the tide was on the ebb, and eventually it left us stranded in a pool of water with about half of our original catch still squirming in the ruins of the net.

There were fish everywhere, for by now the net had ceased to function as such, many of them making a getaway to the sea.

In his anxiety to prevent that sort of thing, Smithy started to grab them by the tails and sling them up the beach, forgetting in his excitement that many of the fish in those waters can hit back.

Throwing himself on a big one which was just giving a last contemptuous flick of its tail before heading out to sea, Smithy caught it by the tail and headed for dry ground. Suddenly he gave a startled yell and, dropping the fish, came racing back.

'It's bit me! It's bit me!' he shouted, throwing grammar to the wind.

It had, too, for the blood was running down his hand and dripping onto the sand.

I was about to laugh at Smithy's predicament when, inadvertently grasping a small fish which was flapping about at my feet, I gave a shout as a red-hot needle was plunged into my hand, once at the base of the thumb and once into my middle finger. Richard, too, fell a victim at about the same time by treading on one of the fish which jabbed him in the foot.

Most of the haul were catfish and were armed with three poison prongs – one sticking out from each bunch of whiskers and one straight from the skull – from which they injected a fluid which caused intense pain for some hours.

All that night I lay awake, cursing the catfish tribe back to the first generation. Susy Ann was not sympathetic either, and gave me no solace in my travail, while Fishooks mewed disdainfully and, had he been gifted with speech, would have said: 'For God's sake, shut up and let us get some sleep!'

After this episode we ceased to exist as fishermen, for our net was a total ruin, and there was no possibility of repairing it.

21

Soon, however, my period of splendid isolation was to end, and when that happened my interest in fishing died.

Brigade, who occupied the best site in the area overlooking the Straits, were being pushed out by the Japs and immediately took possession of the police station by serving eviction papers on all who had set up house there. This meant the end of my domestic independence, but by that time, I was not sorry, for Fishooks had deserted, leaving Susy Ann in a state of rebellion, and the shadows of the dead Chinese hung wraith-like along the Creek below my window.

Taking what belongings I thought I should be able to find room for in my new quarters across the road, I said good-bye to all of my old associations and departed.

As a final gesture of independence I hung Susy Ann up by her crimson sash behind the door, and felt better for it, for she, too, had cheated me. On the velvet creaminess of her neck was the legend: "Made in Japan". And I had accepted her into my household as a bereaved Malay maiden who might be willing to share my loneliness in the long days of captivity ahead.

Chapter Three

Nai Soon

IN a camp such as Changi, where officers were as plentiful as pigeons on St. Paul's, the insistence by Brigade that 'Officers shall be saluted at all times' was one of the main irritants during our first months of captivity.

The various company headquarters which, despite the changed circumstances of their environment, adhered to their normal routine in so far as bureaucratic bull was concerned. They enforced Brigade's decree with enthusiasm. As a consequence, there was an ever-increasing number of janker-wallahs doing penance for their crimes of omission.

One of the favourite clichés going the rounds at Changi soon after our arrival was the spurious morale booster: 'We are all in the same boat and must pull together.'

This worked rather well until the officers realised, doubtless with a shock to their self-esteem, that they were travelling steerage in out floundering ship of state. The saluting order was the first move in their campaign for rehabilitation; it put distance between them and the other ranks even though we were living in close proximity to what was known euphemistically as the officers' quarters.

Officers still had the services of a batman, though this was more a status symbol than a necessity. The batmen were happy with the arrangement: it excused them from other camp duties. Also there were the perks that went with the job, such as leftover rice and the occasional cigarette.

Not all of the officers insisted on their status quota. Many were as annoyed as the rank and file about the saluting order. In a lecture on discipline our C.O. implied that saluting should not be mandatory. When he appealed for the cancellation of the order which was causing so much disharmony in the camp, Brigade disagreed with his suggestion.

These pedants with their conspicuously displayed notice, 'All enquiries at the rear entrance,' considered saluting to be as important as the bully beef and cigarettes which were denied the ordinary P.O.W.s, and of which they had an apparent abundance.

Many months passed before petty officialdom – and it was petty in the circumstances – was forced to accept that it no longer held the supreme mandate at Changi. That it had fallen from its pedestal of grandeur and was now of little more importance than the ordinary prisoners whose future welfare depended entirely on the dictates of the new masters of Singapore with the power of life and death in their hands.

Another major irritant at Changi in the early days was the weekly R.S.M.'s parade; held as a morale booster, we were assured. On these parades, turnout was expected to be up to a standard it was impossible to attain. K.D. had to be clean, boots polished and men had to be clean shaven.

The fact that the majority of the men at Changi possessed only the clothes they wore at the capitulation was not accepted as an excuse for slovenliness. British soldiers were expected to be neat and tidy at all times. They had a reputation to maintain. Reputation? That went down the drain with the fall of Singapore.

Although we were not aware of it then, the time was not far distant when formal dress for all P.O.W.s would be a 'Jap happy – an outsize diaper.

A back-up to the R.S.M.'s parade was foot drill and saluting practice for men, many of whom had been in the army for ten years or more and were now prisoners and realised it, unlike the pedants who still found it necessary to go through the motions of a charade that should have been thrown into the dustbin of Singapore along with the other bull that continued to irritate long after we had arrived at Changi.

Eventually the R.S.M.'s relaxation was stopped, not because of its unpopularity, but by the Japanese that decreed that prisoners were not to perform military exercises: they were expected to work. If there was insufficient work available, the I.J.A. would make up the deficiency.

Having reasserted their authority, the Japs then ordered parades for their own glorification when visiting dignitaries visited Changi to view the fruits of their army's success.

These mandatory parades were tainted by bureaucratic bull. Instead of taking advantage of the situation and so make known just how impoverished we were, Brigade ordered: 'Everyone is expected to have a good turn-out for this parade. Men not in possession of a full rig-out should endeavour to make up their deficiency from those who have spare clothing.'

This misguided policy was not indigenous to Changi: it was repeated with enthusiasm in every camp where the Japs held obligatory parades. On these occasions the Japs took photographs, evidently to prove how well they were looking after the prisoners' welfare.

For these publicity stunts, the best-dressed and fittest men were selected to parade, not by the Japs but by the British camp commandant, who evidently was trying to prove to a palpitating world how the defeated British were maintaining their stiff upper lip.

Bullshit!

On the first I.J.A. parade ordered in Changi, the route through the village was lined by well-dressed and mainly browned off personnel for two hours before the Japs came. When eventually they came rattling up the road from Singapore in an old lorry tied together with many pieces of wire and string, they were not the important people we had expected.

On this occasion a senior Jap officer was to inspect us, and not the three privates and one lance-corporal the truck contained. Perhaps the senior officer was not too sure of his reception in Changi, and had sent the other ranks to draw our fire, if there was any. But he need not have worried: everyone had been warned to be on his best behaviour so as to show the Japs just how much we were liking their hospitality…

Soon after these show-off parades were initiated, all prisoners were ordered to parade every evening for a check-up by the Japanese, who, up till then, had been content with a routine company parade under our own officers.

Now things were different. For the I.J.A. roll-call each group paraded under its senior officer, who reported to the Jap *shoko* or *gunso* present.

Saluting on these parades was very punctiliously carried out, especially by the Jap official present. Choosing the highest vantage point in the vicinity – when there was not one high enough, a saluting base was erected – and at rigid attention, he took the salute from each company before it was dismissed. Officers only saluted, while other ranks turned their heads and looked directly at the representative of Hirohito, who pivoted around so that no one should miss the honour being bestowed on him.

The next move in the strategy for subjugation was the general order that all ranks of the I.J.A. must be saluted by all P.O.W.s, and once more we were entangled in the saluting craze which appeared to be of more importance to both sides than winning or losing a war.

The officers did not accept this new decree without a protest. It hit them where they were most vulnerable – their pride. It reduced them in their own estimation to the status of the other ranks. This was a severe blow to their prestige – if they had any left after Singapore.

Anxious to avoid losing their status, the officers made a formal protest to the I.J.A. They were anxious to avoid their first encounter with a Jap private soldier when they would have to initiate the gesture that would signify their inferiority – the salute. A counter-suggestion that commissioned ranks of the old I.J.A. only should be saluted by officer P.O.W.s was rejected.

The Japs were adamant that all ranks of the I.J.A. must be saluted by all P.O.W.s but, like many other decrees, there was nothing watertight about this one. Every camp used its own interpretation of the order. In some. Jap officers only were saluted by commissioned P.O.W.s. In others, sergeants and warrant officers had to receive the accolade. Then the Jap lower ranks, rankled by not getting their share of the general obeisance, instituted a face-slapping programme to ensure they were not omitted from the saluting merry-go-round.

One of the bugbears of life in Changi at this time was the increasing number of times one was compelled to salute as the Jap presence in the camp increased while our officers continued with their asinine insistence that other ranks should continue to salute them at all times. On occasions an extra hand would have come in useful…

Eventually, worsening conditions at Changi, coupled with the growing realisation among the other ranks that their lives were just as valuable as the life of a man with a 'pip' on his shoulder, brought to an end to saluting among the P.O.W.s. Yet it was with reluctance that General Salute eventually was lowered into one of the yawing holes that began to gape vacuously in the cemetery beside the road on the way to Singapore.

The cemetery was the final stopover for many of the wounded who were part of the influx into Changi after the white flag was hoisted over the euphemistically named 'Fortress Singapore'.

Transferred directly to the ex-military hospital, which was part of the Changi complex, many of the wounded who died would likely have recovered from their wounds had they received adequate medical care. This was not available, the hospital having been stripped of most of its equipment and medical supplies by either the previous occupants or the I.J.A., who were disinclined to grant medical supplies to the hospital when requested by the British medical officer in charge to do so.

Everything possible was done to save the severely wounded, but as the medical staff were working with one hand theoretically tied behind their backs, the majority of these men died.

These were the vanguard of the many who were destined to die at Changi before the majority of the inmates were transferred to die elsewhere.

Dying at Changi had its compensations. One had a roof over one's head and likely a bed in which to expire, plus sufficient rations to ensure that death was not caused by starvation. Then there was a team of medics doing their best in straitened circumstances to keep you out of the cemetery. When they failed, as they frequently did, there was the 'Flowers of the Forest' lament on the bagpipes to accompany you to the piece of Singapore island that, hopefully, would be forever yours. So you see, you did eventually get something out of your misfortune.

Dying in other, out of the way locations was not so formal. When you came to the end of your endurance you simply lay down and died or, if you were reluctant to exchange a realistic hell for a problematical heaven, you soldiered on until the final grain of sand trickled from the hourglass, and with it your options: you died.

Occasionally there was a shortcut in the dying process: you committed some indiscreet act and had your head lopped off as a penalty for your indiscretion...

There were many ways to commit a head-lopping indiscretion, the most foolhardy being a refusal to salute a Jap officer. As the officers were the direct link with Hirohito, the divine Emperor, in much the same way as British officers are representatives of the king through the King's Commission, you were insulting the emperor by not saluting his representative. Fortunately Jap officers were thin on the ground, so the opportunity to commit suicide was not readily available.

You could, however, do yourself a mischief by not paying due deference each time you passed the guard-room. The drill was for the N.C.O. leading the party to give an 'eyes right' before he himself offered the obligatory salute. If you were passing the guard-room by yourself you turned your head right or left, saluting at the same moment or, if you were the abasing kind, you stopped, turned to face the guard then bowed deferentially. This manoeuvre depended for its motivation on the number of yellow blood corpuscles you had in your system...

*****

As the Jap commissariat did not consider it necessary to issue an adequate supply of green vegetables with the rice ration, an intensive gardening campaign was started. With Sommers, Smithy and Laverton, I enrolled in this horticultural enterprise as a substitute for our bankrupt fishing project. From our efforts, minimal though they had been, it was evident that there was sufficient fish in the straits off Changi Creek to make a worthwhile contribution to our scanty rations, had they been harvested.

Possibly neither the I.J.A., who were great fish eaters, nor the British administration realised that an opportunity to repeat the Galilean fisherman's tale was waiting on their doorstep. All that was necessary were a few nets and the enthusiasm of an ample supply of pseudo-fishermen.

However well-intentioned the horticultural enterprise had been at its initiation, it soon became apparent that its total output could never make an appreciable difference to the contents of the jungle stew that complemented our rice ration now, thankfully, no longer a wet dollop liberally sprinkled with mouse droppings and maggots. The cooks had finally mastered the art of cooking the rice dry, and the M.O. assured us the maggots were a valuable source of vitamins, we accepted them. As he made no comment on the mouse droppings, we tended to ignore them…

Insufficient as were the rations issued by the I.J.A. from a warehouse adjacent to the hospital, they were further depleted before reaching their destination by the rations party who collected them on a flat-bed lorry without an engine.

In the army, scabbing (pilfering) had always been taken for granted.

Small items of equipment, cigarettes and money were likely to disappear if left exposed and unattended. Though petty, the perpetrator of such minor breaches of trust was severely dealt with if apprehended.

In the environment of a P.O.W. camp even a petty larceny could have serious repercussions for everyone – especially where food was concerned.

The men manhandling the rations truck, a laborious job, considered their scabbing, which was minimal, as justifiable perks; the morality of their actions did not enter into the equation. After all, what did the odd sweet potato and handful of rice matter? No one would starve because they were missing.

Possibly not, had that been that extent of the scabbing. Unfortunately there were others who had a mercenary interest in the rations lorry. At each checkpoint on its journey to the cookhouse a few items were removed from it to be recycled via the black market.

It was taken for granted, as it always is, that the cookhouse staff pilfered the rations. Certainly they had 'extras', to which they were entitled, having cooked the stuff. I had 'extras' myself on occasion – the scraping off the bottom of the utensil in which the rice was cooked, but this was only as a reward for fetching wood for the cookhouse fire…

Brewing up in the evening (making tea) was a pleasant relaxation if you had the facilities to do so, and a supply of the astringent black tea, presumably a native blend and the only brand available. Initially this tea, without the addition of milk or sugar, which were not supplied with the rations, was most unpalatable.

Time, however, changes everything, nothing more so than one's habits to suit the prevailing circumstances. This was true of the unpalatable tea; soon it became the highlight of our gastronomic intake.

If you had the necessary money, you could always find something on the black market to cook with your cha, thereby providing an additional ration to your legal entitlement. The fact that your 'extras' were probably scabbed from the rations truck did not produce a conscience block. If food was available, you had it and left your conscience to ruminate on a full belly.

As in every circumstance where people are herded together living a day-to-day existence, there were the lucky few for whom money, apparently, was no problem. This affluent circle controlled the black market which was quickly established in Southern Area, the north-east corner of the island occupied by Changi.

Those without the necessary money to patronise the black market relied on the camp's natural resources to add to their official rations.

One of the 'natural resources' was the hibiscus shrub, whose bell-like flowers flamed red in the hedges surrounding what had been the gardens of Changi. The leaves of this shrub, boiled with a pinch of salt, if it was available, made a most appetising substitute for 'greens', and was a welcome addition to the daily rice and jungle stew diet.

In addition to the hibiscus shrub, there were a few papaya and coconut palms in the camp, and also a few Malay cherries and an odd clump of bananas.

In an endeavour to conserve these natural resources it became an offence, punishable by varying degrees of jankers, to take any of them as they were, officially, reserved for the hospital.

In the early hours this order was respected by the majority of the men. Later, when it became evident that the officers' mess, through some self-imposed right, had a monopoly of this fruit, Changi's natural resources disappeared like young corn before a plague of locusts.

The moneyed people – those who had been in a position to feather their nests before the capitulation and who had not been stupid enough to destroy their valuables, including currency – were not concerned with our natural resources, but left them to their poorer brethren.

Between us John and I had ten dollars which we held on to with a miserly persistence, outraging still further our stomachs which were clamorous for some tasty morsel to break the nauseating monotony of rice and hibiscus leaves.

*****

Some little way along the coast south of the village in a palm grove fringed by thick shrubbery lay the nerve centre of the black market. In this kampong the natives had accumulated large stores of tinned foods – formerly the property of the Army authorities – which they sold at exorbitant prices to anyone with money to buy them. Cigarettes, too, could be bought here. To men reduced to smoking dried cherry leaves, no price was too high for the pleasure of satisfying, for a time at least, the persistent craving for a good smoke.

To get to the *kampong* it was necessary to break bounds by going out through perimeter wire, then across the road and so to cover in the scrub surrounding the *kampong*.

When we first came to Changi there had been no confining wire to keep us within bounds and I had roamed about more or less at will, provided there were no fatigues to keep me immobilised. Then Brigade moved down from the hill and there was a general re-allocation of billets to the individual units in the camp, and soon after this the first wire made its appearance.

Under the conscientious supervision of Captain Bell, the perimeter wire soon became an almost impassable barrier to the outer world though, when we had erected it, care had been taken to ensure that numerous 'boltholes' were left for the use of those men who daily, and nightly, ventured into the outlying districts beyond the perimeter, or to the black market *kampong* down the road.

During his periodic tours of inspection of the perimeter to ensure its impregnability, Captain Bell discovered these unofficial exits and had them closed, thus making it necessary to find another way through the wire each time someone went out.

So conscientious was the captain that I often thought he had some ulterior motive in keeping the wire intact. I reasoned that if it kept us in it would also serve the dual purpose of keeping the Japs out, should a situation arise when it would be expedient for us to do so.

There was no substance to this reasoning, however. The captain was just another of those unfortunate people who react automatically to every order given them without the formality of first ascertaining the sensibility of doing so.

Driven by the urgings of my stomach, though my pockets were almost empty, I decided to visit the *kampong*. Perhaps I would be able to get something useful – sugar perhaps – for my few dollars. Or more entertaining still was the thought that I might be able to scab something, for in that respect my conscience was well blunted by this time, especially where the natives or other racketeers were concerned.

There was also a second, but not at the moment so pressing a reason for my decision to visit the *kampong*. The possibility of escape had not faded from my mind and I was anxious to make some outside contact that would, perhaps, be useful to me in this respect, in spite of my former resolve not to be dependent on the natives unless absolutely forced to do so.

After a careful review of the position John and I, with Laverton and Smithy in close contact, had decided that the time had come for an investigation of the possibilities of outside assistance in getting away from the island, for daily it was becoming more apparent that this could not be accomplished solely on our own initiative.

There was little difficulty in getting through the wire in spite of the conscientious Captain Bell. It was just a matter of waiting patiently for someone to make a hole, and then to follow on his heels as he went through.

As I scrambled through the thicket surrounding the *kampong*, a half-dozen fellow prisoners were busy among the bushes, bartering with the natives for anything they had to sell – and at whatever price. They were assured of a handsome profit on anything edible they got back to camp.

This eagerness of the inmates of the camp to get food or cigarettes had its inevitable outcome in the skyrocketing prices, which jumped in dollars daily.

Thus a packet of five cent cigarettes which, on my first visit to the kampong, cost one dollar fifty cents had jumped to three dollars two days later.

As they bargained, the men cursed and swore at the native shylocks – and paid their price if they had the money.

If the invective expended on that *kampong* can be taken as a guide, the people of Singapore must have had a sorry time when the Japs took control of the Lion City…

Avoiding the hagglers in the bushes, I ventured along the coast to where an arm of the sea cut inland like the mouth of a river. Drawn up on the sand, and screened from view by a line of stunted trees which made it impossible to see unless one walked on top of it, as I had done, lay a flimsy native canoe. Sitting beside it, with his back to a tree, was a Chinese youth of about eighteen engaged in the pleasant relaxation of sucking condensed milk out of a tin.

With eyes riveted on the tin of milk, I stood for a moment dreaming of all the plates of rice it would make palatable while regretting the one I had lavished on Fishooks.

Becoming aware of me standing on the fringe of the scrub, the youngster removed the tin from his lips and placed it negligently on the sand beside him. In his demeanour there was nothing to suggest that such a luxury was not commonplace, and I felt my belly begin to ache with desire as I followed his every movement.

'Hello, Johnnie,' he said, cheerfully.

'You're a surprise,' I admitted, still looking at the milk tin and estimating how much I might offer him for it. 'Enjoying yourself?'

'Milk,' he said unnecessarily, lifting the tin from the sand and twirling it in his long brown fingers. 'Very good.'

Before I could say yes or no he rummaged beneath an old sack lying in the canoe and handed me an unopened tin. Looking at the label I read: "Nestles Condensed Milk Sweetened."

Sweetened! That word meant more to me than any other word in the English language just then, and conjured up a brief spell of riotous living for John and myself. Maybe, too, there would be sufficient to include Laverton and Smithy in the banquet. Then my visions of uncontrolled gluttony evaporated at the realisation that in all probability the milk would cost more than I possessed.

'Very nice,' I conceded hopefully, placing the milk on the sand. 'But money –' and I shrugged my shoulders expressively and hoped for the best.

Nor did he belie my faith in human nature. Picking up the tin, he handed it to me again but said nothing, and on his face I could read nothing that might give me a clue to his intention.   Taking the plunge, I enquired with a hopefulness I did not feel:

'This for me?'

'Yes, for you. You have no money, so I give it to you.'

When he said this I could almost feel the three dollars burning a hole in my pocket in an endeavour to express their indignation.

Almost overcome by my good fortune, I sat down on the sand beside the canoe and absently smoked the cigarette that followed the tin of milk. The cigarette, though very acceptable, pricked my conscience, for I knew that John, who had been a very heavy smoker in other days, had not had a smoke other than dried leaves for a week. But, after hiding the tin of milk in my shirt, I did not feel like doing the same with the cigarette which the Chinese youth obviously expected me to smoke immediately.

Watching him, I realised that he appeared to have forgotten my presence.

Sitting on his haunches with a lighted cigarette wasting away between his fingers, he was looking out over the Straits to where a small island reared its dim bulk out of the water. He sat like a day-dreamer looking out into vacancy and, though he appeared to be gazing at the distant smudge of land, I felt he was not doing that, but was looking inward as at something that had happened recently.

Watching him covertly as the wasted smoke curled about his fingers, I wondered what vision of yesterday was engaging his attention. He was an odd youth, I thought, for to my knowledge, day-dreaming was not a vice of the practically-minded Chinese I had encountered on Singapore Island, neither was the bestowal of free gifts which could be sold for hard cash a general practice of theirs. Looking at him, I saw something I had not before noticed, and immediately my attention was focused on it.

On a small shrub where it would catch the sunlight, lay a sodden and stained soft felt hat of the type worn by young Chinese men in Singapore and elsewhere before the Japs came. The youngsters who slaved in the offices of the big business houses as clerks for a few dollars a week, acquiring free a European education better in many respects than the people who indirectly taught it to them.

For some reason I could not clearly define, this salt-stained hat fascinated me. I felt that in some way it explained the presence of the Chinese youth on this deserted strip of beach and that he was living over again some episode that had affected him deeply in the not too distant past.

The hat had the appearance of having been in the water for some time, but I could still see that not so long ago it had been a new hat.

Then, in a flash of inspiration, there came to me the recollection of another occasion on which I had seen many hats of a similar pattern being flung about by the incoming tide – after the execution of the Chinese on the beach below my first billet, overlooking Changi Creek.

Remembering, I saw again those pathetic reminders of the murdered Chinese littering the sand and waiting for the tide to carry them on into the Straits and eventually to the sea. Could this hat, I wondered, be one of those and if so, who was this youth who had obviously taken it out of the water and hung it up to dry in the hot sun?

As though he read my thoughts, he suddenly forsook his pose of immobility, turned his head away from the sea and said simply, and without any prior explanation:

'My brother's hat.'

That was all. Just 'My brother's hat,' as though he expected me to accept the explanation without question. Which I did. Nonetheless it took me by surprise and I blurted out:

'Then your brother was – shot up there?'

'Yes, Johnnie. He and others I knew...'

'I'm sorry that had to happen,' I retorted, feeling I was saying the wrong thing. 'I was most upset at the time and,' I added with truth, 'so was everyone else who witnessed the massacre, for that's what it was.'

'There is no need for sorry,' he assured me philosophically. 'He was one of the many who have died because of the Japs. Doubtless many more will die, and we cannot be sorry for them all, Johnnie. Maybe even I, too, shall die but what matter if I can accomplish some small measure of retribution against those who continue to murder my countrymen. My brother has already forfeited his life for being a Chinese, so why not I?' Then he added, serving from his philosophy, 'Now I come to find this,' and he gestured nonchalantly at the bedraggled hat, 'and take it home. It is all we have left of Ah Tek and sometimes my mother weeps...'

I confess I did not know what to say in reply to this confession of so much sorrow in so few words. Evidently he had known all about his brother's execution and where it had taken place and I wondered at that, for on the open strip of beach there had been nowhere for him to hide, presuming he had been in the vicinity. He must have known, because it was evident that he had not come upon the hat by accident, but had been searching for it and anything else that might be identified as belonging to his murdered brother.

Wondering about that, I thought of the canoe hidden in the scrub beside me. Was it possible he had come over from one of the islands in the Straits? That was unlikely. Paula Ubin, which stretched its bulk out there before had been heavily shelled before the capitulation. Doubtless the others, too, though of lesser importance, had received their quota of high explosive from both sides.

It was not improbable, of course, that he came from Johor, showing faintly through the blue mist that hung over the rubber on its heavily wooded coastline.

It did not matter to me a great deal where he came from as long as it was from somewhere outside Changi – preferably from beyond the Straits. He had a chance, and with a bit of judicious questioning I thought I might be able to get some information from him that would give me an inkling as to what the chance of co-operation would be in any escape attempt.

In such an eventuality the canoe would be invaluable, provided, of course, he was willing to let me make use of it when the time came. From what he had just said, he had a deeper animosity towards the Japs than I had, despite my circumstances. Should he be instrumental in assisting me to escape when the time came he would be making a gesture against the Japs who owed him so much.

Reflecting on the possibility of his co-operation, I decided to approach him on the matter. But I should have to be noncommittal about the venture. The Japs were a crafty lot, especially when it came to planting spies among the locals.

It was not beyond the bounds of possibility that this innocent-seeming youth was just such a person who was using the massacre of his fellows as a means of enlisting the confidence of any P.O.W. he encountered outside the perimeter wire.

The more I considered such a likelihood, the more uncertain I became about the truth of his exploit. It was such a bizarre venture. Go searching along the shore for the hat of a brother who had been riddled with Tommy gun bullets. But then, the Chinese were an inexplicable people whose lives were closely intermingled with the Japanese, who for decades had been their oppressors. Likely, he was telling the truth.

'You knew about your brother's death?' I asked, tentatively.

His reply was as startling as the announcement, unasked for as it had been, that the hat belonged to his brother.

'Yes,' he said unemotionally. 'I saw it happen.'

'Saw it!'

'Yes. With these,' and he brought out from his shirt a pair of powerful binoculars which, when I focused them on a pin-point of land in the far distance, brought every tree and shrub rushing up in clear relief before my eyes.

'In that case,' I asked for want of something better to say, 'you probably know where he is buried. Or did the sea take him?' I added unthinkingly. 'I know some of the bodies were swept out on the ride...'

Again he surprised me.

'I know where he was buried,' he said. 'The sea did not take him. I also know where he is buried now.'

'Where he is buried *now*,' I repeated, puzzled by the implication that this youngster had dug the body of his brother out of the sand and interred it somewhere else. He was proving an amazing youngster indeed if what he was telling me was true. The amazement, or unbelief, was so unnoticeable in my voice that he smiled, probably reading my thoughts in the disconcerting way he had.

'Yes. Ah Tek was buried in the sand with some others, but I did not care to leave him there where the Japanese had put him, so at night time I came with two others and took him away. It was not easy to distinguish him from the others. There was much blood, and it was dark...'

He paused in his recital for a while, and I could see he was living over again that pilgrimage of his to the hole in the sand where his brother's outraged body lay mingled in the same grave with so many others.

It must have been a difficult and unpleasant job, even though it was undertaken for love, and the thought of such an errand in the dead of night, when the least noise heard on the road where the Japs watched beside their machine-gun would have brought a hail of lead about his ears, and in all probability have sent him to join his brother wherever murdered Chinese foregather, filled me with admiration for his coolness.

As I watched him, a slow sad smile spread over the smoothness of his young face. A smile with more pathos in it than the whispering of the breeze among the tombstones in a churchyard, and he explained:

'Ah Tek lies at peace where only my mother and I know. The Japanese have done all they can to him; they can hurt him no more...'

Then, rising abruptly to his feet, he took the hat off the tree stump and said, 'I must go now, Johnnie.'

As I, too, got up, clutching at my shirt where the precious tin of milk was hidden, he added:

'In this *kampong* I have an uncle – but he will not give you any milk!' and he laughed; a carefree laugh which belied the re-awakened sorrow in which he had been steeped but a moment before. 'Perhaps I will bring you some more one day, if you care to risk the displeasure of the Japanese by coming through the wire. I shall be here again in three days.'

'I, too, will be here,' I promised as he bent and began to drag the canoe from its hiding place. As it was now apparent that we should meet again, I deemed it advisable to wait until then before mentioning my wish to escape from Changi. If he kept the tryst and brought me another tin of milk, I should accept it as a good sign of faith, though not without reservations, and put my life in his hands.

In the meantime, Sommers would have to be consulted, but that would be a mere formality. John would be as keen as I was to breathe some life into our dormant plans for a bid for freedom, even though by so doing we should probably be laying our heads on the chopping block. There was ironically a touch of whimsy about that possibility: Chopping blocks were no longer in vogue. They had been replaced by the samurai sword...

The canoe was now in the water, and as the young Chinese lifted the paddle, preparatory to moving off he said, as though it were an afterthought:

'My name is Nai Soon and I have another uncle over there,' he gestured towards Paula Ubin, 'but I live in Singapore. I like the English, though some Chinese do not. I was educated at an English school, and probably it is because of that, and a hope for the future, that I believe the Japanese will not always live in Singapore when so many of my countrymen believe otherwise. Time will prove who is right. Good-bye, Johnnie,' and off he went, leaving me sitting on the beach, not sure that I had got his name right as Chinese names can be a bit complex to western ears. I decided, if I ever saw him again, to call him Nat. That would simplify matters…

Chapter Four

The Sikhs Get One

For the tenth time I picked up the tin of bacon, turned it round in my hands and read the table, though I already knew every word written on it. Beside the bacon stood a small tin of peas and one of carrots. The last two I had resigned myself to parting with, but the bacon – that was different. I had not had bacon for such a long time; nor peas or carrots either, for that matter.

John had been so jubilant when he returned from a foraging expedition outside the wire with the tin of bacon, which we had now for over a week waiting for Smithy to get over his attack of dysentery and be discharged from the hospital.

Had Smithy not gone to the hospital, the bacon would have been safe, and I should not have been in the unenviable position of having to decide whether we should eat it or give it away, for that was the problem which was causing me so much indecision.

On a visit to the hospital, which was crammed with wounded and men who had fallen ill since the capitulation, Smithy had shocked me with a casual:

'Jackson's alive.'

So he was, but with nothing to spare.

Lying on his stomach, with his face screwed round on the pillow, and his eyes, big and bovine looking, roving round restlessly as if in quest of something, he gave me a look of semi-recognition as I came and stood by his bed.

What that something was, I soon learned. Jackson, who should have been dead and partly rotted by now, was hungry. But then, so was everybody else in the ward.

When a visitor entered, the patients who had sufficient strength, or a strong enough will-power, turned to stare at him with the appeal, 'have you brought me anything to eat?' writ large on their faces. If the visitor was carrying a parcel, scores of hungry eyes became riveted on it in an unblinking stare of covetousness. In the majority of instances, when a parcel was brought in by a visitor, there was nothing in it but a few tattered books, though even these were a welcome addition to the bleak monotony of life in the hospital.

While rations were always poor in the main camp, the hospital diet was improved slightly by small quantities of food the Japs allowed some of the officers to buy for that purpose. This extra food was not in sufficient bulk to make a great deal of difference to the men in the hospital who, owing to their circumstances, could not eat any old thing, as could their more fortunate fellows outside. Consequently, in the early days of Changi they suffered a greater privation, and had a more monotonous existence than the latter, who were at least free to enjoy the fresh air, the sunshine and an occasional unofficial pouch-up (cooking).

Jackson was one of those unfortunates whose hunger was always acute. And on top of that, he had a grievance.

'The blood orderlies,' he bleated, 'eat most of my grub. They think that I'm dying and that the grub'll be wasted, so they eat most of it.'

Then in a whisper: 'I should like something nice to eat, Mick, even if I do kick the bucket afterwards. It would be nice to go out with a fully belly!' And then, with a laugh that had nothing funny in it, he added: 'Be a treat for the worms! As it is they won't get much pickings off me.'

'You're not going to die, Jacko?' I asked hurriedly, and, surprisingly, he said 'No.'

'My guts are all right. That's what makes it so bad feeling hungry. Those bloody orderlies... But my back – can you smell it?'

Could I smell it!

I had been finding it difficult to keep from retching at the smell that pervaded the ward like a miasma over a pestilential swamp. From his colour I judged Jackson to be three parts dead, and that he should be worrying about food amazed me. Also, the smell he talked about led me to believe that his wound was gangrenous, and if that were so he ought to have been past caring about his empty belly long since.

'No,' I lied. 'I can't smell anything other than the ward. It could do with a good wash down in a strong carbolic...'

'You're tellin' me,' he said. 'But what's a bit of smell more or less? It's always being hungry that gets me, Mick.'

It was then I had my first doubts about eating the tin of bacon which we had salted away against the day Smithy got over his dysentery and re-joined us outside where, at least, the air was fresh.

'If I brought you in some food, would you eat it, or just waste it, Jacko?' I asked, hoping he would say no to the first half of my question. 'You're not so well,' I pointed out, trying to make sure, and at the same time appeasing my conscience. But Jackson did not bite.

'I know that,' he said, spurning my insinuation, 'but I'm hungry just the same. Can't a dying man be hungry, Mick? Don't you get hungry? Even if you do you're not dying like me. But I'm not dead yet – not by a long chalk. Those blasted orderlies are waiting for me to snuff it so they can hog all my grub. And what grub! Not fit for a pig, let alone a dying man! But I'm not dead yet...' and so on until I began to wonder if Jackson might not cheat the Japs who had sent him that last-minute souvenir after all.

His voice was strong enough, even though he looked a death's head .And then there was the stench of his festering wound, which did not seem to worry him much. He had had it so long, I supposed, that he had got used to it in the way that we were getting used to mouse droppings and maggots in our rice, and the multifarious unpleasantness of life at Changi.

It was just a matter of living long enough. Given time, one could get used to anything, and look upon it as part and parcel of existence – something not to be moaned at, but taken for granted.

Jackson was doing plenty of moaning, but he was justified.

'You know that mess tin you gave me just before this happened, Mick? I should like that full of Irish stew. What became of it, by the way? It's not in my kit...'

'I don't know,' I lied again. It was becoming easy these days. 'I'll see what I can do about the stew, if the orderly thinks it's all right to give you any extra grub...'

'Never mind him; just bring anything you can get your hands on – if it's tasty. I'll eat it.'

Jackson's orderly, or the one who looked after him, was in agreement that he would eat anything that was edible. Apparently his pack had protected his back to a slight extent in so far as the shrapnel had not entered his stomach and so settled his eating problems once and for all. This was no cause for satisfaction to the orderly, whose chief plaint was that Jackson, forever hungry, was eating food that might have gone to someone more in a position to benefit from it.

'If you have any spare food, you may give it to him if you wish, but don't. Eat it yourself. There's nothing we can do for Jackson. He could have been

41

saved, though, if we'd had the gear, and a good many more, too. Smell this place. It stinks! But what can we do about it? Water won't get rid of the smell, and there's no disinfectant nor much water either, come to that. You should see the dysentery ward! But you have, I saw you in there. Your pal Smith should be out in a couple of days...'

For this assurance I was grateful, and when I returned to Smithy, whose large frame looked a bit shrunken, he assured me he did not care for tinned bacon. Give it to Jackson, he insisted, giving the semblance of a grimace to dislike. John, too, had taken a sudden dislike to bacon when I mentioned Jackson's hunger to him.

'I'll scab a papaya from the officers' mess garden and we can make him a pie,' he suggested, taking it for granted that such an exotic fruit still existed in Changi. 'I think I can cadge some flour from a contact in the mess. Have you any cigarettes?'

'Yes – two. I've been saving them for a special contingency. I reckon this is it.'

And so the fate of the bacon was settled in so far as they were concerned. It was all very noble for John and Smithy to say to infer they did not like bacon – that fooled nobody. I knew they had been anticipating a special tit-bit and I had spoiled it for them by getting sentimental about Jackson's skeletal appearance.

Then unbidden came the thought that perhaps he would be dead by the time the pie was ready. This thought, which was only that, not a hope, persisted all the time I was manufacturing the pie. Unlike Smithy and John, I had no illusory dislike of bacon, tinned or otherwise.

As I stuck a knife into the tin I said aloud, 'Damn Jackson!' and meant it.

Difficult as it had been to decide to part with the bacon, it was positively traumatic to watch Jackson devour the pie we had made. He reacted like a man who had not eaten for a week or, conversely, like one about to go to the gallows. As he wolfed the pie, I hoped sincerely that his skeletal body would sustain the shock of so much food at once so that the ordeal of watching him eat it was compensated for by his survival.

Nor was that the worst part of the ordeal. When I entered the ward and unwrapped the pie, an almost audible moan of frustrated longing went up from the beds, and as Jackson, still lying on his belly, drove his spoon into the crust and let out the aroma, I found it impossible to bear the stares from dozens of hungry eyes that were turned towards me.

Without a break he ate the whole pie, which normally should have been sufficient for two. Then, wiping his mouth on a corner of a blanket, he said, with a sigh of gluttonous satisfaction:

'My God, that was good, Mick! Thanks.' Then he sighed and appeared to go to sleep, and I left him like that to live or die as the gods willed.

*****

An early innovation in Changi camp was the detention barracks, organised and run by our camp police, and in which the Japs had no hand. If we wished to make things more irksome for ourselves, they did not mind. They weren't particularly interested anyway.

With such a hide-bound bureaucracy such as reigned at Changi, the detention barracks was a necessary evil. Or so the administration thought; not that they considered it an evil, or an unnecessary imposition on men who were finding life sufficiently full of trials and tribulations without the added threat of being shut behind walls because of breaking some petty mandate which never should have been law.

In an existence where freedom of movement was the main factor that made life bearable, to be shut in detention barracks, which was operated on the worst glasshouse system, was a heavy imposition.

Had the people in charge of us had begun early to realise that infringements of orders were inevitable in the circumstances and had they also not issued so many orders which had nothing but their nuisance value to prop them up, the detention barracks would not have been necessary.

It was not the law-breakers who were at fault, but the law-makers. Unfortunately these gentlemen did not realise this all the time we were at Changi. Conditions there were such that, shorn as they might be of some of their previous authority, they still retained some and endeavoured to make up for what they had lost by misusing that which remained to them.

Probably the most stupid order ever issued by a British commanding officer in a prisoner-of-war camp was the one about hats. It was something like this:

'In future Army issue type hats only will be worn. That is, caps, F.S.A.R., or the regulation type Australian army pattern. Other hats will not be worn.'

The hats order was doubtless inspired by the fact that men who had arrived at Changi without hats were wearing any headgear that would give them protection from the sun. As the army side hat, or cap F.S.A.R., was useless for this purpose, they were jettisoned whenever something more suitable, such as a soft felt or an Australian non-army type hat, could be obtained.

This unauthorised departure from precedent did not please the big shots in Brigade who arrived there with all their kit, and a lot more besides, and who wished to camouflage their humble position with an outward show of magnificence at the expense of the men.

As usual, the various C.S.M.s were sedulous in enforcing the order, and the consequent friction was grist for the detention barracks where the offenders of authority made an unpopular attraction as they doubled out to wash in the mornings or on the way to the latrine, while a couple of military police kept close watch to see that they did not loiter.

Richard Laverton was a guest in the detention barracks for non-compliance with the hats order, or rather in consequence of what had arisen from it.

On a particularly hot day while gardening, he was ordered to get rid of the hat he had been wearing since arriving at Changi. This was a large slouch hat, ideal for keeping off the sun. When he demurred, pointing out that it was the only hat he possessed, and was not, therefore, going to throw it away as ordered, the C.S.M. went to the Q.M.'s and brought him a tin hat.

In the ensuing battle of words, the C.S.M. came off second best, but only for a time. Later, Laverton went to the cooler to reflect on the strange run of fate that had made him an inmate of a prison within a prison.

Unlike many of the men in the detention barracks, Laverton was a man of sound logic and knew when he was beaten. In consequence, he behaved himself while an inmate and did not have to undergo the further indignity of being tied up to the wall or generally maltreated as some of the more recalcitrant detainees were.

Jobs on the detention staff were eagerly sought after, as on the slightest pretext squaddies undergoing detention were put on the equivalent of bread and water, while the staff benefitted from their normal rations. They with the hospital orderlies comprised the best fed section of the inmates of Changi plus, of course, the various cookhouse staffs and food distributors.

Human nature being what it is, the strongest urge in any community threatened by starvation is self-preservation. Individually this trait is not general. It is only when men get confined, compelled to undergo privation, that the urge to survive, even at the expense of one's fellow man, manifests itself.

Individually, the men of Changi camp were considerate of the misfortunes of others, frequently sharing any spare clothing or food they managed to amass. It was when they got together in cliques that the urge to prey on their neighbours, even to the extent of stealing rations, became manifest.

As time passed, it became the norm for the individual to consider his survival as being more important than that of the unit generally. The dictum, 'If I don't take it, someone else will,' became the unwritten law of survival. Consequently the pernicious practice of scabbing at every opportunity anything that could be eaten or sold for cash to buy food on the black market became an integral facet of our social order.

Food, inevitably, was the focal point of our existence at Changi in the early days – primarily because there was not enough of it. Many were the ingenuous stratagems used by the individuals to supplement their rations untroubled by the fact that their success would decrease the amount received by someone else.

Survival was the name of the game. The only part of the earth some of the meek would inherit was a patch in the cemetery down the road.

Apart from its scarcity, the food was initially almost inedible, mainly because the army cooks were unable to serve up the staple diet – rice other than as a stodgy mess with no additives to five it flavour, discounting the maggots and mouse droppings with which it was liberally decorated.

Had the transition period between normal Army rations and a rice and jungle stew diet been gradual, the large number of deaths from malnutrition in the first months would doubtless have been much less. Also, the ability to combat the many afflictions that daily were becoming more apparent would have been greater.

Our misfortune, in so far as food was concerned, was in being prisoners of an Oriental power to whom rice was the staff of life, and who in the main had little interest in European food.

When we arrived at Changi, there were few, other than the Malay Volunteers, who knew how to cook rice. Instead of preparing it so as to produce a 'dry' end product the camp cooks turned out a stodgy mess that was inedible; until, that is, hunger took the edge off our taste buds.

While the "natives" washed their rice at least four times before cooking it, our medical advisers disapproved of such refinement. According to them, washing rice detracted from its all-important vitamin content. Consequently, it was the general practice not to wash the rice at all.

Perhaps this was sound logic but, unfortunately, the mice which infested the godowns where the rice was stored were note at all particular where they left their trade-mark, so that often our rice was more like a currant pudding than any other dish.

Apart from the mouse droppings there were great juicy looking maggots in the rest, but these, said medical opinion, were a source of vitamins and were therefore a blessing in disguise.

The majority of the men would have preferred to go without their vitamins in that form but if one went to the trouble of picking out the maggots and other 'foreign' bodies in one's dollop of rice, there was little left to eat. It was a matter of choosing between the lesser of two evils, and gradually we grew accustomed to eating anything that was available without first extracting the 'extras' from it.

Hunger is a great slayer of convention. It reduced the finicky and the fastidious to the same level as the individual who ate his peas with his knife as a matter of course and saw no reason why he shouldn't.

To the man who, in other days, would have raised his hands in horror had there been a hair in his soup, hunger smoothed away his artificial veneer, and made of him the common mortal he was meant to be. And in time he came to eat maggots, mouse droppings and any old thing that happened to be in his food with an impartiality that could not be improved on.

So we continued to exist on our rice and *gippo*, a weak soup made from whatever was obtainable – hibiscus leaves, for instance – flavoured with the few scraps of meat that occasionally came out from the cold storage in Singapore.

In the matter of the cold storage, too, our luck was out, for the machinery had broken down, or was deliberately wrecked before the white flag went up.

This, however, was but one of the idiot tricks perpetuated by the garrison who, had they been blessed with the veriest particle of foresight, should have known that in the days to come the cold storage plan would be necessary to their well-being.

Before the capitulation, large quantities of tinned food were destroyed by the troops bayonetting the tins, which lay about in heaps for months after, as a reminder that such a belated 'scorched earth' policy had done them more damage than it had the Japanese, who, as a rule, made little use of such stores for their own food requirements.

The natives, too, were affected by this stupid destruction of food in so far as it gave them less to sell in the black market to the men who were now risking their lives daily in the hope of getting something tasty to eat from the kampong outside the wire.

Success or failure in this respect has signalled at night time by the presence or absence of cooking fires in the billets of the foragers as they prepared for a pouch-up on what they had taken such a risk to get.

It was not so easy to get out of camp these days, as Captain Bell's wire had spread all over the area and impeded the free passage of prisoners from the camp to the outside world. The craze for barbed wire had also spread to the individual, so that soon every section had its own "defences." Where before had been the open camp unhampered by boundaries, were now well-defined sections through which it was impossible to pass other than by the pathways left open for that purpose.

It was an offence, both in the eyes of the Japanese and our own authority, for anyone to go outside of his own particular area boundary. Anyone found doing so would be fired upon by the former while our own people were prepared to take the necessary action to prevent a repetition of the occurrence were anyone caught breaking bounds by the camp police.

Actually, the Jap guards were not very sedulous in keeping an eye on the camp other than for an occasional patrol that made the rounds of the perimeter wire at odd hours. It was not so much the patrol that had to be feared, as their practice of not keeping to a routine detail.

Our own police, of course, worked to a routine and were the more easily by-passed on that account. There were, too, police guards at all entrances to the camp, and these men worked in conjunction with the Japs to keep us within bounds.

Also there were the Sikhs, indigenous or otherwise, who had thrown in their lot with the Japs, and were given the honour of guarding the sahibs who formerly had been their overlords.

Many of these Sikhs were believed to have been in Malaya some time before hostilities with Japan commenced. They were not necessarily Indian army personnel and many of them were not, though some obviously were.

Where compliance with the saluting order was concerned, the Sikhs were stricter than the Japs. Failure to salute a Sikh was a guarantee of a bashing, whereas a Jap might be content with administering a few swipes across the face accompanied with some Jap invective.

Initially, getting swiped across the face was degrading but after you had been through the routine several times it became the norm and was accepted as part of day-to-day existence. Of course if you had the spirit, minus the common sense, that wins V.C.s, you could strike back when you were 'degraded' and possibly lose your head as a consequence.

The Sikh guards were instrumental in our first shooting fatality among the boundary-breaking fraternity and also of a mystery which, to the best of my knowledge, was never resolved.

One night, two P.O.W.s visited the *kampong* where I had met Nai Soon, and on their way back to camp fell afoul of the Sikhs who happened to be at the wrong place at the right moment.

In the ensuing scrimmage, shots were fired and one of the P.O.W.s was killed. At least a body was later found but, strange to relate, it was not the body of the second man who had visited the *kampong*. He was missing and, so far as I know, he remained missing.

This incident caused a bit of a kerfuffle. The camp guard commander, a sergeant, lost a stripe while the Japs took the Brigadier to their H.Q. for a heart-to-heart – minus the brandy and caviar. The Japs were upset, not because a P.O.W. had been shot, but because one was missing.

Death by shooting caused little more than a hiccup in the routine of camp life. Once the body joined the others in the cemetery down the road the incident was closed. Certainly it caused no dismay among the fence-riders: they already knew that their errant behaviour could be ended any time by a bullet if their luck ran out.

Before the shooting fatality I had paid another visit to the *kampong*, hoping to contact Nai Soon again. I had been disappointed, though I did have a bit of luck in being able to buy a pound of flour and, more importantly, a half-pound of sugar. This was a blessing for Smithy who was still in the dysentery ward.

With the flour, and a pinch of the precious sugar, John and I made fritters, frying them in some oil he assured me was coconut oil. It tasted more like a mixture of turpentine and castor oil even though it fried the fritters to a golden brown.

For once John's acumen had let him down. Had the oil been of any value it would not have remained for such a long time in the wrecked shop in the village where he found it.

Richard Laverton, who was still in detention, had the satisfaction of seeing one of the police, who had confiscated the fritters we had smuggled into the detention barracks, have a bad time after eating them. John and I, whose stomachs were not so finicky, ate our share of the fritters. Though not a gastronomic delight, they were eaten with relish…

Chapter Five

Smithy Yearns For a Coconut

Early in the third month of captivity a new interest entered the lives of the inmates of Changi Camp. The first outside working party left for Singapore, and was quickly followed by others.

These working parties were detailed for various jobs, such as reconstruction work and the cleaning of rubble from the streets. The docks, too, came in for a fair share of work and though much of it was of a military nature and should not, therefore, have been carried out by us, the Japs paid no attention to our complaints on this score while we, on the other hand, made good use of our opportunities to raid the godowns in quest of food at every available opportunity.

On these first working parties to Singapore, the Japanese encountered were many and varied. One outstanding feature of their make-up was their obvious lack of 'hate' for the English. The word 'British' did not appear in their vocabulary. One was either an English soldier, or an Australian, or maybe a belated American. Later, of course, there were also the Dutch, who as yet had not arrived in any strength at Singapore.

The general feeling of the Japs appeared to be a reserved amiability, and a conversation I had with one, a corporal, on my first day at Singapore on a working party, may serve to explain their apparent wish that the good relationship between Japan and England prior to the war had been maintained.

This corporal was in charge of the job we were working on – clearing rubble from a bombed area. When some of the men, not too sure about how the Japs would react, started to run in order to keep up with the bogies which were dumping the rubble into an old canal, the corporal became quite concerned.

Perhaps he was still under the influence of an inherited inferiority complex and had not got used to his elevated position as ganger over a bunch of white men.

Whatever the case, he went up to the men concerned and, pointing to the sun, admonished them.

Going through the pantomime of running, he said:

'No good!' and in sign language, for his English was very limited, advised them to take things easy.

Every hour he gave us a break, making sure we all remained in the shade while it lasted. He talked about the war and things in general, while all the Japs in his party crowded round and took part in the conversation to the best of their ability. Most of them knew some English, and they were all adept at sign language.

'Before the war,' said the corporal, 'Japan and England...' and he gave the clasped hand of friendship. 'Then war came and Japan and England...' and here he pulled his hands apart in a gesture that was as expressive as any words.

Here another Jap chimed in to say, 'English all right, but Churchill...!'

Evidently Father Churchill had upset the little men, for they certainly were most resentful towards him.

Churchill, in their opinion, was no better than an American – and that was bad! They did not like our ostentatious cousins one little bit!

On another occasion I had a talk with a three-star Jap, whose English was better than my own. This fellow was quite frank in his assumption that Japan would lose the War.

'Japan,' he said, 'has not the resources to successfully engage in a long war. England and America have everything. We have nothing but our determination and courage, and these are not enough...'

These two, the corporal and the three-star, may have been exceptions and, of course, they were not yet tainted by the general 'hate' that eventually got into the majority of the soldiers of Hirohito. But they are a proof that, even after the fall of Singapore, there was no spontaneous hatred for the British – that had to be acquired as time passed and their propaganda machine got into its stride.

*****

Work in the docks area became the plum which every party going to Singapore hoped to pluck. Even the officers in charge of the various working parties were as keen as the men to get into the docks, allaying any twinge of conscience they may have experienced about the legality of our employment by the announcement that, as Japan had not signed the Hague Convention, we were at liberty to assist in their war effort with a clear conscience.

There was little time given to wondering about the destination of the cargoes of shells and bombs we unloaded in the docks. After all, what was the use of idle speculation? We were the victims of adverse fate and our own folly could do little about it.

Such were the depredations of the original working parties to visit the docks that the Japs had to put on an extra guard whose sole duty was to keep us out of the godowns and food dumps. But men who had daily risked being shot at Changi were not to be deterred by a few sentries, when there was all manner of food to be got for the taking.

Many of the Jap sentries were astonished when we showed them the food we had brought from Changi. Some of them would not believe us when we told them we were not getting enough to eat, and did nothing to improve our rations. There were others, though, who gave us tins of milk and jam, or anything else that was available. In the matter of tea, too, they were incredulous and disinclined to believe that we could drink such stuff.

Every working party was allowed two 'tea boys', whose sole duty was to brew tea – or *ocha* as the Japs called it – for the workers. There was, of course, no milk or sugar, and I shall never forget the surprised expression on the face of the first Jap I saw sampling our tea.

Their *ocha* was a pale, sickly sweet beverage which they drank cold, while ours ranged through all the different shades of brown to midnight black, and was often as rank as a brew of senna pods.

Spitting out his tentative mouthful of tea, this Jap inquired in evident surprise, *'Sato hi?'*

Then muttering *'dame, dame,'* he went off and fetched about a gallon of sugar which he tipped into the tea.

'O.K.?' he asked. And we said: 'Number one!' which was our way of expressing satisfaction in the vernacular and, at the same time, giving him the impression that he was a great guy.

And so he was, for he gave us sugar every day...

When the Japs on the job were kindly disposed towards us, they gave us permission to go into the town during the *Yasumi* period so that we might buy food and cigarettes.

Owing to the scarcity of money – for at that time "pay" was 10 cents a day, and the majority of the men were without money when the white flag went up – these shopping expeditions degenerated into scabbing forays, and were

51

eventually stopped.

In Singapore the shopkeepers were not philanthropically disposed towards us, and charged a black market price for everything.

It was with a clear conscience, therefore, that we scabbed anything we could get our hands on, and the Japs were not at all sympathetic to the plaints of the tradespeople. Indeed, there were many occasions when they compelled a shopkeeper to make a refund when he had grossly over-charged.

This, of course, was not a general practice of the Japs, but it did happen as a proof that in every community – even among the Japanese – there is a percentage of decent individuals who, if given the chance, will behave in a Christian spirit and do what they can to assist anyone who is not in a position to maintain his rights.

Unfortunately for us the percentage of Japs kindly disposed towards us was small, even at Singapore in the early days. And as time passed, and the War developed into a temporary stalemate, this fraction grew smaller and eventually became almost non-existent though, right to the end, there was always the odd one or two who remained sympathetic...

*****

As at Changi our own officers were in charge of the working parties going to Singapore. With each party there usually was one, or sometimes two, Jap sentries who lounged about in the shade and paid scant attention to us, provided we got on with the job.

Like Captain Bell, some of the officers were all for appeasement, and frowned on our scabbing activities. At the same time they made sure they did not return empty-handed to Changi when the workers went back in the evening.

We did likewise, in spite of a sometimes strict supervision from both sides, and on those first working parties to Singapore a great quantity and variety of food was scabbed from the godowns and made its way to camp.

This made an opening for another black market as, for a time, the same units were going to Singapore and bringing back food which sold in the camp at exorbitant prices, forgetting that but a short time previously they had been cursing the natives in the kampong across the way for a similar extortion.

As well as food, Singapore exported items of news, supposedly the real thing, to swell the unceasing rumours that were a feature of life at Changi. Originated mostly in the latrines, and known as borehole news, these rumours in substance were as authentic as those brought back from Singapore, and did their part to maintain the flagging interest of all and sundry by the hope, tenuous as it might be, that our days of captivity would not be prolonged.

The credulity of the men was amazing. The more fantastic and improbable the news, the more avidly was it listened to and believed.

Unreliable as was our borehole wireless it never lost its appeal. Disappointed by the non-materialisation of some change for our betterment, we readily found comfort in the next batch of rumours promising speedy relief, and sometimes liberation.

As early as June in our first year, a very strong rumour set our imaginations aflame. Hitler had abdicated and his S.S. troops had taken over in a last endeavour to stem the advance of the British on Berlin!

For a while I believed this piece of news myself, having spoken to the sergeant who had, according to his own admission, listened to the wireless from which it emanated.

He must have been drinking sake! And I must have been a fool!

So persistent was the news of imminent liberation, supposedly picked up on secret wirelesses, that I have often wondered if for some obscure reason the Japs, knowing that there must be a set or two in the camp, broadcast this false information four our consumption. It is quite possible, though doubtful, that they did do this in the belief that we should be more easily supervised if we thought it was but a matter of months before we regained our liberty.

*****

Richard Laverton had finished his detention and was looking a bit more peaked when he went in. To celebrate his release, a pouch-up was decided upon, but on what to feast was another matter.

In the larder was a small amount of flour which had been scabbed from the black marketeers; also two loaves of bread, the first to enter our billet since our coming to Changi.

We might make do with that, though the resultant meal could hardly be described as a pouch-up in the real sense of the phrase.

A meal was only a pouch-up when there was something extra special about it, and at the moment our larder did not contain anything that might cause an ecstatic rumbling in the stomach of a hungry man just released from detention.

However, there were ways and means of altering this state of affairs if one had the nerve, and there was plenty of this in my billet, though it did not always improve the position in the larder when it undertook to do so.

Thinking about the money I had paid for the few odds and ends I had bought in the *kampong* at different times, I came to the conclusion that the natives owed me something, though they would think otherwise if I mentioned the fact to them. The obvious thing, then, was to say nothing, but to make up the deficit myself to the best of my ability, if that were possible. And it was.

On my last visit to the *kampong*, where I had spent John's last couple of dollars for a few cigarettes for Smithy, who had come back to use apparently none the worse for his attack of dysentery, though looking more bony than when he went into the hospital, I had noticed something interesting.

In the *kampong* were several henhouses and a large number of ducks ran quacking about the place. One henhouse in particular, and the largest of the lot, was half-concealed in the shrubbery at the edge of the *kampong*. I had often wondered if Nai Soon's uncle owned it. Not that the possibility gave me a twinge of conscience. If his uncle, according to Nat, would not give milk to the needy, there was little point in my asking him for a chicken or even a fat duck. Solution: take one.

This decision was an indication of the breakdown in the moral standards that afflicted everyone in the camp. If an opportunity to increase your food intake presents itself, take it. Only the timid or the few who still retained a strong sense of integrity would choose to remain hungry. As my moral integrity in the matter of food had long since been blunted, Nai Soon's uncle was about to lose a chicken or a fat duck.

I found Smithy loitering at the foot of a coconut tree, trying to make up his mind about scabbing one of the half-dozen nuts that still hung twenty feet or so above his head, and risk a spell of jankers if Captain Bell or one of the camp police caught him in the act.

In normal circumstances a coconut has little gastronomic appeal. Alter the circumstances and it becomes a mouth-watering tit-bit.

As I watched Smithy I could well realise how his belly was urging him to break the order regarding the natural resources of the camp.

'Even if you are caught,' it was saying, 'you'll have had the coconut. They can't take that away from you after you've eaten it, and what is a couple of days' jankers anyway…?'

'You remind me of a well-known advertisement,' I called from where I was grubbing in a patch of rank weeds, hoping to unearth some lemon grass or ginger. 'You know that one of the two hungry looking kids standing outside a pie shop with their noses pressed to the window and imaginatively eating the pies within.'

54

'Meat pies, do you mean, or just pies? I don't believe such things exist anymore,' Smithy shouted back. 'But that coconut up there – that's real and substantial. Tonight it will be in my belly – and maybe yours if you co-operate.'

'Tonight, Smithy,' I insinuated, 'there will be more than a lousy coconut in your belly if things turn out as I have planned.'

'Don't tell me you are going to that *kampong* again, Mick,' he said, suddenly serious. 'It's not worth the risk. It's much better to have an empty belly than one full of lead.' Then, to belie his wisdom he added: 'But what have you got in mind? There's no money in the house, is there?'

'No, the last of the money went on you while you were swinging the lead in the hospital. To show your appreciation of our generosity you will have to help me out tonight. Laverton has come back to the fold, and you yourself have not been back many days. Then there was that bacon and stuff we never ate, so this pouch-up I have planned is long overdue. Are you game?'

'You know I am, Mick, but I think it's silly just the same. What are you after?'

'How would you care for a chicken?'

'A chicken!'

'Sure, if you are willing to help me scab it – but I know you are; you've just said so.'

'A chicken!' repeated Smithy, as though he were looking at something ethereally beautiful on the far horizon. 'A real chicken...'

'Yes. Just think what you could do with a whole chicken, Smithy, or maybe a duck. I like a duck, don't you? It would give you a new lease of life and help you to get back some of that fat you left behind in hospital. How about it?'

'If you honestly believe there is a chance of getting either, you can rely on me to help you out, Mick. Where is it, and when do we get it?'

'Well,' I said casually, coming over to join him beneath the coconut tree, 'it, or they, is or are in the *kampong*. Let us hope the plural applies in this case.'

'Oh! The *kampong* – just what I thought. You might get shot, you know.'

'You've said that before, Smithy, and don't forget that you might get shot, too. The Japs are not particular when they see anyone snooping about outside the wire after roll call. But then many a man has been shot for less than a chicken – not that I intend getting either of us shot. I know the layout pretty thoroughly by now and there is little danger if we keep our wits about us. Some of the chaps who go out there are a bit too brazen and take too much for granted. When they meet trouble they are usually asking for it...'

'There's something in that, I suppose,' agreed Smithy with a pensive wage of his head, and I could see the chicken was troubling him. 'All right, I'm with you,' he said, suddenly determined. 'After all, a chicken is a chicken – or maybe a duck. What do you want me to do?'

Leaving Smithy sitting beneath the forgotten coconut to digest the plan I had outlined to him, I went back to my quarters where John was already making preparations for the coming feast.

*****

There was no moon that night as Smithy and I left our billet and by-passed the 'prowlers' whose duty it was to stalk about the camp after dark and ensure that no one scabbed anything, or left his own particular area.

'Threading a way through the barbed wire that straggled about on all sides, we safely negotiated the first barrier lying between us and the road. On the far side lay a further barrier of wire, while the hut of the camp police guarded the outlet through the perimeter wire which bisected the road. Should we fall afoul of the police going out, we should be in for a dose of jankers; not that that would matter a lot. It was during our return journey, provided we were successful, that we should have to move with great circumspection for if the police apprehended us they would confiscate whatever we had been able to get in the kampong, and that would be a greater punishment than all the jankers they could get us.

'From the police hut the perimeter wire stretched in a half circle to the sea on the left, while on the right, it joined up with the boundary wire of our neighbours, in whom at the moment we had no interest. It was outside this wire that the Jap or Sikh guards might be encountered. They seldom came inside it, so that up to the point there was just our own police and the prowlers to contend with.

'Little strategy was needed in outwitting these guardians of a law that was obviously made to be broken, and Smithy and I arrived safely at the outer perimeter.

This barrier was at best a frail affair, being of the Danuk pattern. That is to say it was laid down in coils like an extended spring, two at the bottom surrounded by a third. Frail as it was, the barrier was noisy to get through, and in that lay its nuisance value. The least commotion was likely to bring the police from the road, or a Jap patrol should one be in the vicinity.

The easiest method of negotiating the wire, and one that had been popular in the early days of its existence, was to throw a plank of wood on top of it and walk over. In the present instance this method was too noisy, so I had decided not to go over the wire, but under it.

This was a simple feat, and the means of accomplishing it were provided by a large tree, the branches of which spread out over the wire and made the undertaking possible. Also, the staples that anchored the fence in position were few and far between at this point and allowed plenty of play in the wire when it was hoisted from the ground.

Clambering up the tree, I lowered one end of the strand of fine but strong wire I had brought for the purpose, and Smithy quickly made it fast to the barrier, which I then hauled up sufficiently to allow a free passage underneath.

It was possible, of course, that the wire I had fixed to the tree might be spotted by the patrol if they came up that way; if so, Smithy, who would be stationed by the tree, would be in the soup and I should have to find some other way into the camp. It was a chance we had to take, and there was little likelihood of anything going amiss in that direction.

When I descended from the tree, Smithy shinned up it and a few moments later I was skulking in the shrubbery on the other side. Knowing the layout of the *kampong* pretty well from my previous visits, I quickly approached the hen-house I had chosen as my objective.

A mangy old pariah dog which I had met before was sniffling about, causing me to lie low and hope that it did not wind me. Once these pariahs start to howl they continue indefinitely, sometimes not stopping till the morning.

Fortunately this decrepit creature had little howl left in him, but there were others in the *kampong*, and he might set them off if he got wheezing in alarm.

The snuffling of the old dog was the only sign of life about the *kampong*, and soon even he ceased to roam about and allowed me to gain the hen-house where the most difficult part of the undertaking was waiting for me.

Often during the long trek down Malaya prior to the fall of Singapore, I had scabbed a chicken from some native hen-roost. Now I was a bit perturbed by the knowledge that, as soon as I got among the chickens, there would be an immediate cackling of protest.

The usual native affair, the hen-house was constructed from plaited bamboo and thatched with *atap*, while the door was a flimsy affair kept in position by a bamboo pole. Opening this I instinctively waited for the chickens to get going, but nothing happened. Almost conspiratorial in their supineness, they did not even say 'hullo,' and in a matter of seconds I had depleted their numbers by one, which reclined in unprotesting co-operation in the sack I had brought with me. Also in the sack was a fat duck whose only comment on its change of quarters was a hoarse quack or two soon stifled by the thick sack.

There is an old proverb which I have often found to be true, as it was in this case. It goes something like this: 'Give a fool an inch and he'll take a mile.'

Having acquired my bag so easily, I was not content to call it a day and make tracks for home, but must hunt round in the darkness for eggs, with disastrous results.

Putting too much weight on the hen-roost while I leaned over to search among some wickerwork baskets in which the fowl laid, the bamboo roost came out of the slot in which it was fixed and I went sprawling beneath a shower of outraged poultry. Even the hitherto complacent ducks in the corner became alarmed and joined in the hub-bub with discordant quacks.

Freeing myself from the fluttering chickens, I grasped the sack and ran for the cover of the shrub, pursued by the mangy pariah which had come to life and was yapping hysterically at my heels.

Turning quickly before I gained the bushes, I aimed a kick at the mongrel and with a yelp of astonishment he turned tail and scurried back to the kampong, where one hysterical hen was still complaining noisily of my intrusion.

Approaching the wire with caution, I lay in the scrub awaiting the all clear signal from Smithy, who for weeks past had been practising the call of the bittern that hung about by the sea shore and jarred us nightly with its pile-driving call – something like the noise made by a man driving a pole with a wooden mallet, or two stones being knocked together.

Smithy's technique, for which he used two pieces of hard wood, was not perfection, but it was near enough the real thing to pass in an emergency. Three notes would indicate all clear, and two, repeated twice, danger.

Lying in the scrub, trying to stifle the indignant cluckings of the chicken, the duck being still complacent, I was keenly conscious of the brightness of the stars, which had made their appearance in myriads, and all the night noises which, in the excitement of the moment, I had not before noticed.

In the swamp bordering the shore the bull frogs were sending up their nightly chorus of discordant croakings in competition with the chee-*chee*-chee of the multitudes of lizards that shared the swamp with them.

By my watch I knew that the half-hour's grace allowed me before the signal was given was past, and as I lay wondering if something perhaps had miscarried, the swamp orchestra suddenly stopped, and I knew before Smithy's alarm came beating through that uneasy silence that someone was approaching along the shore.

58

As if sensing that help was near, the duck started a muffled quacking which was as suddenly cut off as I felt for its neck and pressed tightly. Profiting from this show of brutality, the chicken remained quiet for the ensuing quarter of an hour before Smithy's all clear came to relieve the tension and seal the fate of the inmates of the sack.

Hurriedly I scrambled beneath the wire which Smithy let down behind me, and in ten minutes we were safe in our billet in the camp.

*****

Though the chicken scabbing foray had been a success, there were others who were not so fortunate in their visits to the *kampong*. Some days later the inevitable tragedy of the unknown man who had been shot by the Sikhs was repeated.

Three men were caught outside the wire and taken into custody by the Japs. After a trial they were shot, and for a while the line-riders were discouraged by the summary execution of their comrades for an offence which they regarded as a minor infringement of camp regulations.

Everyone who went out through the wire knew, of course, what the penalty could be were he apprehended.

Collectively we took it for granted that, sooner or later, someone would pay the penalty for our rashness. However, fatalistically everyone thought: 'Even if someone is caught it won't be me.'

This attitude towards our personal safety was engendered by the knowledge that, basically, we were living a day-to-day existence. Eventually, taking risks became normal procedure, thus putting your life on the line for a few cigarettes or some extra rations was not considered heroic. It was routine for those who took the risks.

It was not only the lure of cigarettes and extra food that entice men to break camp. Some of the men who had been garrisoned at Changi barracks went as far afield as the next village where they got in touch with some of the local bints and so renewed old acquaintances.

In the circumstances, answering 'the call of the wild' in this fashion was foolhardy, especially as the men taking part in it were dressed in civilian clothes, thus making them liable to be shot as spies if apprehended.

It transpired later that the men who had played the major role in the triple executions were in civilian clothes. This gave the Japs the legal right to execute them on the assumption they were spies. Though for whom they could have been spying was a problem not solved by their deaths. Certainly it was not for

Changi camp, where the borehole wireless kept us in touch with current events, even though most of the 'news' was wishful thinking.

It was never clearly established where the civilian clothes came from. The most likely source was the kampong whose residents had profited from the bounty left behind by the garrison of Changi barracks when it evacuated the area prior to the capitulation. Likely they also were responsible for the wreckage caused in the shops in the village where earlier I had unearthed Susy Ann and the clock that went when I carried it...

Civilian clothing was a problem for the camp concert party who put on some stunning performances in the Globe Theatre.

Of such a high standard were the Globe players that it was not uncommon to have Japs, including officers, in the audience; possibly, as admission was free, in order to save face the Japs eased restrictions on the Globe obtaining material and make-up from outside the camp.

Wherever they got it, the end result was outstanding and the artistry exemplary. On occasions the 'ladies' in evening dress looked so authentic, many in the audience felt a revival of emotions they chose to suppress...

Chapter Six

Advice in the Afternoon

Since meeting Nai Soon in the *kampong* of his uncle I had been three times through the wire to wait on the strip of beach where I had first met him, hoping that he would come again. But he did not come, or if he did, it was while I was absent from my hiding place in the scrub overlooking the Straits and Paula Ubin, where I assumed he lived.

Though the executions were distinctly discouraging, they did not deter us from going again to the *kampong* of Nai Soon's tight-fisted uncle: they were not final enough for that. I did, however, agree with John and the others that it was no longer advisable, or sensible, to go through the wire on the off-chance of getting a few cigarettes, or maybe some food. Frankly, the possibility of gratifying my appetite at such a risk to my continued existence no longer appealed and, for the first time since coming to Changi, I realised that my life was of more account than I had before deemed it.

There was, however, one factor for which I was still determined to take the risk of going through the wire. That was the possibility of meeting Nai Soon again.

He was my one hope of liberation, and should I lose my life in contacting him – well, that was just one of the possibilities I should have to contend with if I should ever leave Changi in an escape bid.

There would be little difficulty in leaving the actual camp – that would be just another boundary-breaking episode. It was ultimate escape from the island we wanted and, with Nai Soon's assistance we hoped to achieve that. What befell afterwards was beyond our reckoning, and we could therefore make no provision for it.

Fostered by the borehole wireless there was in met at this time a growing conviction that contact with our own forces might be made in Thailand where, according to rumour, British and Chinese forces were engaging the Japs in the vicinity of the Malay border.

Like most of the other camp gossip this news had no foundation on fact, though there were many in the camp, including myself, who believed there was some truth in it.

I did not consider at the time what would eventuate if all the news coming into the camp were false. Sufficient was it that the tempo of our plans to escape was speeded up by I and by the possibilities of Nai Soon's assistance.

The difficulties of getting to the *kampong* of the Chinese youth's paternal uncle, about whom Nai Soon did not show that affection generally accorded their elders by all young Chinese men with whom I had previously come in contact, were piling up daily.

Since the treble execution our camp police were more diligent in patrolling the fence; also, the Jap and Sikh patrols were noticed more frequently outside the perimeter. In spite of these precautions, many of the fence-riders still went out: though mostly under cover of darkness.

To go at night time was of little use to me, for Nai Soon was not likely to be along the shore in the dark. To leave the camp in daylight was to court disaster. It had to be done, however, and there was little profit to be got from worrying about the consequences if I were caught.

Some days elapsed before I found the obvious solution to my difficulties: and one that would lessen the risk of detection. To enter the *kampong* at night was not too difficult; therefore I decided to leave the camp before daylight and remain hidden in the scrub on the edge of the *kampong* during the day, returning to the camp again when night fell.

Morning and evening roll calls were a snag to this plan; the evening one especially which was supervised by the Japs. Morning roll call was just a routine parade under our own officers, and it was possible to wangle this. It was also possible to wangle the Jap check-up, too, as the camp staff, such as police and cook-house personnel, were excused parade. Given sufficient incentive, one of these could be bribed to take my place.

Even then there was the not improbable complete check-up by the Jap guards who periodically got everybody in the camp on parade so that the whole complement could be verified. Should they choose the day on which I intended to remain in the *kampong* it would be a bit of bad luck. Even then I might get away with it if I made some lame excuse to account for my absence. This had been done before, by men who were genuinely absent through forgetfulness or some other cause, not necessarily dependent on their absence from the camp. Usually if a man were absent and turned up later the Japs were so relieved that they let him off with a slapping as a reminder not to do it again.

If my deception on the morning roll call was discovered it would, of course, mean jankers, both for me and the man who was deputising for me. To explain the reason for my absence would profit me nothing. Would-be escapees were not encouraged by the camp commandant, so that it would be useless to say I had been out reconnoitring the ground.

In fairness to our camp administration, I must admit there was a certain amount of truth in their plaint that none of the men who broke bounds were actually endeavouring to escape, but were visiting forbidden *kampongs* and even Singapore. This was in some respects true. There were however, individuals like myself ever on the look-out for a chance to get away, so that it was scarcely fair to condemn everyone who went out of camp because of the slight unpleasantness that would arise with the Japs if anyone were caught - as, for instance, when the Brigadier was thrown into the cooler after our first fatality.

On that occasion he owed his imprisonment more to the failure of anyone to identify the body than the fact that there was a body to be identified.

*****

Early on a morning when the heavy ground mists were still drifting sleepily before a strong on-shore breeze, I left the camp and went to the *kampong* of Nai Soon's uncle.

By then I had a surfeit of Changi and everything connected with it. The urge to get away was stronger than ever before.

Since leaving my first quarters in the camp a great feeling of despondency had been upon me. Daily this was becoming more demoralising owing to the continual bickering over food, and the all too obvious realisation that our own administration, more than that of the Japs, was responsible for so much misunderstanding in the camp.

Indeed, I found at this time that my urge to escape was fostered more by a desire to get away from the influence of the camp administration than from the Japs who, to give them their due, did not pester my waking hours with red tape and bullshit, even though they did try to starve me…

Again, every day that passed brought me in closer contact with a doctrine I despised. That practised by the 'old soldier' prisoner who scabbed from all and sundry and found a great sense of personal satisfaction in boasting of his exploits, usually of a sordid nature and conferring little distinction on anyone, old soldier or otherwise.

Gradually I could feel myself being drawn into the vortex of prison life where to be honest and fair dealing was a distinct disadvantage and, indeed, a lessening of one's chances of survival.

I had no objection to living by my wits, assisted by the grace of God, for I was not content, as so many were, to exist on rice only, as to lay the foundations of a big belly. I did, however, set myself a boundary which I did not cross in my scabbing activities.

Sommers, Laverton and Smithy also had their moral code and kept it intact.

I did not relish the reflection that I was becoming a part of the muddy torrent of petty spite and underhand dealing that was sweeping through the camp. Bitter as was this realisation, I benefited from it in that I was more determined than before to make a getaway. John, too, was browned off and praying for something to happen, while the complacent Smithy set his course by our reckoning, and was willing to tow along wherever we steered.

Laverton had taken Smithy's place in the hospital, having gone down with dysentery shortly after his release from the detention barracks, and would have to be left behind if our plans matured before he recovered sufficiently to travel.

Lying in my hiding place in the scrub bordering the *kampong*, I thought of all this and hoped that Nai Soon might come sometime during the day.

At the threat of the hot sun beginning to peep over the horizon, the mist along the shore began to lift, leaving me damp and shivering in my hiding place.

There had been a threat of rain in the morning sky but this, too, vanished before the sun, which drenched the cold swampy scrub land with a pleasant warmth, and sent me off to sleep in the first hour.

A feeling of acute hunger and indefinable sense of someone not far away brought me back to consciousness and the realisation that I had committed the unforgivable sin of falling asleep at my post. The sun was when well up in a cloudless sky. Down the Straits a Jap warship was slowly steaming towards the Pacific, while nearer in shore a small coastal steamer, crowded with a mixed cargo of Chinese, Malays and Tamils, chugged along towards Singapore. All eyes on the steamer were turned in the direction of Changi, where the prisoners could be seen strolling about the village and on the surrounding hillside.

At first I thought it was the traffic in the Straits that had brought the threat of danger to my slumbering consciousness. That this was not so became apparent as my eyes ran along the shore to where the wire cut off the village from the *kampong* in which I was hiding. At this point a Jap patrol was slowly picking its way along the shore on my side of the wire.

There was nothing unusual about the patrol; indeed, I had expected to see

64

one or two during the day. But seeing it in retrospect and in reality engendered two different states of emotion and as it came along the beach towards me, I felt that my hide-out was the extreme in transparency.

Normally the patrol did not trouble about the beach and only traversed the perimeter outside the boundary wire. Why they should pick this particular day to deviate from their routine inspection was filling me with uneasiness as I watched them draw nearer along the shore. I wondered, too, what would happen if Nai Soon should choose that particular moment to arrive.

Even as the thought came to me, a canoe swam into my line of vision half way between the shore and Paula Ubin. Approaching at an angle that would bring it in line with my hiding place about the same time as the patrol arrived there, if they continued on towards me, the canoe, when within a hundred yards or so of the shore, swung round abruptly and headed down the Straits, and I was sure that its occupant was Nai Soon.

Thankful as I was that he had seen the patrol and not landed, I was still perturbed by their proximity, and by the thought that Nai Soon might not now come to the beach where he had tentatively promised to meet me.

I need not have worried about the Japs discovering me, for they passed within a dozen feet without even a glance in my direction, and went along the beach towards the kampong.

Evidently I was not the only trespasser, for shortly after the patrol had passed, a shot came from the *kampong*. This was followed by a crashing in the bushes behind me, as one of the men from the camp broke cover and ran along the beach towards the wire.

I knew him by his red hair as a fellow called Ginger Parsons, one of the most daring of the fence riders, and possibly one who had paid more visits to the *kampong* than anyone else in the camp. In order to get to the kampong, Ginger had apparently followed the same plan as myself, but had not been so fortunate as I in remaining hidden from the patrol.

Ginger was one of those individuals who took unnecessary risks by taking things for granted. Normally no Jap or Sikh patrol was to be seen during the hottest hours of the day, though this did not mean, of course, that there was not one in the vicinity.

Having failed to encounter any at this time of day on his many visits, to the *kampong*, Ginger had taken it for granted that he never would. Now he was finding out the danger of such a state of mind as he ran for the point where the wire debouched into the water.

Watching him, I had little fear for his safety. Ginger had been chased from the kampong before, though not at this particular hour, and knew the ropes pretty thoroughly.

My concern was for myself, for, having raised one hare from the covert, the patrol might make a search for another, and I should be in the soup. Ginger, however, scotched such a possibility by his actions and, as I watched the chase, I forgot my momentary fears and wished him God speed.

As the tide was out he was forced to run across the sand for some way before coming to a point where he could take to the water and swim over the barrier. When he had accomplished this he had then to run back on the inside for a couple of hundred yards or more before getting to cover among the mangroves and rank grass that grew along the edge of the swamp.

As he left the water and ran across this open stretch, the patrol burst from the scrub and ran on to the open beach. With cool deliberation two of them stopped and, raising their rifles, fired at the running figure. At the same time there arose a confused babbling and shouting as they called him to stop. Ginger, apparently, had other ideas, or else the deliberation of the Jap marksmen had not been as cool as I had thought, for Ginger dived into the bushes and disappeared.

I expected the Japs to follow the way he had gone. Instead they held a heated argument, or so it seemed to me, and then made off along the wire towards the road and, I was sure, a general shindy in the camp.

The police at the barrier would bear the brunt of the patrol's displeasure. The guard commander at least would have his face slapped, which was hardly fair in the circumstances. But then, he ought not to have volunteered for such a position, and I supposed the police were more prepared to take the rough with the smooth being, by virtue of their office, racketeers in the best tradition, and usually getting the pick of whatever was going.

Ginger's escapade would, in all probability, mean a Jap check-up for the whole camp, so that my absence, if it had not already been discovered, would soon be verified. There was nothing I could do about that at the moment, so I left it and returned to the more pressing business of Nai Soon's whereabouts.

He had disappeared as completely as had Ginger. For an hour I watched the Strait hopefully, but the canoe did not re-appear. Numerous craft passed up and down, but not that of Nai Soon.

At the end of another hour, when the sun was half-way down its homeward path, I ate a handful of cooked rice I had brought with me and chewed a piece of sweet potato reflectively with one eye on the sea. Still Nai Soon did not come. Another twenty minutes passed, then suddenly he was here, standing by the tree stump on which he had hung his brother's hat to dry.

For a while I made no sound, thinking he might not be alone. Watching him, I saw he was studying the sand where the patrol had passed, then in the sudden way he had, he turned round and said:

'You should not walk on the sand when you are going to hide near at hand, Johnnie. Where are you?'

'Well, I'm damned,' I said meekly. 'It's a good thing you were not with that patrol, Nat. I'll call you Nat, if you don't mind. Nai Soon sounds a bit – well you know what I mean…'

'That's all right, Johnnie,' he said unconcerned. 'And you? What is your name, if you do not mind?'

'Mick Stirling.'

'Well, Mick, I hear the Japanese have been shooting some of your people. Is that so?'

'Yes, unfortunately. They were caught outside the wire.'

'Yet you venture out knowing that. Not for that tin of milk I promised you. There must be something else. Is there something I can do for you?' and he squatted down on the spot where first I had seen him.

'Yes,' I said eagerly. There *is* something you can do for me but it would not be pleasant for you if the Japs discovered that you were – doing something for me. Would it?'

'No. Nor for you if they knew you asked me. The Chinese and the Japanese are not good friends. They are, of course, Chinese men who take Japanese money. Some of them earn it, and some of them do not. I might be one or the other, but I am neither. I have not yet forgotten Ah Tek. Now, if you will tell me what I can do, I will listen…'

Thus encouraged I took the plunge and told him of my plans to escape, omitting nothing but the names of the others who were likely to accompany me. When I had finished he was silent for a while. Then he said with a finality that made me feel cold inside:

'You cannot get away, Johnnie. You could maybe leave the camp and hide out in the jungle, but would that be much use? Food would be scarce; as scarce as it is in your camp. Also, you would get malaria. Then what would you do? It is better that you remain where you are until something happens to improve matters. The Japanese have all Malaya and Thailand, and are not fighting in Burma, so where can you go? Nowhere.'

Yes, it was final and, by the way, I felt inside I knew he was speaking the truth! Yet I persisted, hoping he would give me some encouragement, however slight.

'I had hoped the Japs were not in full control in Thailand,' I told him. 'We had new that our troops were being assisted by Chinese in fighting somewhere near the border. Is that not true?'

'It is not true, Mick. There are, I believe, a number of guerrilla troops in the jungle in Malaya who annoy the Japanese a good deal. You might leave your camp and join them perhaps. But do not forget that you are a European, Mick, and would not last long in the jungle in such conditions. Talk over what I have told you with your friends then come again to this spot, though it is dangerous to do so, and I will meet you if chance wills it... I, too, would like to escape from the Japanese, and like you, I have nowhere to go. My mother is a cripple, and I am her only son. And I am worried about the, Mick. The Japanese are ordering all the people to work for them. Those who refuse are being taken away from their homes, and no one knows where they are going. In Singapore the people are beginning to feel sorry the British have gone – the Japanese are not good masters. I do not go there often. I am afraid for my mother, for if I should be taken away she has nothing but my small sister...'

'You are in as bad a plight as I, Nat,' I replied, appreciating his anxiety for his people. 'I had not realised things were so bad outside. Neither had I realised the obvious truth of what you say about escaping. I should like to try nevertheless, though I cannot say what my friends will decide to do when I tell them what you have told me. Should they still wish to go, will you help us?'

'I will do what I can, which is little, though it will not please me to see you go. But maybe you will change your mind –'

'Thanks, Nat. I'm afraid I owe you an apology, for I had felt distrustful towards you after our first meeting. You know how it is with some of your countrymen...'

'I know,' he said with no sign of offence. 'And you will be foolish, if you do not distrust everybody. There are many people in Singapore and Malaya who would sell you to the Japanese if you put yourself in their power. That is why I say you cannot hope to get away just yet. Later, when the people get to know what kind of a master the Japanese will make, things may change. Now they are not sure and hope to make themselves safe by appearing to like their new masters. Soon they will wish the British back, for they were easy-going and not so domineering as the Japanese, who think too highly of themselves – especially now.'

'Why now?'

'You should know the answer to that,' he said. 'Aren't you one of the reasons for their present feeling of importance?'

'Yes, I guess you are right, Nat. I had not thought of it that way. Obviously the Japs will be a little swollen-headed after Singapore, though it's not worrying me much at the moment. My concern is in getting away from them, and I'm sure we must have a few friends left outside...'

'Yes,' he agreed readily enough, 'but only to the length of helping you with food and tobacco – at a price. Were you to ask for help to escape, many of these seeming friends would not know you – their fear of the Japanese is too great for that. Also, if they did agree to help you there would always be the possibility of you being betrayed...'

'I can see you are as suspicious as I am, Nat. Why?'

'Why?' he repeated, as though it were silly of me to ask such an obvious question. And I suppose it was. 'Everyone must be suspicious of his neighbour in these times, Mick,' he said. 'And not without reason.'

Then he went on to tell me about a party of Australians who had got in touch with a Chinese, who supplied them with a boat stocked with food and water. The Aussies had paid the Chinese some thousands of dollars for his co-operation, and had managed to put to sea.

That was as far as they go, however, and one survivor was brought back the following day by the Japs, who had intercepted them.

The general opinion in the camp after this incident was that the Chinese who took their money had betrayed the unfortunate Aussies. Now, here was Nai Soon – a Chinese – substantiating that opinion!

Noting my crestfallen look, he tried to be consoling:

'Wait awhile and hope that things may change,' he said. 'In the meantime, should you come here again and I am not in the *kampong*, leave a note for me. I shall do likewise. If we bury it in the sand at the base of the tree stump on which I hung my brother's hate – remember? – It should be safe. Will you do that, Mick?'

This was a good idea, and one which I ought to have thought of myself. I agreed to it with alacrity and Nai Soon, glancing quickly at the sun, which was hovering just out of reach of the sea, said warningly:

'It is time you were getting back, Mick. You must have been here a long time before I came, and you will be missed.'

'That has already happened, I'm afraid. In any case I cannot get back safely until it gets dark, which will not be for another hour yet – and I'm hungry...'

'That can be put right if you will wait here while I go to the *kampong*. I have something for you.'

The sun was dipping into the waters of the Straits when he came back. In one hand he carried a piece of old sacking with something wrapped in it. In the other hand he held a bowl of rice in which were two hard boiled duck's eggs. In the sack were a tin of milk and one of jam, and I was not sure at the time which of the hands held the more acceptable gift, though John, when he saw the jam, had no doubts about it.

Nai Soon stayed with me while the twilight crept in from the sea; then, before its last flickerings had merged into the quickly falling night, he said good-bye and went back to the *kampong* and his canoe.

When he had gone I sat for a while to allow the night to get a firm grip on the perimeter wire before venturing through into the camp from which I had been absent twelve hours or more, and where John and Smithy were waiting impatiently for my return.

Chapter Seven

The Quick and the Dead

Gradually the routine of Changi was being disorganised as the Japs' demands for ever-increasing numbers of workers broke up the various groups of friends that had drifted together for companionship or, more materially, because it was beneficial to muck-in with someone in preference to living a lone wolf existence.

John and Smithy were standing by to go to Singapore on a permanent working part. Having just returned from hospital, Richard Laverton was remaining at Changi while, much to my regret, I too, was excluded from the working party owing to my imminent admission to hospital with malaria.

With the departure of John and Smithy, our group would be split in two, and the possibility of our getting together again before some months elapsed was remote. It was necessary, therefore, for me to go again to the *kampong* if we were to realise the ideal for which from day to day we lived. Soon it would be too late, and Nai Soon might have left a message for me. Something that would bring a reprieve from dissolution and keep us together...

Always the theme of escape was running as an undercurrent to our existence, and the possibility of fulfilling it was something that remained constant. It was a light in the darkness of our lives, and it would one day, we hoped, be a blaze in which we could destroy the stigma of our defeat.

Nai Soon was the spark from which we hoped to light our fire, and in a last-minute effort to start the blaze before John and Smithy's departure for Singapore, I went again to the trysting place, and found that the spark had been temporarily extinguished.

Nai Soon had been true to his promise. The note he had buried in the sand filled me with a deep sense of frustration and the realisation that our escape plans were again in jeopardy. At the same time, the note pleased me with its sincerity.

Apparently the Japs were regimenting the people of Malaya to their war effort, and Nai Soon was expecting daily to be conscripted into one of the labour gangs that were being organised. To delay a measure which, he had made plain, was inevitable, he had decided to take his mother and sister to relatives in Singapore.

Why where I could not imagine, though I realised that he was more in touch with current events than I could hope to be. For him the safety of his mother and sister was paramount. Inevitably, no matter where he chose to live, he would fall into the Japanese net for, having already executed his brother, probably for subversive activities, he himself would be under suspicion. Leaving the isolation of Paula Ubin would be no more than a temporary reprieve.

With his farewell note, in which he urged me to have faith and believe in the future, he left two tins of milk, two of jam and one filled with sugar; also three packets of cigarettes. A veritable bonanza!

Conscious of the danger and intrigue in day-to-day existence, and the possibility of his note being discovered by someone else, he addressed me as 'My dear friend' and signed the note 'Nat'.

John's disappointment overcame his relief at my safe return, and even the munificence of Nai Soon's farewell gift could not cheer him.

He and Smithy were off to Singapore the following day, and he had hoped for a last-minute reprieve for the integrity of our party.

Smithy, more complacent and practical-minded, made a fire as a first step to a farewell banquet which Nai Soon's thoughtfulness had made possible.

'We might as well make the most of our last evening together,' he pointed out. 'There is a feast here good enough for the gods. Cheer up, John!'

Then to me:

'I suppose it's all right to have a last pouch-up, Mick? You and Richard'll probably be needing the grub...'

'Go ahead, Smithy,' I said disinterestedly. 'I'm not feeling like grub.'

And I wasn't.

Two hours after John and Smithy had gone down the road with their possessions slung about them like a couple of old troopers setting off on a long campaign, I picked up my bedding roll and headed for the hospital to occupy the bed in the dysentery ward but recently vacated by Laverton. All the other beds were full.

*****

That first period in the hospital was but a monotonous interlude in the unending days of captivity, made more bitter by the reflection that my former hopes of escaping had been dissipated by Nai Soon's decision to go to Singapore, and the breaking up of the individual communities that had been an inevitable part of existence at Changi in the first months of our lives as prisoners.

There remained nothing now but to keep true to Nai Soon's admonition, and hope that someday we might perhaps rebuild our plans for escape on a more solid foundation...

Looking back on those first months at Changi, I cannot but marvel at the credulity of the average prisoner confined there.

The possibility of imminent liberation was fixed firmly in almost everyone's belief. Every scrap of news coming into the camp, or originating from the borehole wireless, was avidly discussed and, in general, believed.

Indeed, the more unlikely the truth of any rumour, the more quickly did it become an established fact in the credulity of the multitudes, waiting only in the marching events to put it into effect.

Unfortunately events, other than the accelerating tempo of day-to-day existence, marched slowly, and at times stopped altogether for want of the stimulus of fresh news to move it forward.

While so many waited in idle complacency for deliverance to come marching up the road, or perhaps, out of the so empty sky, the Japs had been busily planning our future – a future which made no provision for imminent liberation.

The working party on which John and Smithy had gone to Singapore was the first step towards the new future that was opening up for us. No longer were we to spend our days in a perpetual round of fatigues and counter-fatigues while the bureaucrats who ruled Changi filled our days with dissension and disaffection.

And for that every 'other ranks' was glad.

Laverton and I were pleased to say good-bye to Changi soon after my discharge from the hospital, and here we were slogging it down the road to Singapore, strung about with pots and pans and other miscellaneous pieces of gear which we could not afford to leave behind.

John and Smithy had gone to Bukit Timah, where they were working in what had been called the Ford Company's motor works before the Japs took over, and where Laverton and I hoped to join them.

Apart from our wish to renew old acquaintances, we had an ulterior motive in wishing to get to Bukit Timah. Food was reputed good at the camp, and Bukit Timah was therefore the Mecca to which everyone leaving Changi hoped to go.

The Japs had other ideas, however, and it was many a long day before we encountered our muckers.

With an eye to the future, and perhaps also for sentimental reasons – for in spite of their 'other-worldness' they have a certain amount of sentiment in their make-up – the Japs were erecting a series of monuments, or shrines, to commemorate their achievements, and, more indirectly, their dead.

It was to prepare the terrain for one of these shrines that Laverton and I, and five hundred odd others, were struggling down the road from Changi on a hot and sultry day with the temperature taking fitful pecks at the hundred mark.

Unlike, say, the British, the Japs were not content just to clear a site and stick up a thing of stone and mortar with a long list of the glorious dead on it – the whole surrounded by a stereotyped railing – and call it a shrine.

No. They were more comprehensive in their hero worship.

The site for the actual shrine was on an island in McRitchie reservoir, around which lay the extensive Bukit Timah golf course, which, in turn, was flanked by jungle as tangled as that to be found up-county.

When it came to building shrines the Japs were no respecters of property, and soon the golf course resembled more a prospective building site in course of development than a pleasant haunt where old men dallied of an afternoon before going back to the golf house for a gin sling, or whatever else they drank in those days before the Japs came screaming through the rubber which, in all probability, laid the foundation of the fairways which we were now about to despoil.

Our job was to construct a network of roads which radiated like a spider's web from the bridge which ran across the reservoir to the site of the shrine. Up the hill stood the empty golf house, the gaping holes in its roof adding to its mournful and somehow offended appearance, as it looked down with a blank stare at the work of spoliation that was heralding a new age, and a new people not yet sufficiently sophisticated to appreciate its position of prestige in the old community.

The road-making gang went into residence in what had formerly been a 'European' housing estate. All the former occupants had fled, and unfortunately they, or the looters, had removed everything from the house, so that we had to start again from scratch when setting up house. We did, however, have a better lighting system than existed at Changi in that the electrical corporation of Singapore was still functioning on one cylinder, and so gave us an erratic

74

illumination.

On leaving Changi most of us thought we were saying good-bye to the pretty irritations of existence under Southern Area administration. That was not so, although until we got organised our new camp was a free-and-easy sort of place, in which the food was comparatively good and interference by the Japs almost negligible.

Soon, however, our new administration, which included a brigadier, complete with red band, got into its stride and the damp became a bit more lively – but in a different way from what it had been before.

From the camp to the golf course was roughly a distance of two miles, and I shall never forget that first morning we marched along the road, where already the grass and weeds were beginning to obliterate the handiwork of man as the jungle, which fringed the road, sent out its first reconnoitring parties in its reconquest of man's domain.

The morning mist had not yet risen, but shrouded in the trees in ghostly patterns that fitted into the somehow unreal, and unearthly, landscape.

No effort had been made to clean up the debris of battle which littered the wayside, and here and there the hastily dug graves of the slain – friend and foe alike – peeped at us from the mist and grass of the roadside.

At one spot some Australians, who occupied the camp next door to us, were re-interring two British dead they had excavated from a shallow pit in the ditch. As we went past the partly decomposed entrails of the dead were being shovelled into their new resting place, and no man raised his hat or made any sign that he had just seen what might have been the last mortal remains of a friend...

Marching through this former battlefield – where a good deal of the worthwhile fighting had been done – past the gloomy, haunted-seeming woods where the dead lay yet unburied, or, at best, under a thin coating of soil scraped over them in a hurry, I experienced a strange awareness of the men who had fought and died here amid the verdant greenery of the tangled undergrowth.

Marching down the road along which they had struggled in defeat on the way to build a monument symbolic of their defeat – and mine – I felt that unhappy spirits were peering at me from among the trees, and mourning their inability to march again with the living. I felt, too, that these unhappy ones were saddened by the enterprise on which we were bent.

Those spirits were more substantial than the spook creations of an overworked imagination. I had known some of them in the flesh, and as I passed through the unsanctified wilderness in which they lay, I felt somehow that those unhappy souls would be held in bondage until the grass which was beginning to overrun the road was cut back, and the highway echoes once again to the clank and bustle of traffic, heralding the new battle that was yet to come before these dwellers in the mist would be at rest and allowed to depart on their several ways…

As we left the road thousands of fellow prisoners were converging on the golf course, for there were several camps in the neighbourhood which sent men to the road-making. In a surging mass we bore down on the half-dozen sword-begird Jap officers, and a number of smaller fry, who were waiting to put us through our paces.

Before they could explain what was required of us the rain came slashing down in a sudden torrent of indignation, and in a couple of seconds everyone was soaked to the skin. But it takes more than a shower of rain to wash the enthusiasm out of a Jap once he has set his mind to something.

Ignoring the downpour which was transforming them from immaculate fashion plates into bedraggled scarecrows, the Jap officers got us sorted out into groups, and we set to with a will.

It was cold, and to work was the one way of keeping warm until the sky relented and the sun came back to a sodden landscape.

As this was our first big job, and was not to be compared with the daily working parties to Singapore, everyone was curious as to how the Japs would react. There was, too, a certain amount of uneasiness mixed with the general curiosity.

While at Singapore we had seen what the Japs were capable of when displeased – though admittedly, their displeasure on those occasions had centred more on the Chinese dock workers than it had on us. Just the same, there remained that feeling of uneasy expectancy. Momentarily, the individual was expecting to be sorted out and given a hiding each time a Jap came along.

Fortunately, there were such large numbers of men on the job that the dozen or so Japs were totally inadequate to the task of keeping an eye on everyone. As that fact became established, consequent on the cessation of the rain, our first feelings of enthusiasm began to wear off and a general slackening of individual effort resulted.

As on the daily working parties, each group had its own officer, who received his instructions from the Jap in charge of the job. It was then left to him to organise his men and get the job done to specifications, or as near to that as circumstances, and the general standard of intelligence, would permit.

Dependent on the mentality and temperament of the individual group officers – and some of them were just plain stupid – the men had an easy or

76

difficult day in which personal supervision from the Japs was often non-existent.

In those days the conduct of the officers who went on working parties was all-important. The average Jap, in contradiction of our initial trepidation, had not yet overcome his inherent sense of inferiority in the presence of British troops, prisoners or otherwise. He was inclined, therefore, to follow the lead of our officers in so far as it affected our working conditions.

Thus, a party officered by a man with sufficient guts to stick up for the rights of his men – though such rights in the circumstances were for the most part theoretical – got through the day with a minimum amount of unpleasantness.

Conversely, any group – and there were some – who were unfortunate enough to have an officer who was scared of his overlords, or who still thought he was as important in the general scheme of things as when he was chucking his weight about on the barrack square, had a thin line.

The general tendency to take it easy whenever possible was frowned on by the latter type of officer, who appeared to suffer from the delusion that we were in honour bound to work just as hard when the Japs were absent as when they were around swearing at us and urging us on to greater efforts.

In time, of course, our inherent sense of discipline wore off, and this type of individual was brought to heel in no uncertain fashion. But before then countless doses of jankers and forfeitures of 'pay' were imposed on the men who were gradually coming to the realisation that a man was not necessarily a god, particularly in a prisoner of war camp, just because he had a 'pip' on his shoulder…

Returning along the road in the evening, muddy and tired by the unaccustomed hard work after my prolonged spell of semi-idleness at Changi, I paused for a moment by the upturned soil of the new grave where the remains of the two who had been taken from the ditch lay newly buried in less cramped quarters, and where the stench of the morning no longer befouled the air and made one realise what a horrible thing can man become when the spark of life is taken from him.

On the grave lay a rusty rifle and a battered tin hat, and on the crude cross constructed by the Australians was written:'Sergeant B---- and one unknown'.

Whether it was because of my own weariness, or because of the sorrow that only a lonely grave can bring, there came to me those immortal lines of Laurence Binyon's:

They shall not grow old as we that are left grow old:

Age shall not weary them, nor the years condemn.
At the going down of the sun and in the morning
We will remember them.

Comforting as was this promise of immortality, I knew only too well that it was but fleeting and theoretical. When a man went down in battle he ceased to be an entity that moved and had its being among a number of similar entities, dependent on one another for mutual protection. He became instead an impediment – a piece of driftwood that got in the way and was flung aside at the first opportunity, and almost instantly forgotten.

Nor was this forgetfulness a momentary lapse engendered by the force of circumstance. It was not. It was definite and long lasting, and made no provision for a 'fond remembrance' in other days.

As soon as the hurtling chunk of metal, or the more merciful bullet, cut you down you'd had it. That was your lot, and away went your immortality contrary to Laurence Binyon's wishful thinking.

Lucky were you if you found a sheltered grave in the lonely earth that drank your blood and eliminated the last smear of your existence as definitely and as conclusively as the spring thaw scrubs out of the winter snow...

To the men marching past the new grave the poor remains in it might never have had life. They might never have moved among us and partaken of our joys and our sorrows. They were as completely blotted out as though they had never been.

The sergeant and his un-named companion were equals: they were both unknown...

*****

For the first couple of weeks, life on the road-making gang meandered along at a not too accelerated tempo. The Japs were content to let us set our own pace and, provided we made a fair showing, left us alone. Occasionally one would come along and exhort us to 'Speedo! Speedo!'

This theme song of theirs, however, was soon accepted as but another of the petty irritations of existence, and little notice was taken of it.

In the third week a new Jap 'charge hand' made his appearance, and the speedo regime became intensified, and was given more substance by a series of 'incidents' and irritating annoyances.

Anyone who even looked as though he might be slacking got his face slapped, or received a smart clout across the backside with a stick as a reminder that he was not working trade union hours.

Mad Harry, as we called the new overseer, was a three-star private in the unfortunate position – for us – of a man who had made up his mind to get a stripe.

His enthusiasm for the job in hand was such that the least hold up or sign of opposition threw him into a frenzy of endeavour that swept us along in a series of feverish outbursts of activity. Then, when he had gone round the corner, we wilted and ceased to cringe with expectancy, but kept a sharp look-out for his return.

Being mechanically minded, Richard Laverton got himself a job as a truck driver on the bogie line, our one piece of mechanical equipment on the job. Running along the flat for about a hundred yards, the line dropped suddenly into a steep incline along which the laden trucks went hurtling at a great speed to tip their loads of excavated soil on an embankment that was being built up to take the roadway.

Descending the gradient was both hazardous and exciting. As none of the trucks was fitted with brakes, the 'drivers' used a length of wood that had to be scientifically jambed between the wheels to check the forward rush of the truck. But, in spite of that, most of the men on the bogie line took the gradient full out, chancing disaster for the thrill of doing something risky and forbidden.

Faster and more reckless became the descents, while Mad Harry shouted in mocked disapproval. Provided the trucks remained on the track, he was not particularly interested in the possibility of someone being killed or maimed. The embankment was going up fast, and that was all that mattered.

Having safely negotiated the slope with a minimum use of the 'brake', Laverton discarded it altogether and came tearing down with a heaped-up load of earth – out for a record.

He got it.

Hitting the bend at speed, the heavy truck tore the flimsy line from its foundations and, turning a somersault, crashed into the jungle twenty yards from its destination. Fortunately for Laverton, he was thrown clear, and came to rest in a clump of shrubbery.

Mad Harry was an unsympathetic spectator of this mishap. Grabbing his stick, which was always handy, he ran over and belaboured the luckless Laverton, after which he tied him to a tree with wire and left him to repent his impetuosity.

This was but an unpleasant incident in the day's toil, and Laverton soon got over it. His grudge against Mad Harry was of a longer duration than the hurt of the physical chastisement he had received.

Mad Harry was becoming a general nuisance. Unlike the others on the job, he was not content to sit in the shade and take things easy while we worked. His ambition would not let him rest. That stripe, so tantalisingly near, he would have. To prove his capabilities, he would make his gang work harder than any other gang on the job.

In theory this logic was fool-proof. But Mad Harry, like many of his fellow countrymen before him, had overlooked, or not been aware of, one major consideration.

The ability of the average prisoner to appear to be working industriously, when in reality he was doing nothing, was a factor that produced in Mad Harry a growing sense of bewilderment.

Instead of his gang, harried as they were, accomplishing more than their neighbours, whose overseers were not fired by the driving urge of ambition, Mad Harry's party were gradually falling behind in their productive efforts.

As the Japs could not be everywhere at once, the system of signalling we had perfected to warn of his approach at any point nullified his continual 'Speedo! Speedo! Speedo!' even when he used his stick with an impartial liberality.

In the end I think he must have thought he was going crazy. Always when he came along we were working like mad, yet for some reason too deep for his understanding, there was practically nothing being done when he compared our efforts with those of the gangs further along the road. Even his embankment had ceased to grow, and the trucks no longer tore down the slope at breakneck speed.

Eventually the day came when Mad Harry realised that all his shouting and running around were getting him nowhere. And on that day, contrary to all precedent, he went and sat down on the bank muttering to himself in the way Japs do when they come up against something that baffles them.

As the percentage of Japs to prisoners on the golf course was roughly one to two hundred, a close supervision could not be maintained. Consequently, anyone who was prepared to take the risk of getting a beating could spend most of his working time asleep in the jungle or foraging for food in the neighbourhood.

To many this was a popular pastime, for there was the possibility of finding a food dump that had not been cleared by the natives or confiscated by the Japs. No such find was ever made, however, though isolated tins of bully beef and an occasional tin of jam were unearthed.

Apart from food there were other interests in the jungle which had a morbid

80

fascination for many of the men, and sent them searching through the undergrowth when they ought to have been at work on the road.

The remains of the slain held pride of place in this respect and many of the searchers got a kick out of finding a bleached skeleton, and the ensuing theorising as to how he died, and what he was before he died.

Next in point of interest was discarded ammunition, of whatever calibre, followed by rusty rifles and useless machine-guns. It was noteworthy that whatever the 'treasure' unearthed in the jungle, nothing that had previously belonged to the Japs, including skeletons, was listed.

The reason for this doubtless lay in the different states of emotion in the contending parties when they had passed over the terrain on which we were now labouring.

Questing through the jungle on a day when Mad Harry was at his best, I discovered a miniature Golgotha, where a number of Chinese guerrillas had been executed, whether before or after the fall of Singapore I cannot say.

From the remains I estimated that there had been about twenty of the Chinese. But unlike the slaughter of those at Changi earlier, these chaps had not been machine-gunned en masse.

Their skeletons lay in the undergrowth near to one of the roads we were making, in groups of fours and fives. All the heads were detached from the bodies, and as the spinal columns appeared to have been severed in each case, it was apparent that the men had been beheaded. This was the usual form of execution practised by the Japanese upon the locals when they were not in too much of a hurry to get the job done.

Shortly after I found this spot, some of the other foragers came along, and soon there was a crowd of prisoners prowling among the bones, looking for souvenirs in the form of rings or gold teeth. None was found, however, and I was glad of that.

It was not nice to see the poor bones being kicked around by a crowd of souvenir hunters who had no thought to spare for the undeniable truth that they were at least indirectly responsible for the execution of the men who had died, and whose bones had been given no burial…

Whenever the toil of work on the roads became too irksome I was in the habit of slipping off into the jungle and going for a stroll in the twilight woods when the mosquitoes permitted.

Oddly enough it was not the threat of the hiding I should get if I were discovered on these unofficial vacations from work that deterred me from going more often. It was the mosquitoes which, since the advent of the

Japanese, had multiplied in appalling numbers.

But for these pests it would have been possible to sleep in the undergrowth all day long had one been prepared to take the risk of discovery, not so much by a prowling Jap sentry as by our own people who frowned on that sort of thing.

It was not only the officers and senior N.C.O.s who did not encourage absence from work. Many of the men did likewise, but they were principally the chaps who had not the courage to take time off, and envied those who did. Their plaint was that 'it was not playing the game,' and made more work for those who kept their noses to the grindstone.

Theoretically this argument was correct though, in substance, it was indefensible. With the Japanese system of working where the efforts of the individual were scarcely noticed unless he were given an isolated job, the absence of a dozen or so from the diggings made no appreciable difference to the remainder. Indeed, at times there were so many men on the job that they got in one another's way, so that a few absentees were a blessing in disguise.

Apart from that, if a man were willing to risk a beating for the doubtful comfort of a stroll in the woods, that was entirely his affair.

The mosquitoes were definitely on the side of the Japs. They made sleep too uncomfortable to be tolerated, or even a quiet rest in the shade for that matter.

It was more profitable, therefore, to wander about in the woods, which in that locality had been the scene of much activity during the Jap advance on Singapore.

On the golf course, and in the surrounding jungle, there had been some sharp fighting by both sides. Round about were the graves of the Japs who had fallen, with their monumental posts covered in hieroglyphics. Here and there a cruder grave marked where a soldier of the Allies lay, some in the shadowed dusk of the woods, and some in the full sun on the green hillside or by the still waters of the reservoir.

Here and there they lay, the East and West commingled and at peace. There were some who would never know a covering for their bleached bones until the jungle vegetation, temporarily slashed aside, grew strong again and covered them with a blanket of green.

During one of my absences from work I discovered some of these old remnants which, judged by the passage of time, were not so old. Appearances were against them, however, and were it not for the tattered raiment that still clung to the bare bones, they might have been lying there when the trees of the jungle, which reared up hundreds of feet above them, were young.

82

On one occasion I discovered two Australians, for as such I identified them by their tattered clothing, lying side by side behind a little hillock as though endeavouring to hide their naked state from the rude stare of the chance passer-by such as I.

Lying in a wilderness of loneliness, they appeared still to give each other the mutual protection they had done before death came clawing through the greenery. In death they symbolised friendship, and in life they must have been as close as John and I...

Soon it was commonplace to unearth the remains of the poor dead: British, Colonials, and Indians. Strangely, no remains that might be identified as Japanese were found. But, perhaps, this was not so strange, for the Japs appeared to have been very methodical in the burial of their dead. Again, they had had more time than we had during the skirmishing in the surrounding jungle; also to the man on the losing end of a battle, a dead man, even though he were but a moment since a friend, is just so much rubbish. Let him be buried when the time is more propitious.

Frankly, I got little satisfaction from unearthing this human debris scattered about in the scrub and jungle. What interested me more was the probability of finding a cache of buried army rations. In this respect, however, I had little luck, finding only an odd tin of bully beef and once a tin of jam. Nevertheless, I was well compensated and the time wasted in looking for food was time well spent for to visit a battlefield, even though it be one where the fight was lost, and such a minor one as that of Singapore, is a chastening experience. It makes one realise, perhaps more forcefully than any other experience, how unimportant one is in the general scheme of things. It makes one feel, too, just how really human one is, and how dependent on the vicissitudes of an unpredictable fate is man for his continued existence...

The principal tool used by the road gangs was something similar to an oversize Dutch hoe, and called by us a 'chunkle'. It is used extensively by the natives, and is much preferred by them to the more orthodox pick and shovel of the West. There were a number of these, too, but in time we came to favour the chunkle and found it the more serviceable for the job in hand.

As the trolley line was not universally used, the usual means of conveying earth from one point to another was by means of small wickerwork baskets and so primitive, or so wholly native, were the methods of working that the efforts of the individual were scarcely noticed. As the long straggling lines of basket carriers moved lazily back and forth along the embryo highway, with many a pause on the way, dependent on the exact location of the Jap on the job, it became apparent that it was not the effort of the individual that mattered, but of the thousands of workers as a whole.

Watching any of the men at work when there were no Japs about, it was obvious that he was scratching the earth with about as much enthusiasm as an over-fed hen scrabbling about on a dunghill. But in spite of the individual effort, or maybe because of it, the roads gradually took shape, making long, unsightly scars as they cut through the green of the fairway and bit into the jungle.

I often wondered at the time what the former members of the high-toned Bukit Timah Golf Club would have said had they been suddenly catapulted into the scene of operations and found us, fellow Britishers, though not necessarily fellow equals, busily engaged in ruining for all time the signpost of their importance and the keystone of their standing as Big White Tuans in Singapore.

Doubtless they would have looked down their refined noses at our handiwork, and mentally blamed us more than they would the Japanese for the desecration of their shrine.

At that they would not have been far off the target...

During the initial weeks on the roads so many chunkles and shovels were 'lost' that the Japs suddenly became concerned at the growing shortage, and made everyone remain on the job until all the tools issued during the day were accounted for.

In those first weeks it was a common practice for men to throw their chunkles or shovels into the reservoir at the end of the day, or to leave them in the jungle alongside the road.

To counteract this simple sabotage, the Japs made each group officer personally responsible for the tools issued to his gang, and if there was a shortage at the end of the day, the whole gang was kept on the diggings until the lost article was found.

Needless to say, anyone who lost anything after this was distinctly unpopular.

As soon as the tools were checked and the O.K. given, the stampede for camp started. And what a stampede! Like cattle that have long been held back from water, the road gangs went streaming over the golf course, each individual doing his utmost to get to the front as though some special prize were to be awarded to the men getting first back to camp.

At the head of the straining mob was the officer in charge doing his utmost to maintain some semblance of order, and usually failing.

All this rush to be first was occasioned, not so much by the desire to get back to camp as by greed, pure and unadulterated. To be first home meant being first in the food queue, which automatically qualified one for a first place in the lagi (extras) queue.

When the men arrived on the road the real trouble began, for here, rightly for a change, order was enforced, and we were made to march along in a more or less soldierly fashion, while the solitary Jap who had brought the party out from camp mounted his bicycle and literally wiped his hands of us as he rode off, doubtless being glad to get away from so much un-understandable disagreeableness.

As soon as we hit camp and were dismissed, there was another frantic scramble for the food queue. This generally resulted in a heaving mass of sweaty bodies pushing and shoving at one end to be first, while at the other extremity the more well-behaved stood back and waited for some sort of order to come out of the chaos, knowing that in the course of time they would eventually get their food, though their chance of getting any lagi was nil.

While at Changi I had looked upon the scramble as being an amusing, though at times nauseating, spectacle. Here in the road construction camp it was more in the nature of a bull fight every time food was served. Heaven knows why, for whether a man was first or last, he was generally assured of his ration.

The bucks system, and the stupidity of those who brought it about, was one source of blame. Though greed, and the lack of self-discipline, was the predominant factor in the general unruliness of the food queues.

The breakfast queue at the road construction camp was a source of amusement, to anyone in a mood to be amused at that time in the morning. In the grey light of each dawn a long line of huddled figures stretched along the roadway by the food point. These were the 'be firsters', the individuals who thought it of more importance to tumble straight out of their beds into the breakfast queue, and to sit there unwashed, and with the night's sleep still befuddling their senses, until the cooks were ready to bring out the food.

To these men, general cleanliness had little place in their personal bag of tricks. And to the various camp officials who allowed that sort of thing to continue while they concentrated on issuing senseless rules about saluting, and other unnecessary chores, little praise can be given...

The food was much better than it had been at Changi. There was a good deal more meat in the diet; also many more vegetables, which were of more importance. Once in a while, too, we had fresh fish, and, equally rarely, real potatoes.

In spite of the improved food, or perhaps because of it, there was still a good deal of discontent over rations. First, there was the inevitable bad army cooking, which did not improve just because we were prisoners; neither did our grousing about it make any difference, though it relieved one's feelings to let off steam now and again. Secondly, there was the usual bone of contention – the officers' messing. It was the general opinion that, as they did no work, even their own chores, it was scarcely right that they should have more and better food than the other ranks.

This sort of thing was as inevitable as the bad cooking, and was usually taken for granted until something occurred to fan the smouldering flames of class consciousness.

There was, for instance, the day when we had an unusually large meat issue. On that occasion the officers were served with a nice juicy steak, plus their usual ration. That sort of thing was not appreciated, and the men were not slow to say so.

Neither were the efforts of the officer who was in charge of one of the neighbouring groups. This gentleman, to give him his assumed title, had one other officer in his group and, to use his own words, 'I am an officer and I intend to have my own messing.'

Doesn't sound much, I know. But when it is remembered that this simple statement entailed the building of a separate cook-house, and the finding of cooking utensils to stock it, plus the extra work entailed, it may be appreciated just how unnecessary this insistence on separate messing was…

The wire-conscious Captain Bell had not the administrative ability necessary to keep a group of browned-off prisoners in a good humour. For one thing he was too scared of the Japanese – hence his conscientiousness where their interests were concerned.

Also, he had not sufficient sense to keep his nose out of our private affairs. Thus, if we had a meat ration and suggested a meat pie, for instance, he would assuredly veto the idea and say we had to have something else.

This inability of our superiors to avoid poking their noses in where they were not wanted, and could do no good, led to a good deal of discontent in the camp. That, and their continued assumption that they could order us about as though we were free men in an English barracks, and not, like themselves, prisoners of war, and in no mood to be chased around. Besides, we got a surfeit of that sort of thing from the Japs daily.

For some reason or other the more lenient were the Japs, the more military minded became our camp administration.

Luckily, the average Britisher is long suffering, and we were not in any one camp long enough to get worked up sufficiently to throw over the traces and raise hell with the administration...

As at Changi every precaution was taken to prevent us breaking bounds which, in this case, meant going outside the theoretical wire that surrounded the camp. We were constantly being reminded what the Japs would do to us if we were caught outside our particular area, and exhorted to be goody-goody and behave ourselves.

Just as these threats and reminders proved unavailing at Changi, so did they at Singapore, and the fence-riders were soon on the job again, going out of camp more or less when they willed.

Also, as at Changi, there was little danger of falling foul of the Japs if one went about the undertaking in the correct manner. Responsible for over 2,000 prisoners, the guard in the camp consisted of half a dozen Japs who lived in what became known as the Jap House, and who spent much of their spare time fooling around with anyone who was prepared to co-operate with them.

As the species go, these Japs were a friendly lot. It was not uncommon to see a P.O.W. teaching the sentry on duty the English way to do arms drill, or maybe learning to do it the Jap way.

It was as though this isolated group of Japs had not yet become accustomed to their total supremacy over the men whose destiny they held in their hands.

Possibly they were just fair-minded individuals who happened to be Japs...

Chapter Eight

Jim Sing Drinks a Toast

One day at the *meshi* break Mad Harry came running along the road.

'All men campo!' he shouted. 'All men campo! *Yasumi*! Speedo!'

The Jap's evident excitement quickly communicated itself to the men, and in a matter of minutes the wildest rumours were being bandied about and given a certain credibility by the unexpected order to stop work and return to camp.

Then, when we were told to take the handles out of the chunkles, picks, and shovels, and to beach the two boats that were used on the reservoir to facilitate the building of the bridge hat was to connect the shrine with our road network, conjecture became almost a certainty.

Some had it that the Americans had landed up country, and that the Japs had all been recalled to repulse them. Another rumour said that the combined Allied Fleets were converging on Singapore, and that the Japs had fled, leaving us behind as a peace offering. A very unworthy one, too, I thought but, I hoped, none the less acceptable.

It could not be denied that the Japs had gone. That much we found out when we got back to camp. Unfortunately, before going they had omitted to provide for their guests during their absence, so that soon we were beginning to feel the pangs of hunger even though we were not working anymore.

As our 'reserve' dwindled and disappeared we hoped that our deliverers, whoever they might be, would not be over long in arriving. In the meanwhile, camp administration continued to issue proclamations mainly dealing with the penalties to be incurred for leaving camp. Whatever else they might be they were at least determined to pass out of existence with all flags flying, true to the great tradition for damn-foolery they had built since becoming gentlemen of leisure in a prisoner of war camp.

Hungry men are not too particular about obeying orders that are not worth the paper they are written on, and at the end of the second day's semistarvation, the routine fence-riders were reinforced by scores of others, as it became definitely established that the Japs had indeed gone from the neighbourhood.

After a couple of days of enforced idleness, and encouraged by hunger, most of the men left the camp daily to go foraging in the neighbourhood, and then eventually to Singapore, about three miles distant.

The first day out, Laverton and I concentrated on the local kampongs, but with little success. The local Chinese were as tight fisted as ever and disinclined to part with anything that could not be paid for.

Getting into Singapore early the following day, we found that an almost miraculous change had come about. Hitherto it had been almost impossible to obtain food of any description without paying for it. Now the reverse was true and it was difficult to pay for anything.

Nor was that the only change. The Japanese, and there were quite a few of them about, appeared to get a great satisfaction from seeing us walking around in hundreds doing just as we pleased. And, provided one saluted religiously, one could apparently go anywhere.

Inexplicable things happened, apart from the change of heart evident in the Singaporeans. Japanese gave up their places in barbers' shops and restaurants to prisoners who went in for a haircut or a cup of coffee, and invariably, paid the bill. Actually this was not necessary as there was no charge unless a Jap offered to pay. Then the money was taken.

Brothel *bints* gave us the tip to wait outside while they entertained their clients – Japs mostly – after which they came out and handed their takings over to the prisoners waiting on the kerb. Many of these chaps were, of course, old clients themselves, but that is by the way.

As we walked along the streets amid a populace suddenly and unaccountably smitten with a definite urge to give things away, I began to wonder if indeed the Jap overlordship of the city was about to come to an end.

It was not only the prisoners who wondered about this possibility. The Chinese, who formed the bigger part of the community, were was bewildered as were we about the strange state of affairs, and kept asking why the Japanese allowed it. We were not unduly bothered about the answer to that just then. While there was food and smoke to be had for the taking the phenomenon that brought it about was of little moment. If the Yanks were coming, let 'em come! In the meantime, fill your belly and hope for the best.

Yesterday everyone had been hungry, and today there was no need to walk about with an empty belly. To get a meal all one need do was linger a moment outside one of the numerous eating houses and look hungry. Then out would come the proprietor to invite one in for coffee and biscuits or whatever was on the menu.

Outside eating houses which were already full, groups of prisoners clustered on the pavement, while the owner's wife and children handed out refreshments. Then, with their bellies full, the prisoners went to the tobacco shops to fill their pockets with cigarettes and cheroots handed out by the suddenly big-hearted tobacconists.

Not all the shopkeepers had been smitten with the urge to give. Many of the Malays and Indians were as tight-fisted as before. These gentlemen had also an affected unawareness of our existence. When we entered their shops, they remained seated in a pose of stolid immobility, refusing even to answer when spoken to. Definitely, unlike their Chinese prototypes, they were not interested in the ex-*Tuans*.

Fortunately this type of shopkeeper was in the minority, and the sudden wave of philanthropy that had taken the town in its grip was little affected by their unwillingness to co-operate.

This invasion of Singapore by the prisoners from the road construction camp must surely be unique in the annals of prisoner-of-war history. Had we been so minded, I feel sure that the town could have been taken over by us, and had there been any certainty that the news of an American landing up country was true, something of this nature would have been attempted. As things turned out, no friction was caused by our haps, and we were allowed to continue our free shopping for a week before the Japs put an end to our activities by getting reorganised.

Successful as was our first day's shopping in Singapore, the ones that followed became increasingly more lucrative. Old Chinese coolies of the female variety appeared on the streets and gave out handfuls of money, ranging from ten cent bills to five dollar ones. Others hung about with sacks full of loaves which they distributed at the rate of two per man.

Little *chickos* standing in the gutter selling slices of pineapple held up their little hands full of the succulent fruit and said: 'Present, Johnnie.' Tiny tots with dirty faces but big hearts came toddling to offer a five cent piece or even one cent piece in a grubby paw.

Standing on the corner of Bencoolian Street with Laverton on the second day, a toddler came and plucked at my trouser leg. In an extended hand he held a one cent piece.

'You take, Johnnie,' he lisped. And when I patted him on the head and, not knowing any better, said:

'No, you keep it and buy some sweets, little man,' he burst into tears and ran sobbing to an older brother who was squatting on the pavement, watching.

Frankly, I have never felt so mean in my life as I did when that *chicko's* little face screwed up in disappointment, and the tears started to well out of his eyes. Laverton didn't help any, either.

'Now look what you've done,' he said. 'You've tumbled his castle out of the air.'

'Damn it, Richard,' I expostulated, angry with myself, and seeking an excuse for my inability to appreciate the situation. 'One doesn't take pennies from kids...'

'Listen,' he said. 'The unusual ethics of life no longer apply, Mick. These people, for some obscure reason, are out to do things for us, and if you do not accept their advances, double-edged as they may be – well, they won't like it. That *chicko*, for instance. It was a big moment for him when he offered a one cent piece to a British Johnnie. What a reversal of our social laws, Mick,' and he laughed uproariously, causing the big brother squatting on the pavement to grin in half-understood appreciation.

I wasn't feeling like laughing. I felt too self-sorry for that. I had hurt that youngster's feelings, and was bitter about it. From then onwards I resolved to take everything that was offered to me. Cents, half cents, slices of over-ripe pineapple, bananas, sticky sweetmeats, Chinese 'wedding cake', any damn thing that came my way went into my sack or my pocket, and I was rewarded by the smiles on the faces of the donors whether they were old coolie women or toddling *chickos*.

Many a *chicko's* eyes shone with an inner light in those days at Singapore when a 'Johnnie' patted him on the head and said:

'Thanks, *chicko*!'

Had anyone familiar with life in Singapore before the war been parachuted into the town he would have been amazed, and probably disgusted, by the complete reversal of the social order as appertaining to whites and natives.

Where before the *tuans* had so rarely noticed the average Singaporean – apart from the women – and would have felt nauseated by the mere thought of eating a meal in a low-class café or eating house, they now welcomed the opportunity to do so and took advantage of the populace's generosity to the fullest extent.

Even the rickshaw coolies, who often in other days had been the butt of the rowdier element among the troops, were now our benefactors and gave of their hard-earned money indiscriminately.

The urchins in the streets, who in former days had been a nuisance because

92

of their begging propensities, now put us on a level with their former slaves. Only in this case we did not have to beg: they gave to us whatever they had, and with a liberality that knew no comparison.

Once only did I meet with a beggar who was not of my own tribe. This was a young crippled Tamil boy, who asked for a cent. Perhaps he had slept late that day and awoke thinking the old days were back and Johnnie had been returned to power.

Hanging about was the usual group of youngsters, and as soon as the cripple asked for alms they descended upon him like a flock of swallows on a hawk, and commenced to pluck out his feathers, calling him many unsavoury names as they did so. Had I not intervened, this rash youngster would have had a bad time.

When I had rescued him and sent him off to safety, with a dollar surreptitiously pressed into his hand, the swallows surrounded me in a shrieking mob and chanted:

'He's a greedy------! Johnnie. You must not give him anything. The greedy ------!'

This coming from a group who formerly had been as ravenous as a swarm of locusts newly descended on young corn, in their insistence for cents, caused me to wonder more than ever what was coming over the land.

A revelation in itself, this spirit of the Singapore urchins showed how thoroughly the feeling of benevolence that had become on the town had taken hold. I hoped it would continue indefinitely, even if the Yanks did not arrive.

Unfortunately, it did not, neither did the Yanks come strutting across the Causeway as we half expected.

*****

Walking along Chulia Street one day, we met only the Tamil not immunised against Singapore's unexplained epidemic of generosity. White haired, and with the kindly face usually to be found on these people when they are no longer young, this old chap's lamentations on our behalf were so seemingly genuine that I was willing to accept the hospitality he offered and to forgive his race much for their shoddy response in Singapore's week of giving.

At the end of his first chapter of lamentation, the old Tamil invited us into a café and gave us a feed. He then went across the road and brought back several tins of pineapple and packs of cigarettes which he presented to us.

Nor were we the only ones to benefit from this old gentleman's benevolence. As other prisoners came in sight along the street he went out and brought them in to the café, so that we finished up with quite a party. All the while he kept urging us to eat more and continued to deplore the unkind fate that had brought about such a state of affairs. But as he said: 'Had that not happened you *tuans* would not be lunching with me today.'

How right he was!

As was to be expected, there was quite a crowd about the doorway of the café, and when one of the guests, with a false sense of the rightness of things, pulled out a watch and asked out host if he would buy it, there was a surge forward to look at it.

For some reason or other the Tamil was not eager to buy the watch. Neither was a fat and prosperous-looking Chinese who took it away to be valued.

The price asked for the watch was two dollars. Not much in the circumstances, but more than anyone was willing to pay, until a young Chinese stepped forward and laid the money on the table.

Naturally, the owner of the watch thought he had sold it, but no. The Chinese youngster patted him on the back and said:

'You take the money, Johnnie. I do not want the watch. You have no money so it is but right that I give you some…'

'Well, what do you know about that?!' exclaimed Laverton, but I heard his voice only as a remote echo.

Here I had been gallivanting about Singapore for three days and I had not even thought of Nai Soon! Such was the self-satisfaction engendered by a full belly, and a lessening of restraint!

Had he come into the café at that moment, I think I should have gone on my knees to him, and so caused a sensation that would not soon have been forgotten in the back streets of Singapore.

Instead, I concentrated on the young Chinese who, by his generosity, had reawakened my slumbering and over-fed recollection and brought back Nai Soon to flog my shrinking conscience.

To the general eye this youngster was just another Chinese kid, but a keener perception soon discovered that indefinable quality which hallmarks the educated Oriental.

Nai Soon had that quality, and so had this youngster.

He was a little younger than Nai Soon, I judged, though I may have been wrong. It was difficult to assess the age of many of the younger generation in Singapore in those days. Many of them had acquired a crafty, worldly-wise outlook that added years to their legitimate age and made them seem older than they were.

To me it was obvious that this youngster was no coolie's son, as were many of the other kids in the crowd about the café. When he moved about among them they slipped out of his way and let him through without any of the usual jostling and argumentation.

Watching him step back from the table on which he had placed the two dollars, I tried hard to think of some pretext to speak to him. I wanted more than anything to contact him without arousing any undue interest in the crowd of onlookers, for I felt that he might be instrumental in bringing Nai Soon and myself together again.

What a fool I had been to forget Nai Soon! How could the opportunity to indulge in a session of unrestricted gluttony have dulled my senses, and made me unaware of the opportunity that daily was slipping through my fingers?

Frankly, I didn't know, and as there was no profit in further self-recrimination, I muttered an excuse to Laverton and hurried out of the café on the heels of the youngster who had brought me back to the stark realities of my position in Singapore at that moment.

He was a dozen yards away when I emerged on to the pavement, and walking by himself.

There were no Japs in sight and, acting on sudden impulse, I quickly overtook him and said, without preamble:

'I should like to speak to you privately somewhere,' and went on up the street.

Looking back when I had gone two dozen paces, I saw he had stopped outside a tobacco shop, where there was a case of evil-looking black cheroots on display.

At the same moment a Jap sergeant-major came round the corner just beyond me and my heart did a guilty dance.

The momentary panic was unnecessary, for the Jap. W.O. was not interested in me. Punctiliously returning my dutiful salute, he passed on down Sarangoon Road to the brothel on the corner, while I watched his progress with a certain amount of trepidation.

I thought that he might be on the way to the café, where the old Tamil's party was still in progress. In that case there might be some trouble, and I did not want that to happen just then.

There was no need for uneasiness, however. With another salute, doubtless in acknowledgement to one from inside the café, he went round the corner, and my eyes came to rest on the *chicko* who was pressing slices of sticky water-melon into my hand.

I was about to repeat the insult of the day before, but remembered just in time and took two hunks. Before the *chicko* could sort out a conglomeration of biscuits, Chinese 'wedding cake', doubtful looking sweets and over-ripe bananas, I gave him a dutiful pat on the shaven pate and went back as far as the tobacconist's, where I received a handful of the evil-looking cheroots, one of which would have put me on my back for a week. However, they were grist to the mill. Laverton would smoke them when he was again dependent on dried cherry leaves and anything else that would make a smoke.

My quarry was talking to the shopkeeper, and as the latter returned to his stool, after giving me the cheroots, he said:

'If you follow me to the book shop some little way along the street, I will speak with you…'

This youngster was taking no chances, and I felt reassured on account of that. By the way, he went about reaching his final destination in a beer shop in a side street not a hundred yards from the New World. He was evidently uneasy.

I realised he was not taking anything for granted, and that even I might not be fully trusted yet.

Instead of going into the book shop, as I had expected, he turned into an adjoining alley, and from that into another, to eventually reach the beer shop three streets away from the café.

Apart from the Jap warrant officer, I encountered no other, and I began to realise that their conquest of the city was not so complete as one might suppose.

Here in the back streets the men of the I.J.A. found life too precarious to permit them to stroll about in ones and twos as they did in the more open reaches of the town and here the repercussions of the new order in Asia were just beginning to be felt.

Squatting on the pavement outside the beer shop were two muscular Chinese of the coolie type. As my quarry drew level with them, he said something in a quick aside and passed into the shop while they, after one sharp glance of speculation, spat a stream of betel juice into the roadway, whether in approval or as a mark of their disinterestedness. I didn't know. Neither did I care – much.

In the half light of the shop he was waiting for me. As I darkened the doorway, he passed through into the back, and I followed him.

As though by pre-arranged signal, an extremely elderly Chinese entered through another door as I came into the room, bearing, of all things, a tray

96

containing a bottle of brandy and two glasses!

The last brandy I had seen was at the big house where John and I had drunk ourselves insensible as we sat in dreamy indolence between the graves of the two defunct gunners beneath the frangipani tree.

The brandy bottle recalled the ghostly nightmare I had had on that occasion and circumstances were such that, for a moment, I wondered if perhaps I was not undergoing another hallucination.

There was nothing figmentary about the young Chinese I had followed from Bencoolian Street, however. Noting my abstraction, and, doubtless, aware that I was not feeling over-secure, he poured out a liberal measure of the sparkling brandy and handed it to me with the admonition:

'You may speak here, Johnnie. Also,' with a smile, 'the brandy is very good!'

And it was! There was nothing 'native' about that brandy. It was hallmarked, and it went down extremely pleasantly.

Before it fulfilled its destiny, however, my host looked with a deep introspection at his own glass, then at me.

'It is the custom, is it not, to drink to something on occasion such as this?'

'Yes,' I said. 'A toast. But to what – or to whom? We might drink to the Chinese people of Singapore, who are being very kind to us just now, and the continuance of the unusual circumstances that make this possible,' and I lifted my glass and sniffed ecstatically at its contents.

'That gives me an idea,' he said, and raised his glass so that the liquid glowed as with an inner fire. 'Let us drink to liberty.'

'To liberty is it,' and as our glasses touched in the gloom of the back room, the amber liquid shimmered and then was gone.

'This,' I thought as the brandy fanned out like a sunbeam caressing my inside, 'is an extraordinary state of affairs; this drinking a toast to liberty with a young Chinese to whom I have not spoken a half-dozen words, in a back room in a beer shop, with the Japanese not two hundred yards away.'

Had Nai Soon come through the doorway at that moment I should not have been in the least surprised.

But there was no anti-climax such as that.

Replacing his glass on the tray, the youngster said, dispassionately:

'It will not come for a while yet, Johnnie,' and I supposed he was speaking of the elusive liberty to which we had just drank.

'Am I right in supposing you are not a friend of the Japanese?' I suggested tentatively.

'Well,' he hedged, 'you can put it that way if you wish. The Japanese are a difficult people, and their Co-prosperity Sphere is not compatible with what we in Singapore desire. However, that is not why you followed me here, is it?' and he lifted the bottle of brandy and contemplated it in abstract speculation as the liquor trickled slowly into the glasses.

For a moment, recalling Nai Soon's admonition to tread warily, I was dubious about mentioning his name, but as it was for that reason I had followed him from the café, I decided to trust my intuition, which told me the youngster was trustworthy. Should my intuition be wrong, Nat's head might be in jeopardy, and I hoped we would forgive me if it came to that...

Taking the plunge, I said, 'When I was at Changi camp I had a Chinese friend who used to give me cigarettes and food. He came to Singapore some time before I left Changi, and I am anxious to get in touch with him again. Perhaps you –'

The words with which he interrupted me were so reminiscent of Nai Soon that I knew my intuition had not let me down.

'All Chinese are not friends of the English,' he said. 'Many of them are in the pay of the Japanese. It is as well to remember that,' and he handed me the refilled glass.

While I told him about Nai Soon he listened without an interruption then, as I came to the end, he gestured at the brandy bottle and went out to where the old man was pottering about in the back regions.

For ten minutes they talked in a half whisper, then he came back.

'It is true about the Chinese Ah Tek Soon,' he said. 'He was one of those executed at Changi and was a staunch adherent of Chiang Kai-Shek. If the younger Soon has returned to Singapore as you say, it should be possible to find him. Say tomorrow, at the café in Bencoolian Street...'

And with that I had to be content. The prospect of waiting another day, with the possibility of not being able to come into the town again, was far from pleasing.

Richard said, when I told him, 'We are right at the centre of things here, Mick. If we can contact Nat again, and if – more improbable – the Japs allow us to come in to the town more indefinitely, we might be able to make something out of what at best is a rather hopeless situation.'

Chapter Nine

Little Flower

BACK at the camp the Brigadier and the rest of the administration were having nightmares. Not, as one might suppose, on account of the probability of the Yanks suddenly coming round the corner, but because of the large numbers of men who were continually leaving camp to go to Singapore shopping.

Although our people did their damnedest to enforce their edict that we remain in the camp, they did not go to the lengths to which our neighbours the Australians did.

Each time an Aussie was caught outside his own wire, which, like ours, was mainly theoretical, his commanding officer fined him five pounds and had it entered in his pay book.

Whether this ridiculous measure was upheld later I do not know. Actually if it did not act as a boomerang and give the individual responsible for it a terrific headache, justice will scarcely have been done to the men who refused to starve to death rather than go out and forage for their food.

The complete absence of the Japanese forces from the camp and surrounding area speaks well for the complete faith they had in the British administration. Apparently they took it for granted that the latter would keep an eye on things while they were away. That our administration did not completely succeed in this respect is not their fault. They did their utmost to persuade us to be good boys and remain at home while the master way away – even going to the length of confiscating the food and cigarettes given to us by the kindly people of Singapore.

This was a good racket for the camp police who, as usual, were taking pickings from both sides, while for anyone unlucky enough to be caught and showed in the guardroom, it was a bitter pill to swallow when his bag of swag was taken away and he got jankers on top of that.

But it would have taken more than a dose of jankers to keep men who had tasted the comparative freedom of the past few days and, in spite of an increased vigilance on the part of our camp police, there were more men out of camp than in it.

For Laverton and I there was now the probability of meeting Nai Soon again – and we were not going to miss that.

Our three days' free shopping in Singapore was beginning to have an appreciable effect on the food situation in the town. The Singaporeans were not now so eager to feed us as they had been, and their philanthropy was being hard pressed to do justice to itself. Fortuitously, however, it found a new outlet which did more than compensate for the sudden scarcity of food.

Apparently there was no shortage of money in the town – the Straits Settlements dollar being still in circulation – and a lot of it started to come our way. Later this was converted into food, and the efforts of the townspeople to safeguard their larders were nullified.

Standing at the junction of Lavender Street and Sarangoon Road on the morning after my meeting with the young Chinese, Laverton and I got into conversation with a Portuguese, who came along the road pushing a pram.

This fellow European had no time to spare in sympathising with our bad fortune. He was all eaten up with his own worries. He found it impossible to buy the food he had been used to, and the imminent starvation of the city was, to him, a black cloud on his new horizon.

Poor chap! I could have knocked him down with the greatest of pleasure, even if he was the first European to whom I had spoken since becoming a prisoner. Or, maybe, because of that.

My instinctive antipathy was not aroused by the fact that he had no word of condolence for us, or because he gave us nothing – not even a cigarette, though he smoked all the time.

He was too evidently satisfied with the new regime – that is, when he could forget his belly – for my liking. Richard was not sympathetic either and making disparaging asides that evidently perplexed the Portuguese, who kept bowing and waving to the Japs as we walked down the long stretch of Sarangoon Road to the Cathay Cinema, while Richard and I strutted along the street as though we owned the place.

Stopping outside the Cathay, which had been taken over by the Japs, we told the Portuguese about the generosity of the Chinese, emphasising the word Chinese, but still he did not bite. Then as a Jap three-star came over and gave us a packet of cigarettes, Richard pulled out a ten cent note and, leaning over the pram, pressed it into the hand of the brown-eyed chicko inside.

'Here you are, son,' he said. 'Take this and buy your old man something to eat!' and off we went to the café in Bencoolian Street, where I hoped the young Chinese would be waiting.

He was there, sitting by himself sipping black coffee. While Richard went to order, I took out one of the Jap's cigarettes and fumbled in my pocket for a match.

'Got a light, John?' I asked, crossing over to his table.

He had. But that was not what I wanted. Then, sensing the warning in his eyes, I turned casually away and went back to Richard, who was putting coffee and biscuits on the table.

Outside on the pavement were two Japs. They were looking enquiringly at us. I saluted in my best military fashion, and they came in as Richard stood up and I began to feel tense inside.

They were both corporals – big shots in the Japanese army.

'You Australian soldier?' asked one of them, looking at Richard.

'Nie,' he disagreed. 'Me English soldier.'

'You English soldier O.K.?' he asked next, turning to me.

'O.K.' I replied. 'Me English soldier.'

'O.K.' repeated the Jap. 'English soldier O.K., Australian soldier campo.'

Which meant that it was all right for us to be having coffee and biscuits in Singapore. Had we been Aussies, however, we should have been sent, or taken, back to camp, and there would have been no Nai Soon that day.

I had encountered this discrimination before. Evidently the Aussies were in disfavour with the Japs for some reason or other. Maybe they had fought better than we had. But had that been so, Japanese psychology being what it is, the Aussies' prestige would have been higher than ours...

Of more importance was the disturbing fact that the Chinese at the other table had slipped away during the cross-examination, and there was no sign of him for as far along Bencoolian Street as I could see.

'He'll be back,' Richard encouraged, sampling the biscuits, for which he had had to pay. 'That old geyser behind the counter isn't giving anything away today...'

'Those bloody Japs *would* come in!' I lamented. 'Chances are we shall not see that kid again and that means no Nai Soon!'

'Don't worry, he'll be back,' assured Richard. 'If he is what he says he is.'

That was a thought, and I pondered on it for the next ten minutes. Then he was there, standing by the table and returning my earlier greeting.

'Could you give me a match, please, Johnnie?'

As I held the flame of the lighter to his black cheroot, he murmured:

'The Green Circle, Lavender Street, in half an hour.'

I expected him to leave then, but he didn't. He sat down where he had been before the Japs came in, and ordered another coffee.

I knew I could get to the Green Circle in roughly ten minutes. But to make certain, I left early for there was always the possibility I might be stopped and interrogated.

I was stopped, but that was pre-ordained and not my fault.

Richard had remained in the café to, as he put it, 'keep an eye open in the rear.' I think he did not altogether trust the young Chinese...

There were a lot of Japs hanging about the New World, and as I came opposite the Victory Café – the name was no longer appropriate – just beyond, one of the men from the camp came out laden with Japanese baggage. He was a youngster named Terry Reynolds from my own unit, and had been in hospital with me at Changi. I thought I might give him a hand with the baggage as I had ten minutes to spare. Then a moment later I had no option.

Following Reynolds was a Jap sergeant who, as soon as he saw me, opened up with a preliminary '*Kura!*'

When I went over to see what all the fuss was about, he added, indicating Reynolds' overladen figure:

'English soldier – you take. Speedo!'

'O.K.' I said, and thought, 'Keep your bloody shirt on!' It was a nice shirt too. White silk. Similar to those Jap officers wore.

'Where are you bound, Terry?'

'Hullo, Mick. I'm glad somebody has arrived. This gunso had had me running around in circles for the last hour. Wants his stuff taken to the police station in Sarangoon Road...'

'Good. I'm going that way in any case. Oh, shut up!'

This to the *gunso*'s oft-repeated 'Speedo – hurry!' He knew a little English and, like many of his kind, was not content to keep it to himself.

Just before we got to the Green Circle – the Lavender Street conception of a night club – a rickshaw passed. In it was the Chinese from the café. There was no sign of Richard.

'Let's grab this rickshaw,' I said to Terry. And to the Jap, 'Rickshaw O.K.?'

He was in two minds about it, but he said, 'Rickshaw O.K.'

In a matter of moments we had piled all the *gunso's* paraphernalia into a rickshaw, and he was on the way up the street behind the not too please coolie, while Terry and I stood on the pavement outside the shuttered one-time hot spot of Lavender Street. Of the Chinese there was no sign. Neither had Richard showed up.

What to do with Reynolds was bothering me. I couldn't very well tell him to push off, and I was not particularly keen on taking him with me when the Chinese popped up again.

'Thanks for helping me out, Mick,' he said, fumbling at a packet of cigarettes the sergeant had given him. All he had given me was a half-hearted *arigato*. 'Have a smoke?'

'Look, Terry,' I said, 'I'm supposed to be meeting a Chinese I knew at Changi. Do you have to wait? There'll be trouble if the Japs get on to it,' I added vaguely, hoping he would take the hint.

But he didn't. It was not meant that he should.

The Jap *gunso*, with his irritating fatigue, was but an unsuspecting instrument utilised by unpredictable fate to put Terry Reynolds athwart my path when I was on the way to a reunion with Nai Soon.

I knew, of course, that Nat had a sister. What I didn't know was that she was a jewel scintillating against the squalid background of Singapore's Lavender Street. Neither did I suspect that destiny was drawing her to the side of the youngster who stood in momentary indecision outside the Green Circle, while the wheel went round a fraction, and the Japs passed up and down the street.

'I'd rather go along with you, Mick – if you don't mind,' he said, and the die was cast...

The Chinese came out by the side door and crossed the street to the vacant piece of ground running up to the backs of the houses that fronted on to Sarangoon Road.

I followed with Terry, wondering what had become of Laverton; then remembering that he had no idea where the Green Circle was.

Poor Richard!

Nai Soon was sitting on a case of empty beer bottles as I came through the door set in the high wall that flanked the alley at the backs of the houses.

Terry remained outside while I went into the courtyard. The Chinese who had guided me passed on into the house without a word.

Nai Soon was his unemotional self, but I could not altogether hide my satisfaction at meeting him again.

'It's good to see you, Nat!' I exulted. 'How is everything?'

'Hullo, Mick. I was wondering if perhaps you had come to Singapore. Why are you allowed so much liberty? I hear a lot of rumours…'

'We do, too. But I'm afraid it's mostly hot air – though frankly I can't explain it.'

'I'm glad for your sake, Mick,' he said, sincerely. 'And I'm glad, too, that the Chinese people are being kind to you. We had some English soldiers along this way yesterday, and we gave them some bread. Say Leen made them coffee.'

'Say Leen?'

'Yes. My sister.'

'Of course. You mentioned her to me – but I had forgotten. And your mother –'

'My mother is dead, Mick.'

It seemed futile to make the conventional reply, so I said, to cover the awkward pause, 'You and Say Leen are alone then?'

'Yes. And I have managed not to be conscripted by the Japanese. Things are getting bad in Singapore, Mick, though you may not realise it,' and he smiled, visualising the inroads we had been making into the reserve rations of the Singaporeans. Little wonder Richard had had to pay for his coffee and biscuits that morning!

'Nat,' I said, feeling selfish, and overcoming that emotion by a makeshift apology, 'I don't want to make things any more difficult for you but I am still keen about getting away…'

'I thought you would be, Mick, and I have made a point of getting as much news as I can. Though I am afraid it is scarcely more reliable than that you used to get at Changi Camp,' and he smiled in a gesture more expressive than any words.

Mere borehole wireless, I thought, and was anxious to hear it just the same.

'So far as I can ascertain with any certainty, the Japanese are in complete possession of Burma,' he said. 'The Japanese-controlled papers are making a great splash about the coming conquest of India. In the circumstances, Mick, you are pretty well – what is the word?'

'I could give you many that would serve,' I said, feeling like some of them, 'but you probably would not understand their different shades of meaning. The

104

one you probably want is 'stymied'.'

'That's the word,' he said, pleased. 'Something to do with golf, isn't it?'

'Yes. If you imagine me as a golf ball trying to get into the semi-security of India some two thousand miles away, with the armies of Japan acting the part of an uncrossable bunker in between, that's it…'

'And I'm afraid as your caddie I can't give you much help,' and he laughed, then shouted something into the house, and the Chinese, who had brought me there, came out with a tray and three cups of coffee.

No brandy this time!

'This is Jim Sing, Mick. His brother died with Ah Tek at Changi…'

'For your friend outside,' said Jim Sing, indicating the third coffee cup, reminding me of Terry Reynolds waiting out in the alleyway, and sending the wheel of destiny round another notch.

I was sitting on the empty beer crate, with Nai Soon squatting on the ground, when a shadow passed before the open window. Following my gaze, Nat said, 'That is Say Leen. I will bring her out.'

I wish he had not said that. I wish he had let Say Leen remain in the house, even if she was peeping out with something more than idle curiosity. Had he done that I should have been spared many an hour of acute anxiety on her behalf. And Terry Reynolds – well, I'm not sure but he, too, would have been better without the unsettling influence of the Chinese girl in his life.

But who am I to quibble about the dictates of destiny?

Say Leen and Terry were made for each other, even though they were hemispheres apart and, at Nai Soon's call, she was quick to respond and stepped out into the bright sunlight to meet him, where he sat with me on a crate of empty beer bottles in the untidy courtyard not a hundred yards from the police station on the corner.

Before her coming I had seen many outstandingly attractive Oriental women, though the fact that they were Orientals – and therefore "new" to me – enhanced their appeal.

There was nothing like that about Say Len. She was an original and, strangely, the first thing I thought of as she came across the courtyard to her brother's side, was Susy Ann, whom I had mollycoddled at Changi.

Say Leen had her milk and cream complexion; she also had her china-like fragility, but the perfect lines on which she was built was something that Susy Ann's creators could never hope to duplicate.

She was dressed in the European style – I had somehow expected that –

and, but for her eyes and the exquisite delicacy of her features, she might have been English.

Unlike so many Chinese girls, she was not built on the 'straight up and down' pattern, and the blouse and skirt she wore showed off the symmetry of her figure to perfection, though I doubt if she were aware of that fact.

If she used any artificial aids to beauty which, in her case, would have been an unnecessary pandering to convention, she did it so skilfully as to make them undetectable.

Reynolds was standing behind me as Nai Soon spoke to her in his mother tongue. 'My God, Mick,' he said, 'she's beautiful!'

Surprised, not by the words, which, after all, were but a poor compliment to Say Leen, but by the tone of his voice, I looked round and was startled by the expression on his face. His mouth was partly open, and he was looking at the Chinese girl with an intentness that compelled her gaze, and made me feel suddenly uneasy. Then Say Leen's eyes lifted from her brother's and something almost visible passed between her and Terry. It was something intangible, yet I could feel it as an emotion made so intense as to be electrical. Then Nai Soon spoke, and they were themselves again.

'Say Leen understands but little English, Mick,' he said, 'and she is shy...'

She was, too, for all her interest in young Terry, and was trying to hide herself behind her brother.

When he spoke to her again, she held out a hand that was more like a piece of delicate sculpture, so perfectly moulded was it. And when I took it in both of mine and looked at it in undisguised admiration, she gave a shy smile and withdrew it, making some remark to Nai Soon.

'She wants to know why you are so interested in her hand, Mick,' he interpreted.

'Tell her,' I said, 'that she has the most beautiful hands I have seen. And,' I added, unabashed by his evident amusement, 'you can also tell her that I am going to approve upon the English interpretation of her name. She is too fragile for a lily which, after all, is a substantial plant: I shall think of her as Say Leen – the Little Flower...'

Whether he told her all that I do not know, but she gave me another smile – not so shy this time. Then her eyes passed on to Reynolds standing expectantly behind me.

As their hands met in salutation, I could feel that intangible emotion building up around them again, and Nai Soon, too, was affected.

106

'She appears to like your friend,' he whispered, and I was not sure that he approved of the possibilities the assumption opened up. Perhaps I was jealous. And not without reason, for Say Leen's interest in Terry was so patently obvious as to leave me out in the cold.

For want of something better to say, I asked:

'What age is she, Nat?'

'Fifteen.'

'That is about eighteen by European standards, and young enough to give me a fatherly interest in her. I hope you will keep her out of sight of the Japs, Nat…'

'I do, Mick – but it is difficult. When she goes out she dresses in old clothes and makes herself not so like your English interpretation of her name.'

'Little Flower?'

'Yes.'

In spite of her lack of English, she and Terry evidently understood each other, and had not Jim Sing come shouting to the door, Nat and I might have continued our conversation indefinitely for all the notice they took of us.

At Jim Sing's shout, Say Leen hurried into the house as Nat went over and shut the door in the wall giving access to the alley at the back.

'You must get away, Mick,' he said. 'There has been some more trouble in the town and the Japanese are searching some of the houses…'

'Come this way, Johnnie…,' urged Jim Sing, and Terry and I followed him into the house. There was no sign of Say Leen.

Nai Soon came in behind us.

'Some Chinese have raided a rice store,' he said, 'and the Japanese are annoyed about it. If you are in Singapore tomorrow, Mick, come here and we will have another talk…'

'Yes,' I agreed! 'And I hope nothing happens in the meantime. Good-bye, Nat, and keep your eye on Little Flower. Come on Terry,' and we were out in the broad Sarangoon Road.

*****

The street was uncomfortably empty. When I had passed along it a couple of hours previously it had resounded to the *clip-clop* of numerous pairs of wooden *cloppers* as the Singaporeans perambulated aimlessly up and down.

Now there was the excited chatter of a group of Japs standing at the cross-roads by the police station. Fortunately, a number of fellow prisoners bound for the camp with sacks of food slung over their shoulders were coming up the road.

Joining a group of these we came to the barrier slung across the street by the police station, and, after a cursory 'You English soldiers?' we were all passed through and sent on our way with a 'Speedo! Campo!' from the corporal in charge of the party.

A mile beyond the town we were stopped by a Jap patrol, and made to pose for our photographs, while two Jap officers worked their cameras. The officers were quite cheerful, though we were a bit sceptical about the unusual proceedings, wondering what was behind the photographs.

I supposed the pictures would make good propaganda, but there was nothing we could do about it – and the *shokos* were generous, as well as cheerful. They gave us a cigarette each, and we went on up the road not in the least depressed at being chosen as the subject matter in some first-class enemy propaganda.

Outside the camp something of a more serious nature was happening. Here there was a new Jap sentry in full war paint, and from the look of him as we came up the road, he was on the warpath.

In an effort to by-pass this gentleman, about half our party made off into the rubber. The Jap did not like that, and began to shout and gesture with his rifle. As he had already roped in about a dozen men from the camp, Terry and I decided to take a chance and keep to the road.

It was not until then that I remembered Laverton, and wondered what had become of him.

The new sentry was more interested in the men who were attempting to by-pass him than in those who kept to the road. It was a slur on his authority, and he didn't like it.

For some reason or other he wanted to establish our identity, and anyone who had a paybook was allowed to proceed into camp after the Jap had jotted down his number.

I had no paybook; neither had Terry, and knowing the credulity of the average Jap, I showed the sentry an old envelope on which was the total of a colossal bridge score piled up over a period of weeks. This was sufficient passport, and I got through with some half dozen others.

A similar number of men, in whom he was fast losing interest, were detained by the sentry, who was getting all worked up over the chaps who were making off into the rubber.

Shouting '*Bageru!*' and '*Dame, dame!*' he let off a couple of rounds and ordered all the men on the road into camp, where the police were waiting to carry on from where he left off. In camp the officers were running about like a lot of broody hens who had lost their chicks, though some of them were more like hawks on the lookout for easy prey.

A few of the men fell victim to these scavengers, and were put in the lock-up, being further penalised by having their 'shopping' confiscated.

*****

The Jap on the road was one of a new guard who had arrived to take over, and at a check roll-call the same evening, a hundred men were missing. Consequently, there was a bit of an uproar in the camp until the information came out from Singapore that all the absentees had been rounded up and thrown in the cooler.

The following day the missing hundred, Laverton among them, were brought back to the camp under heavily armed escort. Anyone taking note of their guards might well have made the mistake of thinking the prisoners were to be executed out of hand.

In fact, there was a persistent rumour going the rounds that they were to be shot after a trial by the Jap Commandant, and I was beginning to get uneasy about Laverton. That is, until I got a close look at Laverton.

For a man who was standing on the threshold of infinite space he looked much too cheerful. The other ninety-nine were not in the least downcast either, and I felt that I was being unnecessarily pessimistic.

Instead of being butchered, the men were kept in theoretical confinement for a week on the equivalent of bread and water. At least that was their sentence, but it did not work out that way. Richard, with a party of twenty, was detained in the Jap House – now under new management.

For a week they lived in complete idleness, listening to the Jap wireless, and playing badminton with one of the sentries who had a craze for the game, while the remainder of the camp went back to the job we had thought finished.

Soon after Laverton came out of his comfortable seclusion the camp administration started another tightening-up campaign. Apparently the new Japs were too lax for these gentlemen, and our appreciation of relative values was going to piece.

During the campaign all the old dos and don'ts were resurrected even to the one about saluting.

Brigade appeared to think we were going to the dogs. No longer did we salute our superiors with the free and easy abandon of other days. Why?

No use trying to give the answer to that one. Brigade just could not realise that we were unable to see the necessity for saluting men whom we were living among and meeting at any odd moment of the day. In the circumstances, to salute was but a travesty of what it was meant to be and an insult to our intelligence. So that when the threadbare notice, 'Officers will be saluted at all times by other ranks. This order will be strictly adhered to,' came out the usual friction followed close on its heels.

To complicate matters the new Jap commandant was not particularly interested in feeding us, and, after our recent taste of freedom, we resented the scantiness of the rations that were issued to us, and were not in the mood to be dictated to by petty authority enthroned in Brigade with a red band round its hat.

Sitting by the side of the road one evening disinterestedly eating a meal, consisting mainly of rice, I saw the red band, accompanied by its shadow, a staff captain, who, in his opinion, was nearly as important as his immediate superior, approaching.

Normally I should have stood up and saluted as the august pair came along. As times were not normal just then, and as I had not my essential quote of vitamins, I was not in the mood for acting like a puppet, so remained seated.

'Stand up!' thundered the staff Captain, going a shade redder in the face which, incidentally, looked extremely well fed.

Disregarding the order, I continued mournfully to masticate until the Brigadier, somewhat out of countenance, demanded:

'Are you as lazy as all that, or are you ill?'

'I am not lazy,' I denied. 'At least not usually. I am hungry...'

'Humph!' snorted the great one, and stalked off followed by a much more indignant satellite, leaving me to my rice and reflections, which, at best, made an unappetising savoury.

Two days later administration excelled themselves in stupidity, and I supposed my affront to the Brigadier was responsible. On that day the whole group was mustered on the road that ran through the woods where the bones of the dead lay as yet unburied, and the graves of the newly dead made brown triangular patches amid the greenery. We were then marched up and down the road and given a quarter of an hour's saluting drill.

The fact that the majority of the group were regular soldiers, many with fifteen years' service, makes this saluting parade all the more ludicrous, and shows to what length petty authority, given a free reign, can go.

There we were then, on this bright May morning, having but recently lost one campaign, making sure we also lost the next.

'Salute to the front by numbers... Salute. Up, one, two, three, down... Salute to the right. Salute to the left...'

About this time the Japs had instituted a two-shift day. Half the camp going to work in the morning, and the other half in the afternoon.

When the saluting parade was enforced, whichever shift was in camp took part in it when, in accordance with Jap agreement, they were supposed to be resting, that being the reason for the introduction of the shift system.

Another new institution at this time was a revised roll-call parade which, I think, must have been based on the old nursery rhyme: 'Here we go round the mulberry bush.'

Previously this group had been paraded as one unit for roll-call, each man answering his name as it was called. This was not now considered good enough, as the fence riders were still getting away with their unofficial visits to the outside world. To make things more difficult for the fraternity, some bright lad with nothing better to do had discovered that it was possible for Private Jones to answer for himself *and* Private Smith, thus leaving the latter free to get on with his business outside the wire.

The new roll-call went something like this: The group was split into sections, each section being under the direct control of an N.C.O., while the sergeant major and the officers stood on the high ground overlooking the arena to see that there were no tricks.

On occasions the group commander, Captain Bell, would take the parade from the window in the gable of his house – a budding dictator waiting only for the day when he should burst into full bloom.

At the time appointed each section lined up behind its respective leader, who stood a couple of paces out in front. At the command 'Call the roll' from the grandstand, the section leaders about-faced and called the names of their men. As one's name was called one had to come to attention, wheel round the remainder of the section and take up a fresh position behind the leader.

Thus, as the section moved individually from one position to another, as the names were called, it was impossible to stand in for a comrade who was absent.

Even this procedure did not completely satisfy the jacks in office who were determined to make the roll-call absolutely foolproof.

Soon the section leaders were shorn of some of their glory, and were not

111

allowed to call the roll. This honour was transferred to the sergeant-major; otherwise the procedure was the same, except that it was more like follow-my-leader than before.

And so we went on from one piece of lunacy to another, while the Japs sat by scratching their shaven pates in bewilderment at our antics, and wondering what the mad English were up to…

With the new Jap administration came an increase in pay. Five cents per day for all privates and lance-corporals and ten cents for other N.C.O.s, while the gentlemen got fifteen.

At first this was a welcome addition to the budget but it had its disadvantages, for, as soon as it came into force, the senior N.C.O.s ceased to work, and became, like the officers, supervisors.

Apparently the Japs were learning fast, or else someone in authority had taken a course in human psychology. No sooner were the N.C.O.s made supervisors than they became more diligent than the officers in pushing the work ahead, and the men who actually did the work were more harried than before.

Such is the undermining influence of authority – even enemy-inspired – when invested in an individual not mentally qualified to use it. In this respect one of our officers has surely earned a niche in the shrine which frowns upon the Bukit Timah golf course across the placid waters of McRitchie reservoir. This chap, a major, was known as the White Tojo, owing to his insistence that the job be done as speedily as possible and with a minimum of *yasumis*.

Since the start of the job it had been the practice to work for a stipulated period, when the Jap in charge of the job would shout: 'All men rest,' or just: '*Yasumi*.' At the end of the rest period he would call: 'All men work,' probably adding a 'Speedo!' or two if he felt like it.

On the whole this system worked satisfactorily, and, unless there was a particularly irksome Jap on the job, we got our rest periods regularly. When the Jap was not present, it was our officer's job to see that we got our *yasumis* at the correct intervals.

The White Tojo, like many others, appeared to think we were working for the British government, and cut down the rest periods accordingly.

Unfortunately, the Japs soon discovered this officer's propensities for keeping us going, and they in turn reduced the number of *yasumis*.

Another imposition for which the White Tojo was responsible was the order prohibiting any of his party to smoke during work hours.

Here again the Japs – always on the lookout for something or someone to copy – planned their conduct on the pattern set them by our major and, while men on the White Tojo's party were having their faces slapped for smoking, their neighbours were allowed to smoke until their cigarettes were exhausted.

This no smoking order, and its consequences, is illustrative of the readiness with which many of the Japs were willing to take their cue from our officers when administering discipline, and the man who was instrumental in bringing it into force is entitled to little credit…

Had the White Tojo been man enough to admit that he was frightened of the Japs, and, therefore, not fit to be in charge of a working party, no one would have ridiculed him. After all, there were many of us a bit shaky, and he would have made but one more.

Unfortunately, he was not that type of man, and continued to issue unnecessary orders, aimed at conciliating the Japs and so making himself feel more secure, while the men in his charge were ground further into the dirt by each imposition he inflicted on them.

A typical one, after the no smoking order, was to the effect that two men carrying one basket of earth was one man too many.

These baskets were our only means of conveying soil from one point to another when we outdistanced the trolley line, and were very cumbersome when carried by one man. Two made it an easy job, and formerly the Japs on the diggings had not interfered. Now, however, the White Tojo, in his anxiety not to "waste" labour, insisted on 'one man one basket.'

'Otherwise,' he said, 'it was a waste of man power!'

Perhaps he was right. Maybe the Japs were our allies after all, and we were being kept in the dark for some obscure reason…

Not to be outdone in showing his enthusiasm for the job in hand, our Captain Bell, getting more dictatorial every day, and for the same reason that the White Tojo was working the old appeasement racket with the Japs, started to encroach on our liberties.

Often, when the tools were issued each morning there were not sufficient to go round the group. When that happened the spare men had taken turns *yasumi*-ing. This was now forbidden by the captain. Instead of spending their time in meditative idleness, or scrounging about in the woods, the surplus men were given the job of 'cleaning up the area'.

This meant that they had to pick up all the pieces of paper, match-sticks, dog-ends and various odds and ends that were to be found in the jungle on either side of the embryo road!

I suppose it is impossible for anyone to give a satisfactory explanation as to why men act in this damn silly fashion just because they have been invested with a little authority which, through misuse, has grown shoddy and threadbare to the men who are continually victimised by it.

I should not care to suggest that these individuals were genuinely interested in assisting the Japanese by getting their work done as expeditiously as possible. That would not be doing them justice, for their intention was not to assist the enemy. Rather were they so scare that they just did not realise how questionable were their actions. Neither did they seem to appreciate the truth of the joke, long standing among us, that we were not prisoners of the Japanese, but of ourselves...

Chapter Ten

Fukanda: Child of Old Japan

Periodically the Japs canvassed the camps for skilled workers to assist them in their war effort and, conscience being so easily side-tracked, they had little difficulty in getting volunteers, for the inducements to being a skilled worker were many. Chief of these were escape from the heart-breaking monotony of road making, or some equally tedious job, and an increase in pay.

Since his mishap on the bogie line, Laverton had been on the look-out for something to drive. Anxious to rehabilitate himself as a driver, when the Japs came looking for men to manage a fleet of steam-rollers, he volunteered for the job after coaxing me to accompany him as mate. Little coaxing was necessary. I was glad of the opportunity to get away from the camp in which there was little pleasure and less variety.

The fact that he had never driven a steam-roller did not worry Laverton. It did not worry the Japs either. They took it for granted that he was qualified as they did the inference that petrol was a necessary contribution to the successful working of the roller. Provided the thing operated successfully they were prepared to feed it with milk if necessary. Every day for three weeks, four gallons of petrol were issued from the Jap stores for the steam-roller and, just as religiously, it was sold to the Chinese who paid well for it.

Scabbing petrol was one of the main relaxations at McArthur Camp. Even the Jap guard were in the racket to such an extent that when they caught anyone they had no option but to deal leniently with him in order to cover up their own double dealing.

With no pretence at concealment, one man in the camp – that same Ginger Parsons who had been chased from the black market kampong at *Changi* – carried two full petrol tins out of the camp every day for a week before the Jap on the gate got suspicious. Being a racketeer of the first order, Ginger knew from experience that the easiest way to fool the Japs on the gate was to operate in such an open fashion as to give an appearance of legitimacy to whatever he was doing.

Jap mentality being what it is, the guard took it for granted that he was authorised to take the petrol out of camp and so let him pass unquestioned.

But like so many of his kind, Ginger, had his imperfections as a racketeer. Greed was his weak point. It induced him to carry an extra tin of petrol which he dropped at the feet of the guard, who gave him a slapping and promptly sold the petrol to a Chinese truck driver. Next day Ginger had another racket. Working on a drain outside the camp, he syphoned the petrol out of each Jap truck that stopped by the guardroom, leaving the driver just sufficient 'juice' to get away from the vicinity of the camp. It was impossible to discourage a man like Ginger, and he deserved all the money he made...

Petrol was not the only thing the Chinese were anxious to get. Anything from a lady's hair net – there were thousands of them in the store – to a motor car, found a ready sale.

Not everyone got the opportunity to scab a motor car, of course, but at least on one occasion a new car was taken from Ford's and driven into Singapore, where it was sold for twelve hundred dollars!

Laverton and I did not go in for scabbing on such a magnificent scale. We had secured income from the daily petrol issue, and from many other incidentals that came our way. As racketeers we were small fry, nor had we any ambition to be otherwise.

Life at McArthur Camp was more enjoyable than it had been at the road construction camp. In addition to the opportunities for making a bit on the side, our normal rations were good; also there was an absence of that officialism that was such an irritating factor in the latter camp. Unfortunately, as was always the case when conditions were good, there were a number of individuals who, through greed and a lack of interest in the welfare of the camp as a whole, outraged the leniency of the Japs and caused them eventually to tighten up on our activities.

An example of this was the ration store. On the day someone discovered that a panel in the back wall of the store was removable, it became our Mecca. Here we went daily to take our pick from the large assortment of ex-British Army rations that the Japs had accumulated. Usually a man took a tin of jam, or whatever he fancied, as he required it, but there were some – the men whose god was greed – that were not satisfied with less than a whole case full.

On one of their periodic searches for wireless sets –there was one in the loft over the latrine – the Japs discovered some of these cases of stolen rations,

116

and in the ensuing investigations the vulnerability of the ration store was discovered, resulting in a couple of men being beaten up, as a reminder that we were not free agents...

Instances of prisoners hitting back when molested by a Jap were not uncommon, until a general order was issued to the effect that any prisoner striking a Japanese, for whatever cause, would have his head cut off. This decree was instantly discouraging, so much so that it stopped all retaliation. But before that happened, I witnessed an occurrence that is typical of Jap mentality, and the ability of the average prisoner to 'take it'.

One of the men, an ex-battalion boxing champion, was continually being aggravated by a miniature Jap, who persisted in kicking his shins and hitting him with a piece of bamboo. For three days this sort of thing went on, then one morning the Jap received a terrific uppercut that sent him flying over a large packing case, where he lay "out" for fifteen minutes.

Later the little Jap staggered off to the guardroom, where he recruited an army and returned to renew the assault. There were six of them, armed with pick handles and bamboo poles, and for five minutes there was a glorious free-for-all, during which the mastiff sought to shake off the jackals that were trying to pull him down. In spite of their armament, the assaulting party were knocked over like ninepins, until an unlucky blow from a pick handle ended the fight. Having got their man on the ground the Japs gave him a hell of a beating, after which they dragged him off to the sweat-box.

A couple of hours later, with two of his cronies, the Jap who had started all the trouble took his prisoner out of the sweat box and, as we watched in trepidation, he was led away across a field to what, we felt sure, was his execution.

Nothing like that happened. Sitting beneath a shady tree in the middle of the field, the Japs produced a bottle of whisky, biscuits and cigarettes, and had a party, the while they kept patting their guest on the back and telling him what a good sort he was.

'You number one,' they reiterated. 'You O.K. Number one!'

This was their way of letting him know they were keenly appreciative of the good show he had put up. He had fought well, and they bore no malice. Had he, on the other hand, shown the white feather when they attacked him, he would have been lucky to get away from a beating. And certainly there would have been no party afterwards.

The practice of compensating any prisoner who got a beating was not general, but occasionally the Japs did do it, for they respected courage.

Provided the victim took his punishment with a stout heart, he did at least retain the respect of the men who beat him. Occasionally they would inform their victim that he was number one and give him a cigarette.

Poor compensation admitted, and achieved only through courage...

*****

A complete contrast to the bunch of thugs who beat up the boxer was the Jap in charge of the carpenter's shop in the camp.

Known affectionately as Sandy Powell, this Jap conscript was the most unorthodox Jap I have ever met. A labourer by profession – and proud of it – he wanted nothing more than to get back to his job in Japan, where he had a wife and two children. Everything military was abhorrent to Sandy, and he was contemptuous even of the Emperor, about whom he made the most uncomplimentary assertions – a remarkable departure from precedent.

Whenever a Jap officer came round to inspect the workshops, Sandy took a childish delight in sticking out his tongue behind his superior's back, and he was quite bucked when we showed our appreciation of his daring. And I think, too, he was just a little bit mental.

Sandy Powell's disinterestedness in his job went to extremes. He allowed the Chinese workers to retain the keys of the ammunition store without any assurance that they would not disabuse his faith in them and had there been a massacre in the camp, Sandy would have been responsible. But I don't think he would have bothered much about that; he was too browned off and too homesick and, in spite of his civil occupation, he was lazy in the extreme. Instead of supervising our work, he preferred to go to sleep beneath a large packing case, while we played cards and kept a look-out for any other Jap who might come along.

When a food dump outside the camp was set on fire, we scabbed a large amount of rations from it and Sandy Powell, willing as ever to co-operate, let us use his store as a hiding place...

On a day when Laverton was giving his iron horse a yasumi, we went to Singapore with six others to do a chore for the Japs, and, if circumstances allowed, to visit the house in Sarangoon Road.

Cruising round in a lorry, our job was to collect miscellaneous pieces of furniture, which were taken to a brothel the Japs were re-furnishing in order to impart to it a more home-like atmosphere. Intoxicated with imagination and the joys of anticipation, the Japs were in jovial mood, and inclined to show off before their comfort girls. The bints were not Japanese bints. They had been there before the Japs came and, doubtless, they would remain when their new clients had gone. In the meantime they gave comfort to all who could pay for it, and to us they gave sympathy without cynicism.

One of the girls had given Laverton ten dollars on the day I met the Chinese Jim Sing in Bencoolian Street, and I was grateful for her generosity. As a gesture of appreciation, I wangled a comfortable-looking divan bed for her, and hoped she would spend many a restful night on it, though Laverton did not think she would. He was of the opinion that a Jap did not make an admirable bed fellow, and consequently, the *bint's* rest would be at least spasmodic.

Evidently the Japs were not admirable 'lovers' in other respects. As we moved their furniture around, the *bints* were continually reassuring us:

'Japanese soldiers no good – English soldiers very good.' Accompanying this testimonial was an unmistakable gesture that left no doubt as to what part of the anatomy they were referring!

While the two Japs with our party were trying out the new furnishings, I slipped out of the brothel and hurried up the street to the New World. Traversing an alley, I came to the house where Nai Soon had been staying with Little Flower – and drew a blank.

There was no sign of them. The Chinese family in the house looked at me open-mouthed when I inquired about Nat. None of them understood English – or at least they appeared not to – so that it was pretty hopeless trying to get any information.

Cursing in helpless frustration, I left the house and hurried back to the brothel where the Japs had apparently tested all the beds and were awaiting my return in a good humour.

Laverton had explained my absence:

'One man cigarette speedo, and the Japs were not worrying...

On another fatigue in the town – getting rations for the Jap cook-house – we ran into the tail end of a fracas between the Chinese and our overlords.

Rice was again the cause of the trouble. In Singapore at this time, stocks were dwindling rapidly, and the ration issued by the Japs was not deemed sufficient by the townspeople. As a gesture of dissatisfaction a group of Chinese had made another raid on a rice store, and this time, unfortunately for them, they had injured a couple of Japs.

Reprisals were summary, and as our lorry took us through the streets to the docks, we passed a number of gruesome-looking heads stuck up on poles at points of vantage – a warning to the populace to live on their rations and like it.

In the docks there was more trouble. Owing to the rotted state of some of the sacks, we spilled a good deal of rice on the ground when loading the lorry, and a couple of elderly Chinese coolies came forward to salvage it.

The Jap guard did not like that. The two old men were trussed up to a beam and thrashed unmercifully while we looked on, nauseated by the brutality of this spectacle, and helpless to do anything about it. Our own particular Japs had no hand in the affair and were, I think, a little disgusted by it.

Sandy Powell, who was with us, looked a bit white and agitated, and I could imagine what he as thinking…

Outside a godown further along the docks, three Chinese lay with the bluebottles making whoopee on the bloated faces of two of them. The other face looked down in sullen resentment from an iron spike over the godown that its owner had attempted to enter.

Noting this summary injustice, I could not but compare the punishment these unfortunate Chinese had received with the discipline meted out to us for a similar offence back at the camp.

Prisoners as we were, the Japs were still conscious of our former status and, apart from some isolated instances, did not go to extremes when administering physical punishment. The unfortunate Chinese, on the other hand, never had this interval in which to adapt themselves. They and the Japs were hereditary enemies; between them was a long and bitter hatred intensified by our collapse at Singapore, and in the first months after our failure they suffered much greater hardships than we did.

Later, of course, as our glamour wore off and we became coolies in the best tradition, the Japs did not bother to pull their punches when they were giving one of us a bashing. But those days were not with us yet. They were something which was yet to come. Something we should always remember…

The tempo of life at one of the camps near Singapore may be judged from a notice signed by the Jap Commandant after a number of protests had been sent in about the general shortage of wearing apparel – boots in particular:

'*You have been living with us for some months now. During this time we have become friends, and you are our friends, because you are soldiers, and as soldiers, we have treated you well in the true spirit of Bushido. But you have abused our friendship, avoiding your work.*

'*This should make you ashamed. As soldiers you should know it is your duty to work, and work to the best of your ability. This should trouble your conscience, as it is well known that soldiers can work under any conditions. You say you have no shirts, no boots, etc., but this is no excuse. All soldiers, again I say, can work under any conditions.*

'We shall do our best to improve your conditions, but it must be understood that you must work. From now onwards action will be taken against anyone not working.' – (Signed)

Lt. FUKANDA.

Fukanda's ideology was sound for a Jap, and he was much more amenable to reason than many of our own officers. Imagine them telling us to be good boys and go to work! Had circumstances been reversed our complaints would have been dealt with in the usual high-handed manner, and we should have a stiff session of jankers as a reminder that we had no authority to question their right to expect us to work without proper clothing.

It was not only the workers who rubbed Fukanda up the wrong way. When the officers, excused the roll-call parade so that they might keep their "dignity", trespassed on Fukanda's generosity by playing bridge during roll-call, he issued a stern reminder that, to the I.J.A., roll-call was not just a mere formality.

In a notice posted on the 25th August, 1942, he said:

'During the time I am the orderly officer, I will conduct the evening roll-call with solemnity. (1) When the Réveillé is given under the command 'attention' all ranks must not move, smoke, laugh, talk, or smile. (2) The remainder in the camp, except sick men, must keep quiet for the inspection. They must never destroy the authority of Roll-Call. (3) The soldiers who are free from roll-call by duty if they see the Nipponese orderly officer, they should salute privately. (4) For officers I admit the absence to keep their dignity. But the sacred Roll-Call is not a sham. So if there is an officer sitting in the chair and seeing the sight of Roll-Call, I feel serious displeasure. If there are soldiers who offend the above mentioned, whatever it may be, I will return them with furious training.'

-   (Signed) Lt. FUKANDA.

Another gem of Lt. Fukanda's, following a sharp rise in the numbers of men absent from the working parties because of sickness is the following:

'In the last two weeks the number of soldiers off duty has increased day by day. Of course, this is not because they are idle – they seem to be obliged to be in bed during the working time. Examining the cases of the sickness, I have found a few cases of stomach ache!

'When I was orderly officer, I made a tour of inspection at night and found

121

that many men were sleeping without covers on their stomachs, and I suppose the coolness of midnight and daybreak caused those stomachs to ache. When we see the percentage of cases, this camp has many more than other camps. This fact suggested that there are other causes of the disease above and beyond the cold caught in sleep.

'I think it is caused by the matter that the soldiers in this camp cannot make their spirits high. Though the soldiers of the other camps are all in the same life as prisoners of war, they love their lorries as their fellows.' (This was a reference to the men who were driving trucks for the Japs – one of the skilled jobs.) 'To work for the enemies of yesterday is not cheerful, but the fact that they drive the lorries is that they can give life to themselves by the lorries. As for the repairers, when they have finished their repairing they will be in gladness forgetting their enemies and themselves. On the way of repairing they can expect the gratification of finishing their work. On the contrary, the soldiers of this camp cannot enjoy such gladness: they work only against their will, being obedient to the Japanese soldiers. Then they think that they cannot feel life worth living.

'In Nippon, sickness is called Byouki. Looking at these two Nippon letters the first word Byo already means sickness, originates in mood, uncomfortableness, unpleasantness, and disagreeableness. In Nippon there is an old proverb as follows: 'Illness comes from mood.' Kaiki, which means to make one's mind cheerful. At those points I will decide without hesitation the fact that these many sick men in this camp is caused by the uncheerfulness of their minds.

'Indeed, in rough beds, thinking of the pleasures of the past days, their own native places, wives and children, they will be shut in deep sorrow without exception. Moreover, when they catch diseases the darkness of their minds will increase and the diseases will be serious unto death.

'My dear English soldiers are not short from some points of view. The days of peace will come sooner or later. If the peace comes you can go to your dear country, work for her, mankind and God.

'Although you are grieved, a day is 24 hours. Although you are cheerful, a day is 24 hours. If you are sad or not, the morning comes exactly the same. So you must raise your minds, spending your time without sadness, and thereupon you will expel your illness. I will say again, there is a proverb in Nippon that illness comes from the mind. The converse is true. Make your minds cheerful; drive the illness far away and keep your health in good condition until the day on which you go back to your dear home.'

– (Signed) Lt. FUKANDA

There can be no doubt but that Lt. Fukanda's philosophy was sound. In the dark days ahead I often thought of his exhortation to remain cheerful, realising that a firm determination to survive was the best medicine no matter what the disease.

Unfortunately, a great number of the prisoners allowed themselves to lose interest in continued existence and so become apathetic. When they did that there was nothing our medical officers could do for them, so that they died when they might have lived.

Fukanda was not the only sentimentalist in the ranks of the I.J.A.

On being transferred from Havelock Road Camp, where they had been employed as mechanics in a garage, to Tanjong Rhu, a group of prisoners were sent off with the following benediction:

'Farewell! From the middle of May for about five months we have worked together in this simple garage. I have been always very thankful for your faithfulness and friendship. I am very sorry that we must bid farewell to each other, and you must go to unknown positions. I could not sleep for a long time last night knowing of your deep sorrow. But be not anxious because we all Japanese soldiers are somewhat rough and wild, but in deep parts of our hearts we have warmness and gentleness and kindness. Your new conductors are the same surely.

'Then, from tomorrow please work as diligently as yesterday. The peace will come sooner or later. When the peace comes you can go back to your country, see your wives, parents, children and sweethearts, and work for your country and human beings. So that you make your health cheerful. On the other hand, take care of your bodies and be healthy until you can go back to your native land. Never mind, never mind. Oh! The sun shines even above your heads. Let the sun shine in your hearts also. I will never forget you.'

When Laverton and I left McArthur to return to the road construction camp we were given no such illuminated address. Just the same, we were not sorry to get away from the place – there were too many incidents occurring. Richard has also over-stayed his welcome as a steam-roller driver, and his iron horse was daily becoming more fractious, in spite of its ration of petrol.

During the last few days we were there I thought the Jap in charge of the oil dump was beginning to look at Laverton with a speculative gleam in his unfathomable brown eyes. Each time we went for our petrol ration he seemed more reluctant to part with it, and he was continually muttering and swearing to himself: A very bad sign and one that suggested a speedy withdrawal from the position of driver's mate on a steam-roller that was dispassionate almost as the Jap himself had been. That's what I was afraid of: he was not dispassionate anymore...

When I was the Jap in question being taught to drive a lorry on the road outside the camp, I felt sure that my premonition of impending disaster was justified, and that our benefactor was becoming more mechanically minded, and our deception daily more vulnerable...

Yes, definitely it was time to say good-bye to our iron horse.

Chapter Eleven

'On Active Service'

While Laverton and I had been steam-rolling – without an 'L' sign – camp routine with the road gang had remained more or less stabilised. The newest innovation in the camp was a one man bagpipes band which took us to work the day following our arrival with the reminder: 'In future men on the way to and from work will march in step.'

Personally, I had never tried marching to the bagpipes, and I never wish to again. This undoubtedly is the opinion of many of the chaps who went down the road that first morning, and especially of those who were put on a charge for marching out of step.

The punishment for this sort of crime was usually three days' detention on rice and water, with added loss of pay for the period. Detention was also given to those who were absent from roll-call which, it is to be remembered, was taken solely by our people. In this case the crime was not referred to as absence, but was known as 'desertion'. That is, being absent from the camp without leave.

Thus, if a man decided to go out for a look around with the probable intention of making a break for it, he got jankers if he changed his mind and came back.

Laverton and I had been back three days when we qualified for five days' jankers for being spotted coming into camp after roll-call by an over-zealous policeman.

Life in the camp was so monotonous after the comparatively good time we had had at McArthur that it became necessary to do a bit of fence riding for the sake of diversity. In this camp there was little opportunity for making a bit of extra money, and the main incentive for breaking bounds was the hope of being able to buy food from the locals, who were always prepared to sell it at a price.

Gone were the days when one could get a sackful of food by going to Singapore for it. Those days were as though they had never been, and the possibility of my seeing Nai Soon again was equally remote.

One night on a surreptitious visit to a *kampong* down the road, where we often went for a coffee after evening roll-call, we thought we had made a new contact. The owner of the *kampong* was a very fat Chinese lady, many years bereaved, but with a brood of *chickos* of indeterminate ages, who squatted round in the moonlight making indecent suggestions.

On this particular evening the obese lady had a boyfriend in her kennel and, ladylike, had to show him off to her guests.

The boyfriend, a contented-looking Malay, spoke good English and appeared to be most interested in our hard-luck story.

Laverton, more browned off than usual, forgot his inherent suspicion of everything native, and asked the Malay point-blank if there was any chance of us making a successful getaway from the island. Not unnaturally, the question had a most electrifying effect on the Malay. Drawing his hand across his throat in a most expressive gesture of negation, he muttered something about the Japanese and faded into the gloom of the *kampong* as though Laverton were a poisonous reptile. Even the *chickos* were affected and withdrew from us as Mother Hubbard came out of her hut in evident displeasure.

What she said was not clear, for she had no English apart from a few words dealing with food and money. Her gestures were expressive, however, and realising we had made a serious *faux pas* we got up and departed into the night.

'That old bitch!' lamented Laverton as we skulked back up the road. 'I bet she is in cahoots with the Japs. Better keep away from her lousy *kampong*, Mick…'

'Might be just as well,' I agreed, thinking of Nai Soon. 'Nat was evidently right when he told me we should have difficulty in persuading any native to help us get away. I'm afraid we are stymied after all.'

It didn't help any when we walked into the arms of an M.P. and got those five days' jankers.

We were not the only ones, however. Many of the fence riders got regular doses of rice and water for being outside the wire which was still mainly theoretical. But that did not make us any the more appreciative of Captain Bell's illiberality…

Perhaps the most absurd instance of a man being put on a charge was the case of the individual who was docketed a day's pay for chasing a young pig that came nosing around near to where he was working. Granted, he had no good intentions towards the pig, which was to be expected, as roast pork at that time was but a memory growing daily more mildewed, and the pig probably did things to his belly that only a hungry man could appreciate.

Then there was the episode of the janker-wallah who refused to work unless his diet of rice and water was strengthened with something more substantial. When the A.P.M. and his staff were unable to persuade this fellow to change his mind, the co-operation of the Japanese guard was requested.

When the guard arrived, a sergeant and a private, they went in to the detention room and had a free-for-all, during which an elderly lance-corporal, who also was in detention, was punched in the face, his false teeth being knocked out – making me think of Smithy and his idiotic precautions on Changi beach.

During the fracas our provost staff stood on the road with an expression that said: 'That'll show 'im.' To them it was a jolly good show. They enjoyed the fun. Undoubtedly the Japs enjoyed it too, while for us it was but another reminder that our own administration was more to be feared than the common enemy.

Since the opening of the construction camp the Japs had been working on the old all-in company scheme whereby men spent their pay in the store of the firm for which they worked.

Our Jap-sponsored canteen, run by a couple of Chinese, the European interpretation of whose name must have been Shylock, took all our hard-earned money and gave little in return. Soon, however, and fortunately for us, their monopoly of the camp trade was threatened.

Beyond the little stream that marked the southern confines of the camp, a black market was sending out feelers. So far as our interests were concerned, there was nothing black about this institution. On the contrary, its prices were 50% down on the canteen, and on that account much of the camp funds were soon going across the stream instead of into the Jap canteen.

As well as being a welcome source of much-needed nourishment, the black market gave us daily a great deal of amusement, which was fully appreciated by those in a position to benefit from its comicality.

About an hour before the market was due to open, crowds of eager shoppers gathered on the near bank of the stream; then, as the first native vendors appeared among the bushes on the other side, the market was automatically open.

As usual, it was a case of first-come, first-served, and gradually the buyers and sellers mingled in the middle of the stream while they haggled and gesticulated, forgetful of the Jap House 200 yards away. Whenever a native with any particular delicacy, such as bread and eggs, came along he was immediately surrounded, being fortunate if he were not submerged in the stream by the over-eager buyers.

There were other things than food peddled along the boundary stream. On the far bank a Chinese soap-box orator lectured us on the Yellow Peril – in this case the Japanese.

This feature of our black market was extremely out of place in the circumstances, and let itself open to the assumption that the agitators were in the pay of the Japs, while they masqueraded as the saviours of mankind – the British prisoner of war taking pride of place in the new salvation they preached. However that may be, I listened to them with a still tongue and derived little comfort from their exhortations.

Once the camp canteen began to show a deficit, the death of the black market became imminent. As soon as the adverse balance was brought to the attention of the Japs, they issued an order to the effect that all trading outside the authorised channels were forbidden.

Having issued the order they sat back and left our administration to put it into effect, knowing their interests were in capable hands.

They were.

Additional police were recruited to stamp out the black market and to lurk along the road as we marched to work, and in the evenings when we returned, to prevent our buying anything from the vendors who lay in wait for us.

Previously it had been the practice to buy cigarettes and tobacco, or maybe an egg or a loaf of bread from the native youngsters on the way home from the diggings. Now the camp police brought this trading almost to a standstill so far as the workers were concerned. They, however, took full advantage of their position to start a black market of their own, and thrived accordingly.

Temporarily the riverside market closed down after the edict forbidding it but the Chinese, who, composed the greater number of vendors, are not easily dismayed by threats, and gradually it opened up again, in spite of all the efforts of our police to suppress it.

Technically the first round went to the black marketeers. Round two was opened by the canteen Chinese, who, when the market first opened, were not above walking down the hill to the stream to buy goods which were later sold in the canteen at a profit of 50%.

The canteen wallahs now started a spying campaign, and kept their patrons, the Japs, informed of the trend of events. Shortly afterwards the guard made a sudden and salutary swoop on the black market, killing one Chinese and severely beating three others, including a youngster of twelve years who later died.

For a couple of days thereafter the market was closed; then the vendors came sneaking through the bushes in the early morning and at night time when we returned from work. Outwitting our police, who religiously searched the shrubbery along the stream and chased away any native they encountered, they came to the stream at the risk of their lives to sell to us the things we were so much in need of.

Three days after the Jap swoop a young Chinese cycled into camp with a basketful of loaves of bread. Unfortunately, he stopped outside brigade to sell some to the officers and was taken in charge by the police who handed him over to the Japanese.

Rather a high-handed action on the part of the A.P.H., as the Chinese were supposed to be our allies, and to turn one of them over to the Japs was, in the circumstances, tantamount to a death sentence.

*****

On the terrace above the cook-house, the dysentery patients sat like a row of bedraggled old vultures waiting with infinite patience for some animal to die so that they might devour it.

The routine treatment for dysentery being a diet with a very close affinity to total starvation, the men down with the scourge were always ravenously hungry. At meal times the smells from the cook-house, such as they were, brought them to the edge of the terrace to peer down in hungry expectancy at their more fortunate fellows below.

At Changi I had had a 'taste' of this starvation cure, and knew just how hungry were the men up on the terrace.

Their plight was worse than mine had been, for at Changi there had been an occasional drink of milk or some other 'extra', to help the patients through the initial period of the curse. Here there were no extras or, if there were, the dysentery patients did not get them.

A diet consisting of sugarless black tea twice a day, plus two platefuls of what was grandiloquently described as beef tea, but what resembled more the water in which the hospital staff washed their greasy plates, was not an inspiring menu for a sick man. Once in a while the morning 'meal' of black tea was turned into a banquet by the addition of a teaspoonful of sugar.

The camp hospital was definitely not a happy place in which to spend a vacation. There were no beds and the patients were compelled to lie on the concrete floor on whatever bedding they possessed. Usually this consisted of a torn blanket and an old sack. Many had to manage without the blanket.

By way of contrast, some of the gentlemen in brigade slept one to a double bed – the real thing – with all the trimmings, and expected us to salute them when they showed up on our shoddy horizon...

When a man died in the dysentery ward, he was rolled in his dirty bedding and carried the short distance down the road to join the others who had beat him to it, while on the road alongside the cemetery his mates were acting like a lot of bloody half-wits trying to salute.

On a visit to the hospital with a couple of old newspapers I had picked up on the diggings – paper was as scarce as food, and was a first essential in the dysentery ward – I noticed a sorry-looking individual lying almost naked on his soiled blanket in a corner. He looked like nothing more than a bundle of dirty washing thrown down and forgotten. Looking at him, I could not imagine his being clean again.

Unwashed and alone he lay there while death peered at him from around the corner. The apotheosis of pity, he had no friends; no one to be offended by his sorry plight... I did what I could for him, but that was not much, for there was so little time and he had not long to stay.

Next day while I was in with another newspaper, death pounced on him. Yet even then he was not freed from that which had stolen his life.

Unwashed as he was, a sack was hurriedly pulled over his head and shoulders and another over his legs. Then rolled in his filthy blanket, he was taken down the road to where the notice board said: 'British Military Cemetery.'

*****

June 10, '42 is a memorable day.

After the morning roll-call a notice, or proclamation, was read to us. This message was from Sir Archibald Sinclair, the G.O.C., and in it he stated that as from June 1st we were to consider ourselves as on Active Service!

If this was not a case of eating your cake and still having it, I don't know what is.

Prisoners of war on Active Service!

After fierce discussion of the momentous announcement, the bulk of the men were of the opinion that we had been given our new status, even though it was only theoretical – so that the administration could get at us with the full weight of the King's Regulations behind them.

This supposition was borne out later when men were given company office for offences which, prior to June 10th, were not considered sufficiently grave to warrant a dose of jankers. On the other hand we, in turn, were not allowed to benefit from the new regulation.

It was definitely a one-edged sword, and was always turned against us.

Administration lost no time in using their new lever. As a result, *yasumis* in camp were less sought after than they had ever been before. Even the sick men not in hospital preferred to go to work rather than remain in camp doing a lot of irritating fatigues thought up for the sole purpose of keeping them from 'lolling about' – as Brigade described a *yasumi*.

In circumstances such as ours it was generally agreed that too much free time was not beneficial to the morale of the individual.

There was little danger of that position arising, however. The Japs saw to that, and kept us busy on six days of the week. Sunday was a *yasumi*, and we were grateful for the occasion.

Then Brigade, anxious lest we become demoralised through too much leisure, thought up a little chore for our Sunday entertainment – and it was not church.

Around the camp were immense hedges of hibiscus – the plant that had nourished us at Changi. On our rest days we had to trim these hedges with table knives, there being no other weapon available. When we were not chopping down the hibiscus with our knives, they were being used to cut the grass or any other old thing to which Brigade took exception.

Another job reserved for off-work days was the wood fatigue. As the cook-houses had to be supplied with fuel from outside the camp, it was the general practice for each man to bring back a log of wood from the diggings.

Apart from this there were numerous dead trees in the woods across the road, but Brigade would not allow us to utilise these.

They apparently thought we enjoyed going for a route march on our *yasumi* days to another stretch of dead forest two miles from the camp.

All things considered, working on the roads was to be preferred to a day in the camp, and had the Japs abolished the Sunday yasumi as they did later when we had left the camp, no one would have been disappointed. That is, if one excepts Brigade. Had the Sunday yasumi been terminated, these gentlemen would have been unable to pass their time playing at silly buggers, utilising us as pawns on their grotesque chessboard.

Fortuitously, after our elevation to Active Service status, we were not destined to remain long in the road construction camp. The Japs had found another use for us and we were going back to Changi to forget, if possible, our dual personalities. To the Japs, as to us, the supposition that we were still on Active Service meant nothing. To them we were still prisoners. We knew that, unlike our administration who were prepared to go on believing in their own inviolability, kidding themselves with thoughts of the past while they overlooked the present...

To many, the order to return to Changi was a keen disappointment. I, too, was disappointed. Return to Changi meant an end of any immediate hope of seeing Nai Soon again, and that was something that left a bitter taste in my mouth. For the others, they had no wish to go back to the old way of life in Southern Area, where the supreme irritants, bullshit and red tape, were likely to have still a loud voice in the councils of the administration and to be much worse than ever they had been in the road construction camp.

When the day came for our return my personal feelings in the matter were crowded out by the knowledge that, if the move was not expedited, I should have difficulty in returning to base under my own steam. Dysentery was peeping up over the horizon again and, like a bird at nesting time, I was collecting all the newsprint I could get my hands on.

Chapter Twelve

General Salute Goes to a Tea Party

IN the cool dusk of the evening, with the moon hanging huge and burnished over the rustling palms, we came into the village which had not seen us for ten weeks. In the moonlight Changi looked barren and there was a strangeness about it that had not been there before.

The native huts huddled in the palm groves that fringed the road had a peaceful and shadowed beauty in the quiet night that was coming down the sky, but it was an uneasy pace – a peace implied by the mystery of the unchanging moon. It went no deeper than make-belief. Underneath, there was fear and shrinking induced by sudden acts of strife that had left a sombre desolation behind them.

Many of the kampongs which, at our going, had been populous with an uneasy throng were now ruined and deserted. In the time we had been away something had happened – something that had left a feeling of suspense to mock the beauty of the filtered moonlight. What that something was I did not know, but it was apparent that the Japs had not been kind to the natives who lived on the fringe of Changi. And I wondered about that, feeling the sadness in the suggestion of decay given off by the silent *kampongs*...

Round the corner a more personal transformation showed, where the bougainvillaea flamed red beneath the moon. When we had passed that way before, the cemetery had not been overcrowded, and there had been ample room. Now, it looked swollen and obscene as though it had achieved repletion from a gluttonous feasting.

Where before the graves had been numbered in twos and threes, they now ranked in dozens and scores. Ghostly in the moonlight the crosses stuck up gaunt and bare, bringing a deep realisation, accentuated by a sense of shock, of the possibilities inherent in a prisoner-of-war camp.

The camp, too, was changed. Where before at all hours of the day and far into the night had been the noise and bustle of a great throng, there was now a quietness. Where previously the hibiscus hedges had been kept neatly 'plucked' and the grass cut short, these were now growing wild to over-run the once neat gardens and give to them the appearance of neglect and decay associated with the *kampongs* further down the road.

'When I realised the reason for this decay, I was filled with a sense of deep satisfaction, and wished that John were with me in the moonlight to share it. Laverton, too, was enthusiastic.

'This is just what we have been waiting for,' he exulted. 'It's a bit of bad luck missing the first party to go up-country. Worse still, you'll be going into hospital again. Don't stay too long, Mick. We must get on the next party.'

'I wonder if John and Smithy are back yet?' I wanted to know. But there was no one to tell me just then. Later, when I learned that they had come and gone, my enthusiasm about the up-country party was replaced by an acute sense of frustration.

Would they never end, these hidden obstacles that were continually tripping me up and turning momentary elation into the bitterness of defeat?

Standing there in the moonlight with Laverton, in the desolation that was Changi, I yearned for John and the placid Smithy; for Nai Soon, with his steadfast philosophy and his keen appreciation of my doubts and fears, so similar to his own. Then I thought of Little Flower and Terry Reynolds, who had been sent back to Changi on a stretcher while I was masquerading as a number two on a steam-roller.

'Where are they?' I wondered. And where was the multitude who had swarmed about Changi in the first weeks of captivity? Where especially were the men who had gone up-country, and about whom I was just now hearing?

Those questions were not answered that night, though I did learn that two large parties had gone from Changi. No one was quite sure where exactly they had gone; neither was anyone sure why they had gone. Sufficient it was that they had left, and Changi knew their faces no more.

They were the pioneers of the great exodus of prisoners just getting under way from Changi and Singapore. The forerunners of the thousands who followed them, they left Changi filled with the excitement and expectation that had thrilled so many pioneers before them. Gladly they departed –as we did later – on a journey which, to so many, meant death.

With them went John and Smithy, who had been back at Changi three weeks, so that we were still divided and out of tune…

It was nice in hospital – with a niceness that had not been there before. The smell, as of dirty washing dumped in a corner and left there, had been whittled down by a liberal use of underproof disinfectant, supplied by the Japanese after a long period of disinterested inactivity during which the combined stinks of gangrene and dysentery hung as a noxious miasma about the wards.

Now organisation, and a military precision which lined up the beds with a piece of string, had come out of the initial chaos, bringing a shabby gentility, almost suburban in its respectability.

Water ran once more out of the taps – for two hours in the morning, and for a similar period late at night – and gave of its blessings to a stinking humanity that was dependent on it for decency and a sense of respect.

Another improvement was the canteen – when you got well enough to go that far. Here you could buy peanut toffee and Chinese biscuits, and, sometimes, eggs – not guaranteed. Also, if you had the money, you could buy jam!

Unfortunately, you did not have the money. Not after some Ishmaelite of an opportunist had relieved you of your petrol dividends as you lay beside the Styx, waiting for a fool of a boatman who never came to take you to a somehow preferred Hell. Then, when you decided you did not require his services after all, your dividends were gone, as were also your hopes of acquiring a tin of jam, so that Heaven and Hell were as remote as ever.

Still, there were other things besides the disappearance of a sum of money, doubtfully come by, to occupy one's attention, after floating about for a week in the ethereal plane of existence, which qualified one for a place on the 'seriously ill' list.

For instance, there was Billy Crane three beds away. Billy had come back on a stretcher from a working party at Singapore as soon as the Japs could be induced to take sufficient interest in him to supply transport for the journey. By then it was too late. Billy was already occupying my place beside the Styx's sombre waters, and this time the boatman was waiting.

For three days Billy kept him splashing his oars in fuming impatience; then, after reviewing the odds stacked against him, he jumped into the boat and was off to see what lay on the other side.

Early in the morning it was – at the time so many men have died. He had been lying quiet for about an hour after the pain of the night. We were the only two awake in the ward – the one who was going, and the one who had not long been back.

It was very quiet, with a sense of waiting in no way connected with the night's orderly vigil, which was about ended. Two moths chased each other round the smoky lamp by his bedside; every once in a while they went ting against the glass, and the tiny sound rang sharp and clear in the silence of waiting.

As I watched, the dying man's head slewed round on the grubby pillow and his eyes came questing for mine with a pathetic appeal for understanding. Then his head turned back again, and his eyes went away – eyes full of wonder and a great uncertainty, like the eyes of a young child – and he was dead.

Waiting in his cubicle at the end of the ward, the orderly seemed to sense the going out of the final spark and came with the red screen, synonymous with death, to minister to the dead with a conscientious attachment seldom given to the living.

Later, when the slight, blanket-swathed form was carried out on the stretched that had brought it in, the knowledge that I should never see him again left an unexplainable ache in me that was continually being aggravated by a vision of his large and child-like eyes peering with an ineffable uncertainty into the future. Stripped of his covering, his bed reminded me of the trees in the park after the first winter gales. Bare and lonely it stood at the end of the ward, waiting for a new cover to conceal its barrenness. But it did not wait long.

Soon Billy's bed regained its air of respectability and another pair of eyes, with nothing child-like or uncertain about them, were questing round the ward, and finding me unfriendly and perhaps hostile…

Pleasant as it had been in hospital – and it was pleasant if one did not become too concerned about the regularity with which death came a visiting – it was more satisfying to be back in Southern Area. There the air was not dependent on a weak disinfectant for its freshness; also at night time when one sat up on the hill overlooking the Straits, the moon shone on the water and made a crazy pathway leading away to a yesterday that no longer existed.

In spite of its non-existence it was pleasant to leave the hill in quest of yesterday and wander along where the moon pointed; maybe as far as the lip of the Pacific, where the lights of the Jap ships twinkled invitingly. Then, after a pause pregnant with uncertainty, a quick return to the hill to watch Paula Ubin's shadow shrink to nothingness and to think of Nai Soon, and, so thinking, come to imagine his canoe rippling through the quicksilver flung into its path by the moon – so consistently friendly and yet so supremely indifferent…

But there were other things to think of besides moonlight and shadowy imaginings.

During the time I had been in hospital the unit had become once more turn-out crazy; also General Salute was making his rounds again, and I had thought I had left that gentleman wandering about the labyrinth of roads we had made on the Bukit Timah golf course – a monument to our striving that will probably outlast the Jap shrine reflected in the unruffled waters of McRitchie reservoir.

On my first parade on returning to the camp I listened to Captain Bell harangue us on the need for a good standard in saluting, while Billy Crane's eyes kept appearing in the heat haze hanging over the *pedang*.

Said the disciple of Bullshit Unlimited:

'The new area commander is not satisfied with the general standard of saluting. Men are not saluting correctly.' (Here was had a demonstration showing how it should be done. 'Up, one, two, three, down.') 'Men are not saluting at all. In future all officers will be saluted at all times...'

Amen!

To bring about the state of sublimity in which every officer would be assured of the obeisance due to him by reason of his greater value as a prisoner of war, and to bolster up for a little longer his shattered ego – shattered by the Jap order to salute all ranks of the I.J.A. – patrols were to be organised to police the camp. It would be their duty to assure that the men behaved toward their betters with a servility befitting their station.

For a while the 'saluting police' had a gay time, and the number of janker-wallahs went up to a new height. Also, our standard of intelligence, as defined by Captain Bell, did not improve to any appreciable extent.

Terminating his lecture, the doughty captain had delivered what I supposed to be a misdirected Parthian shot.

'Of course,' he said, 'none of you has the intelligence to realise the importance of saluting in our present circumstances...'

When someone said, 'Hear, hear!' the captain did not question his right to interrupt. Handing over to the R.S.M., who was dutifully waiting to give one out of the book, he hurried back to his *charpoy* to recuperate from the exertions of the morning...

Not many weeks after this last lecture in saluting in Changi a new order from the I.J.A. brought us so close together as to make it impossible to get one's arm up, even had there been any desire to salute.

Someone at the top of the I.J.A. tree, with a penchant for ancient history, had decided it would be a good thing to get all the prisoners to sign a non-escape form. This, he hoped, would nullify any slumbering tendency for escape on the part of the individual if the out-dated homily about an Englishman's word being his bond that still applied.

It didn't. Those days were of the irrevocable past, apart from the fact that a promise given with a gun held at one's head was not considered to be in the best traditions of international relationship.

Their first tentative feelers to get our reaction having drawn a 100% vote of non-co-operation – that is, if one excepts the half-dozen men who had built up a feeling of reactionary spite against society as represented by the prisoners outside the detention barracks –the I.J.A. issue an ultimatum. Translated into camp phraseology, it meant: 'Sign, or else…'

Well, there was no harm in trying and, after another election the administration, which, for a change, had the complete backing of its constituents, decided to accept the or else clause and hope for the best – though the worst was expected.

Captain Bell rather spoiled the effect of this pronouncement by suggesting that it would be no hardship for him to vacate the "cowshed" in which he was living.

Personally, I had always thought his bungalow, shared with another officer, a comparatively sedate residence…

Losing no time in registering their disapproval at our temerity in turning them down, the I.J.A. commanded that all prisoners refusing to sign the parole were to evacuate Southern Area and proceed to Salarang Square, about three miles south of Changi.

This order was received on the same day, September 1, 1942 – by the Australians, who were billeted in the Salarang area and who, like Changi Camp, had voted for non-compliance.

Salarang Square, with the barrack blocks around it, was in peace time occupied by a battalion of approximately one thousand men. Here, on the evening of September 2, some seventeen odd thousand men were jammed, without distinction of rank or physical classification.

All through the day of September 2 the roads leading to Salarang were congested by the migrating multitude. Slowly the over-burdened and sweating throng poured onto the square until it would hold no more but still they came, and the day was but half finished.

Fortunate was he who on that day possessed the soap box on wheels of his childhood days, or any other wheeled 'vehicle' that could be pressed into service to transport kit. Apart from the possessions of the individual there was all the equipment from the various cook-houses to be transported to the square by means of man-powered trucks, or, when they gave out, man-power unassisted by wheels.

Probably one of the strangest sights I saw on that day, or any other day for that matter, was the spectacle of three senior officers, very sweaty and flustered, hauling behind them a square of wire netting on which their kits were piled.

Where, I wondered, were their batmen? And immediately I realised that this was a foolish conundrum, for on that day at least it was every man for himself and God for us all.

At least we had reached that state of equality wherein we were all travelling steerage in that hypothetical craft about which there had been so much highfalutin talk during the first months in Changi. This time there was no first class saloon. No priority was granted our gentlemen prisoners. We were one and indivisible. And somehow the realisation made my load lighter and the sun less intense...

Later, when the throng on the square had pushed and shoved itself into a position of semi-permanency in which each individual had at least sufficient space in which to sit down, I saw another entertaining sight.

In after days when the poison had worked out of my system, I was of the opinion that the figure on which my gaze was centred should have been the object of my sympathy, instead of my amusement.

Sitting with Laverton beneath a wisp of canvas we had erected to ward off the sun, which was being truly Japanese in its attentions to our discomfort, I saw a figure slowly forcing a passage through the densely packed, and none too amiable, ranks of humanity that hemmed it in and opened reluctantly to give it a begrudged passage. As he came closer I saw that he was a major. A very hot and flustered major. Bowed beneath the weight of his kit, some of which was trailing along in the dust behind him and being trodden on by those who pushed and shoved to fill the blank left by his passing, he came level with me where I sat in comparative comfort in the shade of my canvas awning.

It was the White Tojo.

Unchristian though it may be, I was glad in my heart at his predicament, for the memory of his unpleasantness on the road gang was still fresh in my mind, and excluded all possibility of compassion. Not a commendable attitude, admitted, but the White Tojo had made us sweat unnecessarily. And now it was his turn.

Quits.

Beneath a bougainvillaea vine five yards away Captain Bell had set up house. By the look on his rather wolfish face he was not well pleased by the way things were going. Noting his evident discomfort, I wondered if he would still expect to be saluted, and I wondered, too, if he were regretting his 'cowshed' in Changi.

He probably was. I, too, was regretting my byre.

In spite of the make-shift awning and Laverton's fussing, the sun remained hot, and I had to be constantly on the move to keep out of its glare. So much so, in fact, that I began to begrudge the saturnine Captain Bell his bougainvillaea vine, while as for the White Tojo, the heat of the sun had ceased to worry him.

Every spare piece of clothing that could be erected between the sky and the hot earth on which we squatted was put up to act as a sunshade. Soon the square became like a very crowded, and very untidy, fairground where it was literally impossible to move a foot in any direction without treading on someone.

To cater to this seething mass of bodies the cook-house had to be erected, and then it had to function if we were to go on living to back up our small show of defiance.

Somewhere on the edge of the throng a chicken squawked in shrill protest as someone wrung its neck; then a goat bleated, a banshee wail of despair as it felt its throat being slit by a not over-sharp knife. The cook-house was in action. When it arrived the jungle stew would have the merest bouquet of chicken and the more astringent goat in celebration of our first meal on Salarang Square.

Food was not the only essential in short supply on the Square. As the Japs had made no provision for drinking water when they invited us to change our address, the seeds of an incipient rebellion were beginning to sprout despite the thirst. Although there was sufficient water to supply the cook-house's needs, after the R.E.s had located the existing water main and tapped into it the pressure was so low it could not be utilised for the minimum number of stand-pipes to supply drinking water to the throng on the square.

Fortuitously, before the seeds of rebellion could flower, the Japs increased the water pressure allowing the R.E.s to erect a dozen stand-pipes for drinking water only – no washing.

Inevitably, two of our ever-present scourges, dysentery and malaria, soon became active. As there was no room on the Square for a 'sick bay' some of the more fortunate who had taken up residence in the military barracks were ejected to make room for the sick who normally would have been sent to the hospital at Changi. But that was not on. The Japs were using the hospital as their trump card...

Having no self-contained incinerator to consume his garbage, man is faced by the major problem of dispensing of his waste as soon as he has solved the problem of getting something to eat. In that respect, we were no exception –

even though our intake was minimal.

Sanitation was a major problem. The only solution available was to squeeze the crowd of men on the Square into a more compact mass so that space would become available for latrines.

A series of trenches approximately 15 feet long by 6 feet deep were excavated in the centre of what, in other days, was hallowed ground where dropping a cigarette paper was likely to result in seven days' C.B. for the culprit: the barracks' parade ground.

The latrines were a relief, literally, and a hazard to everyone, especially if you were a somnambulist and walked in your sleep. They were also a repulsive reminder of how we had degenerated. Coolies wallowing in our own filth – almost...

Two men and an officer did actually fall into one of the latrines, but by then it had a soft, gooey cushion of excreta at the bottom, and apart from the unpleasantness of the episode, the unlucky ones were none the worse for their misadventure.

Very soon the presence of the latrines could not be ignored, and whenever the breeze blew in our quarter, there was a great wrinkling of noses as we conveniently forgot the fact that we had contributed to the stench which was hourly getting worse.

Bad as things were for the majority, they were much better off than the unfortunates who, through lack of anywhere else to bed down, had to stake a claim on the edge of these none too fragrant slits in the ground.

Eventually, make-shift covers were put over the latrines, and the stench was reduced in proportion to their effectiveness – which was problematical.

*****

When darkness blanketed the sky over Salarang and rescued us from the blazing overtures of the sun, we recaptured the energy soaked out of us during the day. Then recuperated, we sang and catcalled as the moon poked up over the roofs that hemmed us in, friendly, and with an approving grin on its face. It seemed to say, in a voice too far off to be heard, but understood nevertheless:

'That's the stuff, chaps! Don't let those little so-and-sos get you down!'

The moon would not say 'Bastards'. It was too much the perfect gentleman.

We were no gentlemen...

Bedlam is the only word that may adequately describe the noise let loose on Salarang Square when the Japanese sun went out of the sky. Every ditty that has been composed from the first Eve-inspired piece of doggerel was bawled into the night, interspersed at more sober moments with 'God Save the King' and 'Rule Britannia,' while the Japs stood passively by.

Unlike their Occidental counterparts, who throw a slipper at a dog when it starts to howl at the moon, the guards paid no attention to our caterwauling. Behind their machine-guns, or mooching along the perimeter road, they listened to the noise and remained impassive. Not even the national anthem bawled into the dusky night produced a murmur of protest. In their seeming unawareness of the disturbance, these Salarang guards, Japs and Sikhs alike, were sublime. But for all that, no one ventured too near the road after dark, for the Jap is a peculiar individual and extremely touchy on occasions.

Given an order to shoot should any of the prisoners step over the boundary line, as represented by the road, he would not hesitate to do just that – if the Sikhs did not beat him to it. As to our singing and shouting it was to him incomprehensible in the circumstances. At that date he was just beginning to learn that the British have a peculiar habit of being happiest when conditions are blackest.

If we wanted to sing and shout, when we ought to have been sitting in gloomy introspection – like Captain Bell, whose threadbare dignity would not allow him to take part in the general hullabaloo – that was our affair, provided – and that was important – he had no orders to keep us quiet. In the meantime, the only comment he would make on our misplaced high spirits was a muttered, '*Dame, dame! Bugaro!*' And so, satisfied in his own mind that we were mad, he would let us bay until 'lights out' came to put an end to our moonlight serenading...

*****

On the second day of the Salarang Tea Party a foretaste of things to come, if we remained for any length of time on the square, intruded itself into our hungry jollity. On that day six new cases of dysentery were reported to a harassed medical staff, who had nowhere to isolate any contagious disease that might break out on the close-packed square.

This was but the beginning of their troubles, however. Thus far, the hospital had not been interfered with by the I.J.A. But finding us still reluctant to bend to their will, a manifesto was issued to the effect that, unless we signed the non-escape form, the patients in the hospital, without exception, would be moved to the square.

Coming as a rumour on the third day, this thread was confirmed on the fourth. Thus the Japs, by utilising a trump card no gentleman – not even an Oriental one – would have played, knocked the tenacity out of our determination to resist, and so caused us once again to hoist the white flag.

In the evening of that day we were assembled in companies and ordered by our respective commanders to sign the parole. First, however, we were informed that the order to sign came direct from our G.O.C., who was prepared to accept the onus for our conduct – whatever that might mean. We were further assured that in the circumstances we might sign the parole without in any way undermining our honour or conscience as British soldiers.

By that time we had little of either left, so the parole was signed on the tacit understanding that it made no different to the determination of the individual to escape should the opportunity to do so present itself at any time in the future.

It is a debatable point whether, in the circumstances, we ought not to have signed no matter what the outcome. Had we not done so, and had the Japs fulfilled their threat to move the hospital to Salarang, no power of ours could have prevented a serious epidemic. Hundreds, if not thousands, would have died in the passive battle to regain some measure of the prestige we lost with the capitulation of Singapore.

Laverton was firm in his belief – and I supported him, though neither of us deemed it advisable to ask Captain Bell or the White Tojo for their opinion – that, by capitulating again, we were not being true to the spirit of doggedness that made the old-time British trooper famous. As Richard pointed out, if history is to be believed, no thought of accepting the enemy's proposals would have been entertained, no matter what the outcome, by troops placed in a similar position, say fifty years earlier.

However, it would appear that history is not always as truthful as it might be. Perhaps then, our second capitulation, when we might have waved our fallen flag in the face of the I.J.A. at Salarang, will be judged not too harshly by the nit-picking historians of posterity…

At no time, apart from the first few weeks when I lived with Susy Ann, have I been so appreciative of Changi as on my return from Salarang. But there were dark days ahead, and many who might have died at Salarang in a worthy fight for redemption were to die in out-of-the way places as yet unnamed. Places which waited on our coming to put them on the map, and to define their borders by the milestones of our graves which soon began to sprout in the dank wilderness of their terrain.

Chapter Thirteen

God Looks Over My Shoulder

The two strands of barbed wire came between me and the distant Johor. Theoretically, they guaranteed that I would not go beyond them – down the hill to the edge of the mangrove swamp, and beyond that the water, misty in the heat of the day. No one had told me that the wire was the outer boundary of my domain. The wire itself implied it, though its confining influence was more symbolical – with a symbolism that is peculiar to barbed wire all the world over – than it was practical. For that very reason the two sagging strands were as effective a deterrent to breaking bounds as they would have been had they been increased a hundred-fold.

Indeed, in the latter care, the mere fact of their existence would have compelled many of the men in the house overlooking the Straits to get closer to the distant Johor – not because of any particular urge they might have had to get away from the house, but because of an inherent instinct to go where it was obviously forbidden to go.

That was why the two strands of wire were so effective, in spite of their obvious inability to prevent anyone getting closer to the Straits. They were not a challenge as would a more formidable barrier have been. They implied, with polite suggestiveness, that it was not politic to get between them and the mangrove swamp. They did not try to enforce their assertion with a loud voice that, instead of over-awing, was an incentive to endeavour and a challenge that could not be left unanswered.

It was not Jap sagacity that put the two strands of wire between us and the Straits. They had been there before we returned to Salarang out of whimsical memory – this time not to drink mythical tea, but to provide the fuel necessary to the brewing of its more material sister.

Changi had burned most of its available firewood and the Japs, with no sentimental attachment for their new rubber plantations, had agreed to a party of prisoners going to Salarang to cut fuel for the cook-house fires. Obviously, the I.J.A. had not the commercial ability to re-organise the rubber industry, and so harness it into their war effort. But perhaps they had sufficient rubber in reserve; certainly a great deal of it went out of Malaya before the war. Just as certain, many of the plantations were not in need of much re-organising – the owners had scooted too quickly to have done any extensive damage. Not that the Japs appeared to be concerned one way or the other. Indeed, the more rubber we cut down, the better pleased they appeared to be...

It was pleasant in the house at Salarang, mainly because our days were filled with an interesting and useful labour in which the backbiting and despondency of Changi had no part. Then, too, there were the peaceful evenings when the day's work was done, and the scantiness of the last meal was forgotten – dispelled by the beauty of the magnolia tree on the front lawn, and the moon coming up big and wistful behind the coco palms that obtruded themselves between the house and the mangroves, where the swamp orchestra were turning up for the night's entertainment.

Hazy in the dusk of the evening, the tree-crowded Johor peeped at me between the blue of the Straits like scratches on a negative.

In the hush that came between the dying of the day and the birth of the night, my thoughts went out from beneath the magnolia tree to the distant Johor, nor did the wire seek to detain them. Gracefully it withdrew into the background of the night and let them pass.

In the mist of the distant mainland they found a problematical – and certainly an insecure – freedom that might be had in return for the temporary security of the house behind my magnolia tree. Here was a bed of sorts, a menu that was frugal in the extreme – and many mosquitoes to make the nights seem long and sleep uncertain.

Had Nai Soon been there with his canoe to ferry me across, I should have gone unhesitatingly with my thoughts – not because of the canoe, but on account of Nai Soon. With him I should feel secure and, too, the possibilities of retaining freedom once tasted would be not so problematical as if he were not there.

But of course he was not there; he was just another memory growing shadowy with the passing months, sometimes mingling with my thoughts as they went snooping along the blurred coastline of Johor, hoping for things they knew could not be yet.

Usually they were recalled by the more material-minded Laverton lying in the grass, smoking a cigarette of brown paper and dried leaves. To him the beauty of the magnolia was unimportant – its smell was something you could not eat, neither did it relieve the craving for tobacco, often more intense than the craving for something tasty to relieve the nausea in one's belly.

Unlike Laverton, I preferred the magnolia tree and the dreams it brought. To me it was both meat and tobacco. It filled a definite gap in my life – though I would have chosen a frangipane tree had there been one in the vicinity – by implying a suggestion of beauty where there was none...

Laverton would leave me steeped in dreams for a while until, with a fine disregard for my sensibilities, he brought me back to a more fundamental reasoning.

'It's no use mooning about what's going over in Johor, Mick. Even if we were to get across the Straits, I'm convinced it would do us no good unless we had some outside assistance. Now, if Nai Soon were here –'

'Exactly. But he's not. And don't smoke any more of those blasted cigarettes – the smell annoys me...'

That would be all there was to it. But Laverton's corroboration of what I knew to be true had shattered my dreaming for the remainder of the evening and he, knowing my partiality for the magnolia tree, took his noisome cigarette away to the roadside, from where it glowered in cynical reproof for my churlishness.

Then it was time for the swamp orchestra to start their inharmonious discord – they were already waiting on their conductor – and in a moment the night would be hideous with their tuneless revelry, which would last until the dawn, pausing only when some foreign element, or some suggestion of danger, intruded itself into the mangroves.

Crouched in the rank grass at the edge of the swamp, a giant bullfrog would open the revel with a few preliminary semi-quavers. Then, as his *basso profundo* boomed out over the swamp, it was taken up by a multitude of pulsating throats that sang for hour after hour in a dozen different keys.

At intervals during the night there came from the mangroves the hoarse scream of something caught – something momentarily tortured, and as quickly stilled. At other times man-made sounds came in across the swamp – noises that were more potent than all the harsh screamings and croakings among the mangroves – as the Jap's aquatic patrol snooped along in the semi-darkness looking for something they knew they would never find, and not knowing that the necessity for their vigilance was nullified by the existence of the two strands of barbed wire between them and the house on the hill.

To justify their presence, and to let us know they were keeping a lookout, the patrol made a lot of unnecessary noise when they came level with our house, shouting and beating about on the fringe of the mangroves to the annoyance of the swamp orchestra impatiently waiting to resume the metre of their suspended symphony...

In a kampong, just discernible among the palm fronds that shimmered about it, the Japs had established an outpost where the Straits disappeared round the bend into imagination. Being remote from our two strands of barbed wire, this guard was almost outside our interest – but not quite. Realising that one day the knowledge might be useful, everyone had fixed the location of the kampong in his mind, and kept it there.

On a night when the mosquitoes had driven me from the house to sit beneath the magnolia tree, I watched the moon pick out the bayonets of the Jap patrol as it neared the *kampong* among the palms.

'Rookies,' I thought with self-complacent satisfaction, not knowing that the night was waiting on tragedy.

It was just one more lovely night with the moon adding a camouflage of goodwill to the picture postcard effect. The old moon had done a good job of it, too and, as I sat drowsing beneath the magnolia, only half consciously aware of the ululations from the swamp, I was ready to accept the moon's camouflage as the real thing, and to grant that peace reigned in the land.

Then a dog barked and I came awake as the swamp sank into a make-believe sleep and a mosquito plunged its dagger into my cheek.

Though the moon still shone and the palms waved sleepily to their reflections in the Straits, there was no longer peace in the scented night.

Following the bark of the dog came the despairing wail of a child, and a confused shouting – even at that distance I could recognise the thin inflection of an excited Chinese – suddenly cut short by a fusillade of rifle shots.

After the shots the child still cried and the dog barked with a renewed intensity until a single shot replied to its challenge. Then it, too, was still and I wondered, as I rose to my feet and swiped at the mosquito which was coming back for more, in what new devilry the Japs were indulging.

The answer to that was just round the corner in my mind. I had seen the Japs at play, as well as hearing them, and knew just how they reacted when pleasure gave an artificial stimulus to their sense of duty. Truthfully, I was not particularly concerned about what was going on in the kampong. Just then I had made a most interesting discovery, though there was nothing original about it. I had found nothing new. But to me it was interesting, with an interest outweighing the probable fate of the people in the *kampong*.

148

For the first time I realised that the bark of a dog and the crying of a little child are the same the whole world over and for some reason I could not define, the knowledge perturbed me more than the fact that across the way the Japs were showing the locals just what was meant by the Greater East Asia Co-Prosperity Sphere.

*****

I saw the long-legged, chicken-like creature scurry across the path and disappear into the grass beyond the wire and, as a shadow to its passing, I was through and after it, though at no time was there the remotest hope of my catching it. Enthusiasm for the chase was stimulated by the reflection that chicken for dinner would be a revolutionary change from rice and a tasteless imagination. Not since my raid on the black market *kampong* at Changi had fresh chicken tickled my palate, though I had acquired a tin of the curried variety while at Singapore. But if Providence did not intervene, this fowl that was leading me such a dance outside the wire would never recline in juicy submissiveness in the old petrol tin in which Laverton did our private cooking in the evenings.

But where was Laverton? Why was he not helping me chase this ridiculous fowl that kept waiting for me with a cool insolence that was infuriating; then, when I was about to grab it, stepping aside from my clutching hands to disappear once more among the grass.

For three evenings now Laverton had been sneaking off somewhere without telling me where he was going. I was sure he was not on some scabbing expedition – he could not be so consistently unsuccessful.

The only alternative I could think of was that he was chasing a woman in one of the outlying *kampongs*. And that thought was not particularly inspiring; besides, I knew it was not true. For all his cynicism about my magnolia tree, he retained sufficient sentiment to exclude him from surreptitious *bint* hunting.

'Where then was he?' I wondered. 'And to hell with this damned chicken! I'm browned off chasing it…'

It was all very well thinking like that, even if I did think aloud, to the evident gratification of my quarry which, after taking me down the hill to the edge of the mangrove swamp, also got browned off and disappeared, this time for good.

It had done its job, however, and as I looked at the little chapel to which it had brought me, I wondered if perhaps the chicken-cum-partridge-cum-will-o'-the-wisp was not all will-o'-the-wisp having existence in my imagination only.

149

Screened by a wall of mangrove, the little chapel leaned against two coconut palms, and was as much out of the place as a man eating peas with a knife in a swank restaurant. It looked tired and dispirited and appeared to derive its strength to endure from the tree which held it up at either corner and spread its fronds as a protective screen above the flimsy roof.

Constructed from *atap*, with a framework of bamboo, the chapel had been built with the maximum of attention to detail, and its reproduction spoke of hours of infinite patience given to capturing the slightest detail of the original. Looking at its flimsy contours, one expected to see cherubims and angels looking down from the stained glass windows which were not there, so realistically was the *atap* fashioned.

Inside it was a revelation. It was not empty, as I had thought. Laverton was there, sitting before the home-made altar with its cross of hammered brass.

I did not know what to do. It was so unexpected, this finding Laverton in a chapel that, in itself, was sufficiently unexpected without his presence to complicate matters. I thought about withdrawing, but he knew I was there, and spoke.

'It's quiet here, Mick,' he said, and I understood from the inflection of his voice that he did not expect a reply.

Yes, it was quiet – and peaceful. Though I had not noticed it until then. Chasing the chicken that had brought me there had been warm work, and I was still hot. There was a feeling of rest about the place which made one want to sit down and think – not about anything in particular, but about everything in general. I went down the aisle – sand beaten into the clay floor – and sat with Laverton on the bamboo rail that served as a seat before the altar.

The brass of the cross was stained by verdigris, and I felt I wanted to get it down and polish it. But I didn't; the thought was sacrilegious, so I left it alone, and Laverton said nothing. He was still thinking about whatever it was that was occupying his mind. I knew what that was, for I was getting that way, too.

Laverton was thinking about someone whom he had not troubled lately. I was like that, too. I had not troubled much about Him, either, even when I sat dreaming beneath the magnolia tree. But God was too firmly in possession of the little chapel to be denied. You had to think about Him, and it made you feel awful. There was a mist before your eyes, and you thought the sun had gone down behind the coco palms, though you knew it would not do that for half an hour yet, and you did not like to admit, even to yourself, that it was the blur of tears not far distant that brought the shadows before their time.

Then suddenly you were all right again, and the sun shining through the atap touched the other cross in the corner and you felt you could get up and examine it. There was no verdigris on it. It was made of wood. There were names pained on it, instead. Names of dead men – Australians. The cross did not tell you whether they had died fighting, or as prisoners. But somehow you knew they had not been free men – the chapel had not been built by free men. It was too painstakingly perfect for that...

Laverton stopped thinking about God and came over to look at the wooden cross, although he knew the half dozen names off by heart.

'It's strange to find a place like this here,' he said. 'I found it by chance.'

'I did, too,' I told him, but I said nothing about the chicken – if it was a chicken. I was still thinking about that, and I did not want to discuss it.

'I shan't come here anymore, Mick. It depressed me. It makes me feel somehow unworthy, if you know what I mean...'

I did, and I tried to help him out. But I'm not much use at that sort of thing.

'This place was built by devout men who needed the comfort of its sanctuary. They came here to worship and to be with God – God whom we had conveniently forgotten, Richard. My piousness is measured by the yardstick of memory which, as you know, is short. On most of the occasions I think about God, it is because He intrudes Himself into my consciousness, as he has done in this make-shift place of worship which vibrates with His presence to a greater degree than many of the churches I have been in at home. Even to me it is obvious that that is not the right thing to do. You, too, feel that way about it, I think. That is why you are feeling so self-conscious about coming back here, Richard, and I sympathise with you, for I feel that way myself, though not to the same degree.

'You see, Richard, you have done as a great many people do. You have let God frighten you. Which, of course, is a nonsense. It's all very well being frightened if you have something to be scared about. And I don't think you have... at least not to the extent your imagination would have you believe. It's futile to reason that God is continually chalking black marks against you because you don't more often go on your knees and raise your hands in hypocritical Hallelujahs.

'Self-abasement is all very well, Richard. But too often it is the result of an inner prompting for outward show, instead of being the other way about...

'I am satisfied that my fleeting moments of communion – though I admit they should more often be self-inspired – are as worthwhile, and as acceptable to God, as the automatic responses of the many who daily send up their stereotyped prayers for redemption.

'There, Richard,' I finished lamely. 'I have given you a lecture on religion, to give it its generally accepted attribution. Has it made you feel any different about things?'

'Yes,' he said uncertainly. 'I – I thought we might come back sometime and clean the place up a bit. Perhaps we could get rid of this grass and put some fresh sand on the floor. Why,' he added, getting jubilant, 'we could have it for our group church – but, of course, we have not got a padre…'

'A padre is not always necessary, Richard. In fact, I prefer the place as it is – even to the grass and verdigris on the cross. Let us keep it to ourselves. I feel I shall want to come here on occasions, and I shall want it quiet and peaceful as it is now with the evening shadows chasing out the sun. And then later, the moon to people it with spirits of the men whose names are on the cross in the corner… I wonder why it was never erected by their graves – wherever they are…'

'I wondered about that too, Mick…and I think you are right about leaving the place as it is. It has more – more what would you call it? Sentiment! Yes, it has more sentiment as it is. To pull up the grass and to put fresh sand on the floor would make it just another camp chapel, and I don't think it would like that, Mick…'

This last rather self-consciously, for Laverton was not a sentimentalist. He left that type of emotionalism to me, and was inclined at times to be cynical about it.

As we went back through the dusk to the wire straggling along the hillside we talked of anything but the church by the mangroves…

For some weeks longer the hidden chapel retained its remote integrity. On occasions I returned to sit and dream before the altar, though my dreams were more temporal than spiritual. Sometimes they were a combination of the two, and I know the little chapel did not mind.

Sitting on the bamboo rail in the quiet dusk, I thought of John, Nai Soon and Terry Reynolds, whom I had not seen since that day in Singapore. Thinking of him and the shocked look on his young face when Say Leen came into the courtyard, I also thought about Little Flower, and wondered when these two were destined to meet again. Meet again they must. I felt that was inevitable, even though Nai Soon and I might for ever be apart. Then there was the sincere, easy-going Smithy, so willing to help where help was needed, and so reluctant to give offence. He and John were as remote almost as time itself. They had returned along that road which at times I visualised myself walking with John while Nai Soon hovered wraithlike just out of reach.

152

On these journeys John and I were always alone with the spirit-like Nai Soon. Smithy and Laverton were never with us as we continued our interminable walk, which never seemed to get us anywhere. And I wondered about that, though not for long.

Going down to the mangroves one evening after an especially arduous day, I found the little chapel had vanished. Even the altar and the cross had gone. Someone more materially minded than I had discovered its hiding place and had torn town its frail walls, on which so much patient and laborious craftsmanship had been expended, to feed the cook-house fires that prepared my evening meal possibly.

*****

As a proof that money was no safeguard against disease, Ginger Parsons, scabber-in-chief of Changi Camp, was dying in the dysentery ward.

That was one of the places I had not expected to meet Ginger. In the kampong on the beach, yes. Or scabbing petrol from the Japs at Singapore, but not in the hospital. He had too much money, and seemed to live so well. It was not likely the commonplace diseases that afflicted the average prisoner – dysentery and beriberi – would ever come to roost on Ginger's shoulder. But here was dysentery, and Ginger's light was going out fast.

Realising that, I almost forgave the thief who had scabbed my petrol dividends. Perhaps, I consoled myself somewhat belatedly, it was not advisable to have a lot of money in the circumstances. Given sufficient money – and it had to be a considerable amount – one was prone to forgo rice, and to exist mainly on 'extras' bought from the canteen, or from any of the other sources of supply.

Ginger had been in the habit of doing that. To him rice was fit only for menials – men without the means of supplanting it by something more palatable. And Ginger was an aristocrat: he had money. Probably more money than anyone else in the camp. And now he was dying because he had not built up a resistance against disease. He had given his rice away, preferring to live as a white man when, to all intents and purposes, he was a native – as we were all natives. He had run counter to the dictum 'When in Rome, do as the Romans do,' and would not like to see the white ramparts of Dover and the green fields behind them.

Perhaps Ginger's mode of life made no difference to the final outcome – many men had existed solely on I.J.A. rations before finding a place in the shadow of the bougainvillaea vine that flamed red by the entrance to the cemetery below Changi. However that may be, the theory was interesting, and gave me something to work on while I lay three beds away from Ginger waiting for the final moment that would decide whether he was to live or die. Also, there was the consolation for the loss of my bank account when I had been in hospital before. It was difficult, though, to convince myself that consolation was sufficient compensation for the loss of a hundred dollars, which, after all, was not a large enough sum to make any appreciable difference to my standard of livelihood as a prisoner. Frankly, I could have done without the consolation...

Ginger was one of the first guinea pigs to try out the dysentery wing's 'death ward' – a recent innovation – and he did not like it any more than the others who followed him.

Psychologically, the death ward – a half dozen beds at the end of the main dysentery ward, to which the patients with one foot over the threshold of Eternity were transferred before they could pick up the other foot – had nothing to recommend it. It was an evil that could have been avoided had anyone, other than the patients, been sufficiently interested in its existence. But for it many of the men who left the dysentery ward to go down the hill to the cemetery would have spent a more comfortable last half-hour in this world.

Usually the patients who were transferred to the death ward died, hence the bad psychological effect on the other patients. For the thought was never far away: 'If I go there, I am finished.' It was not a pleasant thought to feel so confident about. Neither was it pleasant to lie alongside a man who was dying – and some of them did not take kindly to dying. They appeared to think they were leaving so much behind them, poor devils, not realising that their life was all before them. In this respect the death ward had its uses in so far as the men not on the seriously ill list were concerned, provided they did not get to having hallucinations about it. Many of them did, and for that reason it was distinctly unpopular.

No man had a greater terror of the death ward than Ginger Parsons. To him it was synonymous with death. He had been in the hospital sufficiently long to assess the chances for recovery of any man who was sent to it and those chances, as he knew, were infinitesimally small.

Three days after my re-admission from Salarang, Ginger began rapidly to go down the hill, and it became obvious that he would not stop until he reached the cemetery. In those last days of his life Ginger's mother meant more to him than, in all probability, she had done since he had left his childhood behind him. Continually he appealed to her, as though she were God, to save him in his extremity. Although his beseeching bore no visible fruit, it did at least reawaken the memory of a mother in the hearts of many of the patients in the ward. I, too, realised again that my yesterdays were not a thing of the past, whatever opinion I might hold to the contrary. There was little else to live for but yesterday's memories; they were ever present even though one cheated and tried to shove them aside. And they made life more liveable then the hope for tomorrow, and the day after that. Whatever uncertainty there might be about them, there was none about my yesterdays. I had had them, but still they were not irrevocable, as the slang interpretation of the phrase implied. I would continue to experience their joys, and their fleeting disappointments. They would uphold me and bring me out victorious under the new sky that must one day appear.

That is, if dysentery or one of its parasitical followers did not get in first to ley me out in the shade of the bougainvillaea vine, where Ginger Parsons' protoplasmic ghost was already arguing about tenant's rights and the undesirability of having tradesmen call at the front door.

Ginger was semi-conscious when he was transferred to the death ward. He had not called on his mother for two hours, and everyone hoped he would leave her alone during the remainder of his time with us.

He did.

Transference to the death ward gave him something else to think about – and he didn't think quietly.

'I don't want to die!' he shouted with a pathetic insistence that produced nothing but an echo, 'I don't want to die…'

At the hour of the first dawn at which so many men have departed from pleasure, pain, love and despair, Ginger also departed and the ward was still.

There was nothing left but memory…

Once in a while a patient who was an original individual showed up in the dysentery ward.

One such was the chap who set up a record for unorthodoxy in his reaction to the psychological bogey of the death ward. On two occasions this individualist graduated from it back to his former place in the main ward, and so to eventual discharge. Two weeks later he was back with a relapse, which took him again to the death ward. This time, however, he was determined to settle his dysentery one way or the other. Waiting till the orderly was out of the ward, he got out of bed, ran to the balcony and jumped over, to land on the concrete footway thirty feet below.

It is doubtful if he achieved his original purpose by this quixotic leap. Certain it is that he acquired a broken arm and a sprained ankle; also – more remarkable – he got rid of his dysentery inside a week and was discharged a fortnight later.

When he did not come back again I cast many a surreptitious, and sometimes a wistful, look at the balcony. But I had not his courage, or his state of mind. I felt somehow that if I assayed the jump it would be a broken neck I should get, and not a cure for my dysentery…

Soon after this record breaker had returned to his unit in Changi Camp, the drab existence of hospital life was enlivened by the arrival of the first batch of Dutch and Javanese sick.

In preparation for the days ahead, the I.J.A. were moving many of the Netherlands East Indies personnel from Java to Singapore and Changi, where their green uniforms were adding a spot of colour to the unrelieved khaki of the British residents, who at first were reluctant to share their compound with 'foreigners'. The majority of the new arrivals were well clothed and looked well fed. Many of them had large sums of money in Dutch currency which, like the Straits Settlements dollar, was still transferrable. A Good deal of jewellery, including precious stones, also found its way over from Java, and was soon in circulation as the black marketeers and the fence riders got to work.

The coming of the Dutch opened up a lucrative market for the smart guys who are to be found in every society, not excluding a prisoner-of-war camp, and for a time the Dutch got the thin end of any deal that was transacted between them and their agents – the easy money men who undertook to show them the ropes.

Not even in hospital were they immune from exploitation. Dysentery brought many of them among us, and as none of the first comers could speak English – an unusual disability for any party of men from Java – they were the centre of attraction, and had numerous 'advisers' who showed them how to spend their money, and charged a high rate of interest for their advice.

And why not? One man's life is as good as another's, say the realists. If you have more money than I, why shouldn't I have some of it?

As this doctrine was the principle round which existence revolved at Changi, and in the hospital, why not apply it to the strangers within our gates?

Why not, indeed? Soon they would pick up the threads that would enable them to retaliate in kind, thereby completing the vicious circle, and so assuring the happiness of everyone connected with it, as they kidded themselves about their cleverness and originality in repeating a process that was as old as Adam's first kiss…

Following the tidal wave of green from Java came a trickle of Americans

156

from odd corners of the Pacific, and with their coming I began to realise just how complete was the Japanese sweep through Asia. Until I set eyes on the first American to walk into the ward I had inclined to the general opinion that our main hope of a speedy release rested on the realisation of the much-rumoured coming of the Yanks.

Well, here they were. Not as conquerors and deliverers but, like ourselves, prisoners of the Japanese – and no more impervious to dysentery than were we.

It was a case of a lame dog trying to help one without legs over a stile. Even if, for courtesy's sake, you classed yourself as the dog without legs it didn't make the prospect of deliverance any brighter...

When the M.O. came along one day and said, 'You'll be in for a few days yet, Stirling; I'll transfer you to another ward,' I didn't mind. In spite of the Yanks, Dutch, Javanese and 'half and halfs', the old ward was beginning to feel like a shirt that had been worn too long without being laundered. It stank – of petty intrigue, avarice, spite, unwashed bodies, and a fleeting heroism that was being diluted daily as the dying died, while the living surreptitiously sneaked their belongings.

Besides all that, I was browned off lying in bed. What I wanted was a new interest in life – something that would stimulate my apathetic curiosity and give me hours of analytical introspection.

I got all that when I was transferred but, had I had my choice of subjects, I should have picked one not quite so morbid.

My view was not south-east instead of north-west, and this made all the difference between having an interest in one's surroundings and a passive willingness to slide along from day to day in a rut gradually being deepened by sheer boredom.

In that point of the compass to which I now had access stood the hospital mortuary. The focus of the continually arriving and departing funeral parties carrying the dead to the cemetery down the road, which was expanding like a new building site of post-war vintage in the hands of the jerry builder, the mortuary was the main hub of activity in my vision. It supplied an interest which, until it became morbid, gave me many reasons for introspection.

In the cemetery the new arrivals were dressed by the right in the approved army fashion, each succeeding file being farther away from the crimson slash of the bougainvillaea which had made a living wreath above the groves of the first arrivals.

Strange as it may seem, it was pleasant to lie on the balcony overlooking the mortuary and watch some of the funerals depart down the road. The

Scottish burials took pride of place in this respect. Watching the swaying kilts, and listening to the "Flowers of the Forest" as the pipers swung down the hill, it was possible to forget the bier on the wheeled stretcher, and to imagine there was no cause for lamentation.

For a time, too, the prisoners from Java brought a touch of colour to the otherwise drab processions as they followed the miniature poached egg, emblem of Japan's contriving and their subjugation, which was carried at the head of every party, no matter on what duty, using the highway.

This rag of authority was as essential a part of the funeral as the corpse, for without it the cortège might not proceed to the cemetery. Unwanted and despised, and carried because of necessity, the little Jap flag was overshadowed by the Union Jack, whose servant, now retired, lay passive beneath it, and for whom it eclipsed in brightness the rag of authority symbolizing the aggrandizement of the Jap.

Gradually my initial interest in the funerals became subservient to an increasing morbidity and when that happened, I was worse off than I had been before. Sometimes I could visualize my own blanket-swathed form, with the Union Jack giving it a camouflage of decency, lying on the wheeled stretcher as it slowly descended the hill into oblivion.

Definitely, it was time I was getting out of the hospital. I wanted to be back on the hillside above Paula Ubin, with the wind fresh and clean on my face, and the shadows thrown by the moonlight making bizarre patterns on the Straits…

Chapter Fourteen

Youth in Shoddy Raiment

The old man came hobbling across the *pedang*, eyes peering short-sightedly at the ground and his stick biting deep into the earth from the weight he put upon it. Each time he covered a dozen paces he stopped to straighten his back and to look about him, and from the way his head slewed round on his narrow shoulders, so that no detail in his immediate vicinity escaped him, I felt that to him the earth was good and the fresh air was a meal. Always when he raised his head he gulped at the air like a starving man ravening over a feast. When he did that, his thin chest grew rounded and solid looking, and his ribs pushed against the skin as though at any moment they would break through. Then as his momentary rejuvenation passed from him he became deflated and thin chested, and his shoulders appeared unable to adequately support the weight of his head.

Catalogued by his actions, there was nothing ambiguous about his immediate post, for there were many others like him in the camp. Besides, there was the whiteness of his skin.

Only a long spell in hospital, or a soft job with the administration, could explain that, and I was sure his anaemic pallor was not due to the latter cause. The administration staff did not noticeably suffer from malnutrition. Neither were they particularly enthusiastic about fresh air as a diet.

Niggardly as they were with food, the Japs did at least allow us plenty of fresh air and sunshine: Or rather they were there for the taking. Not being within the jurisdiction of the camp canteen, it was not necessary to save up for interminable weeks before one could have a bellyful of either.

Out on the *pedang* the old chap with the stick and the white skin appeared to be the only one who knew there was something going "buckshee." Watching him, I automatically took a deep breath but there was nothing wonderful about it. I did not feel like throwing my head back, as he was doing, in order to suck in more. Frankly, I thought it was poor stuff, and not at all satisfying.

Obviously I had been out of hospital too long…

He hobbled closer, and as I counted the dozen faltering steps that would bring him to the edge of the patch of shade in which I sat before he straightened his back again, I was disagreeably surprised. He was not an old man after all. He was young – younger, perhaps, than anyone else on the *pedang*. Then he raised his head for another gulp at the unsatisfying air, and I had another surprise – though it was more of a shock this time – and something turned over inside me.

Yes, he was young all right – nineteen years young.

It was Terry Reynolds!

Seeing him in that condition, I wanted to get up and curse with a loud voice so that the bubble of emotion inside me might burst and let me see more clearly. I did not do that, however; blasphemy would have been so ineffectual in the circumstances. Instead, I took him by the arm and brought him into the shade of the gum tree.

'Sit here, Terry. You will be getting sunburned…'

'I like to be in the sun, Mick.'

'Yes. But you must accustom yourself to it gradually. Haven't you got a shirt?'

'Yes. But I have slept in it so long… I must do some washing…' Then: 'It's nice to see you again, Mick. It's been such a long time…'

'I didn't know you were in hospital, Terry,' I explained, feeling that I had not done enough to find him after I returned from Singapore. But there had not been much time, and no one appeared to know anything.

'I've been in from the time I got sent back to Changi. Must be three – four months. I came out yesterday.'

'What's been wrong?'

'Oh, a mixture. Malaria, dysentery, beriberi, and things in general. I'm all right now, if it wasn't for my eyes. Hope they get better soon, Mick. It's not nice being half blind…'

'What are they giving you?'

'The usual. Rice polishings, and a bit of extra grub now and again – when there is any. Things were not too bad after that Red Cross boat came in. But, of course, most of the stuff has been used… You've been in again, haven't you?'

'Yes – twice. The usual – dysentery. When I've had it a couple of times

160

more I ought to be immune... You knew Ginger Parsons, didn't you? He snuffed it. Poor old Ginger! You'd think he would have been the last one to die...'

'It's all a matter of luck, Mick,' he said in a small voice that went well with his emaciation, and did nothing to strengthen his optimism. 'You know I feel that, no matter how difficult things become, I shall come through all right. It does not worry me much on my own account, but I should like to live because of my mother. I know she would be awfully cut up if I were to – to follow Ginger Parsons and the others. I'm an only child, Mick,' he added by way of apology, and I felt like swearing again. But what was the use? Let him remain comforted by his optimism about the future. Swearing would not make his chances of survival any greater, even if I did think his mother would be a lucky woman if she ever saw her Terry again...

'That's the way you want to feel,' I encouraged. 'Don't ever think about dying. There are too many of the chaps doing that already, and what happens? They die. Believe that you will survive – no matter what misfortune befalls – and you shall. Anyway, that is my philosophy, and I give it to you for what it is worth, Terry.'

'Thanks, Mick,' he said. 'I will remember that. Perhaps it will help sometime. Certainly, in the circumstances in which we find ourselves, it is much easier to die than to live. I shall feel better, though, when my eyes improve. And if I could only get a letter from home... Do you think they know we are alive?' he asked eagerly, and his eagerness was no more alive than my own. But with what could I answer him? I couldn't say 'Yes', and it was equally futile to say 'No'.

'That is more than likely,' I temporised. 'After all, it is over six months since the lists of survivors were sent in to Jap H.Q. Giving them three months to make up their minds about sending them to the Red Cross leaves us another three for the journey. Yes, I think they know by now, and it's up to us to keep smiling so that our people are not disappointed after hearing that we are alive...'

'Yes, yes,' he agreed eagerly. 'Mother will be so glad to know I am alive! I should not care for her to see me now,' he added wistfully. 'She might think I am worse than I really am, and I would not wish that...'

I was wishing something myself. I wished he would shut up. His young voice, younger even than his nineteen years, was doing googly things to my inside – that part of me that always let me down when it was attacked by sentiment – and his mother's face, with the tears on it, was hanging around in the shade of the gum tree, and I didn't like it. Its hanging around, I mean. Not

161

the face. Besides, I had faces of my own to look at, but I kept them at a distance. It was the only thing to do. I knew they would not be happy at Changi, or any other of the camps, for that matter. Terry had not yet learned that faces in the fire are all right at home. In a prison camp, apart from infrequent occasions, they served no useful purpose.

They were better off at home – waiting.

But what was the use of telling Terry that? He was at the age when he liked to look at faces – in the fire or out of it. Take Say Leen, for instance. I wondered when she would shoulder his mother out of his recollection and give him something closer at hand to think about.

I just managed to formulate the thought before he cut athwart it with another query. As his head came round on his thin neck, so that I could see his eyes peering in misted wistfulness into my face, he asked:

'Have you seen Say Leen again, Mick?'

From the moment I had recognised him through the camouflage of his premature senility, I had been expecting that question and, now that it was here, there was no reassurance I could give him. And I knew he wanted reassurance – something that would imply – even if it did not guarantee – that Little Flower was all right.

Well he would have to be disappointed; there was no use my saying 'yes' when I meant 'no'.

'I have not seen her again, Terry,' I said. 'Not since that day we met her for the first time in Singapore, though I got into the town again later. She and Nai Soon were gone from the house when I went round there. At least there was a strange Chinese family in it, and I could get nothing out of them. Then, about three weeks ago, while I was in hospital, Laverton went down to Singapore with a party to do a small job in the New World. He managed to get round to the house, and there was a crowd of Tamils in it...'

He was disappointed, as I knew he would be. He had been banking on my being able to tell him something definite about Say Leen. Say Leen, who already was shouldering his mother out of the picture – temporarily at least. Knowing that, and also his obvious interest in the Chinese girl, I wondered just how deep an impression she had made on him, and how lasting it was going to be. Circumstances being as they were, I hoped Terry's interest in Say Leen would be too fleeting ever to become deep rooted. It would be better that way. Or would it? On second thoughts, I was not sure.

On my own conscious awareness she had impinged as a shaft of sunlight spearing unexpectedly through the gloom of a dungeon cell, to leave a lasting

162

memory of loveliness, and a premise of tomorrow behind it. Then Jim Sing had shouted, and she had fled to the house, taking the sunlight out of Terry Reynolds' life, and some of mine, with her.

But I still continued to enjoy what was left, though I preferred to take it from the shade of the gum tree, when there was not a magnolia handy. There would be ample time to acquire a coat of tan after I stopped feeling like a decrepit Chelsea pensioner and, in the meantime, there was Terry looking like a little boy who had lost his mother in a shopping crowd. Only it was not his mother about whom he was looking so wistful. It was Say Leen. She had got at him in the way only a woman can, and she was still getting at him.

That was almost as bad as seeing faces. In fact, I did not know but that it might be worse...

'Nai Soon's sister is a nice, kid, Terry,' I said, hoping it sounded casual.

'She is the most beautiful creature I have ever seen, Mick,' he answered eagerly. 'Did you notice how perfect were her hands, like – like something sculptured out of alabaster? I would I could paint her...'

'Don't tell me you are an artist?' I asked, knowing what the answer would be, but still hoping that it might be in the negative. A prison camp was not a particularly happy medium for anyone with an artistic temperament. The inability to express the creative urge might lead to repression, and that in turn could produce anything. Coupled with the symmetrical beauty of Say Leen it could certainly lead to chaos.

'I used to attend art classes at home,' he said. 'I was always keen on that sort of thing. If ever I get the opportunity I shall ask Little Flower to sit for me – but she will have to be in native dress...'

So far as the dress went, I agreed. Say Leen would look good done up in a sarong, or whatever it was she wore when not dressed as a European. However, there were more urgent problems to be attended to just then. Terry Reynolds was not the only one who got his vitamins out of the rice polishings sack in the cook-house.

On that thought, I stepped out of the shade into the sunlight to leave him painting Say Leen on an imaginative canvas beneath the gum tree, and went up the hill for my "vitamins."

Someone has said that money is the root of all evil. Perhaps it is, though I have never been refused it on that account. Certainly, had it not been for my urge to acquire some of it – though, as usual, the money was but a means to an end, and the peanut toffee I hoped to buy in the canteen, at five cents a show, was the real urge – I should have not spent Christmas, 1942, in the camp hospital.

Going back further even than my need for the peanut toffee, was the parsimony of the I.J.A., who had refused the byoki men any pay while they were doing no work. Further back still, in the mists of time, was Captain Bell's decree: 'In future, every man will shave daily.'

Admirable as that sounded, it was not easily put into practice, for the order made no provision for poverty, bankruptcy, or just plain destitution. It was not concerned with the number of cents in the pocket of the individual any more than it was interested in whether he preferred to buy a chew of peanut toffee – or an ounce of sugar if he were well off – to appease the aching void in his belly. An ache which could be put out of action only with something sweet, and there was no sweetness in the rice polishings or 'bran' cakes.

But Captain Bell was not interested in interiors; his concern was for all exteriors, and he preferred them to be beardless. When he said shave, you forgot your empty belly, and did as he said – unless you preferred jankers. It did not matter if you tore the hairs out by the roots or, more tragic, spent the cents you had been accumulating to buy a toothbrush, or a piece of soap, or a razor blade which, after three outings round your chin, turned up its nose and refused to give any further co-operation.

The captain was not interested in the why or wherefore. To a beard of more than a day's maturity he reacted as he did to my new Dutch hat – a green affair with a peak that made an admirable sun blind, and for which he did not share my enthusiasm. The hat was not *pukka*, neither was there anything in Orders to say I might wear it. Good enough! Get rid of it. Throw it away. Do any damned thing with it so long as you do not wear it…

'You say you have no other head-dress, Stirling.'

'No.'

'And that you get a headache if you work in the sun without a hat?'

'Yes.'

'Call me Sir!'

'Yes – Sir.'

'Well, there is nothing I can do about it. The O.C. Company has ordered that you do not wear the hat, and that is all that there is to it.'

'Yes, Sergeant-Major! Thank you, Sergeant-Major! Kiss my arse, Sergeant-Major!'

'What did you say?'

'Is there anything else, Sir?'

And away went my hat and, greater tragedy, twenty-five of the twenty-nine cents I had saved for peanut toffee and soap went with it. Not that there would have been much toffee in any case. At five cents a chew, twenty-nine cents was just one cent short of six chews, and I did not see how I could appease my belly with less than five chews once I started. That left four cents to buy soap at fifteen cents a rub. On that calculation there would be no soap, just as surely as there would be no peanut toffee. Captain Bell's interest in my attention to detail would cost me twenty-five cents for a razor blade – not forgetting my good Dutch cap.

To hell with Captain Bell...

*****

Going up the hill, I met a few familiar faces until I came to that Mecca of all hungry souls – the canteen. Here the faces were unchanged. They were not even sun-tanned. The canteen staff had entrenched themselves in an impregnable position, and there they would remain until the last of the khaki-clad prisoners ceased to roam about the hillside and gaze pensively at Paula Ubin in the moonlight. They were in an enviable position in the camp. They were the cream, the élite, the new aristocracy, and everybody envied them.

But for all that there was a bitterness in their lives. They could not go into ecstasies over a five cent bar of peanut toffee, or a pinch of sugar, as could the more plebeian members of their race who were fast being scattered to the four corners of the compass.

Following their going had come the green-clad armies of the Dutch and their Javanese compatriots, with an odd American thrown in at intervals to spice the international savour of the camp, and to give a proof of the effectiveness of the wide-spread drag net of Japan.

It was edifying to learn from the Dutch that Java had fallen almost without a shot being fired in its defence. That gave me a different outlook. It made one realise that Singapore had not been the only white elephant in the Far East.

Of course, there had always been Pearl Harbor. But that had been different, somehow; at least the Yanks, who came to Changi, said so.

'If we'd a goddamn chance we'd have shown those little yellow bastards a thing or two!'

Funny thing, I never did meet a *yellow* Japanese – and I've met plenty.

In the canteen there was the same old face behind the counter; only now there were three chevrons on his sleeve, where before there had been two.

Business must be flourishing!

'Got any razor blades?'

'A few. Dollar fifty a packet of five.'

'I'll take one.'

'Packet?'

'No. Blade.'

'Hmm.'

'Exactly!'

It had been no use consigning Captain Bell to hell, and sending the C.S.M. after him to stoke the fire. That did not give me even the one cent of which I was diffy, and without it there would be no peanut toffee – not even a "squashy" bit. The sergeant had left no doubts about that.

'The smallest portion we sell is five cents' worth.'

All right. To hell with the captain and the C.S.M. after all, and chance it. I would get myself a job with the ration party. Who knows, perhaps I might be able to scab some toffee or sugar. Others did it, so why not I? If there was nothing doing in the scabbing line, I should at least be assured of a day's pay, and with that I could momentarily stay the hysterical promptings of my belly, which kept nagging at me to get it something tasty to play with, as though it were a fashion-conscious wife clamorous for a new hat.

Ten cents, plus the four I had, would not lay the foundations of a pouch-up, but at least I should be assured of my peanut toffee.

That's what I thought. But apparently someone else thought differently...

Descending the hill from Changi with the heavy ration truck – man powered – I executed a deft manoeuvre, though at the time everyone said it was a daft one, that landed me in hospital just as out second Cross boat was entering Singapore Harbour. Of course, I did not know that at the time, and looked on my mishap as an added misfortune. Later I was not at all sure about that; neither was Laverton, when he got back from his working party.

Terry Reynolds said nothing. He was still busy with that imaginative picture of the elusive Say Leen.

Half-way down the hill, the Japs had mounted a Sikh guard to keep an eye on the men who had been sahibs. In so far as saluting was concerned, these hirsute bastards ran our officers a close second and Captain Bell – it would have to be him – was aware of that fact.

At his peremptory 'Eyes Right!' I executed the manoeuvre that took me into hospital. As my head slewed round, something happened to my feet and in the next instant I was lying on my back in the road with one wheel of the heavy ration truck on top of me. I had been pushing in the cut out between the front and rear wheels.

Needless to say, I got no peanut toffee for that day's work!

At the end of a month someone took my crutches away, and I was sad about that, for Christmas was but two weeks distant, and I had got to thinking about all the grub the Red Cross had managed to get through Jap censorship for the occasion. Also, the hospital cook-house was preparing a menu – as early as that – and it looked exciting, even though there was no French on it. Fortunately, no one was waiting for my bed, and the M.O., looking at my medical history sheet, raised an eyebrow and reprieved me.

'We'll keep you until after Christmas, Stirling,' he said. 'Then you can go back to your unit and make a fresh start in the New Year…'

Fresh start was right; I felt I could do with a new coat of paint, inside and out. That menu in the cook-house would take care of the inside, while the outside did not really matter, and I was not worrying about it.

By way of thanksgiving for the clemency of Providence, and the feast on the morrow, I attended a Watch Hour Service in the old Changi Cinema – two flights of stairs and a lawn away from my ward. Here the temporarily repentant – me among them, but without a borrowed halo – took confirmation with that sanctimonious piousness that only the Church and the impressiveness of ceremonial can give.

I wanted to feel good but, try as I might, I could not recapture that feeling of awareness – as of God looking over my shoulder – that had permeated the little bamboo and atap church at Salarang.

Maybe that was because I was taking but a minor part in the ceremony. I was not taking confirmation and, perhaps, I was too conscious of the camouflage of piety that sat so smugly on the faces of those who were.

Tomorrow, I knew, there would be a great deal of blasphemy and a shattering of the Commandments to compensate for this hour of holiness, and I felt that God had missed our turning and gone round the next street.

But perhaps He would come next year…

*****

Christmas Day, 1942! Hurrah! Sound the trumpets! Let the people sing! Hurrah! Banzai! Blessed be the meek for they shall inherit the earth…

The benediction, at least, was true of Christmas morning. We were all meek. Some, indeed, were even mild and inclined to be reminiscent – drunk on memories. But they were not encouraged.

Nobody wanted memories. They would spoil the day and make less attractive the decorations in the wards.

For a week everybody who could walk, and some who could not, had been busy with nature's paint, and the result was a pleasing camouflage of beauty, where before there had been nothing but grim austerity.

A main background to our colour scheme was the shiny green fronds of the coconut palm, and the lighter green of someone's cherished banana plants. From among the greenery, bunches of flaming red peered to remind us of hibiscus stew and dirty rice. Then, to give a promise for the day, and to add a dash of romance, my old friends the magnolia and the frangipane lent a heady perfume to the wards, and kept the purple and mauve bougainvillaea company.

All normal restrictions, including evening roll-call, which the Japs agreed to do without for one day, were taboo and, after an informal service in the morning, the hospital belonged to the patients for the day.

With the dawn came a fanfare of trumpets to salute the holy day, and to make the sparrows – still British – think the old times had returned to Changi. Though they did not level the walls of our Jericho, the trumpets did give an auspicious start to what must, on more than one account, be a unique Christmas.

Immediately after breakfast, bands of Australian, American, Dutch, Javanese and British carol singers went from ward to ward and serenaded us with song. Throughout the day, friends came in from the camp bringing presents and greetings to the sick in the best tradition. A packet of native cigarettes; a cigar, also native; a few sweets saved for the occasion from the Red Cross issue; a couple of bananas; some peanut toffee; and, to one lucky patient, a packet of genuine English cigarettes.

What a sensation these cigarettes caused!

Passed from hand to hand as though it were a piece of rare china being examined by an enthusiastic bunch of collectors, the packet went round the ward to be fondled and sniffed at by everyone who could get his hands on it.

It is doubtful if those cigarettes ever were smoked. They were, somehow, too precious for that. They were a symbol of what had been, and a hope for the future. To put a match to them was to destroy something that could not be replaced, and to do that was to sever a link with the past – a link which, while it remained unbroken, would hold past and present together, and make the time of waiting shorter, and the burden of blindness lighter.

What eventually became of those cigarettes, I do not know. Daily their owner took them from beneath his pillow to hold before his blind eyes as though he could see them. And maybe he could! How am I to know? Why should he do it day after day if there was nothing but a blackness and a groping in the dark?

There was something more than that. To him the slender cylinders of tobacco inside the cellophane were more than cigarettes. They were magic. They were the key to yesterday, and because of them he could see again everything that had happened in that yesterday. For him the cigarettes brought the vision of memory, and while this magic lasted his blind eyes would see again…

Japanese sentiment being notoriously unpredictable, no one was surprised – though everyone was keenly disappointed – when permission to entertain the children of civil internees in Changi gaol was not granted. Had sentiment won, the unfortunate youngsters would have had a real good time, for every man in the camp was determined to do everything possible to ensure their happiness for that one day at least.

Unfortunately, between the civil gaol and the prison camp was the insurmountable barrier of the I.J.A.'s determination not to let us make contact with the internees. And because of that the seventy-odd children spent Christmas in the gaol when they might have been running about Changi in momentary forgetfulness of the ill fate that made them prisoners at such an early age.

Hundreds of toys had been made for the little internees and these, with a substantial sum of money, were sent to the gaol with the hope that Christmas, 1942, would be the last one they should spend with the Japanese…

Even on Christmas Day the shadows fall at the appointed time, and as they began to lengthen along the balconies it was time for us to congregate in one central group and, when that happened, the inevitable occurred. The 'have you heard this one' type of yarn ousted the more conventional theme song, and thus all spiritual resolve, conscious and unconscious, fled until another season.

Up the stairs came the padre who had taken the confirmation service the previous evening, just as a spicy piece of doggerel reached its climax. Shocked, our spiritual adviser turned sadly away to rejoin his choir on the lawn outside.

These good people had come to entertain us in a true Christian spirit, and we had received them as Ishmaelites.

For a week the padre kept away from us, even though the raconteur had been the M.O. Then one day he came into the ward and gave us a reading from Matthew, dealing with Pharisees and hypocrites.

I wonder…

Chapter Fifteen

Moonlight on Changi Creek

With Christmas behind me and the New Year waiting round the corner, I came back to Changi, where so many memories lingered. Laverton was there and so was a slightly less desiccated Terry Reynolds. Of John and Smithy there had been no news, though rumour said that conditions up country were no good.

Maybe they were. No one had any first-hand knowledge, and the bamboo wireless was too uncertain a medium on which to base a concrete opinion. The time would come when we should know definitely – there was little profit in idle conjecture. In the meantime the Japanese were recalling all the working parties who were scattered about the island, so that it became apparent that a move of major importance was imminent.

If we were all going up country, as rumour said, I was anxious not to be left behind. Life at Changi without John had been none too sweet. With the other away it would be insupportable.

In the meantime we waited on the New Year with a keen expectancy which, in some, amounted almost to a conviction that deliverance would not long be delayed once the newcomer had arrived. To those wishful thinkers, and they were many, that contingency was not too much to expect. They felt sure 1943 would see the end of Japan's suzerainty over them. Roll on the New Year and freedom!

A nice thought, certainly, but so premature...

However, there was no divergence of opinion about celebrating the New Year in traditional style. Home-made rice wine – lamentably limited – and imagination would see us through once the I.J.A.'s permission to celebrate was obtained.

Unfortunately, the Jap camp commandant had other ideas. One celebration in the year was enough. There would be no party; neither would there be any noise after lights out. Purely as a goodwill gesture, he was prepared to issue a small quantity of rum for the occasion. Apart from that the evening of the old year would be just another interval between sunset and sunrise.

Be not sentimental about it.

Certainly the rum ration, when it arrived, was not sufficient to raise a spark of sentiment in the heart of anyone not in possession of a big imagination. In spite of that, the individual group officers made sure that no one would make a corner in rum and so get gloriously drunk.

What a hope! The possibility of buying a rum ration – one tablespoonful per man, issued individually and drank in the presence of an officer – was as remote as the hope for indefinite survival of a snowflake in hell.

But, rum or no rum, with permission or without it, it was a foregone conclusion that the New Year would not be allowed to creep in over Changi unheralded. And had they been more conversant with the little subtleties that go to make the word 'British', the Japs would have known beforehand from which point to expect defiance.

It was all right for them to suggest that the old year be not hurried on its tottering way. Understandably they were reluctant to speed its departure. During its life it had witnessed their greatest conquests and their expansion into an empire. And now it was dying. Would the year about to come out of the cradle of the earth be equally fruitful? They did not know. Neither did we.

Just the same we had no wish to delay its arrival or to prolong the life of its predecessor. Whatever the Jap decreed it would not creep in among us like a thief in the night. It would come in full of vigour, and full of promise, and we should be there to greet it...

In the quiet night the ticking of the clock in the company office sounded distinct and measured as the last grains of sand ran out of the hourglass of time, and the old year started to die. Then there came a metallic whirring, followed by a tinny one, two. There was no three. It was submerged, devastatingly eclipsed by a stentorian Scottish voice bellowing a welcome to the New Year, and a defiance to the Japs. And so we slid into 1943.

Close on the heels of that first cry of greeting and welcome, a loud 'Hurrah!' rippled and spread from group to group until it reached the perimeter wire, where it faded for want of someone to prolong its life. After it came a great burst of cheering that swelled and gained momentum as it raced along, and it was echoed and re-echoed along the village street, the Jap guard deserted their machine-gun post and came at the double to quell the disturbance.

They were too late. By the time they arrived at the spot where Scotland had won another victor, the New Year had been welcomed among us, and the old year had slipped irretrievably away. There was no recalling it. Let the guard

172

shout and threaten; their year of victory had slipped away from them, and we had helped it on its way.

Good luck to the New Year!

With its coming the Sikh guards disappeared from the perimeter wire, and with their departure Southern Area breathed more freely and looked expectantly into the future.

Doubly foresworn by their acceptance of service with the enemy, and their tyrannous misuse of the authority invested in them by the Japanese, the Sikhs were hated by everyone in the camp. On the question of saluting they had always been more strict than their masters. They appeared to know that we resented them more than we did the Jap guards who, after all, had earned their obeisance, and they took a satanic delight in exacting their pound of flesh, and sometimes a little bit over, on every occasion that presented itself.

Many of them, of course, had never been in the Indian Army, but had enlisted with the Japs after the fall of Singapore. On the other hand there were some who unmistakably were ex-army and did nothing to conceal the fact.

Why these latter threw in their lot with the aspirations of Japan was never clearly settled while we remained at Changi, though it was generally understood that the Japs had utilised the considerable resources of their *Kempeitai* to persuade them to change their flag.

If the Sikhs – and the other Indian troops who went into the Indian National Army – did so because of *Kempei*-inspired persuasion, no one who had not had personal attention from Japan's military police was in a position to blame them.

Having become a part of Japan's war potential, it was inevitable that former Allies should be more strict than the Japs whom they served. First, they had to satisfy their new masters of their trustworthiness; secondly, there was the inherent urge in every Asiatic, of whatever nationality, to get his own back whenever God, Allah, Mohammed, Buddha or one of the less well-known deities, delivered a white man into his hands.

To blame a Sikh – ex-army or otherwise – for bashing a de-glamorised Sahib is as futile, and as unproductive of worthwhile effort, as the statements conferring unsinkability on the 'Prince of Wales' and impregnability on that mammoth of white elephants – Singapore.

With their going the Sikhs threw the borehole wireless operators into a frenzy of speculation about the immediate future. Once more release was coming on swift feet down Malaya, but apparently its boots wore out, for it never arrived at Changi that year. Whatever the reason for their withdrawal, the Sikhs were gone and everyone was happier for it, until the more pressing problem of how to keep alive on the steadily decreasing food ration intruded itself.

Vegetables were now almost non-existent, and the hibiscus hedges were once more plucked to the buff. Rice, and not much of that, with a little whitebait or a flavouring of *blachang*, occupied the bigger part of the menu, and no matter what it was called, it still remained rice.

To get away from Changi to the problematical land of plenty that was known as up-country was the wish of everyone in the camp – including the canteen staff.

Where the information came from was never certain, but when Captain Bell blandly informed us that there would be plenty of food and 'better facilities for sport' once we got up country, we were content to take his word for it and to wait eagerly on the day we should say good-bye to Changi.

At that date we were not even certain about the nature of the work we were to be engaged in, though there was a casual mention of a railway the Japs were hoping to build. Not that the work itself mattered a great deal – one job was as good as another. Give us food and we were prepared to build any damned thing from a shrine to a battleship, and to hell with sentiment!

*****

'You're not supposed to be here!'

'I wish I weren't.'

'You're supposed to be dead!'

'Thanks! Sometimes I wish I were... Now, what is it all about?'

'Come and see...'

Following Laverton, I arrived at the company office, where the tinny old clock had inexorably brought last year to its death and then, unable to live without it, whirred itself to destruction and refused to have anything further to do with time.

Evidently the likelihood of imminent departure from Changi had stirred recollection in the administration nest. They had remembered that men had been killed, or just disappeared, before we came to Changi as guests of the Japanese. Probably, too, they realised that one day, Providence being on their side, they might be held accountable for those lives. That is, if the new casualty lists that were being added to daily did not obliterate the one on the notice board from all recollection.

'There you are,' Laverton said tersely, laying a finger on a name. 'Stirling, private, 6140003. Killed in action. I always did think there was something odd about you!'

'That is not amusing, and I hope it is not meant to be, but it explains a lot.'

'What, for instance?'

'Just why I feel so ethereal at times. And I had thought it was because my belly is never sufficiently full to give me a feeling of solidity. That list is a load of bull. It's been compiled from some old records company office has unearthed. I was reported killed at Gurun. Instead, I was taken prisoner and held for a day before I managed to say 'Ta-ta' to my captors. After making it back to the battalion on my own, I was greeted with the salutation: 'You're supposed to be dead!' Well, I almost was, but that's ancient history.

'Do you notice anything else about this belated casualty list that strikes a responsive chord in your memory, Richard?'

'Yes, Mick. I noticed it right away. For such a balls up as the Malayan campaign there are far too many 'missing, presumed dead'. They outnumber the 'killed in action' by at least four to one…'

'Exactly. And I should not be surprised if a good percentage of the 'killed in action' were still alive. Anyway, I hope they are.'

'Do you think that is fair?'

'That depends on what your question implies.'

'You said just now that you sometimes wished you were dead. Then why wish such an existence as ours on any poor devil? Let the dead remain dead.'

'And the living can remain alive while they can, eh?'

'Yes. But if we don't hurry and leave Changi, that won't be long, I'm afraid.'

What fools we were! Changi was a haven – with an empty larder granted – and we were blind to its amenities and its comparative security. In it there were few acts of violence. The Japs were not particularly interested in the internal administration of the camp and left us alone. That was the flaw in our existence – that aloneness. Our gaolers were so pre-occupied that at times they forgot to feed us, thinking, perhaps, that we were still drawing energy from the pouch-up we had had at Christmas – now a month old in memory and too stale to provide any nourishment.

Changi, with its aura of British tradition which endured in spite of its fall from prestige as a military cantonment, was not to blame for our adversity. It protected us to the best of its ability even though we had, like it, fallen on misfortune, and in the last weeks of our stay there, it showed itself to us in gracious mood.

The idea of the Snack Bar was good, if one overlooked its impracticability but, unfortunately, that was too obvious to be denied. Established as a medium through which we could acquire, at a price, the vitamins unobtainable from our unit cook-houses, the Snack Bar essayed to provide fritters and such-like ambrosia to the theatregoers and the men who lounged about before the silent screen; also to anyone else who had the fortitude to queue for an indefinite period, knowing beforehand that the probability of getting a mouthful of whatever was on sale – if there was anything – was extremely remote.

Where there was not enough food to fill the bellies of the prisoners during the day, it was obvious that the Snack Bar could be a theoretical success only, as the unit cook-houses had first call on the rations issued by the I.J.A.

It was a pity about this on more counts than one. To sit in the open-air cinema munching a tasty fritter, as a substitute for the more conventional chocolates, while the Keystone Cops went through their intricate routine, was the acme of entertainment – seldom realised.

Over the crowd milling in hopeful anticipation before the Snack Bar, and the better disciplined in the Glade Theatre and the cinema, a fatherly looking moon smiled an encouragement that was seldom appreciated. Nightly it watched our strivings for food, for entertainment, for anything that would speed the moment and bring the next night closer, knowing that to us the day between was but a void wherein there were no ghosts and so few memories – and no moon...

And now it was the last night. Tomorrow Changi would be a memory. Changi, with its ghosts, its pleasure, and its disappointments. Was I glad about that? I did not know; neither did I know if I wanted to go to the last concert with Laverton. But I did not think so – there was something else I wanted to do.

'Are you going to the farewell concert, Mick?' he asked persuasively, knowing probably that I would say 'No.'

'I may do – later. I want to go up the hill first. You know, we might never see Changi again after tomorrow, Richard...'

'Would that matter?'

'Well, essentially, no but, sentimentally, yes.'

'If you want my opinion, I think you have got too damn much sentiment. And about a place like this –'

'It's not the place, Richard. It's the association of memories it conjures up. John, Smithy, Nai Soon, Little Flower... Who knows, maybe we shall never see any one of them again. That is not a nice thought, Richard.'

'Granted. But you are exaggerating. John can take care of himself while, as for Smithy – well I'm not so sure. He's a bit easy-going for this life.'

'And Nai Soon and Little Flower?'

'Oh they're natives, even though they are – or were – well-to-do Chinese. They'll get through all right. Why shouldn't they?'

'Why shouldn't any of us, for that matter? We'll all be natives if we have much more of this.'

'That's true, and the more native we become, the grater out chance of survival.'

'No. I don't believe that. You have only to watch the reactions of the Dutch – particularly the Javanese Dutch – to realise that survival depends on something more than ethnology.'

'That's a new one on me, Mick. What's it mean?'

'It's the science that explains the difference between you and me and, say, the Javanese in Changi village or, if you like, the natives in that kampong across the way.'

'You mean it proves the Javanese are just as likely to go under as we are?'

'No. I am trying to prove that. In fact, I might go one better and say our chances for survival are greater than theirs…'

'You would, if you had seen as many men die in bed as I have.'

Richard did not like that, and I suppose it was unwarranted.

'Look, Mick,' he said. 'I only asked if you were going to the show tonight. Why inflict all this baloney about ethnics – or whatever the hell you call it – on me? I'm not interested in the possible survival of the Javanese. In fact, I should not care particularly if every Dutchman in Changi snuffed it…'

'Now you are getting mixed up. The Dutchmen are not Javanese; neither are the Javanese Dutch, though they wear the same uniforms and are part of the same army.'

'So what?'

'Also, you are biased against the Dutch because they have different customs from us. They like plenty of chillies in their stew; they speak a different language – though some of them can speak ours a damned sight better than we can – they have different mannerisms and, at last, a lot of them are Mohammedans.'

'That's what I don't like about them. I didn't know white men went in for that sort of stuff.'

'Now you are being childish, Richard. If a man wanted to be a Mohammedan, that's his affair. You might just as well have a down on me because I am a Presbyterian and you are Church of England.'

'Oh, that's different.'

'That is what they all say.'

'Hell, and set fire to it!' roared Laverton, suddenly losing patience. 'Be a Mohammedan! Be any bloody sect you wish! Go up the hill and worship the blinking moon if you want to! I'm going to the concert!' And off he went with his bias in one pocket and his fleeting rage in the other.

Perhaps I had been a bit overbearing, I thought, as I watched him go off towards the Glade. But it was true; he was biased against the Dutch, as were the majority of the British in the camp. Though that was nothing new. Anyone who was not indigenous to the British Isles was considered to be inferior in some essential, and any national mannerism that clashed with ours was frowned on and misrepresented, mainly because the average Britisher could not be bothered to analyse it. The same was true of the language. Everybody expected the men from Java to understand us, while at the same time very few of us troubled to learn a smattering of Dutch. It was all so damned silly…

However, that did not explain my cantankerous mood. It was my last night at Changi, and something I could not rightly explain had got into me. I felt both moody and emotional. While one part of me wanted to go to the Glade, where a farewell concert was about to begin, the other part wanted nothing of crowds, laughter, and noise.

It would be quiet on the hill overlooking Paula Ubin. Nearly everyone would be at the show or the cinema, and I could be alone up there. I knew that was what I wanted. To be alone with my thoughts and a few memories on this my last night in Changi. And knowing that, I went to find them.

By the small plantation that came between the sea and the road, where it wound round the foot of the hill, I stopped to say good-bye to the monkeys moving in furtive watchfulness beneath the coco palms. They moved with a peculiar lethargic, shuffling gait reminiscent of so many men in the camp where energy had run down and whose forward momentum was accomplished only with considerable effort.

Between me and the monkeys was the kinship of want and a mutual antipathy for the Japanese who had made them prisoners of circumstance as definitely as I was a prisoner of war. Also, their hope of survival was no better than mine. In fact, it was less for as yet no one, so far as I knew, had fostered any ideas about putting me into a pot with a few hibiscus leaves, and maybe a

178

sweet potato as the basis of a pouch-up.

Leaving the monkeys, I climbed the hill with the moon and saw for the last time the bulk of Paula Ubin sitting waiting in the Straits. Distantly beyond it the lights of a fleet flickered, and I was not pleased about that – they were too ostentatiously secure. Closer to hand the navigation lights burned steadily, but dismally, in the channel. They were, I supposed, lonely for the ships of a hundred nations that no longer came to give them a purpose in life.

As on other nights the shadows lay heavy on the Channel, waiting on the moon to move them and chase them back to Johor. Then on the Creek, where I had fished to such little purpose, a moving shadow blotted the silver, and it was a canoe.

Swiftly it came down the moonlight, as though anxious to meet the darker silhouette of the Straits, and I watched with a stab of recollection until it found a hiding place where the mangrove blotted out the shore.

Inevitably the canoe linked me with Nai Soon, and I went back to that day I had found him crouched on the sand immersed in the memory of his brother – Ah Tek Soon, whom the Japs had murdered down there where the white foam creamed in along the moonlit sands not two stone throws away in distance, but in time, an age. An age wherein much had happened, and seemingly nothing.

Sufficient time it was for the flesh of Ah Tek Soon to have gone back to dust and his bones to whiten in their secret grave. In that time, too, my flesh had changed. There was not so much of it upon me, but it was firm and well-tanned by the sun. And even if my ribs could be counted easily in the moonlight, they encased a heart which beat warm and steady, unlike that of Ah Tek Soon who had come to the end of the rainbow on the silvered sands below…

Behind me in the long grass where the remains of a 15-inch gun poked forlornly at the sky, something squealed in the agony of death and the ghost of Ah Tek Soon fled from me and left me with reality. If this thing coming out of the grass with a tree rat in its mouth was reality, and not another phantom.

It came closer, and then it was rubbing against my leg in an ecstasy of greeting, while the tree rat lay neglected on the grass, the last quiver of death twitching in its long, squirrel-like tail. But I would not let myself be persuaded too easily. Where was its ear? Yes, there was the laceration I had made when I pulled out the hook all those weary months back.

It only wanted Susy Ann to come walking through the moonshine to put me back from where I had started.

'Fishooks, you devil! Where have you been all this time? And you left me thinking someone had made a stew out of you! Oh, it's grand to see you again, but you nearly left it too late…'

I think he understood, though I was half choked with emotion at the unexpectedness of his reappearance. Fishooks was a tangible link with those first days when life had not been as dull and demoralising as it was now. I had thought him dead and he had passed out of my recollection. Now, here he was alive and apparently prosperous, if the flesh beneath his rippling coat was anything to go by. Evidently he was finding good hunting in the Changi nights, and was filling his belly more often than I was filling mine.

As I stroked him and told him about John and the others, he licked my hand with more affection than he had ever shown before, and I realised that his former spitefulness towards Susy Ann, and sometimes myself, had been the inevitable outcome of youthful impetuosity.

Fishooks was no longer a callow youth. He had brown up and matured. I wondered if he had a wife tucked away behind the fence surrounding the wrecked gun. If he had, I hoped he would have many sons, and that he would live to see the *Tuans* return to power in Changi, though it was doubtful if he would ever see me again after tonight.

A figure came round the corner of the hill, and Fishooks, picking up his supper, departed. He didn't like crowds any more than I did…

Terry Reynolds took Fishooks' place on the grass beside me.

'Was that a cat I saw just now, Mick?'

'Yes. Fishooks – an old friend of mine…'

'It must live in the wreckage of that old gun. I've seen it before.'

'I wish you had told me.'

'Oh, I did not think any more about it, not knowing you were acquainted…'

'H'mp! Why are you not at the concert?'

'And you?'

'I'm asking.'

'Oh, I did not feel like it tonight, Mick. I thought I would come up here and have a last look round instead. Besides, it does not do my eyes any good, though they have improved a great deal.'

'Laverton didn't tell you, by any chance, that I was up here?'

'Well –'

'He did. I thought perhaps he might. Richard has an idea I say my prayers to the moon!'

180

'And why not, Mick? There are more unworthy gods to worship.'

'I agree. It's a matter of sentiment, when all is said. Richard is too material minded. He couldn't, for instance, appreciate my going into ecstasies about a cat I had not seen for a twelve month. Could you, Terry?'

He did not answer that, and I did not expect that he would. He had not come up the hill on his last night in Changi to talk about cats, even though it was sentiment that had beguiled him away from the concert. Neither had he come to say good-bye to Paula Ubin, sitting black and intense in the moon-dappled Straits, any more than he had come to take farewell of Ah Tek Soon, about whom he did not know, and the other ghosts who paraded along Changi Creek when the mist started to rise among the mangroves.

No. Terry had come into the quiet night away from the noise and merriment of the Glade seeking an answer to a problem which, until now, had needed no answer. But now it was the last night, and there must be a solution before the morning so that he might go from Changi and leave no ghosts behind.

Watching his face, which had recaptured some of its lost youth, while he looked behind him into yesterday and then, apprehensive, into tomorrow, I waited to help him over the stile of uncertainty and so along the highroad of endeavour, hoping in the meantime he would be able to read the signpost if he ever came to a cross-roads.

He had gone in deeper even than I had thought.

'What shall I do about Say Leen, Mick?' he asked, simply, and I felt like saying, 'How the hell do I know!?'

That would have been fatal, and as futile as telling him to forget her. Say Leen was something not easily forgotten. And Terry would never forget her. Not that I wanted him to – not now. She, or the memory of her, was something to which he could hang on, even when other memories ceased to give him driving power and the incentive to go on. Something like that was necessary for him if he was not to stop suddenly at the foot of a hill as once already he had nearly stopped.

That was a thought.

'That time you were in hospital, you nearly died, didn't you?'

'Well, yes. But –'

'But nothing. You told me it was the thought of Little Flower that kept you going…'

'That and other things.'

'Well, there's your answer.'

'I'm not sure what you mean, Mick. After tomorrow I may never see Singapore again, and that means no Say Leen...'

'Not even a memory?'

'There will always be that, Mick. But is it advisable in the circumstances? That really is what I want to know. Should I continue to hold on to a memory of someone whom, after all, I have seen once only, and may never see again?'

'With both hands, Terry. What have we left but memories? I remember when the white flag went up at Singapore, I got to thinking that the days behind me were finished; that they would be of no consequence in the life ahead. Believe me, I soon found that was not true. Our yesterdays are all important, Terry, in contrast to our todays and immediate tomorrows. They are something apart from the Japanese. They can never be taken away from us. They hold out a promise for this year, next year, or maybe the year after and once in a while, placed even as we are, we can add to them the memory of a Nai Soon or, perhaps, as in your case, a Little Flower...

'Yes, Terry, hold fast to your memories – the good ones – and you will never be alone. There will always be someone walking by your side even in the darkest places. Memories, in a way, are like faith – they never let you down...'

'I'm glad you said that, Mick. It makes me feel warm and comfortable inside. Do you think I shall ever see Little Flower again?'

'Do you?'

'Not with any certainty of fulfilment.'

'I hope you have not overlooked the fact that I also have an interest in the Soon family, Terry. Like you, I should be glad to see Little Flower again, though not for the same reason. It is not she in whom my interest is centred, but her brother. Nai Soon and I shall meet again – I am quite fatalistic about that – and when we do, I shall be very happy...'

'You think, then, he may be going up country?'

'In all probability. He cannot indefinitely escape being conscripted into a labour gang. Then, too, he must eat, and there is not a lot of food about these days. I think somehow he would welcome the chance of getting out of Malaya. But, of course, there is Say Leen. What would become of her in that eventuality I do now know.'

'That worries me a bit, too, Mick. It is not nice to contemplate those beautiful hands doing coolie labour for the Japanese...'

There were other things it was not nice to think about in relation to Say

182

Leen if the Japs got round to taking an active interest in her well-being.

In Singapore beauty was not at a premium, but most of it was overdone. There was little freshness about it, and daily it grew more anaemic and listless from a too-close attention to the needs of Hirohito's children, who would reach out avidly for Say Leen's fresh unspoiledness, greedy for that which the others could not give.

If that ever happened it would be the end of a memory, and Ah Tek Soon would have another ghost to keep him company – a frail, beautiful ghost who would leave a great heartache behind her. In the meantime I hoped Terry Reynolds would continue to concentrate on Say Leen's hands, leaving her destiny to God, and to me the unlovely thought of what might befall her if God let her down…

As we went down the hill, having seen enough of the silent night, a great cheer came rippling up to meet us. For me and for Terry, the last show in the Glade was over – and we had missed it.

It was good-bye to Changi…

Chapter Sixteen

Dowdy Tuans

'Few people would believe it, Mick, but the Japs and the British have one or two things in common.'

'Such as?'

'Well, take their never-failing insistence in getting up in the middle of the night to start a journey in the afternoon, for instance. Then there is the question of packing as many mortals as possible into a given space so that they may travel in the greatest discomfort possible.'

'You've got something there, Richard, but it's not original by any means. I had noticed it before. Which reminds me of something. Guess what.'

'You wouldn't, by any chance, be thinking of the first time we travelled up Malaya?'

'Just that. Remember how they packed us into the third-class compartments, even to the extent of making men sit in the gang-ways?'

'Yes, I have not forgotten that six hundred miles journey, Mick. After two years the memory of those empty first-class compartments still rankles. What a journey! And what a lot of scarecrows we looked when we arrived at Alor Star!'

'That's one thing we need not bother about this time – appearance. And, too, there won't be an unsympathetic fashion plate sergeant-major to welcome us when we reach journey's end – wherever that is.'

'No. But it is going to be hell in these steel trucks if it does not rain...'

'I don't know about hell. It will certainly be bloody hot, and there is little hope of rain for another month or so. It never does rain in this damned country when you need it most... I hope we have no dysentery wallahs in our truck, Richard; things are bad enough without that. Thank goodness, I am all right in that respect. This journey is going to be a bastard...'

It was more original than that. Every one of its thousand miles was a revelation. It was a triumph of can over cannot. The impossible became possible, and nobody died. That was the strangest thing about the whole journey: the unwillingness of someone – it did not particularly matter whom – to die, so that the historians might have an excuse to glamorise and to write epitaphs.

As it was, there was no glamour; only a damn bad smell and an intolerable heat…

Packed thirty-five to an enclosed steel truck, ventilation being through the door on either side, we ambled across the Causeway and clanked into a silent Johor, feeling pleased that Changi and the Equator were being left father behind with each turn of the wheels that were taking some of us back along the same road we had travelled two years previously.

There was a difference now, however, which had nothing to do with the similarity between our over-crowded state on both journeys. Before, there had been the shouts of a multitude of naked and friendly *chickos* along the way. Now there was nothing but silence and sometimes a sullen resentment to go with it.

Yesterday we had been *Tuans*, over-stuffed with self-esteem, hurrying north to protect the youngsters who yelled encouragement outside every kampong, from the threat of Japanese aggression. Now we were going north again, not so quickly this time and, instead of the crowds of vociferating *chickos*, there were but a few, naked as ever, who scurried into the bushes in evident fright as we passed.

'Why the fright?' I wondered, and left it at that. It was getting too hot to bother about inessentials…

Like the *chickos*, the countryside was bare. Where there should have been bananas and papayas in the *kampongs*, the trees were barren. There was hunger in the land – that much was evident to all who could get near enough the doors to see it.

Even the water buffaloes, so indispensable to every *kampong*, seemed to have disappeared. But more remarkable even than that was the feverish activity with which so many of the natives were clearing new ground. There were too many of them working – and working hard – for there to be any doubts about the food situation. We were not the only ones who were undernourished.

Singapore and Malaya were feeling the pinch of hard times. The Greater East Asia Co-prosperity Sphere was bearing dead fruit. There was little milk and honey in the land, and want was at everyone's door.

Like the *chickos*, the natives clearing the scrub evinced little interest in our passing. They were too desperately anxious to get their new land ready for their former child-like curiosity – as much a part of the native as his chew of betel-nut – to concern itself with down-at-heel *Tuans*, who no longer warranted the name. They had, as it were, grown up over-night, and had found other, more pressing problems to interest them.

Judging from the "sadness" that lay over the countryside like a veil of unhappy memories, I could guess what those new interests were.

In Singapore, as we came through on the way to the station, there had been the same apathetic lack of interest in externals. The people appeared to have withdrawn into themselves, and to be no longer concerned with what we did. They just were not interested any longer. Like their country cousins, they were too pre-occupied with their own affairs to bother about ours. But, unlike the former, their pre-occupation was all passive. There was none of the feverish work of reclamation that was going on along the railway.

Where the vitality of necessity would give the countryman sufficient incentive to clear new land to increase his crops, the townsman would sit on his haunches all day, gazing with philosophical calm on calamity until he died of apathy and *tidak apa*.

Singapore was already in the grip of *tidak apa*, and was sickened unto death. Its vitality had run down so that it just breathed, asthmatically and wheezily. It was dying and knew it, and it needed food. In places its bones were beginning to show. Not the old scars of battle, but a new scarifying caused by neglect. Dirt and disease were everywhere, and the shops looked bleak and vacuous. Many of them had given up pretending and remained closed. Others did likewise; not because they had had enough of pretence but because their owners were dead...

Like their city, the Singaporeans looked hungry and neglected, and many of them showed a meek acquiescence that was not inspiring. Others, the quislings – easily picked out – showed a self-satisfied exterior and an appearance of sleek well-fed-ness that hall-marked their calling and made them the envy of their more old-fashioned brethren.

I was not particularly interested in whether the men on the side-walk were quislings or just common-place Chinese or Malays. What grieved me was the knowledge that we were departing without a word of farewell as a final benediction from a populace who, metaphorically, had turned their backs on us and did not see us go. No shout of 'Hullo, Johnnie!' came to speed us on the way. Johnnie was a has-been, and no longer worthy even of curiosity. Someone else had taken his place, temporarily maybe, but none the less definitely. Granted, the newcomer might be a poor substitute, but he held the reins – he was the master. As such he had to be propitiated even though you stick a knife in his back should he be fool enough to look the other way while you did it.

If he did not do that you pretended to like him and called him *Tuan*, hoping he would increase your rice ration, or give you a soft job in the new administration...

Singapore's railway station was so dead it stank. The only staff visible was a lonely looking old Tamil prowling about among the rustled rails where the grass grew knee high, making the station a suitable location for any ghost train.

During the four hours we waited while the Japs decided whether we were to go today or tomorrow, one freight train carrying a dozen dowdy natives wheezes into the once busy station and came to rest with a groan of thankfulness. Equally thankful at having arrived safely, its freight tumbled out on to the platform in a huddle of reds, blues, and off-white that looked well against a background of egg shells, pomelo peel, banana skins, dog ends, and last year's newspapers.

At Gemas, 150 miles from Singapore, but fifteen hours in time, we stopped for our first meal since leaving Changi. This was supplied by the local Jap garrison, and was much better than the meals we got at other halts, where we were dependent on some supercilious Chinese for a little rice and a piece of dried fish, when there was no vegetable stew on the menu.

Comprising four three-star privates and a corporal, our train guard evinced little interest in our existence and, apart from a roll-call at the end of each halt, left us completely to our own devices.

There were others, however, who kept a wary eye on our movements when the train came to a standstill – which it did frequently – or when it was going slowly – which was more frequent still. A senior N.C.O. or W.O. had been allotted to each truck, and it was the duty of these guardians to ensure that no one left the train without special permission of the train C.O. When we stopped at a station, however, this order was ignored, and no N.C.O. living could have enforced it.

The incentive to get off the train was twofold. First there was the supreme urge – fresh air. Secondly, there was the possibility of being able to buy eggs or fruit from the natives whom the Japs allowed into the station, and no one wanted to miss that opportunity.

And thus our trainload of sweating, swearing, and hungry humanity crawled northward, while each weary mile took a little of the initial excitement of anticipation from us and brought in its place a doubt for the future, and a realisation that our pre-capitulation scorched earth policy had been almost negligible.

At all the larger stations the sidings were crammed with rolling stock, which appeared to be completely undamaged in any way. This was also true of the stations themselves, until we came to Kuala Lumpur, where a bridge had been demolished – whether by us or the Japs I could not say – and was still down.

This bridge was the only piece of major destruction I saw during the whole trip...

And so to Kampar, the bloody memory of where, to many of the men on the train, as to Laverton and me, the scars on the little station had something personal about them, symbolising as they did the only worthwhile resistance we had made to the Japs thrusting down the – if one omits the Slim River and the Argylles, who were outside our sphere of influence – West Coast towards Singapore.

That had been Christmas, 1942 and, for many of Hirohito's men, it had been the end of the trail from Tokyo to the Lion City. A goodly number of Indians and Gurkhas, and a sprinkling of British, too, were lying out there beyond the hills over which the pipeline – at whose other extremity we had seen so much excitement in such a short period – still crawled like an over-fed python.

Perhaps it was over-fed, for a deal of blood had been spilled where it gushed water down the hill onto the road, making an ideal set-up for the Jap snipers who, more than once, disproved the theory that Japs could not shoot...

Sungei Patani – and more memories – came with sunrise next day. Here the Japs were taking great precautions to keep secret the aerodrome they were building. As usual they over-did their precautionary measure, and everyone on the train knew just where the new aerodrome was before we got out of the hush-hush area.

With each turn of the wheels came an old memory made new and liveable. Down the road was Gurun, where I had been held by the Japs for six hours, nine days after their coming to the rubber forests of Malaya – and here I was still alive, while many who had never seen a Jap before the capitulation of Singapore were dead and forgotten.

Was that something for which to be grateful? I did not know... but it was nice to be alive in spite of the heat and the other inconveniences that being alive entailed. Also, Alor Star was taking the place of Gurun in the panoramic vista of my past life, and I was back from where I had started, just over a year previously on the long retreat down Malaya, which ended in a prison camp at Changi.

189

Not as a conqueror or as one who had made good was I returning, but in chains and with the backside out of my trousers. And I was a bit self-conscious about that. Many others on the train felt that way, too, as we came into Alor Star where, before the coming of the Japs, we had been Tuans and men of substance. Now we had not even the protection of a latrine to hide our shame – though frankly, this was fast becoming non-existent – but must perforce squat by the side of the track among piles of egg shells, where others had been before us. Thus exposed to the hypercritical gaze of the locals who not so long since would have been horrified at such a demoralising exhibition, we added our quota to the fertility of Kedah, as others before us had done with their flesh and blood.

Looking at what little of the town I could see from the railway and then at the sentry sitting on a pile of sleepers swapping reminiscences with the prisoners, I found it difficult to believe that the amiable looking Jap on the pile of sleepers had been among the supposedly bloodthirsty horde who came out of Thailand to chase us across the Alor Star river – those of us who were fortunate to get over before it went up in premature ruin – and so eventually out of Malaya.

Standing there, half in the present and half in the past, listening to the Jap and smoking one of his cigarettes, I saw again the scene at the bridge as the smoke cleared and it became apparent that the bulk of our transport was on the wrong side of the river. But before I had time to feel bad about that, a Tamil with a basket stepped on to the line, and as he came closer I rushed back into the present on the thought – eggs!

Laverton, unhampered by the handicap of memory, beat me to the egg-seller, but I was a close second.

'Has he any raw ones, Richard?' I wanted to know, as did he, for that matter. We had not suddenly gone finicky, nor had we yet had a surfeit of hard-boiled eggs, though we had eaten more in the last three days than we had done for the six months prior to that.

As was to be expected, Terry Reynolds was ill. He had not the constitution to stand up to the gruelling hardships of the journey, and had been extricated unconscious that morning from beneath a jumble of bodies piled higgledy-piggledy in the undisciplined contortions of exhaustion, which went by the name of sleep in the over-crowded trucks. Laverton and I had taken him forward to the "sick truck", where the men most seriously affected by the journey were segregated.

The raw eggs were for Terry – but there were none.

190

'I know this old bastard,' said Laverton, referring to the Tamil. 'He's an ex-rubber tapper. Used to do the trees in the camp… I wonder what he would say if I told him we had been stationed here before the Japs done him out of a job?'

'Why don't you? He might give you a few *lagi* eggs…'

He did not care for the idea. I could see that, and I was surprised. Laverton was a sentimentalist after all.

'On second thoughts,' he said, 'I should prefer him not to know. Doesn't feel too good, somehow, coming back home with the arse out of your trousers so to speak…'

'Great minds think alike,' I might have said. But I didn't. The thought was not sufficiently original, so I let it pass and clambered back into the train which was about to start, to concentrate on another one.

It was obvious, in spite of Laverton's wishful thinking, that the local citizenry knew many of us had been stationed in their town before the Jap war lords went big game hunting. It was equally obvious, and more hurtful to the self-esteem, that had we been a trainload of hogs, or maybe shit buffaloes, going up the line, the people who once had stepped out of our path while we lived our little hour, would have taken a more personal interest in our passing. Like their more cosmopolitan kin in Singapore, they were disinterested – and not because of *tidak apa*.

We had had our day. We were not now the fashion. Maybe some other time… Until then do not make too much mess for us to clean up; not that we'll clean it anyway…

Alor Star, with its hard-boiled eggs, for which we were grateful, and its memories of futility, which many in the train did not wish to prolong, was presently behind us, and we went clanking through Chungloon – last outpost of the former days. Here I bought my last bunch of bananas on Malayan soil, and threw my last brick at a Malay pi-dog, which, unlike the humans, was too inquisitive.

Soon thereafter we were in Thailand, first impressions of which were dulled somewhat by the realisation that any money we had left was now worthless – at least for the time being which, by Japanese reckoning, meant a long time. The Thais, independents rascals that they are, refused to have it even as a gift.

Unlike their neighbours, the Thais showed no lack of interest in our arrival. But then, we were comparatively new to them; they had not seen enough of us for their curiosity to have been blunted. They were, however, not so free-and-easy with the Japs as were the Malayans, in spite of the fact that they were supposedly more willing partners in the Greater East Asia Co-prosperity Sphere.

Noting their evident reluctance to get on friendly terms with the Japs in the station, and their wary approach to us, I came to the conclusion that the Thais were not over-pleased about their new alliance. To the least discerning among us, it was evident there was little brotherly love between the partners in the new deal that was going to bring the millennium to Asia, and make every white man regret his Occidental parentage.

Whatever their feelings for the Japs may have been, the border Thais treated us liberally with eggs, bananas, pomelos, and watermelon. Veritably we had come out of poverty and want into a land of plenty, and our enthusiasm for the big adventure, which had died somewhere in the neighbourhood of Gemas, began to revive and grow strong again.

But were these first signs of plenitude a sure indication of what Thailand had to offer? Rumour said 'yes' but a rumour was a mischievous bitch, not too conscientious when it came to choosing between yes and no...

The wise would wait for time – dependable old char lady – to supply the answer. And, in the meantime, we were off into the unknown Thailand behind a continuous shower of sparks from the wood-fired loco that had taken us in tow.

Why Thailand has not been burned to a cinder as a result of her flame-belching locomotives is a question I cannot answer.

Laverton, when I put the problem to him, suggested it was because so much of the country was burned in the engines' fire-boxes as to leave insufficient fodder for the showers of sparks to set a light to.

I could not find any logic in that supposition. It was too much like drawing a bow at a venture and missing the target altogether. Frankly, I think Laverton was not unduly perturbed about the fate of the country through which we were passing. He had eaten too many bananas and these, with a dozen or so hard-boiled duck eggs, were not entirely conducive to clear thinking.

As we left Malaya behind us the Jap guard came to life and took a momentary interest in our existence, and at our next stop they put on a show of force, augmented by the local militia, that was much more impressive than the first close-up of the troops who might have been our allies – and, without a doubt, fellow prisoners – had they been sufficiently devoid of common sense.

From a first viewing the Thai Militia – though in this case they were police – in their loosely fitting chocolate-coloured uniforms looked more like a crowd of apathetic milkmen about to start out on their rounds of a cold winter's morning.

But then, it is not always a good thing – not is it advisable – to judge an army, or even a police force, by its appearance. In support of that piece of logic, witness our own plight. We, who before the Japs came to bring us a new religion, worshipped so diligently at the shrine of the great god Bullshit. Also take stock of the ragamuffins who so abruptly terminated our devotions... though all our priests were not dead yet...

Too late I learned that the show of military might had not been put on as a gesture to welcome us into Thailand. We were, apparently, within spitting distance of the Pacific Ocean, and the Japs were feeling a bit queasy at the thought of some of us skedaddling.

But their vertigo in this instance was not justified. No one on the train was aching for a sight of the Pacific and, besides, the dark unknownness of the night beyond the brilliance of the station lights was no inducement to adventure...

My next lucid recollection of the Thai night was of a village being trodden underfoot as our train, a mobile volcano, rushed devastatingly upon it and, miraculously, failed to consume it.

Dawn put an end to nightmares, imagined and real, and discovered what to us appeared to be one immense forest stretching as far as the back of beyond; then, when we got there, going farther still. But it could not go on for ever, even though we were in Thailand where, it has been said, anything is possible, and eventually a break came in the greenery, new and old, and there was a stretch of the old familiar padi. About them was the camouflage of distance which in that part of the world appears always to be blue. On closer inspection, I knew they would most likely be dingy, and probably desiccated, like an old woman cocking a snook at time through the medium of a silk shift and fur coat. Failing that, they would be luscious in a mantle of a thousand greens, and in their bosom there would be a shade and a quiet repose with the sound of running water to give a caress light as the touch of Say Leen's fingers on my arm...

Variety occasionally stepped from the scrub in the form of a herd of work elephants whose hides looked as devoid of moisture as the padi, and whose tails looked ridiculous. One of these caricatures of nature's bounty was, for a moment, distinctly resentful of our continued advance towards the hills which distance could no longer camouflage.

Taking up a defiant stance athwart the track, this misguided animal prepared to go into action in support of the slogan, 'Thailand for Thais.' Then remembering that elephants were not solely indigenous to Thailand, it used the knowledge as a subterfuge to enable it to retreat before our shrieking, fire-spitting dragon, without loss of that commodity – face – about which one hears so much in the East. With a scornful toss of its trunk, which was elephantese for 'I could if I would – but I won't,' it left the track and waddled off into the scrub, swishing its ridiculous tail in a hoity-toity fashion.

Once in a while a long *kampong* obtruded itself into the greens and browns and occasional puffs of dazzling white – egrets on lazy wings floating on the heat-laden air – that rushed to meet us, and was as quickly dropped behind. Noticeable only because of their isolation, these lonely kampongs were the outposts of the eleven million Thais who lived in the vast wilderness of forest, jungle, scrub and padi, with an occasional range of hills to break the general flatness that comprised the demesne of the legendary Bangkok; which, in turn, conjured up visions of magic carpets; princes and potentates; white elephants and beautiful maidens; heavenly odours and original stinks; gods with jewelled eyes, and gold-roofed temples; Siamese and Japanese; white men free and white men fettered; a night in Lavender Street and one in Leicester Square; then the subtle emanation of a thought: this is all baloney…

Six days after leaving Singapore we ambled into Nong Pladuk, base camp on the Japanese Burma Railway, and back door to conquest. Over the camp the vultures circled in effortless flight, watching and waiting… waiting and watching… knowing that soon something, or someone, would die. If they did not feast today, there was always tomorrow…

Chapter Seventeen

Hail, Jonathan

Through the split bamboo fence the roofs of the huts looked like outsize *kampong* dwellings, only they were neater and arranged with greater precision; they did not straggle all over the banana plantation that made a flimsy screen between them and the railway that was responsible for their being there. About them was a military correctness and an outward solidity which the banana plants could not hide, and more than they could conceal the nationality of the men with the brown faces, and the scanty wearing apparel, who were gathered in expectant groups on the square, as we marched in and halted by the guardroom.

Full of joyous anticipation, I tried, without success, to find John's lanky figure on the square. Smithy was there, however, and I was reassured. Where he was, there would also be John, and soon we should be together again – all four of us – making plans for the future…

But I had overlooked something, and as Captain Bell spoke, a cold dismay clutched at my happiness and gave an uncomfortably accelerated rhythm to my heart.

We were to be searched, and I had not anticipated that!

My precious map – in which was invested all my hopes for escape – my diary, including painstaking notes on Thailand and Burma, and two daggers picked up at Singapore were there for anyone to see if he chanced to look! More important, though not necessarily to my immediate wellbeing, was two-thirds of my MS., "Shoddy Heroes", on the Malayan campaign, written at Changi with Susy Ann looking over my shoulder.

Now I was about to lose the lot and get a damned good bashing into the bargain. But I doubted I should feel that; the mortification at my loss would anaesthetise any additional pain.

It was little consolation to know that I could not have concealed all the contraband my home-made attaché case contained. The map at least could have been put in a place of safety. Now it was no more than ashes on the wind…

What a fool I had been to depart from my golden rule for survival – never take anything for granted – and thus allow myself to be caught just because the Japs had not been over-zealous in their searches at Changi, though they had made a half-hearted attempt to check out kit at the station before we left.

'O Lord, who looks after the welfare of fools and blasphemers against common sense,' I prayed, 'please give this birdbrain another chance.' No? All right, then, I would make the best of a delicate situation. What had Captain Bell ordered?

'Undo your kits and lay out everything so that the guard may inspect your belongings…'

To do that would not be taking a chance – it would be suicidal. And there was nowhere I could hide the case – it was too bulky. My only hope was to leave it standing there, apparently overlooked and innocent, and hope for the best.

That was not very comforting, though. Wasn't there something else I could do to distract the Japs, who were already on the way? Yes – yes! Of course there was! Where was Laverton?

'Richard! Richard! Quickly! Give me a few of those attractive-looking females you picked up at Singapore.'

'What's up? Oh, hell! I'd forgotten. That bloody map! Where is it?'

'In my case. Give me the postcards. Hurry, damn it!'

There! That's better. Spread them out on the bedding – not too obviously though. The one with the most leg on top, and there was not a Jap outside Japan who would not pause to appreciate and speculate…

Here they come, and what a collection they are making. Junk mostly, from their point of view, but to the men who were losing it, invaluable owing to its being irreplaceable. Knives, scissors, hammers, chisels, every notebook in sight and every scrap of paper with writing on it. How futile!

Now the big moment arrived, and I am praying like hell – or should it be heaven? There go my scissors. Damn! I shall have to walk about with the arse out of my shorts in future… Come on, my beauties, turn on the old sex appeal… Yes, your allure is as potent as if you were there in the flesh! Aren't you thrilled as they pass you from hand to hand, their task temporarily forgotten as they delight in what they see, and gloat over all that his hidden?

Not much, admittedly, but sufficient to hold them enthralled…

Hullo! The lady with the saucy legs has found a cavalier – and an English-speaking one at that.

Roses in Billingsgate!

'English-*ka*?' he asks, holding out the photo, and I am quick to defend my countrywomen.

'English girl *nie*,' I say, with a shake of my head. 'French O.K.'

'Nippon you give? O.K.-*ka*?'

I feel it may be unfair to the curvaceous lady if I acquiesce, but there is little I can do about it, and the danger is not yet over. Laverton will not be pleased, but his displeasure will be mild compared with that of the Japs if they discover my map. I must get this lecherous baboon and his grinning hyenas away from my kit, and that is easily accomplished now. A flick of my hand to assure him, and it is done.

'O.K. I give.'

A few minutes later I was with Smithy, who was waiting anxiously to learn the result of the search.

'Did you lose anything, Mick?'

'Yes. A good deal of sweat, a pair of scissors – which were more important – and a postcard.'

'Girl friend?'

'No. That is – yes – in a way. She did me a good turn – and she had nice legs…'

But that was a bit too involved for Smithy, and he passed it by.

'It's nice to see you again, Mick,' he said. 'Your crowd look a bit undernourished…'

'They do more than look it Smithy. They are. What is the food like here?'

While he was making his mind up about it, I looked again at the dark bruise on the side of his face, and wondered if it had any bearing on the change in his demeanour. He was no longer the placid, easy-going Smithy whom I had known at Changi and before. In the months we had been separated he had been wounded emotionally – I knew that would not be difficult of accomplishment in his face – and had acquired a hardened exterior that was as foreign to him as the loincloth about his hips.

'I don't want to give you any wrong impressions of this camp, Mick,' he said, as we crossed the square to the hut where I was to sleep. 'The food is good – much better than it was at Changi. But there are other things that have not improved in proportion.'

Unconsciously he rubbed his cheek, and I understood what he meant.

'Frankly, the Koreans who do the camp guard are a lot of bastards…'

They must be, I thought, if they have made swearing a matter of routine – you who used never to swear.

'They are the ones who searched us, I suppose? I thought they looked a bit different, somehow.'

'Yes. They are good at that sort of thing; though, oddly enough, one or two of them are quite decent in their behaviour. It is strange, that, Mick. No matter how depraved any group of men is, there are always one or two decent ones…'

'Well,' I encouraged, 'the Japs are like that, so why not the Koreans?'

'You will find out in time that there is a subtle difference between a Nip and a Korean. We don't call them Japs anymore. They prefer to be known as Nipponese, and Japan as the Great Nippon, so we have compromised and call them Nips.'

'It's all one to me,' I said. 'I am prepared to call them anything – and sometimes do. If they prefer Nip, then Nip it shall be… What was that you said about the difference between them and the Koreans?'

'The Koreans are just lice. Unfortunately, you will find they are not the only ones in camp, and there are plenty of bugs, too. But to get back to the Nips: They are soldiers – no one can deny that – and men, if you like. I think we can concede them that point, in spite of all the fifth-rate propaganda we heard about them. The Koreans, on the other hand – and I have to repeat myself to say it – are a lot of cowardly bastards, apart from an isolated one here and there, temporarily infused with valour, because they know we are not in a position to retaliate when they get to knocking us about…'

Well, that explained a lot. Poor, inoffensive Smithy had been ill-treated, that was plain. But it was no use offering him sympathy. He would not want it. In fact, he might even resent it.

'What you said about the Koreans is equally true of the Japs, or Nips, as we now call them, surely?'

'Well, no. Not exactly. The Nips have a code of sorts to which I believe they sincerely try to abide. But circumstances are against them – you will admit that I know. Consequently we are victims of the fate that has made the Nip feel – whether he admits it or not – inferior to a white men. Even a white man in our position.

'The Korean, on the other hand, has no code of ethics. He is just scum, and knows it. He knows, too, that the Nips consider him to be lower than a Chinese, and that is pretty low in their estimation. In a desperate endeavour to rehabilitate himself, and with a distorted desire for revenge, he vents his spleen on us, using the refusal of our government to help him out in 1910 as a pretext for bashing us about... But why bother about that?' he broke off, rubbing his cheek again. 'Let's get you fixed up with a sleeping space and a meal. You'll find sleeping accommodation rather more cramped here than it was at Changi but, as I said, the food is better...'

And it was – much better even than I had expected. Apparently the rumours we had heard about food up country were correct. There was plenty to eat in Thailand – comparatively, that is – and while that state of bliss remained, we should be all right. But that it would not last indefinitely was obvious. Thailand would eventually become another Malaya, in which prices would reach fantastic heights while food supplies sank to exhaustion point. In the meantime, it behoved everyone to eat while he could so that in the lean days ahead – if the worst happened – he would at least have a memory to look back on.

After a meal of meat stew – more meat than I had seen for months – sweet potatoes, rice, jam tarts and an egg – this was a special occasion, however, and was not the daily menu – I went with Laverton to look round the camp and, in particular, to find John, having omitted to inquire about him from Smithy, who had gone off on some rush job from which he did not expect to return until late the same night.

Nong Pladuk – as were all the principal camps that came into being along the railway – was administered on similar lines to Changi. Here, however, the Nip staff actually lived in the camp and, in consequence, incidents were of a daily occurrence. As Smithy had said, the Koreans did the camp guard, and also a good deal of the administrative work from which they often took time off to prowl around looking for a pretext to knock someone about.

Despised as they were by the other elements in – the prisoners and the Nips – the Koreans were yet in a position to chastise the former and exact recognition from the latter by virtue of the officer they held. As a guard they symbolised the Emperor and everyone passing the guardroom was compelled to salute them; the compulsion, of course, being applicable to the Nips only. The prisoners had no say in the matter, and were not concerned with the hypothetical halo, Imperial or otherwise, that hangs about all I.J.A. guardrooms, any more than they were troubled by the early morning promises of Hirohito's warriors.

Each morning these sun worshippers faced east to say their prayers and to bewail the fact that they were still alive, promising to die for the Emperor "tomorrow." Unfortunately, these daily assurances were not meant to be taken literally. Had that been so I have no doubt the Nips, being Nips, would automatically have solved the Far Eastern problem by a process of self-immolation that would have wiped them out in a matter of months.

It was a pity, that…

At right angles to the huts of the coolie prisoners, the officers' billets occupied the west edge of the square that separated us from the Nip quarters. Here I found the White Tojo delousing his bed, or at least he was doing that very necessary chore until he discovered us bearing down on him. Then he was suddenly interested in a nail sticking out of the wood, which, at the moment, appeared to be of more importance than the lice which I later found infested the camp.

There were bugs, too, as there had been in Changi; only now they were reckoned by the thousand, where before their numbers had been calculated in scores. As a score of bugs are as irksome in one's bed as, say, a thousand, there was little dissimilarity in sleeping conditions, in so far as livestock was concerned, in either camp.

However, I was not particularly interested in Nong Pladuk's bug population; nor in the White Tojo's efforts to maintain his dignity and pose when caught at such a disadvantage. Laverton, I knew, would be appreciating to the full the situation, and would not be disposed to help the major over his difficulty. He had an old score to settle and waited only for an opportunity.

Then a bug gave it to him.

'Look, sir,' he shouted suddenly. 'There is one! Just there by your right foot; tread on it!'

Dutifully the major did so, but it was an uncomfortable operation. Then he made a gallant comeback.

'This is a job for a batman, you know. Would either of you care for the job? The chap I had is going up country tomorrow.'

'No. I don't think either of us would fill the post to your satisfaction,' I said, forestalling Laverton. 'For myself, it is a position I have never held, and do not intend to hold –'

'Why is that?' he wanted to know. And I told him.

'Because,' I said, 'I have met only two men in the army for whom I should have cared to do batman. One was a Lieut.-Colonel and the other was a regimental sergeant-major.'

'And what did they have to offer that I have not?' he asked.

And before Laverton could say 'guts,' I cut in again.

200

'They were *men*,' I emphasised. 'And I respected them.'

'Oh! And what am I?' he demanded, riding his dignity on a tight rein.

Well, he asked for it, and Laverton was not to be out-manoeuvred indefinitely.

'A louse!' he said. 'And I should like to put my foot on your neck!'

We were half way to the camp sergeant-major's office before I stopped bubbling inside.

'You ought not to have said that, Richard,' I reproved. 'The blighter will probably put us on a charge –'

'No he won't. Can you imagine him admitting to being called a louse? Too many people already know that for his comfort… Let us see if the sergeant-major can give us any news of John.'

He could, but it was not comforting.

John was on the up country party that was leaving the following day. Up country from now on meant anywhere between Nong Pladuk and Burma without reference to the compass.

From both those two points the railway was pushing out like a finger of doom that already had chosen its first victims. And John was going out into that tangle of jungle, hill, and swamp through which it must force a way, if it were to meet, and so put an ultimate crown on the strivings of the men who would work on it.

'Is there any chance of us going on the party, sergeant-major?'

'Not tomorrow. Is Sommers a friend of yours?'

'Yes. I should like to go with him…'

'I can't do anything about that, but I should not worry. Your party will be going to Kanburi in a week or so.'

'Where is that?'

'Next camp up the line. About 30 miles – if you can get there. I don't know where exactly tomorrow's party is going, but it will probably be in the Kanburi area, and in that case you will be seeing Sommers. In the meantime you will be working in this camp or at Ashimoto's – that is the camp beyond the station. Take my advice and keep away from the Koreans – they are not drawing-room pets by any means, and some of the Nips are equally undomesticated…'

'Smithy does not seem to have exaggerated, Richard,' I said as we went back to our hut. 'Nong Pladuk is no home from home, in spite of that feed we have just had. We shall have to keep our wits about us, I can see that.'

'I wonder what it will be like on the railway, Mick. You know, I think I am going to like the job.'

'Me, too, especially if the grub remains the way it is. But don't forget, once we make a start there will be no holidays until the job is finished. That is, of course, unless we fall sick, and I hope that does not happen.'

'How is Terry?'

'He went into the hospital, and I think he will be all right when he has a couple of weeks' rest and some food.'

'He's a queer kid – ought to be at home with his mother…'

'That's the unfortunate part about it. There are just the two of them – father died when he was a nipper, and he is likely to do the same. Damned shame… Oh, well, what about a kip until John comes in from work? Good old John. I shall be glad to see him again, though it is a nuisance he is going away tomorrow.'

'You and John are pretty close, aren't you, Mick?'

'Yes, I guess we are. We were together all through the scramble in Malaya, and got to know each other well. John is a dependable sort, if you know what I mean.'

'I know, but I am not so conservative as you. I make more friends, though perhaps it does not profit me any. They are not all so dependable as John and you, Mick…'

'Thanks for the bouquet, Richard, and we must not leave Smithy out of this. If we stick together things should work out all right.'

'Do you think we shall have a better chance of getting away now?'

'Well, at least we have come the first thousands miles by train, and that is a big help, Richard. Another thousand should put us within shouting distance of the nearest British outpost, but John will probably know more about that than I do at the moment. Let's wait until he comes in.'

Sleeping space in the huts was strictly apportioned, the wooden floors being utilised as communal beds on which the men slept in individual plots approximately 6 feet by 4 feet. Each plot was "owned" by the man who slept on it, but there was nothing individualistic about the bugs. Once they were introduced into a hut, they spread with remarkable rapidity, and were not unduly concerned about whom they visited at night.

These live, I found, were more the stay-at-home type – especially if one had a comfortable bed. They liked a bit of comfort and were not satisfied with the cracks in the floor boards. Besides, it was draughty underneath the huts, which were raised about 4 feet from the ground, making an admirable meeting place for the local pi-dogs, who came through the fence at night to add the sound effects to the nightmare of sleep.

That came later, however. The pi-dogs were too wary to make a racket during the day without the disturbing influence of the moon to undermine their mongrel cautiousness and the bugs, though they did their best, could not keep me awake without outside assistance.

I slept and dreamed again of John battling with the two dead gunners for an empty brandy bottle, and awoke to find him standing there with a smile on his face.

'John!'

'Mick! It's good to see you! I was beginning to despair of you coming in time...'

'But I have arrived, John. And you are not nearly so glad to see me as I you. It feels like an age since I saw you last. Thank goodness we shall not be separated for so long next time The sergeant-major tells me my party will be going to Kanburi in a couple of weeks; then we can get moving with our plans... I've got a map, John!'

'Good! But be sure you don't lose your head on account of it; the Nips are not encouraging to would-be escapees. However, we'll talk about that later – I must have a wash. We get water from the well in the square –'

'I know. I have filled a bucket...'

'That's fine. It's just like old times, having you here. I wish I was not going away tomorrow –'

'You wish I were going with you, you mean. And don't I, too. We can't do anything about it, I suppose?'

'I'm afraid not. The names of all the men on the party will be in the Nip office – they watch that sort of thing.'

'We shall just have to wait then, and hope for the best... This water is damned cold.'

'Just what you need after a day working in the sun. I sweat a hell of a lot. Still, that is a good thing, I believe. You look mighty stringy, Mick. Haven't they been feeding you at Changi?'

'Things have not been too good there for a long while. Not enough food and too many mouths. There will be hard times in Singapore and Malaya, John.'

'We should worry! All our chaps will be coming to work on the line. Let the Malayans have a taste of the Nips' Co-prosperity Sphere. Do them a lot of good. Which reminds me – have you heard any more about that Chinese chap – what's his name? Nai Soon?'

'Yes. I met him in Singapore, and what do you think?'

'I don't pretend to know.'

'He has an absolutely stunning sister!'

'Mick!'

'I don't mean in that way. You never saw anything like her, John. Do you remember that doll I had when we first came to Changi? Well, she is something like that come to life, only she is more perfect in every detail. She has an exquisite beauty that is somehow unreal and makes you feel she might break if you got hold of her.'

'And did you?'

'No. But I held her hand. Such a beautiful hand, too.'

'Mick?'

'Yes?'

'Are you romancing?'

'Of course not. Say Leen – that's her name, but we call her Little Flower – is absolutely perfect. In fact, she is too perfect – she could be too easily broken.'

'That sounds almost fatherly.'

'It is meant to be. She is only a kid, John, and you know what these damned Japs, or Nips, are once they get their mischievous hands on anything worth looking at.'

'I know what you mean, and I hope they never get the opportunity of plucking your Little Flower – though, why that? Doesn't Say Leen mean Western Lily? I knew a girl with that name in Alor Star.'

'You were not the only one. Most of the battalion knew her; though, strangely enough, she was not a *bint*. If you ever meet this other Say Leen you will see why I called her Little Flower.'

'I hope I do, Mick. She should be good to look at, and I always did like pretty things. Lord knows, there is not much glamour about this life…'

Here, I thought, is competition for Terry Reynolds, and I did not want that, however close I might be to John. He could stand on his own feet without the inspiring stimulus of Say Leen's fresh beauty – so in affinity with Terry's artistic temperament – to prop him up. I should have to watch that if they ever came together, which was unlikely. Indeed, it was unlikely any of us would

204

ever see Little Flower again but, while the possibility remained, she was Terry's by right of necessity.

That was the way I wanted it… and that was the way it should be…

With roll-call behind us, and the quiet dusk of the coming night falling over the camp, we talked of yesterday and the day before, coming by easy stages to tomorrow and the future!

'Have you had any contact with the Thais, John, since you have been here?'

'No more than anyone else. Of course, we are not supposed to contact them at all but we do, obviously. Most of the Nips are not very strict about that sort of thing, and allow us to buy fruit and whatever else is going. There are exceptions, of course, as Smithy will tell you –'

'He has had a beating, hasn't he?'

'Yes. A couple. And I'm sorry about that. Not just because he was beaten, but because of the effect it has had on him. You know how easy-going and inoffensive he used to be – well, he has changed a good deal. He's a different chap from the old Smithy who used to fish with us at Changi.'

'That is one of the things one has to guard against in the life, John. Ill-treatment, hard work, squalor, disease, and insufficient food are a strong combination to fight. I am not surprised Smithy should be losing his good-natured inoffensiveness. The four of us must try and get together as we were at Changi in the early days. If you can keep an eye on him until Laverton and I join you at Kanburi, we will have a shot at getting away, if things are favourable.'

'That reminds me, Mick. You must be careful with that map of yours. Should the Nips have a search and find it, anything might happen. Don't get careless just because you fooled them once – the picture postcards might not work next time.'

'I'm not giving them the chance, unless I have to. The map is buried in a piece of bamboo beneath the hut…'

'Good. Keep it there, and don't tell too many about it.'

'You and Nai Soon might be brothers, John. Your counsels have a great similarity and, listening to them, I count myself lucky to have such friends…'

'Don't start getting sentimental, Mick – not tonight. Let us be practical instead. For a start, I'll make a wager you have no money.'

'You're on a dead cert – only dead is not the word.'

'As I thought. Well, this will start you off. It belongs to Ashimoto really, so you need to have no qualms about accepting it.'

'This' was twenty Thai dollars, the first I had seen, and I did not attempt to argue with John – his generosity was too well established in my recollection for that.

'Thanks, John. What is the racket?'

'Ashimoto's. That's the camp over the way. Sort of general repairs shop and junk heap combined. Ashimoto is the Nip officer in charge – hence Ashimoto's. You'll find if you go there on a working party, that there are numerous opportunities for adding to your twenty-five cents a day, and the Thais will buy practically anything. First of all, though, they will be wanting the clothes off your back. I wouldn't sell if I were you, Mick; the Nips are not over-generous with replacements. Another thing… Don't get caught scabbing Ashimoto's belongings – he won't like it; neither will you if you are caught! But I need not tell you that; you have not that lust for acquiring easy money that gets so many of the fellows into trouble…'

'It's not lust, John. It's just commonplace necessity.'

'I don't agree with you. After all, what is lust but greed? Some men lust after money, while others with sufficient money – if that is possible – lust after women or some other commodity. They are both equally greedy.'

'Is this a practical argument, John?'

'Well, yes. It tends to emphasise the fact that necessity should be tempered with caution. In other words, be not over-lustful or greedy when the time comes for you to despoil Ashimoto of some of the loot he has cabbed from Malaya and Singapore. And, too, don't look for sympathy from our people should you be caught. They do not encourage scabbing… Well, Mick. I think I'll have a couple of hours' kip – got to be on the move about four. Shall we say good-bye in case I do not see you again before I go?'

'It's not a nice word, that – good-bye. Let's just make it 'Cheerio' or something equally indefinite. I wish you were not going, John, but as you are, look after yourself, and I shall be counting the days until I join you at Kanburi.'

'Cheerio, Mick. It's been great seeing you again, and I wish you were coming with me even though you are looking very pensive with the moon in your eyes. You are thinking something may happen to me, aren't you?'

'As usual, you are right. But I don't suppose it will; you are capable of looking after yourself, John.'

'Of course I am. And I have got Smithy to help me out. You have Laverton, so that we are equally divided. When we are united again we must make tracks out of this damn country. Good night, Mick.'

206

'Cheerio, John – and God be with you…'

He was gone when I came on to the *pedang* in the morning, and for me there was little beauty in the sunrise that flamed in the eastern sky. As I watched, unimpressed, the guardroom came to life and the chanting of the Nips reiterating their determination to die tomorrow was a promise to Hirohito, and a benediction for John…

Chapter Eighteen

The Flag is Waved

John's picturisation of Ashimoto's was lacking in one essential: it made no provision for that national characteristic which is the backbone of Dai Nippon – the ability to make something out of nothing. Here, where one would have expected to find mechanisation at its best, was instead a conglomeration of broken machinery and assorted junk that would not have been given storage space in a British Army workshop, let alone be expected to provide essential parts for such an undertaking as the Burma Line. Practically all the equipment – including the junk – was loot from Singapore and Malaya. Most of the machinery in the camp had parts missing or broken, and these had been replaced with substitutes made, for the most part, by the prisoner technicians who staffed the camp and executed nearly all of Ashimoto's skilled assignments.

By doing that they made a worthwhile contribution to the Greater East Asia Co-prosperity Sphere from which they could never hope to derive any great benefit, no matter which way the cat jumped – not that any of the prisoners harboured any doubts about the animal's ultimate destination. That is one of the odd things about our British complacency: no matter what catastrophe may overtake us, eventual resurrection is never in doubt and, doubtless, that explains why Ashimoto and his kind never had any difficulty in getting skilled labour when it was required.

Ashimoto might be described as a moderate Nip. By that I mean he did not find any amusement in ill-treating the men who worked for him but, on the other hand, like so many of his kind, he was not particularly interested in the way his staff conducted themselves. Had he been more concerned for our welfare, he would have discovered that many of his subordinates were over-bearing and intolerant – which is another way of saying they were just plebeian Nips – and inclined to the belief that face slapping was their prerogative by right of divine mandate. This sort of thing, however, was usually taken for granted, and was soon forgotten after the initial sting of humiliation had worn off. But Ashimoto's men did not confine themselves to that typical Nip gesture, the *smack, smack* on either cheek, designed not to hurt, but to humiliate. On occasion prisoners were severely beaten for no other reason than an inability to understand an order, or because the Nip concerned was in a cantankerous mood.

Coupled with the high handedness of the Koreans, these all too frequent incidents at Ashimoto's kept Nong Pladuk Camp in a state of uncertainty and suspense. Complaints were made daily to the Nip Commandant, who shrugged his shoulders expressively and made no attempt to put a stop to our ill-treatment. Like Ashimoto, he was concerned only with getting a job of work done, and if in the doing of it we got slightly scalded, why that, surely, was our affair.

Happily, our commanding officer was first a man, and secondly an officer. When it was becoming evident that personal abuse was to be a permanent feature of the camp he sent an ultimatum to the Nip Commandant, who must have been considerably intrigued by such an unprecedented gesture.

It is easy to visualise how this manifesto must have been received in Nip headquarters. To a people who put a literal interpretation on any order from a superior, the presumption of our commanding officer in assuming he could influence their conduct by an implied threat was, in the circumstances, ludicrous and unworthy of notice.

Who were we to question how the soldier of Dai Nippon exercised their mandate? Were we not yet aware that we owed our miserable lives to the restraint imposed on those soldiers by a merciful, and forgiving, high command? Were we so debased in honour that we could not yet realise that every moment of continued existence was a reproach and a condemnation – a lasting reminder that we had failed in our appointed task and, failing, had lacked the courage to wipe out our dishonour by self-immolation?

Having failed in so much, why grow indignant about so little? Thus reasoned the Nip mind, shrugging our preposterous ultimatum into the wastepaper basket. Apart from the ethics of such a document, we were in no position to make threats.

Down, dog, and know thy master.

But British hardihood was not yet cowed into final subjection. It still had one champion willing to wave the flag and order a rally around it.

Two days after the ultimatum went into the Nip office, another man was beaten for some imagined offence, and our commanding officer went into action, and, obeying his instructions, every man in the camp stood fast after morning roll-call on the day following the incident, refusing to fall-in in the usual working parties preparatory to marching out of camp.

When this happened there was a momentary lull of uncertainty, during which the Nips tried to digest the fact that we had gone on strike. Then, their easily aroused excitement catching alight, they commenced to scream and shout, and to rush about the camp as though the Yanks were coming down the line.

Almost immediately an emergency call went out to the other camps in the vicinity. Armed Nips came hurrying to reinforce our guards, hoping, perhaps to overawe us and so make us repent before it was too late – which it already was.

Determined as was our revolt, it was entirely passive, though one shot would have turned the camp into a shambles. I think, too, had a shot been fired, or had anyone been bayonetted, we should not have come off second best in the ensuing free-for-all, in spite of our unarmed state.

Obviously, the inevitable outcome, whatever the result of a fight between us and the guards, would have been disastrous. At the time, however, no one had a thought for that eventuality; everyone was keyed to a fine pitch of excitement, and the fight, had it come, would have been welcomed.

Facing us with fixed bayonets advanced threateningly, the Nips ordered us repeatedly to fall in for work, and when no one made any attempt to obey, their excitement and dismay – which in a Nip produce the same effect – mounted to such a pitch, they quickly became unintelligible even to themselves and kept shouting orders and counter orders as though they were temporarily bereft of their senses.

And they were. Such a thing had never happened before in their recollection, and now that they were face to face with it they had no idea what to do.

When eventually it became apparent we were not going to give way to threats, the Nip Commandant tried a new approach. Picking out all our officers, he had them taken to one of the huts and locked in, apparently with some idea of breaking our resistance.

He thought, perhaps, we would weaken when the guiding spirits of the revolt were removed.

In that he was mistaken. Immediately after the officers disappeared into the hut, we began to realise for the first time just what good fellows they were – without exception. And when a rumour – started God knows where – to the effect that the officers were going to be shot got into circulation, an audible sigh of expectancy ran through the ranks; then, suddenly, it was very quiet in spite of the shouting of the Nips. Everyone was tensed, waiting for something to be said; some word of command in an English voice to break the ache of waiting and throw us into berserk action.

As we waited, many of the men were trembling, and my knees were knocking together as though I had a bout of malaria coming on. But it was nor malaria; neither was it fear that made the others tremble. It was suspense, extreme and acute, and worse than any fear.

The suspense of waiting for the first shot, or the first scream from the hut into which the officers had disappeared, as a bayonet went into shrinking flesh, was awful in its intensity. It was an eternity of time crammed into a few minutes, and then it was all over. No shot came, nor any scream other than the bestial gibbering of the Koreans which we scarcely heard. Then in a moment we were back on solid ground with the quicksands of suspense and uncertainty behind us, having gained a moral victory that brought little material benefit in its wake.

However ineffectual our gesture of defiance in the long term, it reflected credit on the man who initiated it, and was neutralised only because it was isolated. Had there been more senior officers with his courage, conditions in many of the working camps along the railway could have been greatly improved; also British prestige need never have been ground into the dust to the extent it was...

*****

Stooping quickly, Laverton scooped up a handful of sand, and, when the last grains had trickled into the oil drum, he screwed on the cap, pushed the drum over and let it roll down the runway to the men waiting for its arrival.

'O.K.' he shouted. 'That is the last one. Tell the Nip...'

All day for two weeks we had been doing that, and now the last of the damaged oil drums had been emptied, and Ashimoto was the owner of hundredweight of sand which, in due course, would play its little part in further impairing the over-worked Nip transport in Thailand, or perhaps Burma if we were particularly lucky.

'What is the Nip for sixteen, Mick?' Laverton wanted to know as he wiped his oil hands on the seat of his shorts, forgetting that these days he was doing his own laundering. 'Matsumo will want to know how many we have done this morning.'

'*Jiu-roku*. You ought not to have taken this *hancho's* job if you cannot remember your numbers. It will get you into trouble one of these days... Look out – here he comes!'

212

Matsumo, the corporal in charge of Ashimoto's petrol and oil dump, was another unpredictable Nip conundrum with a mean look in his short-sighted eyes which his think-lensed spectacles could not hide. On occasions, he was amiable and inclined to be garrulous in so far as his slight knowledge of English would allow. More often, he was moody and given to sudden outbursts of temper that vented themselves on anyone who happened to be near at hand.

A barometer to Matsumo's temperament during the two weeks it took us to overhaul the petrol dump, the sand in the drums increased or decreased dependent on whether he was amiable or bad tempered. Had anyone been sufficiently interested he would have found upon an inspection of the drums that the corporal had been in a vile temper most of the time.

In so far as his inability to foresee our probable reaction to his temperamental outbursts was concerned, Matsumo was typical of his race. Unable to appreciate the fact that we, as prisoners, did not consider it an honour to work for Hirohito, Matsumo viewed our bondage – as did most of his countrymen – through the clouded lenses of his own reaction to a like state of existence.

To serve the Emperor in whatever way fate decreed was the guiding principle of his life and, to him, our efforts were but a small return for the signal honour that had been conferred on us when we, too, were given the opportunity of furthering the ambitious programme of expansion sanctioned by the Son of Heaven. It was unthinkable, therefore, that we should be so dishonourable as to perform any act that did not serve the best interests of His Imperial Majesty. Working it out that way – if, indeed, he ever thought of it – Matsumo supplied both the incentive and the opportunity for us to do a spot of internal sabotage, secure in his belief that we were honourable men – in so far as our debt to Hirohito was concerned – and keenly conscious of that debt.

Poor Matsumo! We were well aware of that debt, but our method of assessing it was somewhat different from his. How scandalised he would have been had he known we actually got a kick out of insulting his Emperor though, frankly, our little disloyalties were not directed at that old gentleman, so much as at his representatives nearer at hand. If these were sufficiently old-fashioned to believe that an affront to His Majesty was implied every time we broke a shovel, or any other article, that was their misfortune.

Who were we to attempt to give them a more modern outlook? Indeed, even to suggest it was both foolhardy and reckless – something Laverton might attempt when he got annoyed which, for his own comfort, was happening too frequently. One day he would get a hell of a hiding and wonder why, having not yet realised that the Nips are the only people on earth whom no other race

213

can fully understand.

Watching Matsumo approach, Laverton was prepared to react according to the Nip's mood, forgetting that in all probability the corporal would change so quickly from sunshine to rain, Laverton would not have time to get his umbrella up.

Matsumo was happy now, that much was evident as he came along, notebook in hand, pleased to be able to write off another job as completed.

'Finished-ka?' he asked in a satisfied voice that ignored the pools of oil saturating the ground over a wide area. I had wondered about so much obvious waste, and expected another outburst of petulance from Matsumo, but nothing like that happened. The job was finished and he was satisfied. Now he could write down the relevant information in his little book, and hope Ashimoto would give him a pat on the back instead of a swipe across the face.

'Finished-*ka*?' he repeated as Laverton, an unwilling hancho, marshalled his Nipponese.

'*Hie. Jiu-roku* O.K. *Hachi dame dame*......'

'*Hachi dame dame ka*? No good!' muttered Matsumo, not liking the information that for the sixteen full drums we had eight empty ones.

'All right,' said Laverton truculently, unable to be diplomatic. 'Count them. *Ichi, ni, san, chi, go, roku, shichi, hachi.* I speak O.K.', and he waved a hand in a gesture that signified 'bloody fool!'

At that Matsumo's geniality went out like a light. Laverton's implication that he was being a bit of a silly bugger not to believe the evidence of his own eyes, even though they were short-sighted, did not go down well.

'You no speak O.K.!' he shouted, and Laverton got a swipe across the face to teach him to be more tolerant of intolerance and not to over-reach himself.

'Steady, Richard!' I warned as out discomfited *hancho* was about to catch alight. 'Keep your shirt on! I should not like to see you go back to camp on a stretcher.' And to Matsumo, who was inspecting the empty drum to make sure they were empty:

'Gasolene *hachi nie*. Gasolene *go* – oil *san*...'

Assured that only five of the empties were petrol drums – petrol being apparently more precious than crude oil – the Nip grunted a grudged 'O.K.' and a reluctant '*yasumi*,' and went off to his store shed to make the necessary alterations in his petrol account.

'I'd like to strangle that bastard!' growled Laverton, rubbing his cheek where the Nip's hand had left a dirty mark. Then questioningly, he added:

'What did I do wrong, Mick? I always seem to put my foot in it when I try to explain something.'

'Psychologically the Nips are a maze of unpredictable emotions, Richard. I doubt if there are a dozen people in the world who thoroughly understand them. As you may have noticed, a number of our fellows imagine that by pandering to their over-bearing vanity they will keep them in a good humour. I personally do not agree with that line of approach. Even a Nip is quite capable of knowing when he is being patronised and, like anyone else, is apt to get fed up of it. Another mistake very often made, and one which earns a large percentage of our chaps a swipe across the face, is the habit of anticipating what a Nip wants when you are doing a job for him. You know what I mean – I've seen you get clouted for it often...'

'You mean finishing a job without waiting for detailed instructions?'

'Yes. When a Nip gives anyone a job, he likes to feel he is absolutely indispensable to the accurate completion of that job. For instance, if he wants you to dig a hole in the road and tells you to do so, and then disappears for a couple of hours, leaving you to get browned off waiting for him to come back, he is more likely to give you a clout than a pat on the back when he does return and you have completed the job without waiting for precise instructions. You see, it gives him a feeling of superiority if you allow him to believe you are helpless without his personal supervision. Of course, that usually does not apply if you are constantly working under the same Nip and get to know his peculiarities.'

'Silly lot of blighters!'

'That's as it may be. But you simply must make allowances, Richard, otherwise you will be running up against trouble every day – and that is not necessary at this stage of the game.'

'All right. Give me some more psychology.'

'I don't know even if it is that. But I have found one sure way of getting out of a tight corner, though I must admit it is a devil of a job to bring it off in time to avoid trouble when it starts brewing.'

'Tell me about it. I can see the Nips eating out of my hand – almost!'

'If a Nip is going to give you a hiding for some offence, imagined or otherwise, try to make him laugh. If you succeed, which is unlikely, you will be damned unlucky if you get a bashing...'

'I'm afraid that sort of technique is not up my alley, Mick. I'd probably make a muck up of it and get a worse hiding than if I just told him to go to hell and left it at that!'

'I agree. You are too damned impetuous. I think you had better try an alternative approach – one that suits your temperament better.'

'I know the one I should like to stick to.'

'That's just it. You are too self-assertive, Richard. And you lack finesse, which is indispensable if the former quality is to operate with any hope for success. It is no use telling the Nips, by the attitude you adopt, that you do not give a damn for their way of thinking, if you do not know when to be assertive and when to be diplomatic…'

'You mean, I suppose, I am too aggressive for my humble station?'

'Well, something like that. Usually, the Nips will respect the *hancho* of a party or, for that matter, the C.O. of a camp, who makes them understand he is not to be intimidated by their shouting. That does not mean, of course, that you can ride your high horse over their emotionalism without giving a thought to their point of view, and expect at the same time to negotiate all your fences.'

'Do you know what I think, Mick?'

'I might guess.'

'Don't bother. I'll tell you. You are just being kind, thinking, perhaps, I would not appreciate your telling me I am not of the stuff that makes good *hanchos*. Well, I already know that, and if I were in a position to speak my mind, that sod Matsumo and a few others would know it too. What we need is another show-down, Mick.'

'Yes, but think of your pal, the White Tojo. He must have had a fright last time. You would not put him through the same ordeal again surely?'

'That blighter,' said Laverton, in an unkind voice, forgetting Matsumo. 'I have more respect for some of the Nips – not many, mind you, but one or two. Still one must not be too critical, I suppose. The White Tojo is unfortunate in being the servant of his fear and not master of his conscience…'

'Aiming high, aren't you, Richard? Or have you got it inside out?'

'Just what do you mean by that crack?'

'Well, if a man were master of his conscience, I should think he could do just as he wished. In other words, he would not have a conscience to worry about.'

'Oh, shit! You know what I mean. Why quibble?'

'Why indeed! There goes the *meshi* bell, and here comes the *ocha* boy…'

*****

216

Leaving Nong Pladuk's dog kennel station, the new line had the experienced companionship of an elder brother, until they parted company in an ever-widening "V" outside the town of Bam Pong, three miles from the base camp. From the apex of the "V" the old line went on its way unconcerned and assured until it skipped across the river at Ratburi, twenty odd miles distant. About its youngest relative there was none of this assurance; every kilometre beyond Bam Pong was essayed tentatively, and at times unwillingly, and before it also gained the river, it had overcome a multitude of obstacles which provided a comprehensive analysis of what was to come before it acquired the age of maturity.

Along the first half mile of the new line, men from the camp we were leaving were giving the finishing touches to the thing they had created, and, watching them as we waited for the train that was to take us to Kanburi, I was envious of their industry and anxious to start on the new venture that was to take me to John and, I hoped, my happy adventure.

Later, I was to envy them for another reason, and to wish I was back at Nong Pladuk where, at least, there was a certainty of three meals a day, and the supreme comfort of having a roof over one's head in the rainy season. Where I was going there was not that certainty, though I gave no thought to that at the time. I was too concerned with the present and the immediate future to be bothered by uncertainties and the voice of rumour. Time would reveal what lay round the bend at the end of the first half mile.

The sooner our train arrived, the sooner would we be able to appreciate or disparage the workmanship of the men who had gone before us.

With the train's arrival, hours after our early breakfast had ceased to be even a memory, there arrived also a thought to which Laverton had to give expression.

'How long will it take us to get to Kanburi?' he asked, looking at a Thai girl who was hanging about in the background, hoping some of us would find sufficient incentive to brave our guards' displeasure by buying her bananas.

Well, it is about thirty miles. If we travel at even the speed of the Rocket we ought to get there in time for supper.'

'It's possible we might not make even that average speed. I have been hearing things about this railway, Mick, and don't forget, we have not been issued with any grub for the journey.'

'No, but Terry got me some nice *lagi* rice from the hospital, and there are some nice-looking bananas behind you. Go and ask that Nip for a light while I get a bunch...'

Her patience being thus rewarded, the Thai girl gave me twenty-five bananas for twenty cents and these, with the rice provided by the thoughtful and pensive Terry who was not yet sufficiently recovered to join us, would bridge the gap between too early a breakfast and an uncertain dinner.

After a good deal of shouting and swearing, in which the Nips played a starring rôle, we were all packed into the open trucks on top of six inches of coal dust, with standing room only and no home comforts for the journey.

And what a journey!

Laverton's premonition that we might not equal the speed average of Stephenson's Rocket was no misconception, but even he could have had no idea that we were off on a journey which, for slowness in railway history, has probably never been equalled. Sweaty and begrimed with the coal dust that rose in clouds from beneath our feet, we waved good-bye to the men working in the station as we reached the bend that hid our future and, in a moment, our past.

It was there beyond the bend the railway really began. That first half mile was a snare: it gave a promise of achievement and an assurance of stability that were premature and unwarranted.

It advertised the fact that the new line had got off to a flying start, conveniently overlooking the fact that it was a sprinter. Even now, with Bam Pong not in sight, its acceleration was slowing down, and it had begun to stagnate and to feel itself unable to maintain the quality of its initial effort. Furthermore, it was not amenable towards our heavy train, and to show its resentment it hid itself in the rich soil of the *padi*, which had been laboriously excavated to provide its right of way, and refused to co-operate.

Beyond Bam Pong the line looked like a boa constrictor with convulsions, and along it the train meandered, held upright by the proverbial luck of the Nips that always seemed to come to the fore when it was most needed. It would have been much easier for the train to have run down the embankment into the *padi* which, I felt sure, was yearning for it. Had it done that, all its troubles, and many of ours, would have been over and done with. But our train was a good Nipponese: it refused to take the easy way out and we went on our way breathlessly, and with an ache of expectancy as we waited for the crash that must come no matter how long it was delayed.

Frequently the train rested by the way as if to gain strength for its next assault on the half buried track beneath its begrimed feet, and each time it did that one of the guards climbed out to inspect that part of the track visible above the mud. Probably he guessed at the remainder. If so, his guesses were usually accurate, for when the train took another tentative step forward it found the

218

rails, burrowed in and hidden from the sun which in time would turn the mud of the embankment into a good ersatz concrete.

Occasionally the guard could not make up his mind – or else he was not prepared to hazard a guess – that the line actually existed. When that happened, he assumed a look of extreme knowingness, put on for our benefit. Then he muttered a lot of unintelligible gibberish as a further proof of his ability to cope with the situation. At other times he reacted in a more orthodox fashion and cursed the line as though it were a living thing – one of us, for instance – to be brought to heel by invective.

But curses had little effect on the Burma Line. They left it cold in its bed of mud as, swearing and muttering doubtful compliments to the men who had laid it there, the guard clambered back on to the engine, and the train essayed another step forward until eventually the inevitable happened, and we had to join the blaspheming Nips on the muddy embankment. Then, truck by truck, the train was man-handled over the particularly bad spots. Just how bad those oozing muck heaps were, I have no idea. It was all putrid, the whole stinking, shifting thirty miles of it, if one overlooks the decoy half mile between Nong Pladuk and the bend, now ten miles and a day behind us. And to every one of those miles we had contributed a bucketful of sweat and ten thousand cosmopolitan curses.

Maybe the curses were not literally cosmopolitan, but they were at least a mixture of Scots, English, Irish, Welsh, and Cockney, not to mention Nipponese and Korean, plus all the commonplace swear words picked up by the more travelled of our party who had been in India, China, the Sudan, and other outposts of the Empire, before coming to play trains with the Nips on the Burma Line.

Late in the evening of our first day's endeavouring to reach Kanburi, now ten miles nearer, the half-dozen Nips on the train threw in the towel. Metaphorically washing their hands of the train and everyone on it, they went off across the *padi* in search of a *kampong* in which to spend the night, and we were left to curse afresh and with a new vigour. There was no food and, now that there was nothing to keep our minds off such trivialities, everyone began to realise how hungry he was.

Drinking water, too, was minus. During the struggle to keep the train moving, every drop had been used, most of it turning into sweat as soon as it went down our gullets. Now we had no sweat left…

An added irritant was the refusal of our Old Mother Hubbards, travelling in comparative comfort at the rear of the train, to broach the "reserve" rations which were carried about with every party on the move. These rations – usually a couple of sacks of rice and any tinned kit available – were for an emergency. That, in our opinion, had arrived but Captain Bell, lying on his camp bed in luxurious idleness, was not in agreement with our thought processes. Tomorrow was another day, and there would be no food that night.

It was then I began to bless Terry Reynolds for his foresight. What mattered it that the rice was sour and the sweet potato I had not known about was covered in coal dust? With Laverton I could have a meal and forget trouble until tomorrow. Then, too, there were the half-dozen bananas that remained of the original twenty-five. We two, at least, should not go hungry to bed.

First, however, we had to get off the train onto which everyone had clambered before the Nips departed into the night, leaving us unprotected against Captain Bell and his bureaucratic tendencies. Now, as we made a concerted move to scramble out of the trucks, an order arrived from the captain, who had not yet put in an appearance, to the effect that no one was to leave the train other than for 'the purposes of nature.'

Obviously we had no intention of turning our packed quarters into a latrine, even had there been sufficient room to squat down. Neither did we intend remaining on the train all night in order to satisfy the egoistical stupidity of Captain Bell, or any other damned fool in a position to issue orders which were sufficiently inept to be disregarded, and which ran counter to our new franchise. If Captain Bell and his fellow nitwits were not yet aware that we had gained that franchise by reason of our presence on the Burma Line, if for no other reason, it was time they were made aware of it.

It was time, too, they realised we were an entirely new creature from the embryonic caterpillar that had struggled to get out of its chrysalis of convention at Changi. If they were minded still to issue orders and mandates as in the days before the Rising Sun went up over Fort Canning, we were no longer in a receptive mood. All that sort of thing had gone overboard as soon as we rounded the bend below Nong Pladuk station, and so far as we were concerned it would never be salvaged.

In the new life that was before us there would be no place for petty tyranny. We should be having a surfeit of that sort of thing from the Nips – only it would not be petty. All classes and creeds would have to sink their individual egos if we were to survive as a party. No minority, whether by reason of mandate, or of personal opinion, should have the right to impose its tyranny on the mass of its fellows. Every one of us had his life in his own keeping. Even greater than that, he had the lives of his fellows to think about, and that was a big responsibility.

220

To hell then with the bullshit and red tape! Bury them in the stink of the padi, and shed no tears of sorrow on their slimy graves and in the meantime, let us get out of this bloody train in which we have been cooped close as sardines in any tin. If the gentlemen at the rear have not sufficient interest in our welfare to get out of their coach and acquaint themselves with the hardship their order to remain on the train entails, why should we encourage them in their bloody foolery?

Through this process of reasoning our initial browned-off-ness and feeling of hunger were supplanted by the urge to revolt against someone, and Captain Bell was the most obvious objective. Disregarding his order, we began to clamber off the train, much to the increased dismay of our sergeant-major, who had been acting as runner, relaying orders and counter orders from the State coach. In a last effort to preserve unity, this poor man made another trip to the rear, where authority was still reclining on its camp bed, blissfully unaware there was a volcano beneath it. This time he was successful. Captain Bell agreed to our getting off the train, but we were not on any account to wander away from the railway.

This concession came too late to be of any use, as the train was already empty, most of the men having gone off to a nearby banana grove in the hope of getting something to eat, while Laverton and I prepared our supper in the engine's fire-box after which we lay down in comparative comfort and went to sleep...

As the mists of morning began to lift, the Nips came back to the train to find their cargo stretched out along the bunds in the *padi*, in the banana grove, along the track and beneath the train.

With shouts of 'All men no sleep! All men train! Speedo! Speedo!' they brought us yawningly to our feet, and so back to an intense hunger and the realities of misery. But in spite of the Nips' urgency to get underway, our train was not in a hurry.

First, it had to be fed with an enormous quantity of wood before it could be induced to move a mile nearer to Kanburi. The condition of the line was such that it refused to go any farther so that once again we were stranded, and still hungry.

After a cursory inspection of the track and a reiterated '*Dame, dame!*' the Nip corporal in charge ordered:

'All men *meshi*.'

When we chorused '*Meshi nie*,' he raised his eyebrows in disbelief and queried:

'Meshi nie ka?' Adding, by way of emphasis, 'Meshi nie no good. *Dame, dame!*'

'You speak shoko,' he was advised, and ten minutes later the first fire was lit and a party of exuberant water-carriers were on the way to the river, while Captain Bell, prodded into acquiescence by the corporals 'All men *meshi! Bageru!*', was hurriedly unearthing the reserve rations.

Chapter Nineteen

Nice People… and Not so Nice People

Somewhere beyond the hills the day was dying as we arrived at Kanburi station, after a three miles trudge that had its beginning where hope lay buried in the *padi* behind us. In the struggle between our train and the railway, the expectations of the former had not been realised and, carrying our gear, we walked away into the evening with a final curse, leaving the train with its engine leaning over into the padi in the most dejected fashion imaginable.

Plastered with mud, and tired, forgetting for the moment to remember hunger, so glad were we to be rid of the thing that had taken fifty hours to cover thirty miles, we turned a blind eye on its dejection, and listened not to its sizzling plaintiveness. 'Look how I have striven for you,' it seemed to be saying: 'and you reward me with curses and ingratitude…'

Equally fed up, the Nip guard were pleased to get away from the drunken-looking engine. Had it been human they might have beaten it for its inability to achieve the impossible. Certainly they would not have walked away with such an air of finality – such an obvious thankfulness to side-step the suggestion of defeat implied in the train's inability to triumph over the railway, which had squirmed about beneath its weary feet and tricked it into final submission.

Our feet were no less weary as we came into Kanburi, as the sun, in a blaze of glory, mockery, or what you will, went down behind the hills that gave an edge to the flat plain in which the station was being born, leaving us to the unsympathetic Nips and the equally unfriendly night.

From the station a muddy track disappeared beyond the circle of light thrown by the naphtha flares. Braving the darkness which made unfriendly the Thailand Night, we stepped into the mud behind a solitary Nip carrying a home-made lantern in which was stuck a stump of candle – a speck of light that would not stay still, but danced about like a vagrant firefly, sometimes here, sometimes there, and sometimes nowhere...

Along that half mile of track there was enough mud to build a mud house for all the people who live in mud houses. There was nothing special about it: it was just ordinary mud. Yet it was cursed with a curious and, partly, unexplainable abandon in which was an under-lacing of hysteria that gave a clue to the physical and mental exhaustion resulting from the past two days' tussle with the train, and was a pointer also to the uncertainty with which we viewed the immediate future.

Looking back on that night, I feel somehow paternal towards those stumbling, swearing figures trying not to lose sight of a speck of light that seemed always too far ahead no matter how urgently one pressed forward. We were but children in those days, bad tempered and given to mistaken beliefs. Yet real hardship and privation had not yet come our way. We were, that night, tentatively and blasphemously approaching the threshold of despair.

Had anyone suggested such a thing, he would have been howled down for a simpleton; no matter what affliction we should experience in the future it could not be worse than what we had already endured.

That is what we thought – we worldly-wise people who knew so much, yet knew nothing. And that is why I am inclined to feel paternal when I live again in retrospect the days when the ability to curse was not with us any more...

When anyone can curse freely and emphatically for half an hour there is not much physically wrong with him, although he may be quite certain he is undergoing the hardships of a thousand damnations. It is only when the faculty for cursing is no longer there that real hardship and privation have come home to roost.

Perhaps a large slice of our sense of injustice as we stumbled along in the mud was due to the feeling of emptiness and unknownness about us. The appearing and disappearing light ahead was the only sign of life that came through the intense blackness where the trees crowded us close on either hand, and added to the indigo of the night.

That wavering light, seemingly so far away, was our one link with the shoddy civilisation we had left when we abandoned the train. And it had been easy to do that in the light of day, not knowing what lay ahead in the coming night, and no one had felt regretful.

Now I was not sure. The train had had a security about it that only now could be appreciated. Here, in this uneasy night, there was nothing but conjecture, interspersed with curses, and a flicking light which, if it went out, would bring dismay.

224

Thinking that, I wondered if the train were still looking dejectedly after us, or if it had submerged itself into the night and forgotten our impatient curses which were now being expended just as impatiently. Probably nothing so futile as that bothered it, for it was not subject to the fits of depression or of exaltation that assailed the puny mortals who had tried to push it forward over insurmountable obstructions.

Lucky train!

Once the light flickered and disappeared, and instantly we were lost and helpless. There was nowhere to go. To move forward might be to rush upon the fate we felt was waiting for just such an eventuality, while to remain where we were seemed equally risky. What we wanted was the restoration of our light. It meant everything to us, though before its disappearance we had cussed it because of its insistence on remaining so far ahead. Now it had gone and we were helpless and lost.

At Changi, no such feeling of revulsion would have assailed our sensibilities, nor would we have made any noticeable effort to keep up with the light. But here in the unknown Thailand night things were different. Changi was a known and friendly place, made familiar from the years of British occupation which gave it an aura of friendliness that still endured, in spite of its new and alien ownership, and in it there would have been no need for a light to pilot us through the darkness, which there was a friend and a spur to incentive...

Eventually our Nip was fished out of the hole into which he had fallen, and the light shone once more to bring us eventually to the road, which was getting ready to rest after visiting the old town of Kanburi, sitting mellowed with age on the river bank two miles away.

While giving life to the town the river put a period to the road which had been its only competitor until the coming of the railway. Beyond Kanburi it rapidly deteriorated until it petered out at Tardan, twelve miles higher up the river. Here the Thais had endeavoured to continue its life by means of a bamboo bridge, which periodically was swept away, and thence as a jungle track to Burma. Now Japan's intention to open a back door for her troops had relieved the locals of the necessity for maintaining their ineffectual bridge, and gave a hope that the jungle track would one day be equal with the road which ended where it began.

With the feel of that road beneath our feet and the faint silhouette of telegraph wires, we became rejuvenated. Civilisation, though still shoddy and misted by uncertainty, had come back into our lives, making us again secure in ourselves, and ready to sing if need be, and when we came, by accident as it were, upon a dozen camp fires turning the night into friendly star dust, the trials and uncertainties of the past days became as nothing, and we were giants filled with an over-weaning conceit about the future.

Once again there was no yesterday or tomorrow… only today.

Tomorrow came for all that to reveal the fact that our camp, which had looked so cosy in the warm firelight of the night before, was nothing but a huddle of dilapidated tents bounded on one side by the road, and on the other, by the railway and imagination. So far as we, the new arrivals were concerned, the sky was our roof, and the sun our lantern, while plumbing was carried out at the discretion of Captain Bell, and amended as demand necessitated.

Of more immediate interest, however, was the Thai market on the roadside where such luxuries as eggs, sugar, coffee, meat, fruit, and most of their close relations, were to be had for the asking – provided one could pay for them. And in that provision we met temporary frustration which was not appeased by our breakfast, good as it was when compared with an equivalent meal at Changi.

At that time Thailand had not yet begun to feel the effects of the Nip army of occupation, and there was ample food for everybody, including those prisoners who had money to buy it, until one crossed the river at Kanburi and got into the wilderness of hill and jungle where an occasional lone kampong was the only sign of Thai civilisation to be encountered on a day's march. Here there was no surplus and no native vendors to supplement the I.J.A. rations which deteriorated rapidly once Kanburi was left behind.

In the vicinity of the station, however, and in the market outside the camp, there was no scarcity of food but, fortunately for us, the Thais were hungry for other things, things which they had little hope of obtaining other than from us. Theirs was the hunger of man with a full belly and an over-sufficiency of money. Not content with an inner lining of fatness, they hankered for an aura of outward munificence. With little or no hope of replacing their shoddy apparel, they were as hungry for clothing as we were for nourishment. As John had warned at Nong Pladuk, their main object in life appeared to be a determination to acquire every stitch of clothing we possessed. And to that end they put temptation in our path at every turn, being assisted by the elasticity of the Nip non-fraternising orders at the station camp.

Although clothing was a first priority, the Thais were also anxious to buy watches, rings, fountain pens, or anything of value from a diamond to a sewing machine, and nothing barred – provided it was the real thing. To spend time polishing a brass watch chain in the belief that they would accept it at its face

226

value, was to look for disillusionment. However out of touch with our civilisation the Thais may have been, their sense of values was more dependable than ours, and they were not to be duped into believing a glass bead was a diamond.

Not all of us had diamonds or other jewellery to sell, though a surprisingly large number had. These, usually, were the men who had been in a position to help themselves during the scrimmage in Malaya and Singapore, and they were now reaping the reward of their dishonesty – or maybe foresight would be a better word.

Unhappily, I had not been in a position to confiscate any of Malaya's abandoned wealth, and, consequently, had no jewellery to sell. Laverton was equally devoid of adornment though, like me, he was well dressed, and had a surplus of clothing for which the Thais were eagerly waiting, knowing that in time our bellies would prove stronger than our common sense, which whispered of the days around the corner and of cold nights to come.

Conveniently overlooking the fact that we had no money to buy food, the Nips allowed us to patronise the market and, at the same time, warned that anyone caught selling clothing to the Thais would be 'disciplined'.

Futile threat! No one could resist the watermelons, big as footballs, which the Thais paraded before our covetous eyes, nor any of the other things for which our bellies shouted. Very soon there was a regular clothing market established in the jungle lying between the road and a convenient bend of the river, where we were allowed to go in organised bathing parties. Every other bush along the pathway leading from the road to the river concealed a Thai with a wad of dollar bills, which he was anxious to exchange for clothing or, failing that, some trinket of value.

Many of these buyers were youngsters in their teens and some were more immature even than that. But whatever their age, they had one thing in common – an apparently unlimited supply of ready money. Where they got it was nobody's business, and certainly we were not concerned about its origin. As we went along the pathway to the river, youngsters just past the toddling stage came out of the bushes and the long grass to pluck at our clothing and chant, parrot-like:

'How much, Johnnie? How much?'

Faced with such a temptation, it is not surprising that many of the men left camp fully clothed and returned an hour later in a pair of under-pants. Neither is it to be wondered at that an epidemic of thievery was soon in full swing in the camp. Indeed, it had been there before we arrived and, in the circumstances, was inevitable…

*****

Where the hills came down to look at the river a half mile above Kanburi town, and twelve miles below Tardan where the road ended, the Mae Khlong was joined at right angles by an equally turbulent tributary that had its origin in the hills where Thailand ended and Burma began. All the way from its rocky cradle to its juncture with the Mae Khlong, this river paralleled the way the railway was to go and, to a great extent, helped it on its way. After mingling its waters with the stream from Tardan, it seemed to forget the railway and the men who worked on it, until it called in at Bam Pong to say good-bye before journeying on to Ratburi and the Pacific.

Just above the confluence of the two rivers the Nips were hoping to build a concrete and steel bridge that would be strong enough to withstand the fury of the Mae Khlong, when the rains came to turn it into a spiteful, tearing monster that annihilated everything in its path and left no doubt as to who was master during the months the monsoon lashed the jungle with its torrential rain.

On the river bank where the bridge was to be built, the Nips had another makeshift camp, where the men working on a temporary wooden bridge were housed. This was Tamakan, and it was here I hoped to contact John, for he was not at Kanburi. During the three days we had been there, Laverton and I had circularised every hut in the area, hoping to locate him and Smithy, but without success. Apparently their party had not stopped at the station, but had gone to Tamakan. This was an unfortunate move as the bridge camp had a bad reputation, mainly on account of the Nip Commandant – a lieutenant named Sasuki – who was reputed to be a bit of a swine. Running Sasuki a close second was a Korean known as the Undertaker, owing to his prosperity for hastening prisoners on the way to the cemetery, and a couple of other degenerates who specialised in making life as unpleasant as possible for the men in the bridge camp.

Apart from the penchant for brutality of Sasuki and his underlings, living conditions were bad at Tamakan, and illness was getting a firm hold on the camp, and as Sasuki's pet aversion was a sick man, many of the invalids were having a bad time.

Sasuki was the principal exponent of the dictum: 'If a man is too ill to work, let him die,' and he practised it religiously. A fat, swaggering bully, he was well-named the 'Pig', and when later I came within his zone of influence, I realised that for once rumour had not been exaggerated.

From Three Pagodas Pass to Nong Pladuk the fat Nip lieutenant was an abomination and a stink in the nostrils of every man who came in contact with him, and was probably instrumental in causing more deaths than any other Nip on the railway. Should John be at Tamakan, he was certainly not enjoying the same luxuries as Laverton and I were enjoying, and I felt mournful about that and disinclined to continue the gluttony of the past three days, during which we had been yasumi-ing, waiting for the Nips to get organised.

It was not nice to think of John and Smithy being ill-treated, and I hoped they had by-passed Sasuki and Tamakan…

Having congratulated ourselves on having set up house – though the building was but a theoretical establishment – at Kanburi, the information that our first job was to be on the wooden bridge over the river was an unappetising entrée to work on the railway.

The Mae Khlong was the first natural major obstruction to the progress of the railway, and the Nips were in a fever to get the bridge completed so that they would not be dependent on the Thai barges which ferried their equipment across the river.

About two hundred yards long and some thirty feet high, the bridge was being built with a minimum of mechanical equipment and when it was completed, to be swept away later when the rains came, it was a triumph of human striving and achievement in the face of almost insurmountable difficulties.

To drive the piles into the river bed a ram was constructed from a great chunk of iron with a hole in its centre. Through this hole ran a perpendicular bar, one end of which rested on the pile and kept the driver in position. Motive power was supplied by the prisoners hauling on the ropes, which hoisted the weight up the bar and then let it fall back on to the pile beneath.

To the accompaniment of the Nips' pile-driving song, '*Ichi, ne, a-si-o*' – the equivalent of our 'one, two, three up!' – the ram ran up and down the guiding bar with the regularity of a well-oiled machine, and slowly and laboriously the bridge grew out of nothing and assumed the proportions of solidity.

As was to be expected on such a job, where speed was the main essential, there were many accidents. Men fell from the scaffolding into the river and were fished out unconscious. Others missed the water and fell on the shingle, where they sustained injuries varying between a broken ankle to a broken back. The Nips, too, had their misadventures. One went into the river and was drowned, but he had himself to blame for that. Had he been more amiable, the vital moments of indecision which cost him his life would not have come between him and rescue. As it was, no one was anxious to go in after him until it was too late; then there was one Nip less at Tamakan.

Coming round a corner with a pile of planks for the bridge, I knocked into a Nip who was going the opposite way in a hurry. He was a big, swarthy individual over average height for a Nip. Actually he was a Korean. Mouthing a stream of gibberish, he set about me with a length of bamboo then, when I dropped the planks I was carrying, he kicked me in the belly, and that was that. Nice chap he was and, though I did not know it at the time, he was the Undertaker – Sasuki's chief rival in meting out ill-treatment to the men in Tamakan.

Though it was not nice to be kicked in the guts for an accidental triviality, I was lucky, and the Undertaker must have been in a comparatively amiable frame of mind. Before then he had put a number of men in hospital for offences less trivial even than mine. Others – well, they went a bit further than the hospital.

Yes, the Undertaker was a nice chap – to keep away from.

Men like him and Sasuki, and countless others with their penchant for cruelty, were responsible for the generally accepted theory that the only good Nip was a dead one. Strictly, this is not correct, though at the same time it is not widely separated from a factual analysis of Nippon character.

Smithy had spoken no less than the truth at Nong Pladuk. There was always the isolated individual among the Nips who was prepared to deal fairly, and even generously, with the prisoners dependent on him for existence. Unfortunately, this type of Nip was too much in a minority to make any appreciable difference to the welfare of the men on the railway. It was Nips like Sasuki and the Undertaker who left their impress wherever they went, not only on us, but on their countrymen. Sasuki was a martinet whose very presence struck terror into the Nips in his command. When he appeared on the railway they became panic-stricken, and ran about shouting and using their bamboos indiscriminately in an endeavour to speed up the job or to give the impression that they were doing their utmost to get the railway forward. It was not necessary even for the burly lieutenant to come among us to create this panic. Standing in the background with a cynical sneer on his full lips, he savoured to the full the effect his presence had on everyone in the vicinity. On the rare occasions he found it necessary to open his mouth to shout an order or an imprecation, every Nip within hearing almost died of heart failure, while we lesser fry experienced a tightening of the inside which was most unpleasant.

With men such as Sasuki to guide their destiny, brutality among the Nips was an inevitable characteristic. Given a better deal in life they might produce a bigger percentage of decent, fair dealing citizens. But when it is understood that the life of the average Nip is one continual round of physical chastisement after he becomes a soldier, his propensity for ill-treating anyone over whom he has authority need not be classed as an ethnological mystery.

Having become a soldier of the Emperor, the young Nip is literally the servant, or toban, of everyone senior to him – and there is always someone no matter how rapidly he may gain promotion. Classed as a one-star private, he starts his military career as a frightened, browbeaten nonentity, being exceedingly fortunate if his initiation is not accompanied by a damn good hiding.

At the end of a gruelling day's training, he has innumerable chores to perform on returning to camp. First, he must bring his superiors their food from the cook-house, only getting his own when their needs are satisfied. After meshi he must attend to the washing-up, and then there is sure to be a pile of soiled clothing to be laundered at the river or nearest well. Only when there is no further call on his services is he at liberty to attend to his own routine jobs, and by that time breakfast is nearly ready.

As a reward for this industry the one-star is knocked about from pillar to post according to the temperament of the men who have two stars or more. During his frequent bouts of chastisement he is expected to stand rigidly to attention and take his beating without complaint. That, of course, goes for everyone in the Nip army regardless of rank.

In the circumstances, it is to be expected that our one-star will in time become case-hardened and, when he qualifies for his second star, will inevitably vent his spleen on anyone of inferior rank to himself. But no matter how high up the military tree he climbs, there is always someone on a high branch waiting to throw rotten fruit.

Yet with all that he is, in my opinion, the best disciplined, and the most conscientious, soldier in the world and, given an equal share of its resources, would stand supreme as a fighting man, acceding the right of way to no one...

Neither John nor Smithy was at Tamakan and, while I was glad of that, I was also disappointed. They had gone on a survey party and might be anywhere in the jungle and hill country between the river and the Three Pagodas Pass leading into Burma.

Thinking later of my reaction to the new of their departure from Tamakan, I was inclined to disagree with the first part of it. There were too many tales of hardship and privation coming back across the river, and though they might not all be true, a percentage of them certainly was. And that was more than enough. Once the river was crossed one stepped, as it were, into a new existence in which civilisation as pertaining to Kanburi and Tamakan, which was on its outer fringe, was present only in so far as the railway brought it, and when the railway was left behind, there was nothing but a wilderness of desolation through which came the occasional *phut-phut-phut* of a Thai barge fighting its way up against the river with a load of rice for the outlying camps.

Now John and Smithy were out there somewhere, as remote from me as if I were still at Changi. There must be another period of waiting, during which anything was likely to happen, before we could hope to be together again. While no one was anxious to cross the river into the hinterland of unknownness beyond there could be no other solution to our problem. But even that would have to wait on our going with a party from Kanburi. It was futile to do as Laverton – growing impatient beneath the whiplash of Sasuki's cynical cruelty – suggested.

On the evening which saw the bridge completed, he came to me and said:

'What are we going to do about contacting John and Smithy?'

'What can we do, Richard?' I said, knowing we could do nothing but wait on fate or, fate failing us, abandon John and Smithy, and strike off on our own. And I did not want to do that: it was too much like betrayal. They had no map or compass, and we had both.

'We might emulate Mohammed,' suggested Laverton.

'We might, but we are not going to – not yet anyway. For one thing, we have no idea where the mountain is, and for another, you can't just walk off into the jungle and hope to achieve anything. If we knew where John and Smithy were, we might take a chance on picking them up, supposing we did leave Kanburi by ourselves and without the formality of asking the Nips' permission. Instead of doing that, I think it is much more advisable to wait until we go with a party, which may be any day now. What do you say?'

He agreed, but reluctantly, and to me there was no joy in his acquiescing to my wishes. Once more the responsibility for our course of action devolved on me, and I was not happy about it. I was not sure I was doing the right thing in substituting caution for Laverton's impetuousness, and I realised I was biased against any premature attempt at escape because of a tenuous hope that Nai Soon might miraculously materialise to strengthen me and take the initiative out of my hands.

Problematical as was that hope, it was given impetus during the weeks we had worked on the bridge. During that time many coolies from Malaya had gone across the Mae Khlong, but most of them were Tamils, sheepish from frightened expectancy and unwilling to talk to the ex-tuans who contacted them.

That was the only familiar thing about Tamils: their fawn-like docility and their lambent, frightened eyes. They were just so many helpless sheep scurrying before a refractory sheepdog yapping in bad mannered impetuousness at their heels. I could not visualise Nai Soon in such company, though their coming was a pointer to the future and a hope that he would eventually arrive.

Should he come, as something told me he would, even though it was as an impressed labourer, I knew he would walk alone; he would hold himself apart from the rabble of fear-inspired coolies streaming across the Mae Khlong as if anxious to rush upon the fate that awaited them along the jungle trial on the other side. There would be nothing of their sheepish humility about Nai Soon; neither would he exude fear as they exuded it. Like the Thai coolies who laughed at the Nips and kept their independence, he also would remain independent even though the needs of his body put him in temporary subservience to the Nips who had murdered his brother Ah Tek Soon and given me his friendship.

Until he came, I must put a curb on impatience by giving fate, which thus far had dealt kindly with me, a chance. A week or a month would make little difference to the ultimate issue. There was a long period of waiting before the rains came and I could concede half of it to fate, and hold the other half in reserve against eventualities, knowing that every mile beyond Tamakan took me closer to my ultimate goal…

The Nips, however, were not in a hurry to send Captain Bell's party across the Mae Khlong. Others with less incentive than Laverton and I were departing daily, while our party was detained at Kanburi building sidings and renovating the line between the station and Bam Pong. Since our first journey over it little had been done to smooth out the kinks, and the Nips were anxious to have it made more like a railway.

Makawa, the Nip corporal in charge of us, had a keen appreciation of Occidental civilisation, which did not detract from his determination to get the line securely ballasted before the rains came in the last half of the year. Whether he had a personal interest in securing communications between Kanburi and Nong Pladuk I do not know. Maybe, like so many of us, he held to the belief that when the monsoons came the line would automatically go out of commission.

If that were so, he was wrong. Instead of turning the embankment into a quagmire into which the railway would sink irretrievably, the rains, when they came, seemed to bind the soil until it set like cement which, with the ballast we had added to it, made a firm foundation over which the trains ran with a minimum of accidents throughout the monsoon.

233

At strategic points along the railway the Nips built branch lines to the river to facilitate the ballasting of the parent concern. One of these off-shoots ran from Kanburi station along the track to the road, which it bisected, and then on to the river, where groups of Thais were piling up great mounds of sand and gravel against the coming of the first train from the station. Building this spur line was a comparatively easy job, and there was no Sasuki to harass us. Makawa, though not so easy going, was amenable to reason and, when not in a spiteful mood, allowed us to patronise the food vendors who hung about the station eager for our trade.

Many of the women were extremely pleasing to look at, with a natural beauty that was enhanced by the indifference with which they wore it. Maybe their standards of beauty are different from the European conception of that ethereal quality or perhaps we rashly conceded them the crown of beauty because they were akin to that one element which had disappeared so completely out of our lives – woman. Not the physical aspect of woman – that bothered very few – but her companionship and the sound of her voice in the quiet evening after the day's toil was done; these were things that were sadly missed and often yearned for…

Not all the Thai women were good looking. Many of them were betel-chewing shrews whose black teeth and slobbering mouths revolted the sensibilities until, by a process of association, one became acclimatised. All over the place were great dobs of red saliva, as if someone with his throat cut had been running round in ever-decreasing circles waiting to die. But for all their little peculiarities, the betel-chewers made good coffee, and anyone who could do that was forgiven a multitude of conventional sins.

Chapter Twenty

The Calling Hills

Ragged patches of shoddy green, the clumps of scrub and bamboo made irregular patterns on the brown aridness of the padi fields stretching away to the blue hills rising distantly against the sky, while in between an occasional toddy palm reared its shaggy head above the heat haze. Higher still, specks of almost motionless vitality, the vultures hovered on expectant wings… waiting.

The vultures were not waiting for me, however – not yet, anyway – and I stopped watching them, not caring for the association of ideas their presence inspired, as they hung up there in the blue, missing nothing. They knew that men were dying in Kanburi Hospital a mile away, and I knew too, but I did not want to be reminded of that. I wanted to study the sleepy looking hills so that I might get to the root of an idea, or an urge, that had struggled for expression from the day we left our patch of scrub and moved into the old coolie hut beside the station.

Sagging in drunken acquiescence to fate and bad workmanship, the old hut made a shelter for us at night time and, in the heat of the day, a happy hunting ground for the thousands of ravenous flies the coolies had left as a legacy of their insanitary way of life, when there was no white man to keep a paternal eye on their welfare and inspire them to observe the elementary tenets of cleanliness. Had the coolies taken the flies with them, I might never have come under the spell of the hills that rose in an unexpected rampart before me as I came through the bushes into which I had fled from the hut, where the flies made life intolerable. But now they had thrust themselves upon me, rising up out of the *flat* padi country to make a barrier to vision, it was inevitable that conjecture as to what lay on the other side should become firmly implanted in the fertile soil of my imagination. From there it was but a step to a consultation with map and compass, the outcome of which was a growing conviction that I had found the way out, if I cared to take it.

After that there was little peace between me and the hills. Daily they insinuated their blue majesty into my consciousness as a signpost to endeavour and beyond them, I could see the Mae Khlong coming down in a series of sinuous curves that would guarantee immunity from the thirst devils standing on guard against any attempt at escape.

With that knowledge and the spell of the smoky hills to urge me, I formulated a plan and plotted a course that, in theory, would take me from the old coolie hut to Akyab, on the Bay of Bengal, where rumour said was the barest outpost of security. Unless, however, John came back to Tamakan, this would avail me nothing, for his hold on me was stronger than the insidious hills that daily coaxed me to be up and away, and until he came I would tarry.

In the meantime, the Mae Khlong gave me a reassurance I had not before experienced, for with the danger from thirst minimised, the odds against a successful getaway were reduced from, say, a thousand to one to a mere hundred to one. In so far as the actual escape from the camp was concerned, there was no danger. As Laverton had implied, that was just a matter of packing one's kit and heading north, south, east, or west as the fancy took one. Remaining free was the problem, and the penalty for not being able to solve it was death, either through misadventure or at the hands of the Nips.

In the circumstances, it was but an elementary precaution to carefully organise any escape plan before putting it into operation. Also, all relevant information, up to the point where knowledge gave way to speculation, had to be tabulated and memorised. Thus my map told me that a bearing on the hills in a direct line with the old coolie hut that had been instrumental in introducing me to their beckoning, tree-crowned heights would take me to the Mae Khlong some two miles above Tardan. From that point the river would lead me up into the foothills, where it had its birth. Then there would be the difficult climb over the main massif into the Shan States where, if rumour was correct, innumerable bloodthirsty Shans were waiting for just such an eventuality. Rumour, however, was often biased to fit in with any given situation, and I was not prepared to accept it at even its face value. Banking on the pushful diplomacy of the Nips, I felt reasonably certain a few Shans at least, and possibly also a minority of other Burmese, would have a grouse against the sponsors of the morally bankrupt Co-prosperity Sphere, and be prepared to help me on my way, if for no other reason than a wish to vent their spleen on their new overlords.

I hoped John, when he returned, would feel the same way about these remote people of whom we knew nothing apart from the not very subtle propaganda gleaned from the Nip-sponsored newspapers that were sometimes available. Should they be as divided in opinion as my reading between the lines led me to believe, and should I fall in with the right division, it was my intention – or at least it was the plan suggested by the insinuating hills – to cross the Salween and, keeping to Central Burma, aim at Akyab, too many miles away to give any hopes of my ever arriving there without some outside assistance, and to date there had been no promise of that.

Anxious as they were to contact us, the Thais were motivated solely by hope of personal gain, and not, as some might think, by an open-hearted philanthropy. While granting us a sympathetic tolerance, inspired mainly by our misfortune, they were not on our account prepared to take their discrimination against the Nips, for whom they had little admiration, any further than a parrot-like repetition of their stock phrase: 'English number one – Nippon no good.'

Provided the Nips did not interfere with their over-rated independence – which they honoured each morning as the 10 o'clock hooter sounded from Kanburi – the Thais were prepared to work in amicable association with their new landlords. From the Nip point of view that was conceding a lot, and often they were disinclined to make concessions for the sake of harmony. Inevitably, there were clashes, ranging from isolated raids on Nip stores by individual Thais to the organised ambushing of a party of Nip officers at Bam Pong, in retaliation for an unwarranted interference with some of the Mustard Club boys – the yellow-robed priests who roamed about the country calling no man master, and for whom the Thais had a wholesome and reverential respect equalled only by their attachment to their quixotic independence.

In this affair the Nips lost two officers, while Bam Pong lost the bigger part of its Chinese community, who were deported from the town: scapegoats to appease the ruffled majesty of Nippon.

Prepared as they were to contest the right of way with a Nip, in support of their independence, that same independence prevented the Thais taking an active interest in our welfare. Like the elephant that had changed its mind about challenging our entry into the country, they were concerned only for Thailand, and whether we lived or died, they were not particularly interested. They were not prepared to help us do one or the other, any more than the arid *padi* fields were willing to associate themselves with any plan of escape.

Yet, in the Thais, as in their desiccated fields, was a deep-rooted urge to give generously. When the moment was propitious they would do that, but we must be patient and wait for change – it would not be hurried. When that came there would be a metamorphosis. Where the *padi* now lay sun-baked and a-shimmer with heat, would one day be a magnificent carpet of luscious green velvet unrolling in indescribable beauty to the blue hills, where the heat haze hung like a lace curtain between ephemeral beauty and stark reality. But before that happened, the rains must come to turn the scorched fields into miniature lakes on which the egrets flash in dazzling banks of sheer white against the russet gold of the evening sun. Then later, when the water buffaloes had done their work with the wooden ploughs that have not altered in a thousand years, the carpet of a thousand greens would start to unroll as the first ragged patches of young rice pushed above the brackish water.

Before then, I hoped to be away beyond the hills that daily were becoming more insistent, with John, Laverton, and Smithy, plodding on and on into the infinity of distance, with always at the back of my mind the image of the vultures wheeling in endless spirals against the blue vault of the heavens from where they watched and waited and missed nothing...

*****

Before Providence intervened to make it possible for me to go to the hills to that I might see at first-hand what lay on the other side, the railway had pushed across the river, and was taking tentative pecks at the jungle-clad hills – a continuation of the range that occupied so much of my leisure hours. As the line advanced the hills receded before it as though reluctant to accept the thing that was coming out of the *padi* country to foist itself upon their cloud-washed impassivity.

Tamakan, from which John and Smithy were still absent – indeed, I was beginning to despair of their ever returning – was now the largest camp in the area and, under Sasuki, had achieved a reputation of ill repute.

The main Kanburi camp, too, was expanding rapidly, and was being added to each day as fresh contingents of prisoners arrived from Singapore and Changi. In this camp the tempo of life was not so erratic as it was at Tamakan. Major Cheda, the Nip Commandant, was a fat old man not fired with the lustful brutality of Sasuki. Unlike the latter, Cheda did not find a perverted amusement in the sufferings of the men over whose destiny he held the supreme mandate; neither, on the other hand, did he concern himself with making their lives any more tolerable or secure. He was, however, approachable and amenable to reason in much the same way as his subordinate Makawa, who had returned to Nong Pladuk.

Minor growths outside the main Kanburi camp were the individual huts around the station, including the old coolie hut in the *padi*, where slowly, but surely, life was becoming daily more precarious. In the time we had been at Kanburi a metamorphosis had taken place, the most noticeable feature of which was the reversal of the standard of dress in the locality.

On our arrival we had, in the main, been well clothed and well shod, while the Thais had, except for a few isolated individuals, been at least 75% deficient of clothing. Now the converse was true: the Thais were well dressed, while the majority of the prisoners were bare-footed, and hid their shame behind a "Jap-happy" – a piece of cloth approximately six inches by eighteen, and worn universally by the Nips as underpants – which, with a battered straw hat, comprised their working dress.

Clothing was not now the only thing of which where was a shortage. The surplus of food available to anyone with sufficient money to buy it no longer existed nor, for that matter, did the money. Through a natural process of supply and demand, the Thais had got most of the clothing in the group and, also, their money had returned to them. The price of such "extras" as were still available had gone up 100%, and few could afford to buy them. Worse still, the Nip rations, which originally had been comparatively good, were deteriorating rapidly, not only in quality but often in quantity.

Unsatisfactory as was the food situation at Kanburi and Tamakan, it had a certain surety about it that was not in evidence in the camps beyond the farthest point to which the line had penetrated. Men on survey parties and on jungle clearing for the permanent way were dependent mainly on the river for their food supplies: When the barges failed to arrive, or when they arrived late, as often happened, these men went hungry. The further one got from the railhead, the more intolerable life became. News coming back to Kanburi told of men dying of hunger and disease; of a thin trickle of medical accessories, and, more often, none at all, to combat the higher percentage of illness in every group, which had its own cemetery, where daily the little crosses were multiplying.

This was true even of such 'civilised' camps as Kanburi and Tamakan. Here, too, the little crosses were marching side by side as though in competition to see which of the two camps would first reach the hundred mark. Even in the station area, it was no uncommon sight to see a party of prisoners on their way to the cemetery at Kanburi with a dead comrade slung on a crude bamboo stretcher. From the old coolie hut I had watched three men go to Kanburi cemetery that way, and their going filled me with an acute unease for John and Smithy, so remotely out of touch in the jungle vastness of the hills, where life was a day-to-day affair poised on the scales of chance and the ability of the individual to laugh in the face of despair.

John, I knew, was capable of that but Smithy – well, I was not sure. Laverton had said he was too easy-going to survive indefinitely and, though Smithy had lost a good deal of his placidity since coming to Thailand, I felt inclined to think that Laverton might be right.

But come to that, any one of us might look death in the face at any hour not knowing at whom we were looking until it was too late: life and death had equal chances in this game we were playing. Luck was an ace card which might win a trick at a crucial moment, and so decide the winning or losing hand. In so far as my own aces were concerned, I had no regrets; they had seen me through a difficult patch before and, I felt sure, should the occasion arise, they would come to my aid again.

However that might be, I had no intention of becoming a victim to smug complacency by letting fate, or chance, do all the work. The hills were out there waiting for me, and I knew I must go to them sooner or later. If I remained any longer in the coolie hut, they would not be denied; for the memory of John might not be strong enough to hold me back while, as for Nai Soon, he was fast becoming a wraith in the dim recesses of yesterday.

The tenuous hope I had held for his coming no longer inspired me nor, on the other hand, did it any longer bias me against the urgings of Laverton, who daily was becoming more fretful and wanting action.

If only John would return I should feel happier, and would no longer be plagued by indecision. On his arrival everything would become clear cut and lucid, and the hills could have my undivided attention. As it was, I was concerned mainly with what was beyond them, not being satisfied with what the map told me. If John did not return soon I would go and see, so that when he came, there would be no unnecessary delay. But if he did not return – what then? That was something I could not answer. I was too afraid that one day soon I might find it necessary to supply an answer, and for that reason I shied away from it, seeking sanctuary in vacillation and self-deception.

Then the Nips, anxious to speed up the ballasting of the line, put on a night shift to load the wagons at the river, and I found the opportunity to go to the hills and see what lay on the other side.

After the intense heat of the day, night work was a luxury and, though Makawa was no longer with us, we were fortunate in coming under the benevolent jurisdiction of an old Nip ex-sergeant-major, who had served with the Allies in the First World War. Because of an over fondness of *sake*, this old soldier had been reduced to a corporal, and still drank heavily whenever he got the chance, which was not often for, like everything else, *sake* was becoming scarce.

Night time by the river, in an atmosphere redolent of an old-time boom town, had something peculiarly restful and satisfying about it. It had none of the over-heated bustle of the day in which thirst and the shouting of the Nips was an ever-present irritant. When the wagons were full, we were at liberty to wander about among the stalls, where the Thais sold odds and ends of food, including home-made lemonade and various delicately flavoured sweetmeats, which it was inadvisable to examine too closely if one were to enjoy their extreme piquancy.

In the uncertain light from the gas flares and the resinous torches that supplied the only illumination when the moon was on holiday, traders on the lookout for a bargain mingled freely with the food vendors, and coaxed us to sell anything of value we still possessed and, when they could not buy, they were not averse to thievery.

On a night when the moths were sacrificing themselves in thousands in a dance of ecstatic abandon before the gas flares, one of these versatile opportunists brought a momentary hope of fulfilment for my ultimate objective. One of the well-dressed Thais who were to be found hanging about every camp as far up as Tamakan, and who could usually speak English, this fellow was almost over eager to assure me that he did not like the Nips. For him the premier race were the English and more especially that portion of them working their hearts out in Thailand. Overlooking the fact that this was a remarkable departure from precedents, for the average Thai has little time for any national other than his own, I experienced a momentary belief that at least I had found one with a less stereotyped outlook, and the thought filled me with an exaltation I had not experienced for a long time.

Here was the outside contact for whom I had been waiting so long and – happy thought! – He had the semblance of a plan already prepared. What mattered it that the possibility of escape via Bangkok had never occurred to me? It was enough that he had suggested it, and immediately I could see its possibilities though, fortunately, I was too cautious to let him realise I was impressed. Some of Nai Soon's circumspection still lingered, and as suddenly it insinuated itself between me and the persuasive Thai, who was being so unaccountably helpful, the glow went out of me and I felt dejected almost as the giant bull-frog sitting in over-stuffed passivity among the scorched moths falling like dirty confetti from the gas flares.

Later, when I saw this too helpful Thai enjoying a gossip and a cigarette in the Nip guard tent, I realised once more that outside contacts were of a problematical advantage, however necessary they might at times appear. This theory was further enhanced by the old lady from whom I bought my *yasumi* lemonade.

'He is a bad man,' she said, referring to the Thai with whom she had seen me talking and I knew then, without an doubt, he was in the pay of the Nips,

241

for I had heard the phrase before, and knew just what it implied.

Later the same night two of the Nip guards relieved the despondency resulting from this brief encounter by getting drunk on a little sake and a lot of imagination. Emboldened by their Dutch courage, they decided to wave the banner of Nippon's greatness among the hovels by the river, where the Thai coolies lived, and in the ensuing scrimmage, one of them got in the way of a knife which let out all of his imagination and most of his *sake*. Equally deflated, the other Nip ran back to where the ex-sergeant-major, also drunk – but not on imagination – was sitting by the fire, brooding about the loss of three hundred dollars from the guard tent two nights previously.

Never at ease at night owing to the uncertain temper of the Thais, who were not to be browbeaten as we were, the Nip guards were made more jittery by these two incidents, and when tragedy came to lay its hand on our nocturnal striving, many felt the Thais were at least indirectly responsible for its coming.

Our job at night was to fill all the available trucks with ballast and when that was done, we were allowed to *yasumi* until it was time to return to camp in the morning. While the majority of the men lay about the fire, others slept in an old loading bay on the branch line, or anywhere else that afforded shelter from the cold wind that sometimes blew along the river.

A week after the stabbing of the drunken Nip, one of the sentries fired two shots while investigating a noise in the vicinity of the loading bay, as a result of which two men were killed.

These men – an Australian and an Englishman – were proved, upon investigation, to have been shot while lying down, so that the Nip's excuse that he had fired at two Thais, who threw stones at him, was an obvious fabrication. It is more likely that, being in a state of jitters, he fired at the men lying asleep without bothering about the preliminary of first identifying them.

Had they been Thais there would at least have been an official investigation but, being prisoners, the manner of their death did not warrant that. Our lives, from the Nip point of view, were of little value, and death was no novelty. Why kick up a fuss about something that could not be rectified?

In the morning we carried the bodies back to camp, finding in their rigid unresponsiveness a reminder that life was more fleeting even than we had believed and, too, they were an added proof, if that were needed, of the unpredictability of the Nips...

Half way across the *padi* the smoky look began to lift from the hills, then, as I got closer, their final vestige of camouflage fell away, leaving them revealed in their unlovely nakedness. Rising in a series of terraces that might

242

have been man made, so uniform were they, the red sandstone ribs of the hills showed through the sparse vegetation and stunted trees that, from a distance, cloaked them with the mantle of beauty, and gave promise of idyllic repose where there was none. Leaving the untidy piles of rubble left by the builders, I ascended to where there was no longer any blue but sky, and found further disappointment.

Where I had expected to see the Mae Khlong, vital and full of promise, I saw instead a world of hills stretching away in tree-shrouded undulations until distance once again recaptured the smoky blue wistfulness that had beguiled me with its insinuating suggestiveness, and brought me questing across the *padi* in search of a mirage that retreated as I advanced.

Looking back the way I had come, I could see the odd coolie hut dwarfed to a doll's house by distance and, away beyond that, the chimney stack of Kanburi's paper mills rising up out of the plain line an outsize toddy palm.

Of an older vintage than the chimney stack, the Thai civil prison, too, was visible. And, though I could not distinguish any of the fettered convicts who kept alive the spirit of man's inhumanity to man, the recollection of their unhappy state turned me away from Kanburi and back to the missing Mae Khlong.

Even though the river was not visible, I knew it was out there somewhere. My mistake in expecting to see it once I gained the summit of the range of hills, which showed from the railway, lay in the inability of my home-made map to give me in detail all the natural features of the country. Where I had expected to find one range of hills, there were dozens of others for which I had not been able to make provision, not knowing where they were. But now that I knew what intervened between me and the Mae Khlong, my initial disappointment at not being able to see the river dissipated and, momentarily, I was at peace.

For the greater part of the day I remained among the red rocks mapping out a probable route from the old coolie hut over the range on which I was standing, and so into the far distance, where the blue smoke hung against the sky. When I returned across the padi in the late afternoon, well satisfied with the knowledge I had gained, I knew there would be peace thereafter between me and the hills: they had beckoned, and I had accepted their challenge to find them wanting in everything but the promise of what lay beyond the upflung rampart of their rugged barrenness, wherein was none of the allure associated with that remote, unattainable beauty that had smiled at me through the heat haze hanging over the padi…

Though I did not know it, the hills were a bad loser; they relinquished their grip on me with reluctance, letting me go only when they had given me a memento to carry back to the patch of scrub where I had left Laverton asleep. When almost clear of the rubble that littered the edge of the padi at their foot, I stumbled and went down, and the hills must have chuckled in satanic mirth, while I, not knowing that they had laid the foundations of an ulcer that was to plague me for months, let them go with a single curse...

Laverton was not asleep in his arboreal bedroom. He had been detailed for one of the rush jobs the Nips were continually finding, and had gone to Kanburi to unload a barge that had come down river.

He was back almost before I had closed my eyes in sleep, and the urgency of his 'Wake up, Mick!' sounded an alarm in my fuddled senses.

'Wake up!' he repeated. 'Something awful has happened!'

Intuitively I knew what was wrong: that is the price one pays for being too close to someone; as Laverton had said at Nong Pladuk, I was very close to John. My fears were not groundless: some ill had befallen him. But I must make sure.

'Is it John?' I said needlessly, noting with a perception sharpened by fear the harassed look on Laverton's face.

'Yes,' he said. Then in a rush: 'I'm sorry, Mick. I know just how close you were to John...'

There it was again, only now it was in the past tense. But that could not be right. I would not believe that such a thing could happen. Not so soon, anyway.

'Is he ill, Richard?'

'Don't you understand?' he said with a near shout. 'He's dead, Mick!'

So it was true! Not even my unwillingness to believe could side-track such finality. Then unaccountably I thought: 'I wonder if the hills know?' and, turning to face them, found the blue haze more pronounced than it had been. Yet, as I listened to Laverton telling me how death had come to John, the haze thinned out and became as before – smoky blue and transparent – and there were the hills behind waiting with renewed enticement.

Laverton had found Smithy – an emaciated and enfeebled Smithy – with some badly damaged Nips in the barge at Kanburi. Apparently there had been a premature explosion when John's party had been attempting to blast an outcrop of rock that interfered with the survey they were making. Smithy had got a broken leg and numerous bruises while John, apparently, had been killed outright.

'How is Smithy?' I wanted to know, not liking Laverton's description of his condition.

244

'He's in bad shape. Poor blighter is mostly skin and bone, apart from his broken leg. They've been having a damned time, Mick…'

'And John-?'

'Smithy told me John was hit on the head with a lump of rock. One of the Nips was killed too… Smithy says if none of the Nips had been injured, he would not have been sent back to Kanburi, and if it was not for John's death, he would feel thankful for the accident…'

'In that case all those tales coming down the river are true, Richard, and we, too, should be thankful we are still at Kanburi. But John – somehow I can't convince myself he is dead. In a few days, perhaps, but not now…'

Three days after the news of John's death our plans were complete. Sufficient food – mostly uncooked rice – had been amassed to enable us to get away from the vicinity of the railway without having recourse to the Thais, on whom eventually we should be dependent until we crossed the hills into Burma. A two days' supply of sterilised drinking water – a more immediate problem – was also being carried and this, if my reckoning was not too far off the mark, should get us to the Mae Khlong which, thereafter, for a hundred miles or so, would safeguard us against thirst.

Matches, salt, two knives scabbed from the Nips, a parang, a coil of rope, and miscellaneous pieces of wire to tie our boots together when eventually they started to fall apart were also included. But there was one essential missing – a supply of medical kit, particularly quinine, and for this we were relying on the co-operation of Captain Bell, who had not yet been advised of our imminent departure.

Laverton, with a scepticism not altogether unwarranted, was not in favour of taking the captain into our confidences.

'He won't be over enthusiastic,' said Richard. 'Though come to that, I shouldn't be either if I were in his place. There's bound to be a hell of a row when we turn up missing.'

'That is one of the reasons why we have got to tell him. After all, it would not be playing the game for us to walk off leaving him holding the baby, not knowing which set of nappies to put on it when it begins to squall. Another thing, I'm hoping he will cover us on the morning and evening roll-calls so that we have a night and day start before our absence is discovered. Then there is the question of quinine. We must have some. It would be just damned silly to go without it.'

'I agree about that, though actually I had not thought about it before. Malaria without quinine is not pleasant to contemplate. Yes, you are right; tell him by all means…'

After roll-call the same evening, I sought out Captain Bell, and gave him the gist of our plan for making a getaway.

'There are one or two essentials we have been unable to get hold of,' I said, as he sat on the bund between two *padi* fields digesting the information I had imparted to him.

'And they are?'

'Quinine, and a small amount of antiseptic, for cuts and that sort of thing...'

'You know, of course, Stirling, that our medical supplies are strictly limited? However, it could be arranged, I suppose but frankly, I am not at all impressed by your plan. There is, for instance, the question of food. After what you take with you has been used up, you will be reliant solely on what you can get from the natives. What if they refuse to co-operate?'

'That is just one of the chances we shall have to take. After all, in a scheme of this sort there can be no cut and dried course of action. One can only hope to achieve something, while bearing in mind that chance will decide whether success or failure crowns one's efforts. It's absolutely impossible, as I see it, to guarantee any definite result.'

'I agree – to a certain extent. But you can at least make the best provision. I do not think you are doing that.'

'In what respect?'

'Well, apart from food, there is the much more serious problem – water. How do you expect to exist in a country like this without a regular supply?'

'What we take with us should get us to the river beyond the hills. If it doesn't we shall have to manage until we get there.'

'That is just it, Stirling. There is too much supposition about your scheme. I'm afraid it does not appeal to me at all. And, by the way, have you had any experience of jungle travel? Very uncertain, you know.'

That was one point on which I hoped to satisfy him. Since coming to Thailand, I had been in contact with a good deal of jungle; also, there had been an overabundance of it in Malaya before the Nips came. Doubtless, it was there still and was as difficult to negotiate as any other jungle.

I told him that, and he said:

'I have had some experience of operating in the bush, and cannot recommend it. Neither, after consideration, can I approve of your plan. As I said, you are not taking enough food with you, and to survive you would have to ensure that you travel from water hole to water hole – that is vitally important. In the circumstances, I am afraid I cannot countenance such an undertaking – not now, at any rate. I would advise you to wait for a while to see if things improve and, in the meantime, work out an alternative plan – one that is likely to be more successful...'

With that damp squib for encouragement I went back to Laverton who said succinctly:

'Bloody fool! Does he think we are out in the desert? Water hole to water hole! And we're not sure even about the rivers!'

Having failed to win Captain Bell's co-operation, we had no option but to wait until such times as we acquired a supply of quinine, either by honest endeavour, or by the more likely medium for success – theft. Once that was accomplished, we would be off to the hills with or without the captain's consent and with a bit of luck, the railway would see us no more.

It was not pleasant to think about Smithy incapacitated and marooned in the hospital at Kanburi, so I did not think about him – or tried not to.

Laverton, who was now working in the main camp building, a Nip cook-house, managed to visit the hospital and acquaint him with what we intended doing.

It would be six weeks at least before Smithy was on his feet again, and by that time, all being well, we should be on the way to Salween...

How futile it is to plan and conspire and make no provision for the element of chance. Having told Captain Bell that chance was a factor that would inevitably produce success or failure *after* we left the old coolie hut, I made the mistake so many people make by not envisioning the probable outcome of chance deciding to have its fling before we left.

That is what happened. Chance came knocking at my door, and I was absent.

One of the men who had an inkling of our purpose broke the news to me when I came in from the river three mornings after my interview with Captain Bell.

'Laverton's gone,' he said, and for a moment I did not understand.

'Gone? What do you mean?'

'He was put on that party that left today – one of the chaps on it went sick...'

All I could think of for a while was the foolish phrase: 'From water hole to water hole.' Then, for some reason or other, I wanted to laugh when I knew I was nearer to tears.

Without Laverton I was marooned as definitely as the incapacitated Smithy, for to attempt a getaway by myself was something that had never entered into my calculations when analysing the possibilities of escape; neither, for that matter, had I the foolhardy courage necessary for such an undertaking. Life was not yet such a desperate hardship that I was prepared to flirt with death for the sake of novelty or the dubious satisfaction of hitting back at chance for sending Laverton up the line ahead of me. With him there had been a possibility of achieving something – without him there was none.

Salt in the wound made by his going was the knowledge that there had been no secrecy about the departure of a party from the station area. I had known about it for two days, but the possibility of someone on it being replaced at the last moment by either Laverton or myself had not been given the consideration it so obviously warranted. A piece of bad generalship which rubbed me raw, this knowledge, paradoxical as it may seem, took the sting out of my initial disappointment, and replaced it with the bitter alum of self-recrimination.

But Laverton had gone and all the self-recrimination in the world would not bring him back. I could only wait until I, too, left Kanburi and the hills which, with victory seemingly assured by John's death, had lost in a manner I had not foreseen. Thinking of that I wondered if they had had a prior warning of what had just transpired, and looking for confirmation or denial, I found they gave me neither. Between me and them was still the sun-scorched *padi* with the pillared toddy palms rising shaggy-crested above the heat haze, and further beyond, the blue smoke of distance, transparent and utterly remote, beckoning with a lost appeal that would not yet be answered.

Tomorrow, perhaps… but not today.

Chapter Twenty One

'Old Soldiers Never Die'

Behind me was the old coolie hut with its flies and disillusionment. There, too, were the blue hills that rimmed the *padi* in which it squatted, dowdy and over-tired, and with its destiny fulfilled. There also, more poignant than either of these, was the memory of what might have been now gradually merging into what might yet be.

Ahead were the fretted waters of the Mae Khlong, slushing against the piles of the bridge over which the railway ran in triumphant achievement, disappearing into distance where the jungle, slashed through by its savage impetus, drew back a little way to let it pass.

Between the old associations and the new ones crowding them out, lay a finely etched, and indescribably grim, illustration of the price in lives being paid to maintain the stimulus of the railway's surging advance.

In the over-crowded, vermin-infested hospital at Kanburi, where drinking water was rationed to a pint a day, were men in every stage of physical decay waiting, with a patience equalled only by the vultures overheard, for the inevitable as the only means of escape from squalor, disease, hunger, and all the hardships that went with them. It would mean, too, a release from the ruthless uncharitableness of the Nips in whom the quality of mercy was not made manifest by the sufferings of the men whom daily the railway was sending to a premature and unlovely death.

Beriberi, dysentery, malaria, and black water fever were each claiming their sacrifices, but dreaded more than any of these were the tropical ulcers that ate into the flesh with the virulence of an acid, and for which there was no apparent cure. To start one of these monstrosities, the slightest abrasion of the skin was sufficient and, once it had started to expand, there was no telling when it would stop.

Confined mainly to the legs, the tropical ulcers ranged in size from a half-crown to a dinner plate, and often did not stop growing until the complete leg of the victim was enveloped from the knee down. Exerting a corroding action on the flesh, which gradually rotted and fell away until the bone underneath was exposed, the ulcers induced an intense pain that was almost unbearable. Also, they gave off an intolerable stench which filled the hospital with a nauseating effluvium.

Treatment was as varied as the sizes of the ulcers. Each medical officer, after finding the standard treatment universally ineffective, had his own methods. Some scraped away the rotted flesh and applied pure carbolic, when it was available. Others omitted the scraping process and concentrated on killing the ulcer with a frequent application of whatever antiseptic they possessed. Still others assayed to cut out the complete ulcer, hoping by such drastic measures to get rid of the malignant growth, and so effect a cure – but with little success. A final and irrevocable method was amputation – but that came later.

Medical equipment being always at a minimum, and often non-existent, one of the greatest aids to recovery from any of the numerous diseases was the will of the individual provided he wanted to live. Unfortunately, many men, demoralised by hardship and suffering, did not look upon death as something to be shunned and out-witted. Instead, they went out to seek it, knowing it was the only escape from a life devoid of everything that made it worth hanging on to, and once that mental state became a fixture, they were as good as dead; no medical officer, however well equipped, could save them from themselves.

In direct opposition to this philosophy were many men who, according to the law of averages, ought to have died months before they did. Even then they only died because their bodies became incapable of sustaining the terrific impulses put in motion by their will-power.

An outstanding example of this was a scraggy caricature of a man named Sherwood, who lay three places away from Smithy on the bamboo sleeping platform. Sherwood was one of those unfortunate people who get everything that no one else wants. When I knew him he was in with a mixture of dysentery, malaria, and beriberi – quite a combination even for the railway, but not enough to fill him with the apathetic despondency that had killed so many of his friends.

Whenever any of the men in his ward began to lose faith, Sherwood would prop himself up on his bamboo bed and play a flute he had brought from Singapore, and which he used to inspire those who were inclined to take the easier way out.

Heroic in his regard for others, Sherwood was a marvel of endurance and fortitude, and when last I saw him alive, he had shrunk to a mere handful of

'I do now. She is exquisite, isn't she? I have never before seen anything approaching her fragile beauty, Mick. Nai Soon must be mad to bring her to such a place...'

'I had hoped he would leave her at Singapore if he came to Thailand. Now he has brought her you may depend on his judgement. Nat would not put Little Flower in jeopardy if there had been any other way out. What is she doing?'

'She works in the cook-house, though I do not think she actually does much; it is really a sort of hideout for her, I believe, and she seldom is dressed in anything but dowdy coolie clothes. It is only on the rare occasions she dons her finery that you really feel appreciative of so much unexpected beauty.'

Before I could think of something suitable to say to that, he added:

'They have been very kind to me, Mick. Nai Soon, by some miraculous contriving, has got me little odds and ends – a spoonful of sugar, a pinch of salt, once a tin of condensed milk that gave me indescribable delight, and occasionally a few cigarettes – without which I might well be dead. He is a generous friend, that Chinese youth, Mick, and he is ever anxious for your safety. You must contact him as soon as possible. Like me, he has waited a long time...'

'But how, John? I do not even know how far up we are going. This meeting and parting again is horrible, yet there is nothing we can do to prevent it, I suppose?'

'Not now, Mick. Later, maybe. Then you will not be far away, as the Nips are held up by the hills about five miles ahead, and it is there you are going... be careful, Mick; for my sake, and your own, and do nothing rash. Promise me that...'

'Rashness is not one of my failings,' I assured him, as our meshi party, who had gone into the camp to cook rice, returned through the gateway where the bluebottles were now vainly seeking the faces of the dead. 'There can be only one way out, John – together or not at all, and while Nai Soon may help shape my destiny, you are inextricably bound up with it. Therefore, whatever I may do, you shall have a hand in it and, if it should be something rash – well, yours also shall be the blame. Will that do?'

'You have not committed yourself, Mick,' he said, solemn as an owl, 'but I guess it will do. Now, here is a pointer to your future: should you come in contact with a Nip called Black Joe, say your prayers every night and do nothing to annoy him, though that would be impossible. The mere fact of your trying would make him have a down on you. Black Joe is that type of Nip, Mick. Steer clear of him with every stratagem you can utilise. He is a killer.'

skin and bone that looked pitifully inadequate as a cover for his unquenchable cheerfulness. It was on the day I went to say good-bye to Smithy, who was making good progress. Sherwood was lying very still, not wise-cracking and boisterous as he usually was. Then suddenly he sat upright, and in the half light of the hut his almost naked, emaciated body looked unreal and horrifying. Then a bony hand stole out and caressed the flute as he said, in a voice that sounded hollow and mechanical:

'I am going to play 'Old Soldiers Never Die.'

While the last note was still quavering in the hush of expectancy aroused by his playing, he laid the flute on the bamboo and slid down beside it, while overhead the vultures decreased the radius of their timeless circling... and I had another memory to take up the line in the wake of Laverton, who had been gone two weeks.

During that time Tamakan came into the news on account of a double escape attempt, which made me wish that I had been included in it until I learned three days later that the first party of three to leave had been recaptured after only a couple of days' liberty.

These men had taken the obvious and, to me, foolish route along the railway, hoping to get out via Moulmein and Rangoon, apparently overlooking the fact that in those areas the native population would be more sympathetic towards the Nips on account of their close proximity, if for no other reason.

After covering about fifty miles, they were compelled by thirst to visit a Thai kampong, where they were betrayed to the Nips who brought them back to Tamakan from which they had escaped with a good deal of coolness and ingenuity.

From the bridge camp fatigue parties crossed the river daily to gather wood for the cook-house fires, and aware of the inability of the average Nip to see anything suspicious about a circumstance performed openly and without any apparent subterfuge, the three escapees attached themselves to the wood party and walked out of the camp and across the bridges. Instead of collecting firewood, they hurried into the jungle and headed for Burma.

When they arrived back at Tamakan, it was evident these three unfortunates had been maltreated by their Nip guards and, during the time they remained in the camp, the Undertaker and his henchmen filled their days with a savage persecution, which culminated when they were given shovels and, escorted by a party of armed Nips, driven off in a lorry into an impenetrable silence that closed behind them.

The other party to leave the camp consisted of five officers equipped with everything necessary for a successful escape, including arms and a guide to set them well on their course. In spite of that they were caught and brought back to Tamakan. They, too, were savagely beaten, and later left the camp under escort to disappear into the unknown.

While not encouraging to anyone who was determined to escape if the opportunity presented itself, these two examples were a further proof that the main danger against a successful get-away was the willingness of the Thais to co-operate with the Nips in foiling any escape bid.

When later I learned to what an extent the Thai police, and the Thais generally for that matter, were supposed to be co-operating with the Allies against the common enemy, I was, to put it mildly, incredulous. To one who was always on the lookout for such a contact – and there were many others of a like faith – the existence of such an organisation as the Thai underground movement can scarcely be credited. I can only infer that it was so far underground as to be invisible in daylight.

Had any organised plan for escape been in force outside the railway camps, literally thousands of men could have walked off into the jungle, and the Nips would have been powerless to have stopped them. The lack of incentive to escape, which was practically universal, lay in the obvious fact that there was nowhere to go. To take to the jungle without any prior preparation, or without the promise of outside assistance, was both futile and foolhardy, and merited nothing but the inevitable death from exposure or thirst, which would crown such a piece of foolishness.

While our Nip engine driver examined the bridge, I listened to the Mae Khlong fretting against the piles, and wondered about the three men who had been taken out from Tamakan never to return. Between us there had been a mutual affinity which was not appreciated until it was too late to be realised, and now they were gone and their striving stilled for ever...

Sherwood, too, was gone and, listening to the river, I could hear his flute rising triumphant above its rushing spate which fretted at the bridge against which it was powerless until the rains came to send it down in savage onslaught against this man-made contraption that defied its summer strength.

Presently we essayed the crossing and Tamakan was behind, with the jungle and the hills waiting to receive us...

*****

At Wampo, seventy-five miles from Nong Pladuk, the railway caught up with the hills, which until then had made but tentative attempts to hinder its surging advance.

Leaning out over the river which had cut through them in some distant age, the hills raised a barrier of stone against the railway's continued advance into the land of mist and jungle behind them. Across the river their continuation ran sharp and clearly defined above the roof of the jungle to disappear into the blue haze of incalculable distance, and from their wooded crest the howling monkeys screeched their derision, thinking, perhaps, the little men who had come to put an end to their seclusion had met defeat and would be forced to turn back along the way they had come.

If they thought that, they were mistaken. In so far as the railway was concerned, the Nips would acknowledge no defeat. No matter what obstacle arose in their path, they would overcome it or rather, inspired by their ceaseless urging, we would overcome it, as the hills that abutted on to the river were being overcome. No matter how many little crosses spouted along the railway, it would go on through jungle, hill, and swamp until it merged and became one with the line pushing down from Burma and the Three Pagodas Pass. How many men had already died was beyond comprehension, and how many were to follow the pioneers along the trail into eternity no one knew nor, apparently, did anyone give it much thought.

Death had become too commonplace to warrant more than a fleeting curiosity as to who lay beneath the rice sacks on the crude bamboo stretcher on which the dead went to find a resting place in Thailand's sour soil. It was only when it came cloaked in personalities that it showed dark and foreboding against the greens and browns of the hills, where the monkeys moaned at night time and chanted their derisive jabberwockery during the day.

When, was a reward for an undisciplined impetuosity, death came to a Nip, it acted as a stimulus and a reminder that we were not alone in making sacrifice to the railway's rapacity and it, as not infrequently happened, an arranged accident overtook one of the little men to whom the monkeys took such a dislike, and who filled our days with misery and toil, the potency of achievement became heady and intoxicating. For a brief spell we knew reprieve from the desolation of hunger, toil, and disease that made of the jungle a desert, and the hills a haunted wilderness where life was a day to day affair and tomorrow was uncertain.

Where to us the hills were, seemingly, an insurmountable barrier that would not fall before our puny effort, handicapped as we were by lack of equipment suitable to the job, to the Nips they were but an added incentive to endeavour and an opportunity to prove once again, as so often they had done in the past, that it is not the unaided effort of the individual that counts, but the combined nibbling of the multitude. To take a seven pound hammer and a metre long chisel to the foot of the overhanging bluff, knowing that you were expected to prepare the way for its destruction, was to know the meaning of futility but when, aided by a hundred other chisels, you bored into the face of the rock, you came to realise in time that as an individual you were less than nothing, and so realising you began to appreciate your futility as an individual; how little it mattered if the top of the cliff dropped off and found you unprepared. Unexpectedly comforted by that thought, you swung your hammer with a renewed vigour, paying no heed to the blasphemy of the man holding the chisel. Soon it would be your turn, and when the tamp hole spurted a stream of lime water into your eyes, you could swear with equal abandon and, if none of the English-speaking Nips was near, you could damn their ancestors back to the day Commodore Perry gate-crashed their island kingdom, little realising that, almost a century later, you and many of his countrymen would be standing on the brink of Eternity because of that unwarranted, and possibly, unchristian, intervention. But that is the way things occur: people will poke their noses in where they are not welcome, and look what happens...

While the monkeys screamed their simian profanity from the roof, we clawed into the basement of the hills, seeking with hammer and chisel to clear a way along the river's edge, urged on by the Nips who screamed in unison with their country cousins upstairs, and used their bamboos without discrimination as a mark of their extreme displeasure.

Pushed out by the close-packed hills behind, the cliff overhung the river which swirled muddy and angry at its base, as if anxious to widen the gap through which it surged before the rains came to give it an added depth of twenty feet overnight. For uncountable years it had been doing that, and now, with chisel and hammer and a few sticks of dynamite, we were assaying to accomplish in a few days something its swollen might had been unable to contrive during all the centuries it had surged down to Kanburi and the distant Pacific.

Gradually the face of the cliff retreated before us, leaving an ever-widening gap between it and the river, which was beginning to gurgle in satisfied expectancy at our initial success. Our triumph over the wall of rock against which the river had flung itself through the centuries would compensate it in some degree for the years of ineffectual nibbling by giving it a wider passage through the hills that cramped its style when, swollen by the monsoon, it came thundering down in gleeful abandon to smash into the equally turbulent Mae Khlong below the bridge which seemed now so far distant and out of touch.

Presently we should build another bridge – or viaduct – to take the railway on its triumphant way to Burma – back door to India, the Nips' Promised Land, in which they hoped to find the proverbial milk and honey as a reward for conquest and commendable endeavour. Now, impatient at the delay caused by the barrier of the hills, their smouldering impetuousness, always seeking to find a way through the thin veneer of restraint that overlay it, broke in a wave against the cliff to fling us in a series of ill-timed assaults into the breach between it and the river.

Too impatient even to wait until we had driven the metre-long chisels into the rock face, the Nips rammed in the dynamite charges before the tamp holes were half completed, and let them off with an ineffectual bang that did little but break up the holes and make impatient the toil of hours.

When that happened, they assumed a poise of dismayed incredulity as if finding something inexplicable in a situation, which was of their own making, and which could not be remedied by repeating the empty phrase '*Dame, dame!*' and expecting it to bring about the ruins the dynamite had failed to achieve.

'You too much speedo, speedo,' I told the Nip who, for the second time in a morning, had reduced my labour to futility.

'*Chiisai* hole no good. *Taxan* O.K...'

I might as well try to explain to the monkeys gibbering in consternation up in the hills. They, at least, would not swear back – or would they? I was not sure about that, thought I felt pretty certain they would not endorse their remarks with a swipe from a bamboo pole that started a little ball of hate that grew and grew until you thought it was going to choke you. Then gradually, as your hammer rose and crashed on the chisel boring in to make a new hole, the hate ran out at your fingertips until, almost, it had dissipated. But it did not all go. There was always a reminder of it waiting for the next blow; without that reminder, you could not go on: hate was your father and your mother; it was the child of your loins, and you loved it with a devotion that would not let you abandon it to the uncertain love of a foster parent. Sometimes in the night when you awoke sweating with your heart battering like a fist against your ribs, on which the covering was too thin, you spoke to your hate and it answered you and coaxed you back to sleep with the half promise that one day it would bring fulfilment...

That was a long time coming, and the days went by, bleak and unrewarding, while death played skittles along the jungle trials, leaving you not knowing when you might be mistaken for a ninepin. It might be today, tomorrow, or possibly the next day if you got through until then, and then where would your hate get you? Nowhere. It was as ineffective, and as unproductive of result, as your scheming and plotting for a successful get-away had been.

Or was it? Didn't it inspire you eventually to ignore the inevitability of death, and keep you strong when in reality you were weak? Of course it did. It stimulated your over-tired and sometimes unco-operative body, driving it forward in the face of unresponsiveness and the urge to capitulate. It had come athwart your path, and you would be eternally damned if you acknowledged it the third time. Probably you would be damned in any case, but that was no excuse for compromise – the acceptance of a Nip-sponsored way out. Death, if that came, should not be of your seeking. It should be something that was foisted on you: something from which your hate could not keep you apart. Hate and the memory of a skeleton of a man burning up the last flickering impulses from a body already turned quisling to serenade the old soldiers that had gone before, and to inspire those who remained, would make you live in spite of the railways' insidious defeatism…

It was relaxing to lie in the quiet, moon-slashed night and think of all the things your hate could accomplish if it had a free rein, until, gorged with your introspective appetite for revenge, you realised that even hate was insubstantial and fleeting, having a day-to-day existence as fleeting as your own. When that happened you felt better, somehow and, laughing at hate, accepted it for its stimulating effect, knowing that when you were no longer in need of its exhilarating potency, you could forgot it with no resultant sense of loss. And, knowing that, you looked again upon the face of beauty, until in a little while you turned away from it and went to sleep.

*****

Beautiful in its scrubbed cleanness, the stream cascaded down the hillside, free and unrestrained and with a song in its voice, to hang for a moment as an opalescent curtain shot through with the multi-coloured radiance of sunlight where the hill fell away beneath its hurrying feet. Then, passing into the gloom of tree-induced twilight, it plunged onto the track along which the railway would come and from there it hurried, now furtive and no longer singing, to the river writhing sinuous and evil-looking through the mangroves and the jungle.

Beyond the river the hills stood up like chimney stacks, poking their heads through the clouds that hung writhing above the roof of the jungle, to make a downy carpet on which the unwary might well assay to walk. Through the holes torn by the air eddies, the jungle peeped in resplendent grandeur, while the river, which close at hand seemed over-stuffed and evil, ribboned its way around the hills, placid and unassuming and with no sign of the ruthless power latent in its unruffled meandering.

256

Where the stream burst free from the iron cradle, the trees raised mighty arms to the sky, and through them the parakeets chased, streaks of animated colour against the unbroken sameness of the hills' finery. In between, where the stream leaped from the overhand on to the track below, a wisp of smoke trailed lazy and apathetic towards the sunlight, while down below in the shadows squatted the huddle of huts and dilapidated tents that was Tonchan. Senile and decayed looking beside the stream's bounding vitality, they drew no strength from its vigour, nor found any pleasure in its translucent depths.

Personifying everything that had receded into yesterday, the stream implied a restful repose and a surcease from labour. Startlingly out of tune, its scintillating cleanness was almost anachronistic in a land where dirty water was the rule and not the exception. Watching it one forgot momentarily, maybe, but sufficiently long to feel appreciative, that two miles away the railway was advancing, clamorous and irresistible, snaking up the river valley in a series of vibrant convolutions that swept the jungle and the hills aside in a gesture ruthless as the river's down-rushing might. One forgot, too, the squalor, hunger, disease, and the all too frequent death that landmarked the way behind and increased with each step forward.

Listening to the water's hurried descent, one slipped back into a memoried past, where the streams were always clean and where the desolation of want and despair was something new: until, bridging the gap between then and now, the parakeets screeched in the leafy dome above the camp, letting in the tremulous voice of the stream as a conscious recollection of what was embodied in its crystalline depths.

Then, as peace and tranquillity faded, stark realism came to point an accusing finger at the snake winding down the hillside, and to bring a cynical remembrance of a beauty that did not exist.

Here, you thought, looking at the stream for the first time, is balm for a wounded spirit. Here, in this cool depth, I can be re-baptised and made new. Here is something for which I have yearned through the heat of uncounted days: rushing water, silvery in the moonlight and blessedly cool by day. Here is the symbol of everything of which I have been denied since the Rising Sun broke free against the sky over Singapore. It will be both wife and mother and in its arms I shall know peace…

Remembering, you yet remained for a moment, fascinated, feeling in anticipation the stream's cool rejuvenation caressing your palate like a rice wine. Then came the final thought, devastating and conclusive. Here, too, is something hidden, camouflaged with a devilish cunning, making of the stream a mirage of unattainable desire that refuses to fade – a mirage beckoning with a cajoling enchantment and a promise of unimagined delights.

Here is cholera, the hidden death...

With its verdant canopy in which the parakeets flitted, and its crystal fountain in which we dared not play, Tonchan typified the average jungle camp along the railway. Perched on the hillside overlooking the river, it suggested a remote security that was belied by a closer inspection and an acute sense of smell.

Exuding an effluvium of death and decay as perceptible almost as the smoke from its cook-house fires, the camp was a festering excrescence on the hillside.

Even before the cholera came sneaking out from its devious hiding places, coaxed by the first rains, disease and death had made an impress that could not be eradicated. Like an old garment that has been washed too often, all vitality had gone from the camp, leaving it dowdy and anaemic, and, though scrubbed clean, its poverty-stricken shoddiness was inescapable.

With the coming of cholera the grim, unceasing fight against disease and privation became intensified. And while a sketchy medical service, reduced almost to impotency from lack of supplies fought for our preservation, each fresh wave of coolies to break against the perimeter of the camp broadcast a new harvest of death and desolation.

In their inability to observe even the elementary laws of disease prevention, the Tamils, who were arriving in ever-increasing numbers from Malaya, were foredoomed to decimation, if not complete annihilation, by their helpless acquiescence to fate. Apathetic in the extreme, and without any apparent medical organisation, they lived like animals, and died as no animal would want to die.

We, too, were reduced to a mode of existence not very remotely dissociated from that of the Tamils but unlike them, we had the benefit of an Occidental civilisation that struggled to maintain us in the face of an unsound Asiatic philosophy of *tidak apa*, and a ruthless, Nippon-inspired despotism that failed to appreciate the obvious fact that our survival was necessary to its success.

Between us and the Tamils was the bond of servility, but further than that the relationship did not extend. Supine in their inability to compromise with fate or, failing that, to draw inspiration from their own danger, they were militant only in death. Alive, their sheepish complacency frustrated any remaining glimmer of a *tuan*-inspired way of life instilled into them before the coming of the Nips, and, still struggling to see them through the dark period of transition that was suggestive of a close alliance, while keeping us poles apart.

When death came on swift wings to strike us right, left, and centre, the bodies of our slain were not left to pollute the streams with a festering corruption that often lay unnoticed until it had reaped a new harvest of anguish and despair. Neither did our dying creep into the jungle to expire alone and unmourned, waiting for death with an inevitable finality that would not be gainsaid.

That was the Tamil way, but it was not ours...

Having no favourites, cholera, the most demoralising element in the Nips' universe, brought dismay and a feverish activity by spicing their lives with the potency of fear, having as its central orbit a little box in which their ashes would make the journey back to Nippon as an earnest that "tomorrow" had at least caught up with them. But for us there was no box, little or otherwise; only the noisome, water-logged earth in which the poor bones left over from a makeshift creation were stored away against a hypothetical judgement day. There, too, went the Tamils after being fried by the scavenging parties, who had the nauseating task of collecting their over-ripe bodies from their self-sought seclusion.

More thorough in their cremations, when cholera broke through their defences, the Nips burned its victims with an attention to detail that was often lacking in our amateurish experimentalism. To them the disposal of the dead was more of a scientific ritual than an urgent necessity, calling for a finesse we had not yet acquired. But we learned fast – the Nips saw to that – and with an over-abundance of defunct coolies on which to practise, soon acquired the art, though at no time was it a favourite pastime...

In spite of its disappointments and frustrations, Tonchan brought a revived interest in the past and, in small measure, a hope for the future. It was there that Smithy had received his passport back to Kanburi and, searching among the little wooden crosses for John's name, I found no trace of it and wondered about that.

This was the beginning of a hope that, unknown to me, had been lying dormant waiting for something to prod it into life. The absence of a piece of wood with the words "John Sommers" on it was sufficient incentive for hope. John might not be dead, though common sense outlawed that supposition. Still, there was the hope, and hope, I knew, should not be abandoned lightly. I would cling to it for a while and see what happened. If John were indeed alive I should know within the period that fate, unpredictable as ever, would appoint. But that was an emotional thought, and I did not dwell on it over long...

Coming back across the rapidly closing gap between Tonchan and the railhead, I caught up with the tail end of a party of new arrivals straggling in from Nong Pladuk and in that, too, there was hope, for there might be someone

I knew personally and intimately enough to feel pleased about his arrival.

There was someone.

Standing on the spot where I had stood when I first saw Tonchan's crystal stream, fascinated as I had been fascinated by so much cleanness and, I supposed, thinking the same thoughts, was Terry Reynolds. An inordinately self-satisfied Terry with the new sun tan just beginning to obliterate the yellow tinge of long illness. It was the remembrance of that illness that put my pleasure in seeing him in momentary doubt. When I had said good-bye to him at Nong Pladuk, I had not been over-confident of his survival. Now, here he was standing with a grin on his face, waiting for me to say something. Very well, then.

'What the devil are you doing here?' I demanded, trying to sound cross, and not making much of a job of it.

'What a smashing stream!' he exulted, evading the point. Then, before I could disillusion him: 'It's good to see you again, Mick. I've been wondering about you... Where is Laverton?'

'That,' I said, 'is a long story and, as I remarked before, what are you doing away up here? This is no place for invalids, though God knows we have a multitude of them...'

'I was ill,' he said, 'but I am not now. Something wonderful has happened!'

'Indeed?'

'Yes, Mick, I bet you will be pleased. Nai Soon is on the railway!'

Pleased! What an underestimate of my reaction. Nai Soon! The name, spoken outside my consciousness, was a beacon slashing through the gloom of an anaemic despondency that was almost as virulent and as soul-destroying as the Tamil's philosophy of *tidak apa*. Nai Soon, who had slipped gradually and, I had thought, irrevocably down the byways of yesterday to take his place with my other memories, was here within a measurable distance waiting for another turn of the wheel to bring us together again. Fate, indeed, was being kind. First the hope of John's survival, and now this. Little wonder Terry looked cheerful – but he would not be thinking of Nai Soon. Nat was but a means to an end, and I hoped Terry would not be disappointed. What else could I hope?

'Are you sure about that, Terry?' I asked, knowing it was not an intelligent question. Terry would not be satisfied with a mere supposition any more than I should be. If he said Nai Soon had arrived, he was certain of his information.

'Of course I am, Mick,' he said, with an unnecessary assurance. 'A month after you left Nong Pladuk a train load of coolies came through and stopped for a while in the station. There was a party from the camp loading rice, and one of them, a chap named Coleman, got into conversation with a Chinese. It was Nai Soon – I am sure of that.'

'Why so positive?'

'You know Coleman, don't you?'

'Yes. But what happened?'

'The Chinese, or Chink, as Coleman called him, wanted to know if he knew you, Mick.'

'Yes – yes. Damn it man, don't keep nibbling at it!' I urged impatiently, as he dabbled a foot in the stream, feeling at the water as though it were something precious.

'You are impatient, aren't you, Mick?' he admonished, grinning again so that I could have slew him. But he was sure of his ground, and could afford to keep me waiting.

'Coleman assured the Chinese that he knew you, though for some reason or other, he did not tell him that you had gone up country, and was given a note which he brought into camp in his boot. All it said was: 'We will meet again, Mick' and was signed 'Nat'. Is that good enough?'

'It's conclusive, Terry. Yes, it was Nai Soon alright. I wonder where the devil he is? And that reminds me: I suppose you are hoping he will not be alone?'

'Well,' he hesitated, 'that is rather a difficult question to answer, Mick. I know, of course, that you are referring to Say Leen, and I am awfully keen to see her again. But, taking an unselfish view, I hope most sincerely that Nai Soon has not brought her to the railway. Can you imagine her in surroundings such as these? Why, the very idea is preposterous.'

'But, in spite of all that you are banking on seeing her again, aren't you?'

'Truthfully, yes. She did something to me that day I met her at Singapore. But, of course, you know all that; there is no point in my repeating it...'

'Have you finished your picture?'

'Picture?'

'Yes. You started it at Changi, didn't you? Remember? On the *pedang* that day I saw you filling your belly with fresh air.'

'Oh, you mean an imaginative painting – pictures in the fire and all that? No, I have not finished it. You see, it would have to be in native costume, and I have not seen her in that yet. But if the opportunity arises, I am ready. I have made up some colours from odds and ends of stuff I pinched from Ashimoto's, and I have a piece of canvas, too. Who knows, perhaps we shall one day have a portrait of Little Flower to hang in our hut.'

A nice thought, that. Say Leen was good to look at. Even on canvas, she would add a touch of yesterday's glamour to a mean and partly degenerate existence. But Terry would have to move with circumspection supposing she did come to the railway – an unlikely eventuality, but not too improbable to be unrealisable.

Judging external impressions through the medium of his own reaction, he was likely to fall foul of his implicit faith in human nature as applicable to his own kind. Seeing Say Leen's fragile beauty through the curtain of his own reverential appreciation, he yet could not realise that there were other degrees of appreciation, excluding any interest the Nips would show for his dream girl should one of them make close contact with her. With no awareness of the underlying current of frustrated emotionalism, inherent in many of the men who, through force of circumstances and inhibition, were unable to feel an aesthetic appreciation of anything so fine as Say Leen's fragile untouchability without at the same time thinking in terms of intimate conjecture, Terry would find her presence an ever-developing complication that would eventually – possibly when it was too late – bring the realisation that the Nips were not the only ones from whom it was advisable to hide anything of sentimental value.

Realising that, I knew immediately it would be better for Terry, and more indirectly for myself, if Say Leen remained a memory. There she would be safe. Here on the railway her safety would at best be problematical, while her fascinating allure would, in all probability, bring to Terry a negation of all his hopes and the ruination of all his pictures in the fire. And I did not want that to happen if it could be avoided...

Chapter Twenty Two

The Monkeys Laugh

A muddy streak zigzagging across the face of the jungle, the track unwound itself erratically and without any apparent aim. Timid and without the impetuous haste of the railway that crowded close on its heels, it meandered and spiralled, lazy and without the ambition of a fixed purpose. A mile away across the Mae Khlong, it was a road pointing with definite purpose at an unattainable Bangkok but, here in the jungle behind Tonchan, it had lost all sense of desire to get anywhere. Always looking for the easier way out, it faltered and turned aside at every obstruction, adding unending miles to its devious and uncertain length.

Between it and the river was an age-old kinship of a simple way of life that knew no ambition. For uncounted years they had felt their way round the hills and through the jungle without haste, knowing that eventually, and in the time appointed, they would get where they were going. When the hills rose up before them, they turned aside or found an easier way through, and even with the jungle they were not averse to a concessionary solution of their problem. It was only in times of flood that the river, temporarily bereft of its habitual laziness, attempted to overreach itself and grow disputatious until, losing the artificial stimulus of borrowed strength, it drew back into the easy placidity of contented existence from which the truck never departed once it had shaken off, on the banks of the Mae Khlong, the last vestige of its borrowed worldliness.

Unlike either of them, the railway was not conciliatory minded: it was adamant and always in full flood. Ruthless in its power for evil, it trampled down or cleaved apart obstacles which would have made the jungle track or the river hesitate, and eventually turn aside, before unwinding another coil of their sinuous strength. Always with a reserve of power, it charged forward to fresh conquests with a typical Nip disregard for any hurt it left behind in the working camps littering its wake. With no time for sentiment or casuistry, it raced on to the mountains, where the jungle touched the sky, leaving Tonchan desolate, but not empty, behind it.

Keeping ahead of the railway's momentum, the sick men from the camp – those deemed unable to make the two day march to our next halting place – went up on the river's rising crest to an inevitable oblivion when, had there been any humanism to guide their destiny, they would have gone down on the current to Kanburi, and a well-earned rest as a recompense for endeavour. Where they were going they would for the most part remain. Each revolution of the barge's propeller fighting the river's turgid might whittled away so much from their chance of living to see the consummation of all their weary months of toil and privation – months during which they had given of their best without any possibility of reward. Now broken, but not yet wholly eclipsed, they were going forward to appease, and for a little longer serve, the thing that was destroying them…

On the railway's other flank, where the track ran between the wall of greenery that defined it, the "fit" men, too, were advancing from Tonchan to assault the hills that took the jungle up to the sky where the clouds swirled in a vortex of perpetual motion during the monsoon.

With the advent of the first rains, the Nips were marshalling their forces, anxious to get through the hills before the full fury of the monsoon broke over the jungle to bring a new hell where already there were an over-abundance of devils. Concerned only for the success of their project, which was bound up inextricably with our ability to work, they were, paradoxically, not even consciously aware of the inevitable outcome of their policy of total effort from everyone, regardless of his physical ability to give.

In our inevitable inability to continue working if the pressure was too long maintained lay the greatest danger to the Nips' success. Yet they could not appreciate that. All they could visualise was the crowning consummation of our united effort, and its reflected glory blinded them to everything else. Especially to those things they did not wish to see.

An instrument fashioned to help shape their destiny, we were not meant to endure beyond our ability to serve and, provided we knew our purpose, the Nips were not unduly concerned about our fate. With them the railway was first, last and all the time. If, to make it a reality, we were totally eclipsed, to them that would be a small price to pay for such an achievement and, in their philosophy, for us an honour.

Having thus so easily disposed of our desperate plight, the Nips' demands were daily becoming more onerous and more difficult to fulfil. Each camp, no matter how many of its personnel were grudgingly marked *byouki*, had to send a full complement of workers to the railway even if in the doing of it unfit men had to be taken from the hospital to make up the total demanded.

Unable to accept the obvious conclusion that every man on the railway would inevitably be *byouki* – as already most of them were – before the monsoon blew itself out, unless some period of rest was given for recuperation in the initial stages of sickness, our taskmasters were daily becoming more impatient of illness. Concerned only with getting their full quota of workers on every parade, the physical state of their slaves was of secondary importance to the numbers available. If on occasions they did show a momentary concern for the increasingly high death rate – alarmed for the railway; not for the men that were dying to build it – they were soon reassured by the apparently inexhaustible reserves of workers at their command. Provided these reserves were not incapable of filling the demands made on them, the railway would not falter, and its triumph would be a monument to their achievement and an empty tomb for the dead…

With Tonchan firmly implanted in the album of yesterday, I slithered along the track in the wake of an exuberant Terry Reynolds, trying to capture some of the stimulus of his self-satisfaction, and failing dismally. In my mind there was a thought that nullified the pleasure of leaving Tonchan and the anticipatory delight of a possible reunion with Nai Soon.

Laverton was the subject of that thought.

Two days before, I had met him on the railway, an almost unrecognisable and nearly blind Laverton, filled with an abiding joy in his affliction for, through it, he had secured the comparative sinecure of 'tea-boy,' than which there was no more sought after job on the line.

It was Laverton's enthusiasm for his comparatively easy job, rather than his physical breakdown that appalled me by its stark realism. Never at any time a shirker, his obvious belief that his good fortune in being nominated as 'tea-boy' for his group was sufficient compensation for an almost complete loss of sight, due mainly to malnutrition, was a harrowing reflection on the standard of existence on the railway. It pointed also to a moral, as well as a physical, decay that was somehow unclean and more unwelcome even than death.

There was none of the old fire left in Laverton. It had burned itself out, consuming at the same time that urgent unreasonableness that had continually demanded action in the days when the hills held the power to fascinate and promise. Those days were no more; neither was Laverton's urgency of purpose. As his strength had been sapped so also had his spirit of rebellious decisiveness;

nor was it the demoralising effect of his near blindness that accounted for his change of heart. Had that been so, I could have accepted it and suffered no hurt other than a sympathetic consideration of his affliction. It was the breakdown of the old barriers of comradeship and mutual trust that hurt more than anything. Meeting him like that after a separation of two months, Laverton was almost a stranger to me, and when he made a casual mention of Nai Soon's passing up the line with a party of coolies, the inference was complete and the hurt more deeply rooted.

So much was this true that the knowledge of Nai Soon's presence in the neighbourhood did not register with any degree of satisfaction until Terry Reynolds' intense appreciation of the possibilities inherent in his arrival lifted the gloom from a mournful discomfort that was not easily appeased.

Terry's exuberance at our departure from Tonchan was due mainly to the information I had received from Laverton about Nai Soon. For him, too, the railway was still a big adventure, especially now, for round each bend he expected to encounter a too long absent Say Leen. This expectancy kept a softly meditative look on his young face, and recaptured at unexpected moments a smile that quirked the corners of his mouth in an expressive gesture of inner enjoyment.

Coming down a hillside from which I could see the river as a dark streak in the far distance, I found him waiting, lost in evident appreciation of a panorama which, to me, was dead and soulless with the barren joylessness of a long familiarity. Beneath the spreading expanse of jungle, in which the sun flashed from a million jewels left by the rain of the night before, and the unvarying tapestry of the smoky hills, I could sense the desolation and decay of a million years. I could feel, too, the all-pervading unhappiness left by our uncounted dead. Therein was no study for a dreamy contemplation of nature's handicraft, however enchanting it might appear.

But for Terry, the jungle, with all its shoddy finery and affectations, was not yet spoiled. His artistic soul and, maybe, his quixotic love, still prompted him to enthuse about its appealing wistfulness and its possible delights – delights which were as inextricably mixed with evil as Tonchan's crystal cascade, which was now behind us.

To me, the jungle was a harlot, over-dressed and flamboyant, hiding beneath its ostentatious display a promise of disease and degeneration. Not so well acquainted with life's little peculiarities nor so cynical of first impressions, Terry knew nothing of harlots nor did he yet know the jungle for what it was. Standing on the hillside waiting for me he could see it only from the viewpoint of his temperamental artistry and viewed in that perspective, the jungle unfolded in a pleasing and generous panorama that gave no hint of its underlying trickery and deceit that could rise up suddenly, and usually unexpectedly, to belie its apparent placidity.

It was good, I supposed, to see beauty with an unjaundiced eye that did not inquire too closely into its ramifications, and for a moment I envied Terry his enjoyment of something I was no longer able even to appreciate. But the moment was as fleeting as a thought, and when he swung round to inquire with a solicitude I had not expected, it had already gone:

'What's the matter, Mick, is your leg hurting?'

'Not any more than usual,' I grunted. 'But I wish you would not be in such a damned hurry just the same. We are not going anywhere important, and we have all our lives to get there...'

'You know that is not true,' he said unexpectedly. 'At times your cynicism is too patently false, Mick. Why don't you admit that ulcer is hurting like hell and let me carry your kit?'

'In that you do me an injustice, Terry. I am not, as you, appear to think, markedly handicapped by this confounded ulcer; neither, on the other hand, am I weighed down by my kit – it is too scanty for that. If you must know, I am bowed beneath the weight of an introspective conjecture that does not lighten with the passing miles.'

'Laverton?'

'Yes – and offshoots from that source. Has it occurred to you that we may be rushing along this muddy track to destiny, Terry?'

'I had not really thought about it,' he said, puzzled. 'Why?'

'I don't know why I should bring this up, but since meeting Laverton again I have been deeply concerned with a possibility I had not before envisioned.'

'I don't quite follow you,' he said, as we went down the hill together, not wanting to lag too far behind the main body of our party, though we were by no means the last, for all the sick men had not gone up the river by barge. As we splashed through a stream at the foot of the hill, Terry added as an afterthought, having dwelt, perhaps, on the implications of my reference to destiny:

'I realise that things are getting pretty desperate, Mick, and they will probably get worse now the rains have started. Is that what is worrying you?'

'Well, not exactly, Terry. Though we may be approaching a state of privation and hardship not yet fully appreciated and, possibly, an unlovely death. I am concerned more with the possibility of a moral breakdown such as has undermined Richard Laverton's confidence in his ability to meet and conquer and situation that might arise –'

'He's had a bad time, Mick. It's not nice to lose your sight – I know that.'

'I can appreciate that, Terry. And I am not blaming Richard... not for anything. He is not the type that gives in easily. If he were I should not feel so concerned about my own future – my ability to measure up to whatever may arise. Frankly, if I had the option of choosing, I should prefer to suffer physically rather than morally, though, obviously, one state begets the other... so what is one to do?'

'You are not asking my advice, Mick?' he said seriously, concerned at my evident inability to reassure myself.

'I was not actually seeking advice at all, Terry, though if you have any to give, I should of course, appreciate it. My problem, as I see it, can be answered only by myself – by my ability to maintain my self-respect against all opposition. See what I mean?'

'Yes – yes, I think I do, he said, stopping to watch the death throes of a snake that had been neatly decapitated by someone ahead of us. 'And, strange as it may seem, that snake is a good example of what you are getting at...'

'Now it's my turn not to understand,' I said, wondering if there was any truth in the legend of that refused death to a snake before sundown. If that were true, this one writhing in headless anguish in the path before us had ten hours to wait, and it was a hot day.

'Why do people kill snakes?' he asked.

'Because they are afraid of them, obviously.'

'Exactly. And because they are victims of their fear they slaughter without discrimination, killing the innocent as well as the guilty.'

'Well, it's better to be sure than sorry, I suppose. Personally, I never did like snakes, harmless or otherwise. Which is this?'

'It appears to be one of Thailand's few harmless snakes, and were it not for the fear inspired by the species as a whole, it would not have lost its head; neither would I have been able to offer a solution to your problem.'

'Such as?'

'Well, from what you have told me I gather you are not too sure of being able to look yourself in the face in, say, six months' time and be pleased with what you see.'

'Yes. Something like that.'

'As I see it, Mick, there are only two ways a man may lose his self-respect. First, he may let it go deliberately, though in that case I am inclined to think it

268

doubtful he ever had any. A more likely way to lose it is through fear. To me, that is the only way. Fear being man's most primitive emotion, it can become masterful and demoralising and, if given a free hand, it will exercise complete control over any situation in which there is a divergence of opinion between right and wrong –'

'Hence this decapitated snake, which was without the power to do evil even before fear sliced off its head?'

'That is the point I have been trying to make, Mick. I hope I have not sounded too priggish.'

'Good heavens no! You've put it very nicely, Terry. In future I shall make sure before hitting out instinctively at every snake that crosses my path... it will be your fault if I die from a snake bit...'

Where the monkeys called a plaintive disparagement of the railway's continued advance into the seclusion of their age-old solitude, the jungle track brought us to a camp from which hope had fled an where the dead buried their dead.

High on a hillside above the jungle, over which the clouds swirled in mass formation, it epitomised all the evil the Nips had perpetrated since the first working party arrived on the railway. Originally 1,500 strong, the group in this camp had been one of the first shock battalions to go into action against the jungle, and in their offensive a third of their number had died, while the survivors, many of whom were handicapped by the stubborn flicker of life that refused to be extinguished, suffered horribly from malnutrition and disease.

Of the thousand men in the camp, ten were, by Nip standards of fitness, classed as fit – fit in such cases being applied to anyone who could still complete a day's work on the railway without dying at the end of it. Already dead were six stiff figures lying outside the gateway waiting for cremation, an outward and visible sign that cholera was a busy visitor to the camp. Caricatures in skin and bone, the remainder shuffled about between their huts, taking scarcely any notice of our arrival. Devoid, apparently, of any interest in external affairs, their minds and bodies were as dead almost as those of the six cholera victims lying by the gateway. But in one essential they differed. Hallmarked by the brand of fear, the eyes of the living were intense and haunted, gazing into a past from which there was no escape, and into a future without hope. To watch their pathetic shuffling and then to meet their haunted eyes was to know the surging reflexes of an acute emotionalism that constricted the throat and distorted vision.

'There are not men,' you told yourself in a half-hearted attempt to find an explanation of the obvious. 'It is not possible they once were strong and robust, able to laugh or swear as the mood took them. Voiceless and cowed beyond all description, their apathy is so tense as to be inhuman. This, surely, could never happen to me.' And on that thought you experienced another emotion, before which your resurgent hate went down in utter ruin.

Before you was fear, and as you looked at it, you became its slave almost before you realised the purport of the queer, tight feeling inside you. But only for a little while you were lost in a maze, which was not of your own contriving. Unconsciously you had been ready for just such an emergency, and after a short struggle you wriggled out from beneath the crushing weight of a new uncertainty and stood upright again, while the distorted image of a decapitated snake wriggling in impotent agony with ten hours to go till sundown came between you and the fear-haunted eyes looking without comprehension through the bars of a cage.

Then, as a figure appeared in the gateway to pause for a moment while it flicked a grimy sweat-rag at the flies buzzing in ecstatic appreciation of death, your inside turned over in a different way, and you went forward, trying desperately to control the pounding of a heart suddenly gone *hacha*.

'John! Oh, John! Thank God you are alive!'

'Mick,' he whispered. 'Mick.'

Then, as your fingers twined round his, you and he were the only living souls in a dead world. Everyone else had receded into the distance of far off space so that there was no one or nothing between you. For an eon of time which, in reality, was but a moment, you remained like that, standing there above the roof of the jungle, feeling through the quivering reflexes of his fingers all the unkind things that had happened between Nong Pladuk and now.

Then John spoke through swollen lips and, though his voice was low, there was a laugh at the back of it that made your heart sing in unison with his as the other people, temporarily banished, came crowding back.

'You look awful, Mick,' he said. 'Are you ill?'

'Not ill, John, but supremely happy. It's been a shock meeting you like this. You know, I suppose, I thought you dead?'

'I had wondered a bit about it,' he agreed. 'Things went haywire after the accident, and Smithy was taken to the Nip camp to be fixed up before they discovered I could do with a bit of fixing myself. I learned all that later, of course, and, unfortunately, I could not let Smithy know I was still alive before he went down river with the injured Nips. How is he, Mick?'

'Glad to get back to Kanburi, but sorrowful on your behalf. He will be all right. But you, John… this is something for which my wildest dreams would not let me hope… though I did hope, John. Believe me, I never really gave up hoping. And then, when I arrived at Tonchan and could find no trace of your grave – well, then I began to think that perhaps I was not being such a fool to hope you might not have been killed after all. This is terrific, John…'

'Yes, it's great to see you again, Mick. But didn't you meet Frank Manning at Tonchan? I told the silly ass to keep a lookout for you. You knew Frank, don't you?'

'Yes. I knew him all right… He was leaving as I got there – feet first.'

'Poor Frank' was all he said. And there was no other comment worth making. Manning was just another little link with the past that had been severed for all time. He was now forged to the chain of the dead stretching from Changi via Singapore and Nong Pladuk, through the grim wilderness of jungle and hill in which the living were making a chain that would remain long after the dead were forgotten.

Poor Frank!

For an hour we talked of each other, impersonally and in a roundabout fashion, not wishing to thrust too deeply into the other's reserve which threw up a barrier of unwillingness to discuss personal experiences only in so far as they affected people like Frank Manning, who was now beyond all conventional shilly-shallying. In that hour I learned many things, in spite of John's reserve. I appreciated why he looked fat, when in reality his body was emaciated. I realised, too, why his hands trembled, in spite of everything he could do to keep them still: John had been through hell, yet only his body had been blistered, and my heart sang in thanksgiving and joy for that assurance.   John   was   a superman: he had never lost sight of the shining star of hope that symbolised faith and a spirit that would not admit defeat. John would never be dragged down into the mire where hope lay buried, because he would never abandon hope, as so many others had done. Come what may, he would always be triumphant. Looking into his eyes, I felt the certainty of that knowledge and was glad.

'By the way,' he said at the end of a lengthy pause during which the bodies were taken away from the gateway. 'I have news for you, Mick.'

'News, John? You are the only news in which I am interested at the moment.'

'You will be interested in what I have to tell you. Or have you forgotten Nai Soon?'

'You don't mean-?'

'I do, Mick. He is in a coolie camp a couple of miles farther up the line.'

'Has he – has he said anything about me?' I wanted to know, feeling inordinately anxious lest Nat had let me slip from his memory. To do that was easy, I knew. Why, at times John had become a muted recollection in my remembrance. Why, therefore, should not I, too, be forgotten? Nai Soon doubtless had other more pressing problems to contend with than a casual acquaintanceship fostered during what were the relatively palmy days of Changi. But I would not concede that possibility – not yet anyway.

Between Nat and me there was a bond – one of those indefinable associations that materialise without apparent reason, and are not the easier broken on that account – that was as strong as the ties that bound me to John: a friendship cemented by the debacle that gave Singapore to the Japs and made us slaves.

The bond between Nai Soon and me was born out of a mutual rapport that recognised its equal and gave respect to it. Yet there was affection, too: for without one the other could not exist.

Nai Soon was my second inspiration…

'When Nai Soon forgets you, Mick,' came John's voice, solemn and with no pretence at over-statement, 'these hills will be levelled with the jungle down there, and the glories and tribulations of the railway will have been long forgotten…'

'How is he?' was all I could say.

'He is all right – quite well, in fact. He is a sort of *hancho* over the coolies, and does very well from the food point of view – luckily for me. But he has done a very foolish thing, Mick.'

'In what way? His perception is very acute; so acute, in fact, that I am inclined to suspect that you underrate him. I know Nat much better than you do. He is a very canny individual, I assure you.'

'I have found that out more than once. Just the same, I disagree on this one point. Frankly, I think it was just damn silly of him to bring Say Leen to Thailand…'

So she had come, in spite of all my hopes! Yes, I quite agreed with John – Nai Soon had been a bloody fool, to put it mildly. Oh, well, Terry would be pleased. But what about John? How had he become acquainted with Say Leen? That was a thought, and it took me back to Nong Pladuk and the first possibility of rivalry between him and Terry, if John ever met Little Flower. Well, it had happened, but I could not very well be too inquisitive of John's reactions to something I knew instinctively would impress him deeply.

'I was not aware you knew Say Leen, John.'

'In that, he is not an original, surely?'

'You are wrong there, Mick. Black Joe is not just another brutalised Nip. He is a specialist in breaking men, for he is concerned not so much with the body as with the spirit. To see a man radiate fear is his one enjoyment, and in this camp there are numerous specimens of his handiwork. Study some of them, Mick, and be advised in time...'

Having already done that, I had no wish to do it again. Instead I studied John, who had slipped back momentarily into the past. And in that past, I knew, was Black Joe – a malignant and at least once defeated Black Joe.

Watching John living backwards, I tried to arrive at a comparative description of my immediate future with the threat of Black Joe hanging like a shadow over it, and did not like what I saw. It was clear that John's body had suffered in his struggle for self-expression, as it was also clear that Black Joe's conniving had not made him a mental was well as physical wreck. John was still his own master and would, I knew, spit in the face of Black Joe and go down laughing. John was like that: he would put himself in the Nip's way, while advising me to keep clear, in order that he might vindicate himself again and again, failing to see he needed no vindication.

Could I do that? Could I keep fear from corroding the marrow in my bones and turning my disease-ridden bloodstream into something akin to weak tea, in which was neither sugar nor milk? Maybe. And maybe not. True, I had my quota of bashings, as had practically everyone who worked on or for the railway. But in a purely routine physical chastisement and a deliberate undermining of moral stability as practised by the exponents of the art, there was a subtle difference.

The pig, Sasuki, had been good at that sort of thing. And now there was this Black Joe who, if John had not over-estimated his finesse, was a blazing sun to Sasuki's twinkling star, and I was supposed to measure up to that heat and not flinch. Very pretty! Well, John had done it, but could I? Maybe 'Yes'. Maybe 'No'...

John was coming out of his reverie, and I had not yet found an answer, though somewhere in the forefront of my mind was the picture of a snake killed by fear, and the remembrance of Terry Reynolds' unexpected philosophy supplying the only answer to a problem which, as I very well knew, was perhaps a problem only in so far as my imagination made it so. I would leave it at that and wait on eventualities to supply a more definite assurance should the need arise.

John said, shaking his head:

274

'I must have slipped off my perch for a moment, Mick. I see you have finished your rice. It will be tomorrow before you get any more, and there is little body in the jungle stew these days. When the rains come in earnest it will not warrant even the adjective jungle. God help us, Mick; we have come to a pretty pass. I wish – but, what is the use? Forgive my bringing up the past. But when I look back along the way we have come, dark thoughts come into my mind, and they are not good to look upon…'

'I have them too, John,' I said gently, honouring his memory, for it was mine also. 'It would have been such a fine death – and in the best tradition, too. Sometimes I laugh at that thought, John – secretly, and with no amusement. Remember how we were going to make a great slaughter with the little Gurkha bayonets before the end came – just you and me together? It makes you envious, doesn't it, when you realise all the humiliations and the dreadful calamity that have befallen us since we discarded those bayonets unsoiled? That is the most awful part of it, John: the absence of blood, sticky and smelling like spilled wine. But was it our fault? I do not know. And that, too, is an agony which I doubt time will ever heal…

'Find no apologies for the thoughts of yesterday, John. Rather build them up and extract strength from them, lest you die tomorrow.'

'You are worse than I am,' he said, with a good attempt at a laugh, as I picked up my bundle preparatory to falling in behind the column that was moving off again, refreshed by a little rice and a quarter pint of vegetable water. 'I ought to have known our thoughts would still be in harmony. Good old Mick! I'll be seeing you at the end of the trail!'

Looking back, before the first clump of bamboo hid him from me, I saw him standing where I had left him, one arm raised in benediction and farewell and the other hanging limp and relaxed by his side.

Once more our paths had come together for the space of one little hour and now they were dividing again, and all eternity, in which there might be no John, lay ahead.

Momentarily, as the first bamboos came between us, I saw his arm flicker; then it started to fall, and in a second he was back in yesterday and I was marching on into tomorrow…

Chapter Twenty Three

Farewell, Jonathan

Islands in a vanished world, the hills of Kanu raised themselves out of the clouds – atolls in a sea of foam. Clean, magnificent and remote from a plebeian world to which they seemed not to belong, they intimated an harmonious peace into which the uncertainties and hullabaloo of an ambition-inspired philosophy could never enter. To them ambition was a new word, and they knew not yet its meaning. But, though they were old, they were not senile, and they would learn fast...

Like Tonchan's crystal stream, the hills were suggestive of everything that had receded into yesterday. Looking at them you felt – if you allowed yourself to feel – alone with God. Up there with the rest of the world hidden as though it were an affront in the sight of its maker, heaven became a distinct possibility, and was no longer a fairy tale mellowed with age and a too frequent repetition. Whichever way you turned, heaven stared you in the face, finding you sometimes cynically unimpressed, and at others, self-sorrowful, contrite and unbelievably human. Usually your cynicism was the stronger emotion, or you imagined it was, not realising that cynicism was but a subterfuge; an escape from a self-conscious appreciation of something into which you did not wish to inquire too closely.

It was easier if you forgot heaven, which only complicated your emotionalism and, so far as surface essentials were concerned, achieved nothing.

Hell, or its more modern counterpart, individualism, was a meatier bone on which to chew and, in the circumstances, it provided greater sustenance and gave a stronger incentive to go on living. It allowed you to fill your heart with a savage lust – a mixture of hate, fear, irresponsibility and, strangely, an anachronistic compassion that found an outlet even when a Nip was hurt. Or perhaps that was heaven sneaking in and catching you unawares...

277

Fundamentally, your generalising on hell and its attributes was sound, for it had no detrimental effect on your stamina. It was only when you started to sentimentalise – seeing heaven looking at you – that you began to flounder and feel uncertain and not over-strong.

It was easy to stand on a pinnacle above the clouds and, forgetting the turmoil on the hills' lower terraces, exclaim in fervent joy, 'How beautiful!' or something equally apt. Actually, if you said 'How bloody awful!' you would still be right. What you said depended on the ability of heaven or your own particular hell to foster the association of ideas necessary to the formulation of an opinion that would suggest your true state of mind when you beheld the panorama of the hills' majesty.

Standing as it was between two worlds, one in shadow – literally and metaphorically – and the other with nothing but the unbroken blue of the sky above it, you found it difficult to orientate your facts, and so give them the semblance of a truth unbiased by personal prejudice or an outward display of harmonious accord in which nature, unhampered by man's futile industry, was the supreme artist. Forgetting reality you could say with perfect truth: 'Here is a sublime beauty to which ambitious man can never attain. Here is the joy of yesterday and a heartache for today.'

Leaving it at that, for today was too close to be comfortable, you looked for reality and found it beneath a flimsy covering of bamboo and *atap* on the edge of the jungle, about a dozen paces above the clouds that made a girdle around the hills' belly button. In pursuit of reality as being more easy of attainment than an ethereal beauty that would probably let you down if ever you found it, you became inquisitive about an incessant buzzing as of a swarm of bees settling in a new home about their young queen. Leaving your pinnacle, from which you could see too much and yet not enough, you went towards the irregular patch of shadow from which the buzzing emanated until, stopping appalled, you wondered if what you saw could really be in such a sanctuary of isolated peace and uncertain meditation.

At the sight you thought again of Tonchan and the beast hiding in its crystal stream. Then, your nose crinkling in disgust, you realised that here, too, beauty was soulless and without depths.

Yet, for all your disgust, you watched fascinated as the bluebottles, ecstatic in enjoyment, swarmed about the naked and indescribably filthy figures lying on the soiled grass. So dirty were they you did not know whether they were fellow countrymen or just Tamils. The bluebottles did not care much, but you did. Then, as unseeing eyes blinked under the merciless probing of the flies, the lambent depths of their unfathomed brown stare mitigated your horror and, for some obscure reason, you were no longer disgusted. Yes, as their bellies heaved beneath the covering of filth that grimed them, you found you wanted to shout: 'These men are alive!' But instead of doing that you just thought it and thereby achieved as much as if you had gone up on the highest pinnacle and shouted.

Neither heaven nor hell was interested in your discovery. It was just one of those things to which neither of them would lay claim. And when you came to realise that, you realised also that though theoretically you were nearer heaven up here in the hills – 500 feet to be exact – you were, paradoxically, much closer to a blistering and too obvious hell in which the arch devil was a swarthy Nip called Black Joe who fed souls to the flames with an impartial and satanic delight unequalled by any old-world Lucifer.

Recollecting Black Joe, whom momentarily the lofty solitude of the hills had shut out, you began to listen for the symbolic rumble of his voice rolling up out of the mist that was beginning reluctantly to retreat before the heat of the new day. Leaving the flies to their feasting, you passed from sunlight into shadow, coming nearer to the rumbling boom that ran up the hillside to meet you. Eventually you were in a position to look down into the inferno where Black Joe put his victims through their paces in an industrious striving that knew no defeat.

Watching while the clouds rose off the roof of the jungle to give a glimpse of the river distant and swollen, you marvelled at a feverish activity that had something inhuman about it. Analysing it as an onlooker, you found it difficult to believe that two days previously you, too, had been town there swinging a hammer and trying desperately to shut out the pain from a leg ulcer that nibbled at your flesh with the insistence of the chisel boring into the rock each time the hammer swung and crashed down on it.

For a month you had been doing that until, by the grace of God and His not-taken-for-granted heaven – it was at times such as those you thought of God – a part of the hillside dropped off prematurely, bringing darkness and an abiding peace which, however, did not last long enough... But that was two days ago, and tomorrow you would be back down there listening to Black Joe and tasting anew the saliva of hate – a hate that was kindled the first time you heard his name. Recalling that time, a month of yesterdays behind you, you saw again a brave figure, ill and emaciated and with a smile on his face, waving good-bye from behind the bamboos that came between you and it.

Good-bye... good-bye... good-bye... For ever and for a day...

Leaving that friendly wraith, you skipped a fortnight and found Nai Soon, tactful and imperturbable as ever, but with a suggestion of sorrow at the back of his voice. Later, when you knew the reason for that sorrow, you appreciated it and found in it an unexpected comfort.

Experiencing again the bitterness and the joy of that meeting with Nai Soon, you found a twinge of pleasure where, so far as you knew, there was nothing but cold desolation and sometimes the suggestion of despair. It was on a day you had chosen to go to the kampong of one of the few jungle Thais who sometimes came to the railway to stand in open-mouthed incredulity of this reminder of a world which had passed them by. Coming back – hurrying in case your absence was noted – you came round a bend in the jungle track and there was Nai Soon…

Reliving that meeting, so unexpected and so long awaited, you discovered you had to recall your own personality, and to stop thinking as though you were a lonesome ghost speaking to an earthbound you. You and Nai Soon were all that were left of that little band of friends who had known the joys and hardships of Changi, and between you, even in retrospection, there could be no dissembling…

Nai Soon was sitting on a tree trunk that sprawled across the track, and on which where had been no one when I passed on the way to the kampong by the river where I had got two katis of tobacco. Smoking a black cheroot, he appeared much as on that occasion I had met him for the first time, as he squatted on the beach at Changi. As then, the smoke was curling neglected about his fingers while he savoured the mysteries of a deep introspection – but this time there was no salt-stained hat drying in the sun.

Startled by the abruptness of our meeting, I let the tobacco fall from beneath my arm while I gazed at him in incredulous disbelief. Gravely he went down on his knees and retrieved it. Then, handing it to me he said casually, as though we had met the day before:

'Hullo, Mick.'

'Is that you then, Nat?' I had wanted to know, feeling helpless with relief. 'Really you?'

'Yes, Mick. We meet again,' and he smiled with an unmistakable pleasure that warmed my heart. 'I am unexpected, I suppose… but, nevertheless, I am true. How at the Nippons treating you, Mick? And your leg – you have hurt it?'

'Ulcer,' I said, impatient to hear more important things. 'But never mind that. Have you seen John Sommers recently?'

At that, the light went out of his face. After a moment, he said:

'I am sorry for you, Mick. Your friend is dead, This will tell you,' and he

280

handed me a slip of paper he took from a notebook sticking out of the pocket of his shirt.

There was no mistake about it this time. John had gone on his interrupted journey, and yet, I was not surprised. Neither was I so hurt as I had been on that other occasion when the premature news of his death came from Smithy. The note said, simply and explicitly:

'There is no mistake this time, Mick. Nai Soon will take this message to you only if I die, and I shall die, Mick – my body has let me down. Funny thing, it often works out that way, and a man cannot live on his will-power alone. He must have a body to wrap round it. Actually, I was dying when we met last time, Mick, and somehow I sensed that you knew, and I was glad you came in time.

'Do not grieve for me, Mick. After all, there is no cause for grief: I am losing nothing. And, more important, I have lost nothing.

'Remember me to Smithy and Laverton, should you meet them again. While as for yourself, Mick, I can only give you a final good-bye. We have been very close together through the good and the bad times, and we still are close and always will be.

'God bless you Mick – John.'

Then a final P.S.: 'Nai Soon is very sorrowful. He has been a good friend.

Nai Soon added a rider to John's 'Good-bye':

'He is buried up on the hill, Mick, within sound of the railway that took his life. Perhaps one day we shall go there together, you and I... In the meantime, what of yourself? Here we are together again, and I had thought that perhaps it would never happen. But life is strange that way... And you are very thin, Mick. You are not so well –'

'We all look that way, Nat. It is the hallmark of the Burma Line. I am all right apart from this ulcer which plagues me at times.'

'I am sorry –'

'Skip it!' I said brutally, thinking of John. 'Tell me about yourself and where you are living.'

'In the coolie camp further down the line. I saw you following the Thai who sells tobacco... but it is very scarce. Though perhaps that is fortunate, for its scarcity has brought us together again and I am glad.'

'I too, am glad, Nat. Very glad...'

'Oh, Mick,' he said, dropping his guarded reserve for a moment.' It is good to talk with someone who is not a Nippon, nor an ignorant coolie, so frightened as to be unable to speak above a whisper.'

'I appreciate just how you feel, Nat. Unlike me, you are among a people who are not your own and are, I suppose, that much more isolated. But surely there are a few Chinese men with the coolies? And that reminds me. Why did you bring Say Leen to this hell?'

'You know, then?'

'Of course. John told me.'

'Yes. Your friend and she were pleased with each other. She is very sorrowful, Mick.'

'And what of my other friend – he whom you met that day in the courtyard at the back of the house in Sarangoon Road? Is he forgotten?'

'No. I think not. But it is a long time since that day, Mick. Still, Say Leen would be glad to see him again – I know that. And his name – I am sorry, I have forgotten it...'

'Reynolds. Terry Reynolds. He lives but to see her. Men are fools that way, Nat, and he is a friend of mine. You will remember that...'

'Yes, Mick, but my remembering would do no good if Say Leen did not already wish to see him. In that respect women, too, are fools... How is he?'

'Not very well. Too much malaria and not enough quinine. What he needs is a tonic, which gets me back to my original question: Why did you bring Little Flower to Thailand, Nat?'

'Your Terry Reynolds could possibly supply the answer to that, Mick. I did not bring her; she came.'

That had surprised me, for I had not thought such a fragile mortal as Say Leen could be self-willed even with love to prompt her. Before I could make any comment, Nai Soon said insistently:

'Let us talk no more now, Mick. Go back to the railway before the Nippon comes in search of you. I will arrange to meet you again for, unlike your people, the coolies are not closely watched; also I have a position of some authority, and can move about at will. Often I go into the jungle to smoke, and to wonder about what will become of us all if the railway is not soon finished...'

Leaving him on the promise that he would contact me as soon as expediency permitted, I went back to the railway and finished my day's work with my head in a cloud, having shut John's death in the inner recesses of my mind where those things of a too emotional value were stored to be looked at only in times of desperate crisis or when a spur to incentive was needed.

That was a fortnight ago, and Nai Soon had not come and tomorrow I should be back with Black Joe, having profited little from the two days' *yasumi* grudgingly given as compensation for my accident.

Thinking of that, I drew back from the cutting where Black Joe held his devil's court and once more ascended the hill, but not to look again for beauty. Instead, I went with reality to the stream in which the work elephants dropped great dollops of semi-digested shrubbery, and in which the Tamils performed their ablutions. With a fine disregard for the conventions which forbade a man's pissing in his bath-water, they further contaminated the stream which served our cook-house, showing an unconcern for our sensibilities equalled only by the elephants that dropped their dung where and when the urge took them.

Swooshing a bucketful of water over the bluebottles swarming about the two dying Tamils, who looked so lonely in spite of their attendant chorus, I made a mental note of the fact that they were taking a damn long time about it, wondering at the same time how many more bucketfuls I should have to carry from the stream. Though I gave them one a day only, I had been doing that for two days, and it was a fruitless chore, sloshing water over a couple of near stiffs who were too far gone to appreciate it. But I was compensated by the thought that perhaps it cooled them down a bit and, too, the bluebottles did not like it. And there was a certain satisfaction in that...

*****

Shouting an imprecation, Black Joe raised his bamboo and the man who had stopped the swing of his hammer to wipe the sweat out of his eyes went down beneath the blow. Regaining his feet wearily, like an old man staggering under a heavy load, he hoisted himself upright and, gripping the heavy hammer, glared with the passion of near insanity at the sloe-eyed devil before him. Momentarily, while hate over-rode fear, Black Joe stood on the border line between then and now, until fear triumphing, the vice-like grip on the hammer relaxed, and the fire went out behind the now frightened eyes.

In the interval of time necessary for sanity to overcome hate, the other toilers in the cutting remained poised in a fixed tableau of expectancy, waiting for the smack, smack, smack of bamboo on bare flesh, and the horrible animal-like cries of the Nips as they finished what Black Joe had begun. Fearful and yet curious, the men watched from the corners of their eyes, feeling hate and, at the same time, a thankfulness that Black Joe had not picked on one of them. Towards the man who had been struck, they extended a compassion of sorts – a compassion more mechanical than sincere. Being subservient to fear and a never-satisfied curiosity, it did not suggest any concerted action against Black

Joe even when, at the back of their minds was the hope, tenuous and never likely to be realised, that one day hate would triumph, and the swarthy Nip would be split open from the crown of his shaven pate to his boot laces.

Visualising that day, they could see themselves closing in on Black Joe and his half dozen associates. They could almost feel, and hear, the hammers and the long steel chisels thudding on shrieking flesh – battering in a berserk fear until only a smear remained on the rocks among which they toiled in a hopeless despondency – a despondency made bearable only because hate spiced it with a promise of ultimate fulfilment...

It was stimulating to dream like that for a moment, hiding behind the allusion that fear could be overcome. Then the smack of Black Joe's bamboo coming down a second time brought reality and an over-powering realisation that it was too quiet in the cutting – much too quiet.

Black Joe felt that way, too, apparently. Raising his head in ominous inquiry of the unexpected echo from his blow, he mouthed a stream of half-articulate invective and, deflecting his bamboo to a new target, came charging among the idlers, who already were swinging their hammers in a desperate intensity that had behind it the driving power of fear.

Watching Black Joe, and feeling grateful at being out of his reach, I tried to trace to its source the insinuation of a thought that was nagging with the wish to express itself. Then, as Black Joe went out of focus, and the man who had been knocked down took his place, the hammer skidded off the head of the chisel almost decapitating Terry Reynolds, who shouted:

'What the hell! Do be careful, Mick.'

These days, when so much of the veneer of refinement had become chipped and scarified, it was nothing new to hear Terry swear. He was lucky; he was just getting into his stride, and swearing for him – not that he did a lot of it – provided a stimulus which had long escaped the more seasoned exponents of the art. But it was not Terry's puerile blasphemy that interested me; there was something down in the cutting that whisked me from my precarious perch among the rocks on the hillside, and took me back to Changi and a long-forgotten pie. Looking at it I forgot Black Joe, though I could still hear his shouts and the smack of his bamboo livening up the men within reach of it.

To suppose the owner of that scar was Jackson, for whom I had made a pie back in the palmy days of Changi, was to suppose too much. Why, even the worms would long since have lost all interest in poor old Jacko... Then the figure below me turned and looked up, and there was no recognition in the face. It was a queer, brooding sort of a face, and it did not make you think of moonlight on Changi Creek, yet it belonged to Jackson. There was no doubt about that. By some fluke of chance or mischance, Jackson had cheated death to become a coolie for the Nips and the butt of Black Joe's especial spite.

Poor Jackson!

Watching him through the arc of my hammer's swing, I was appalled at his stark emaciation, and wondered at his apparent strength. The way he smashed his hammer on the chisel was suggestive of an impulsive aggressiveness struggling for expression, and the baleful asides he directed at Black Joe, who had come back to stand watching him with a cynical leer on his swarthy face, were a mixture of fear and a hate not yet sufficiently strong to completely overcome prudence.

Uneasy because of a hate that was too apparent for Jackson's continued wellbeing, I went over to him where he sat in a brooding silence during the *meshi* break.

'Hullo, Jacko!' I greeted, trying to be matter-of-fact. 'You did not leave the hospital feet first after all!'

'Why – why, hullo, Mick,' he responded, surprised. 'I didn't recognise you. Wasn't that you up top?'

'Yes. I thought you looked a bit blank, but I am glad to see you. How is the back? Actually, it was that I recognised first. Doesn't look so good...'

'No. It plays me up a bit, especially when I swing that bloody hammer. That bastard Black Joe! I'll get that swine one of these days, if he does not leave me alone...'

Here was the old Jackson, and with a genuine grouse this time. His present antagonism was based on a more certain antipathy than his former assumption that the hospital orderlies had tried to starve him to death. Thinking of that, I wondered if perhaps he would have been better off had they succeeded. Maybe he was speculating along the same line, for he had sank into quietness after his outburst. Then he exploded again.

'Those bloody orderlies!' he shouted unexpectedly, paralleling my own thought. 'I wish they had starved me to death – they tried hard enough. Been better off... I can't stand much more of this, Mick. If I didn't hate that Nip so much I'd pack it in...'

'Surely,' I insinuated, 'You are not going to let a Nip get under your skin, Jacko. We'll have finished here in a couple of weeks; then, perhaps we shall get away from Black Joe and his gang. Why, man, you are a modern miracle to be alive at all...'

'I know that. But what has it got me? And I only did it so that those bloody orderlies would not have the satisfaction of laying me out. I knew they were just aching to roll me up in a blanket, and when they started to get impatient – well, I made up my mind not to die and so gratify them, the swines. But it would have been easy, Mick… it would have been damn easy…'

Yes, it would have been easy for Jackson to have died then, and now there would be no blanket… What a queer admixture. He was to go on living just to spite someone! Well, if he remained long on the railway, he would find it was much easier to reverse his procedure. And what a sublime conceit to imagine Black Joe cared whether he lived or died! So far as the Nip was concerned, Jackson might live or die as he chose, but while he lived there would be enmity between them – that much was obvious. And unfortunately for Jackson, Black Joe held all the trump cards – or imagined he did, not able to appreciate the fact that Jackson might produce a joker that would put the Nip out of business for all time.

Watching Jackson pecking morosely at his rice and scrap of dried fish, the conviction came to me that one day he would attempt to knock Black Joe off his pedestal of arrogant self-assurance. Once his resolve was sufficiently stimulated by acquired hate, the hammer would swing, and there would be no last-moment reprieve for the Nip, as there had been but two hours since. What happened after that would be final and conclusive so far as Jackson was concerned. He would be beaten to a pulp from which any remaining life would be let out by a bayonet jab. Nor would he be the only one to suffer. Every man in the cutting would be held at least indirectly responsible for Black Joe's death. In the ensuing intensified persecution they might, with reason, come to curse the man who had been instrumental in fulfilling their dearest wish. It would be all right if Black Joe would die and leave no unpleasant aftermath. But he would not do that. Potent in life he would, if he were killed, be as militant as a dead Tamil, and Jackson would be his first victim…

Little thought was necessary to convince me that Jackson would have to be dissuaded, provided he was in earnest, from any act of folly, no matter how courageous, that would bring an added hardship to the men in the cutting. It he had to kill the Nip – as I felt he had – then let it be done in such a manner as to suggest misadventure. But even if a successful "accident" were arranged it would be a long time before suspicion was lulled and the Nips stopped prying in an endeavour to find some clue, not necessarily one that could be substantiated, that might point to the individual responsible, supposing it was not an accident.

Looking that far ahead, while Jackson finished his rice, I wondered how he would bear up before the inevitable Nip interrogation. Watching him covertly, I was defeated by the impassive blankness of his stare, finding in it no clue to what I wanted to know. It did not imply any credible belief in his threat that was more a promise, to kill a man. Fascinating as was the assumption that he would kill Black Joe if given the chance, the obvious implications of such an act were too terrible to warrant even the encouragement of moral support, and would have to be discouraged, for everyone's sake.

'Jacko,' I said, 'you can't go about killing Nips just because you have a grudge against them. We all get that way at times. Often I get the urge to smash one of them as though he were a bad egg, but I don't do that sort of thing, even if we had the courage. Besides, what is there to be gained by it? It's only in the story books that slaves kill their guards and get away with it. You or anyone else can't kill Black Joe and get off scot free, unless –'

'Unless what?'

'Unless it is done in such a manner as to give it the appearance of an accident in which we had no hand. You would not want any of the men to get done up for something they knew nothing about?'

'I hadn't thought about that, Mick,' he admitted. 'I was thinking only of Black Joe and myself. I would not care what happened to me if I could get the swine, and I will one of these days if he does not leave me alone. Unless you tip him off!' he added fiercely, glaring as he had done after Black Joe struck him. As quickly as then, the fire went out of his eyes and he said, contrite: 'But you wouldn't do that, would you, Mick?'

'Don't be a bloody fool,' I said. 'And I don't care for your insinuation. Even if I did warn Black Joe he would probably give me a damned good hiding as a reward... you know what Nips are... and I'm not getting a beating for the sake of any Nip I know.'

'Sorry, Mick,' he apologised. 'I didn't really mean that. I get to thinking queer things at times. Maybe I'm going *hacha*...'

'That's more than likely,' I agreed irritably. 'The matter with you, Jackson, is you are brooding on Black Joe's fondness for using his bamboo. Try to think less about him and keep out of his way for a couple of days if you can arrange it. That's the best advice I can give...'

In the days that followed it was apparent Jackson was making no effort to keep out of Black Joe's way. On the contrary, he always chose a position in the cutting that was within easy reach of the Nip's bamboo, every stroke of which seemed to give him a distorted feeling of satisfaction, as if he were counting them and adding up the score against the day of settlement. Normally brooding and saturnine, he had acquired a look of malignant malevolence that was intensified by his shock of unkempt black hair in which streaks of grey were beginning to show.

Withdrawn into himself he sat hunched by the fire in the evenings talking to no one, and wishing for no outside contacts other than the object of his dark and secret plotting, and the continual ache in his disfigured back. No longer did he bother to get water from the stream to boil for his nightly wash, and, unless coaxed to use that provided by someone else, he dispensed with washing altogether.

Gradually a feeling was building up that he was going *hacha*, and I felt sure Jackson got a kick out of that. To him it was the culmination of a thought he had himself expressed and would, therefore, be a source of sardonic amusement.

Maybe his sanity was breaking down – as God knows it had every right to. Or maybe he was building up an aura of impending insanity that would explain some incident he was planning to manufacture.

Only he and I knew what that was likely to be, and there was little I could do other than take on the part of executioner myself. Yet I had no intention of doing that, even though I hated Black Joe for what he had done to John and what he was doing to the men in the cutting, myself included.

Perhaps it would be more accurate to say I had not the necessary foolhardy courage to sink my hammer into Black Joe's shaven pate, though in retrospect the doing of it gave a suggestion of lustful delight.

It was only poor, borderline Jackson who would ever have the courage – fleeting though it might be – to accomplish what so many of us desired to do, yet left undone, fearing a punishment that would, in the end, be a release...

Chapter Twenty Four

Black Joe's Blood Is Red

Little Flower came just in time. No longer could memory and pictures in the fire compete successfully against malnutrition, disease and insufficient rest.

Inexorably Terry Reynolds was being forced to the edge of the abyss into which John had gone and, do what I could, his indifference defeated me. Soon, I knew, there would be another little cross, or maybe a pile of ashes to be scattered for the rain to beat into the earth – another few ounces of fertiliser for the ravenous jungle. Fortuitously before that could happen, I was reunited with Nai Soon.

In hospital, with a too frequently recurring malaria for which there was not enough quinine, Terry reacted in a way I had not anticipated. I had expected him to become excited and possibly reminiscent, for he had not spoken of Little Flower for a long time. Instead of doing that, he slid off the bamboo sleeping platform, divested himself of his shorts and went out into the monsoon that was drenching the jungle in a torrential downpour. For ten minutes the rain lashed his over-heated body; then he came back into the hut.

'That's better, and so am I,' he said. 'A good wash always makes me feel I have put on a clean shirt... Where is she, Mick?'

'In that coolie camp down the line. Why?'

'I am going there.'

'You are not!'

'I am!'

That, at least, was something I had been expecting and not wanting.

'Look here, Terry,' I said, abandoning direct persuasion. 'You have waited a long time for this. I, too, have waited a long time – for Nai Soon. It would be a pity if either of us did something that might bring trouble to Say Leen or her brother –'

'You are right as usual, Mick,' he said, after a moment's reflection. 'I had not thought of that. Sorry.'

'Rather be glad, Terry. In a day or so you will see Little Flower again, and I wish you joy. In the meantime see that you remain on the sick list so that you may have time on your hands, when the moment arrives...'

What happened when it did arrive I do not know. With Nai Soon's connivance they met somewhere in the concealing jungle, and, when Terry came back, there was a light on his face that had not been there before. Also he was buoyant and brimful of life – at least on the surface – and tucked inside the shirt he had donned for the occasion was the piece of canvas I had not seen since Tonchan. Evidently at least one of the pictures in the fire was on the way to becoming a reality.

But reality was never far from us. One evening it brought Nai Soon to me while I was squatting over the fire – our one comfort in a dismal world – optimistically scraping a couple of buffalo feet that had been discarded by the Nip cook-house.

Usually unruffled and placid as the surface of a quiet backwater, Nai Soon was troubled by the storm of a deep emotion that filled me with sudden alarm and scrubbed the possibility of buffalo stew from my mind. While yet beyond the circle of the reaching firelight, he broke into a torrent of vituperative Chinese, startling in its vehement unexpectedness. Though I could not understand but an occasional word, it was obvious he was cursing someone; obvious, too that that someone was a Nip.

'What's the matter, Nat?' I asked, wanting to shake him, and not because my supper had dropped into the fire.

'Say Leen!' he gulped. 'A Nippon soldier –'

'What!' I shouted, feeling a nauseating revulsion that was like a kick in the stomach.

So it had come, as I had known it would! Little Flower of the fragile beauty that was more faerie than mortal, to be made the plaything of some bestial, sex-sodden Nip! The thought was too vile to be given birth, yet it came. It had been waiting there for this moment, and not it was free in spite of Nai Soon's reassurances. What I fool I had been to think he could keep her hidden. One glimpse of her freshness, charm and her too obvious virginity would set the Nips on fire, as would her untouchableness make her all he more desirable... Damn Nai Soon! For the first time I felt anger towards him, and he was aware of it.

'Don't look so cross, Mick,' he appealed. 'It has not happened yet. I know you warned me, but,' and he laid a long brown hand on my arm as though he were asking forgiveness, 'I thought I could keep her hidden from the Nippons…'

'Just what happened, Nat? Tell me everything.'

'Nothing yet. But, Mick,' he added quietly, 'I must kill a man.'

The way he said that was sublime. It was so in character with the Nai Soon I had met sitting on his haunches on the beach at Changi while the hat of his murdered brother dried in the sun. To say so matter-of-factly, 'I must kill a man' was more in character with his philosophical placidity, that yet was deep as a peat bog, than the torrent of incomprehensible abuse that had cost me my supper.

Relieved that Little Flower had escape, momentarily at any rate, from the horrors I had envisaged, I realised just how deep an attachment I had for Terry's inspiration.

Little Flower was such a frail morsel; such a wisp of unsophisticated womanhood; so – so virginal and so unexpectedly determined. There was nothing artificial about Little Flower; her beauty and charm were natural, not artificially acquired to attract.

When she laughed, which was seldom, she transmuted sadness into joy and gave hope where there was none. For Terry Reynolds she was an incentive to live and go on living when to die was more simplistic. Now she herself was in danger. She had been discovered and, like a rare piece of china balanced precariously on the edge of a table from which the slightest tremor would sent it crashing in irretrievable ruin, one misplaced step or one unguarded moment could mean her extinction.

Should the Nips get their hands on Little Flower she would die, either directly or indirectly, and the one thing in our lives that was beautiful would disappear… What a bloody fool Nat had been to allow her to come to the railway!

Come to that, what a lot of bloody fools we all were! Terry, with his crazy idea of painting a picture of his jungle fairy; Jackson, who had not the sense to die and let bygones look after themselves; and me, still dreaming of an escape that would never materialise this side of heaven, or hell either for that matter. And Nai Soon, what did he dream of these days? Sometimes of helping me on the road to fulfilment, doubtless, and sometimes of problems I could not fathom. And Little Flower, what had she been dreaming of before the Nippon soldier shattered the idyllic piquancy of her precarious existence? Of Terry Reynolds, without any doubt and I hoped, just once in a while, of John, who was not bothering me anymore. For Terry, she had reserved a special niche into which no one else could penetrate, and I doubted even if John had ever looked into it.

When opportunity beckoned, she and Terry met in the jungle, to sit holding hands in some sheltered nook. But for them there was none of the childish nonsense I spoke as being the only way I could converse with her. For Little Flower and Terry there was the universal language of love, and between them there were no secrets.

Once, when we all met in the jungle, as we did occasionally, I made a garland of tree orchids which I put around her neck – Terry being too bashful for some reason or other. When I did that she gave me one of her rare tinkling laughs and said something in Chinese to Nai Soon standing by in approving detachment, as he was standing now waiting for my pre-occupation to come to an end.

That had been a pleasant afternoon. It had left a lingering memory and now there was a shadow on it…

'I've been expecting something like this to happen, Nat,' I said at last: 'and I'm afraid I must repeat my disapproval of you allowing Say Leen to come to Thailand.'

'Yes, Mick,' he said without any attempt at defence. 'And now that you have been proved right, there is only one thing for me to do…'

'And that is to kill a man – a Nip? Risky business, Nat. Do you have to do it? What actually happened?'

'Today as Little Flower was washing at the stream, where sometimes she meets your friend Terry, a Nippon soldier came, but she hit him and got away. He followed her to our camp, and I know he will come again – maybe when I am on the railway. The Tamils would not intervene, Mick – they are so afraid of the Nippon – and Say Leen would kill herself. I have given her a knife… He must die.'

'Have you any idea which Nip it was, Nat? Anyone I know?'

'Yes, Mick. He is thick-set and very dark, and his forehead is low and sloping like a – like an ape's. I have seen him often in the cutting where you work. He is a bad man and often beats your friends –'

'Black Joe!' I interrupted, amazed. 'Black Joe the – the – but never mind the adjectives, Nat. There is no point in my contaminating your English.'

'Very well, Mick, but he is everything you say!'

So there was going to be rivalry for Black Joe's head, and the semi-demented Jackson was not likely to get it. Instead, a young Chinese girl of whom he knew nothing, yet who had a kinship with him in their mutual desire for revenge, was to be the instrument that would decide whether the Nip lived or died.

There could be no doubt of the identity of the Nip who had chased Little Flower – he was Black Joe. Knowing that, I now knew to whom we owed the comparatively easy time we had in cutting that day.

While I had been swinging my hammer in slow tempo, and thanking Providence for making Black Joe take a holiday, he had been pursuing Little Flower through the jungle, ravenous as any wild beast and, doubtless, incensed at being frustrated by such an apparently helpless victim. Fragile though she might be, Little Flower apparently had a strong sense of self-preservation, hence Black Joe's frustration.

Terry would be relieved and gratified by her escape. On reflection it would be inadvisable to tell him anything about the affair. Little Flower, while supplying a fillip to his wasted body, could do nothing about the malaria that was sapping the life out of him by turning his blood to the semblance of coloured water. If he found out about Black Joe, it would not be possible to keep him in the hospital hut, where he was fortunate to be. He would insist in going to the coolie camp, and that would be the end of both him and Little Flower.

Nai Soon was all for sticking a knife in Black Joe, thereby terminating the affair before it could gather momentum. Easy of accomplishment, perhaps, but a waste of precious life – Nai Soon's. Here was the impetuousness of Jackson, who was willing to sacrifice his own life in order to destroy his enemy. In Jackson such a fatalistic outlook was to be expected, while in Nai Soon it was to be deplored for its lack of finesse and attention to detail. Now, if I were planning to kill a man...

After all, why not?

If Black Joe had to go down the hill, as apparently he had, then he should go as the result of an accident that would leave no suggestion of foul play in the minds of the Nips who investigated it. That sort of thing would not be easy to arrange though, and to bring it to a successful conclusion, Black Joe would have to be isolated from the other Nips.

Thinking of that, I could see nothing but a blank, uninviting wall which suggested nothing. Black Joe was never alone in the cutting, but when he left it... There was the obvious solution! A solution which, if it worked out right, would put Black Joe's blood on his own head and give my conscience less reason for unease – not that my conscience troubled me much; it had become sufficiently case-hardened to allow me to commit a technical murder. The slaughter of Black Joe would be an unadulterated pleasure – a duty that had been long neglected. Unwittingly, Little Flower had become the instrument that might destroy him. If he turned it against himself, that would be a matter for destiny and Black Joe. John at least would be avenged...

And so we came to an agreement, Nai Soon and I. Little Flower would decide which way the arrow flew, and if Black Joe bared his breast to it, the ghosts that flitted along the railway in the night time would probably think it amusing. I, also, would find it amusing. In fact, it would be a damned good joke...

Sitting in the warm radiance of the fire at night, it was not pleasant to reflect that in a couple of days I should have the blood of a man on my conscience if fate and Black Joe's bestiality willed it. Seeing in advance the blood spurt from his shattered skull – for I had fixed all the details while working near him in the cutting – made me feel queasy at times and wish I had agreed to Nai Soon using his knife. The conscience part of it was not a heavy burden; it was the idea of lying in wait like a baseless robber for the Nip to come into my trap that got under my skin.

Had it been possible to kill Black Joe while I was in a rage and while his bamboo was beating a tattoo about my head, the chore would have been a pleasant one. Failing that, I would have to compromise and stimulate a rage when the time came – and before. This was not very difficult when I visualised Little Flower struggling in his arms, and saw again a shadowy figure waving good-bye through a clump of bamboo. Then, too, there was a more personal incident that made me sweat when I thought of it.

The day following his pursuit of Little Flower, Black Joe had worn a bandage on his forearm where, doubtless, she had bitten him and, in a rage because the head had come off my hammer, necessitating a momentary interruption in its swing, he had deliberately kicked the ulcer on my leg. The pain of that kick was something I should never forget nor forgive. By it Black Joe had cut his own throat, and it would be fun to see him dying...

Nai Soon was agreeable to my plan for exterminating the Nip, though I had to use a good deal of persuasion to convince him I was doing the right thing. He wanted to be the one to strike the actual blow, and I sympathised with his ambition, knowing that my way was not his.

'It would be much simpler for me to stick a knife in him, Mick,' he pointed out, going back to his original argument. 'I could do that without thinking about it, but not your way...'

'And conversely, Nat, I could not do it your way. I can attune myself to the pitch where I can smash his skull with anything that might be handy. Your sticking a knife into him would, I agree, be a more delicate operation than mine, though not necessarily any more effective. Then, too, my method provides for a simple explanation that would not apply if a knife were used. Another thing, Nat; we must not underrate the Nip. He would skewer you as though you were a piece of cheese. I have seen him in action, and believe me, he is a tough proposition.'

'Yes, Mick, I agree he is a very strong man.'

'Then, let it happen as I have planned. I will avenge you, Little Flower, John, and Jackson – but you do not know him – and all the others whom the Nip has beaten. Finally, I shall avenge myself; then perhaps this ulcer on my leg will cease its intolerable ache…'

And so it was agreed.

Little Flower, who was to know no more than necessary of our plot, was to go daily to the stream that gushed out of the hillside about a mile from the camp. It was by a secluded pool of this stream, where she went to wash and sometimes to meet Terry Reynolds who, thank goodness, was still in hospital and in ignorance of what was afoot, that Black Joe had come upon her. It was certain he would go there again with his desire for Little Flower to urge him and, if he did that, it would be the end of the drama one way or the other.

The spot was idyllic for lovers and, paradoxically, a fine location for a murder. Well screened by the jungle, it was sufficiently secluded to be known to only a few – and Black Joe was one of the few.

In a sparkling cascade the water gushed out of the rock to form a little pool where it tarried a moment before tumbling over the edge of a twenty foot drop to vanish into the tangled growth of the lower jungle. At the end of its twenty foot tumble was a pile of rocks on which Black Joe would be found with his brains – if he had any – messing up the scenery around him.

If the affair were well managed, it would pass for an accident, if not too closely investigated. The body probably would never be found, though I hoped it would, so that the suspicion of the Nips, which would be aroused when Black Joe disappeared, would not result in some innocent party – the jungle Thais, for instance – getting the blame. I had seen that sort of thing happen and I did not want to bring it about again.

Looking back on the incident of Black Joe – though usually I prefer to look forward – I am gratified in the belief that fate was working against him. When he outraged my sensibilities by his overdone brutality, he could have had no suspicion that his act was going to be instrumental in his undoing. By that unnecessary gesture, so typical of his race, he made me incapable of standing – as he thought – and, consequently, I was put on the camp byouki list and given another three day *yasumi*.

On the last of those days Black Joe died...

Jackson had been in hospital a fortnight and was still alive. For some time he had not mentioned Black Joe, so that I was beginning to hope he was getting a more rational outlook on what was, after all, an inevitable situation. He was more cheerful than I had ever known him. Also, an outstanding improvement, he had developed a sudden urge to share with the other patients any little luxury that was given to him. This was a different Jackson from the greedy and spiteful individual I had known at Changi and in the cutting. Contrite and without a grievance, he was a model patient and profited accordingly. Perhaps that explained his change of heart but as I was willing to be convinced, I was not too sceptical until Terry said something that suggested Jackson was playing a deep game.

'Jackson has been up to something,' Terry said, when I went in to see him and talk about Little Flower.

'What do you mean?' I asked, not feeling surprised at Terry's obvious dislike. Ever since Jackson had made some scathing comment about the half-finished painting of Say Leen, there had been enmity between then and, had they been physically capable, there would have been open warfare.

'Jackson goes out for a benjo pretty frequently, as you may imagine. More often than necessary, I feel sure. Why, I don't know, but I got suspicious, and two days ago I watched him after he left the hut. He was acting rather odd, Mick,' he apologised, 'and I had a feeling he was up to something. You know, he is a queer cove...'

'Yes, Terry. I know. What did he do?'

'He left the hut to go to the latrines, but instead of doing that he sneaked in among the bamboos and ran off into the jungle. And he's supposed to be very ill, Mick! He was away for more than an hour and the M.O. came round and raised hell. When he came back he said he'd felt dizzy, sat down and fallen asleep. As if he could with all those ants about! He's up to something, Mick. I feel sure of that.'

Terry was not the type to exaggerate needlessly. I should have to check on Jackson, for the time factor covering his absence from the hut might not be coincidental. Two days ago made it the day Little Flower was attacked by Black Joe. It was possible Jackson was tailing the Nip on that occasion when he was supposed to be helpless in hospital.

Unlikely as that seemed, I realised that with a man of Jackson's mental instability anything was possible. It would be advisable to keep an eye on him for a day or two, for if he had been spying on Black Joe he would now know about Little Flower.

Though he could be aware of her friendship with me and Terry, I did not want him making some remark that could put Terry wise to what was being planned. If he found out about Black Joe's interest in Little Flower he would quit the hospital hut, weak as he was, and probably commit some crass act that would totally mitigate our plans for the successful elimination of Black Joe.

'I shouldn't worry about Jackson, Terry,' I advised, hoping he would keep away from the man. 'He is a bit neurotic – slightly *hacha*, I suspect… Probably he has discovered another *kampong* and is after a Thai *bint*. Keep away from him, Terry.'

'I will,' he promised. 'Have you seen Little Flower recently? How are she and Nai Soon?'

Lying on his bamboo bed with a couple of old sacks over his skinny frame, Terry's involvement with Say Leen was both a blessing and an impediment. Where Jackson could live for revenge with some warped idea of killing someone, Terry would survive only for as long as she gave him the incentive to keep coming back from the brink of the abyss into which so many had fallen. If the incentive were to be taken away he, too, would slip over the edge, leaving me with no further commitment but to attend his burial and, metaphorically, lay one more sleeper on the bed of the ravenous railway.

'I saw Nai Soon the other day, but not Little Flower,' I informed him, avoiding his eyes which had the shadow of death in them. 'He came to the camp, but it was too late to visit the hospital hut. Little Flower is fine; Nat is keeping her well out of the way, and the Nips don't often frequent the coolie camp – too scared of picking up something nasty.'

'I couldn't bear it if any harm were to befall her, Mick. Her being there makes like bearable, but the Nips –'

'Don't worry about the Nips, Terry. They don't mix with the coolies, I assure you. Too scared of getting cholera…'

'Yes, of course – cholera. That's something else I had not considered. Do you think there is any danger of Little Flower getting it? Many of the coolies die –'

'There you go again!' I chided. 'See what love does for one.'

That may have eased Terry's concern but it was no relief to me, for frankly I had not even considered the possibility that Little Flower's living in a coolie camp made her vulnerable to the great slayer – cholera – that was dreaded both by the Nips and the P.O.W.s.

'I suppose I do worry a bit, Mick,' he confessed, breaking into my introspection. 'She is so fragile and it is so – so unsatisfying lying here knowing she is within reach and I cannot see her. Perhaps in a day or so when I get a bit stronger –'

'Don't worry about that, Terry. I'll fix it so that she can pay you a visit one of these days. But we have to be careful; the Nips are not the only ones who would be interested if they knew what was hidden beneath those old clothes. In the meantime, I should advise you to get all the rest you can; you might have to go back to the railway any day now. A great many of the men are unable to work, and the Nips will most likely make a check on the hospital soon.'

'I'll do that, Mick,' he assured me. 'Thanks for everything, and especially for keeping an eye on Little Flower. Give my regards to Nai Soon,' and he smiled the smile of a little boy though he was a man...

Jackson was playing patience with a pack of time-worn cards, and a pretended indifference to my presence in the hut.

'Hullo, Jacko,' I greeted, leaving Terry. 'How's everything?'

'Pretty good,' he said cheerfully, throwing the cards on to the threadbare blanket that was his only covering. 'What's it like in the cutting these days?'

'Much as usual. I have not been working for a couple of days. Leg's not been too good. That swine Black Joe damn near crippled me!'

'Oh, him,' he said dispassionately, so that I wondered where all the venom had gone. 'Do you know, Mick, I had it all planned to kill that Nip. And I would have too, if it had not been for you.'

'Me? Nonsense! You would not kill anybody, Jacko,' I said, trying to put him off the idea.

'That's where you're wrong, Mick. He used to make me feel queer in the head, so that all I wanted was to bash him – to sink my hammer into his skull. It was the shouting that got me more than anything. I didn't mind the bashings so much. But I feel better now. To hell with him!'

There was a lot in what he said. One certainly could get used to being knocked about; it was the continual shouting that got on one's nerves, and made one want to do something desperate or silly. Something like smashing a pane of glass or throwing a piece of crockery to the floor. And as there was none of those things handy, the only alternative was to smash a Nip – but that was wishful thinking. It was also suicidal.

It was that stored-up urge to smash something, where there was nothing to smash, that helped me plot Black Joe's destruction. And I knew that when his

298

skull went crunch beneath my blow, a lot of the frustrated emotionalism would go out of me and I should feel better for it just as Jackson was feeling better for his rest. That is, if he was not pulling the wool over my eyes. I should have to find out about that.

'You don't feel like killing someone anymore,' I suggested. 'I told you you would feel much better if you stopped brooding about Black Joe. And I was right, wasn't I?'

'Yes, Mick, he whispered, bending over to pick up the cards. 'Yes. You told me that, and it's true. Black Joe won't worry me anymore...'

Standing outside the hut on the morning of my last day's *yasumi*, I watched eagerly while the working party fell in on the track that ran down the hill. I had done the same thing on the other two mornings, and now I was wondering if, perhaps, Black Joe was going to disappoint me again.

Just before the party moved off he came along the path from the Nip quarters, and there was no water-bottle at his belt. Black Joe was having another day off from the cutting!

Nai Soon came out of a clump of elephant grass as I came limping along the track.

'Is everything ready, Nat?' I asked, knowing there was too much excitement in my voice, and not able to do anything about it.

'Yes, Mick.' Nai Soon was very cool, and I envied him.

'And Say Leen? She has been warned?'

'Yes, Mick. She is ready.'

'Good, Nat! Get back and warn her – I am going to the pool...'

'Good luck, Mick,' he said sincerely. 'And – and be careful...'

But I waved him away and went on along the track without another word spoken.

I was on the way to kill a man, and words did not come easy. As I left Nai Soon, there was a queer, empty feeling inside me, and a mounting desire to turn about and hobble back to the railway.

I fought it down and went on.

'I will not think about this thing I am going to do,' I told myself foolishly, for it was impossible not to think about it. Black Joe's face, low-browed and simian looking, kept appearing in the path in front of me.

Its pathetic monkeyness started a chain of insidious sympathy. But I knew it was a fake: I had no sympathy, no feeling of remorse for Black Joe. It was fear that was pulling at me. I was beginning to be afraid of the task I had set myself. Black Joe was getting at me even before I got him…

'This is no good,' I thought. 'Sympathy or fear will get me nowhere. I must get angry. I must arouse my passion so that fear and make-believe contrition will depart and leave me the strength to carry out my resolve.'

I went on along the path not feeling any better. Then the thought came again and I camouflaged it.

'Who am I to try to stop the turning wheel of destiny? If Black Joe comes to the pool in pursuit of his evil purpose, his blood is on his own head, not mine. I am but the instrument of vengeance, self-appointed maybe, but inevitably picked out…'

Thinking that, I saw for a moment John's face grinning at me from the bushes and I went on, not jubilant, but feeling better…

The pool was there, shimmering cool in its quiet tranquillity. Down the face of the rock the water gurgled in childish delight to linger for a moment in its crystal depths before unbalancing to plunge down on to the rocks below, from where it lost itself in the swampy jungle.

Strutting the pool by means of the stepping stones at the edge of the fall, I came round to the great rock behind which I would hide and await the Nip's coming. Searching for that which should be there, I found it, and it was comforting to my touch…

Nai Soon had gone to some trouble when he designed the club that was to put out Black Joe's life. He had fashioned the handle so that it fitted smooth and snug into my hand. Giving it a tentative swing to test its weight, I thought of Nai Soon squatting on his heels working with a painstaking care. Once in a while he would test the point of his knife and think what a fool I was to prefer such a clumsy weapon as the club.

Soon I began to wish he was there beside me, for my efforts to rouse my passion with dark thoughts of privation and brutality were not a success. Nai Soon would be a comfort…

On the other side of the rock Little Flower's gay sarong lay in apparent discard by the edge of the pool. Coming on her heels through the jungle, Black Joe would see it and cross over to investigate, thinking her in the bushes. As he stooped to examine the sarong, he would keep on going until he finished up in hell and the club lay in my hand would be stained with his blood…

Revulsion swept over me, and I dropped the club to immediately pick it up again. This would not do. I was getting scared again. Fine assassin I was turning out to be!

300

In the stillness the plashing of the stream sounded like the roar of a waterfall. A flock of parakeets swept down from the jungle to inspect the pool, saw me behind the rock and went off in screeching flight.

The day was interminable. It was an eon of time wherein everything but the falling water stood still. Water in which blood would soon be mingled if destiny did not decide otherwise.

'Would Black Joe's blood be red?' I wondered in fretted abstraction. 'Or would it be an obscure muddy colour?'

Elevating the end of the club, I looked at it, but there was no stain on it yet…

I dropped it and another hour went by, while the water still chuckled among the stones and no parakeets came to squawk at me. Then there was the quick panting as of an animal in rapid flight, and a slither among the bushes, and Nai Soon was beside me, squatting at my feet with his knife in his hand.

At his coming the noises returned to the jungle and the tinkling stream was no longer a waterfall…

'She is coming – and the Nippon, Mick!' he whispered urgently. 'She showed herself to him as you instructed. The Nippon looked at her and there was that on his face that made me feel for my knife. I have it here, Mick. Look!' and he thrust it under my nose as though I were blind.

'I can see the damned thing!' I said fiercely. 'Keep it handy in case I fail.'

'But you won't, Mick, will you?'

'No.'

Silence and the plash of the water while I waited, thinking of Little Flower running through the jungle like a scared fawn with Black Joe in eager pursuit.

The picture started to heat the blood somewhere in the region of my feet and, as I dwelt on it and embellished it, the warmness gradually crept up to my heard and I was no longer afraid.

Black Joe could come at any moment and I would be ready…

The bushes across the pool parted, and there was Little Flower poised for swift flight like a nymph of the woods.

In disarray, her black hair made an accentuation mark about the pallor of her face. Her eyes, opened in fear, looked quickly over her shoulder back the way she had come, but she had been swift, and her pursuer was not yet upon her. Her green and scarlet sarong – the twin of the one lying by the pool's edge – was pulled above her knees so as not to impede her flight and her legs shone white as alabaster.

In momentary indecision she stood on the edge of the pool; then the upswept skirt of her sarong fell and quickly she ran over the stepping stones to disappear in the jungle on the other side, leaving behind a tableau of aching expectancy.

Again there was a noise from across the pool, but this time it was a louder, more determined noise.

The jackal had come to slake his thirst…

There he stood in his lustful arrogance mopping the sweat from his face. Evidently the chase had been long and hot, and he was ready to feed.

Ah! There she was, and he put out a tentative but determined foot preparatory to crossing to where the sarong lay half concealed by the rock.

Black Joe's foot was not destined to tread on that stepping stone ever. While it was yet poised in mid-air, an inarticulate shout came from a clump of bushes behind him as a figure rose up in a picture of awful doom.

It was Jackson!

Seeing him, a lightning flash of comprehension shot across my shocked vision, laying bare Jackson's secret plotting in all its crafty cunning. He had been watching Black Joe, and probably Nai Soon and myself. As I talked with him in the hospital he had been laughing at my gullibility in believing he had forgotten his hate for Black Joe. Now, when it was too late, I knew Jackson could never forget. He had been too subtle for me.

As I saw him rise up behind Black Joe, I wanted to shout a useless warning, forgetting that I had conspired to do what he was about to do.

But I could not shout. My tongue seemed fastened to the roof of my mouth, while I stood in full view waiting through that split second of time that Jackson's hands remained swung up in the air.

Startled by the unexpected shout, Black Joe missed the stepping stone and his foot splashed into the water, and he appeared to stumble. As he fumbled at his belt, the chisel in Jackson's upraised hands came down, and the Nip went over into the pool. Simultaneously, Jackson dropped the chisel and ran off shouting into the jungle.

Unaccountably horror-stricken by the enactment of the tragedy in which I had assayed to play a leading part, I waited for the space of a dozen heart beats for something indefinable to happen.

It didn't.

Then, with Nai Soon, wide eyed with incomprehension, I ran out from the rock and over the stepping stones to where Black Joe lay discolouring the water.

Chapter Twenty Four

'His blood is red!' was the first thought that came to me as I bent over him.

Black Joe was dead – horribly and devastatingly dead.

'We must get him over the edge,' I said urgently to Nai Soon, who was hanging back, not wanting to touch the dead Nip. But I persuaded him, and together, we dragged the body to the edge of the fall and pushed it over head first. As it went there was a lull broken by Nai Soon's 'I don't understand, Mick. I don't understand…'

Then the muffled thud of the body hitting the rocks came up to us, and Black Joe's list had earned its reward.

Slowly the red in the pool thinned out and it became again clean and translucent. The blotches on the grass where Jackson had flung the long steel chisel were eliminated, and the chisel I buried in the jungle on the way back to the railway. Black Joe's cap, which was floating half submerged in the pool, I was about to fling over the edge of the fall when Nai Soon stopped me.

'Don't do that, Mick,' he said, plucking at my arm.

'Why not?'

'There is blood on it – inside. The Nippon's –'

I turned the cap over. There was blood on it.

'I'm a damned fool after all, Nat,' I said, feeling grateful. If the kempis ever came to investigate Black Joe's passing and found that cap, they were smart enough to know that blood on the inside of it could mean but one thing. Thank goodness, Nai Soon had his wits about him after all. What a ghastly blunder!

'I'll hide it on the way back,' he said, taking the cap from my willing fingers.

Where Jackson had crouched concealed the bushes were broken, and there was not much we could do about it. Most of the footprints were obliterated or camouflaged, and we hoped the rain would complete the job before Black Joe was found – if he ever was found.

Then, clutching Little Flower's gay sarong, Nai Soon went off through the jungle to the coolie camp, while I hurried in the opposite direction, as anxious as he to get away from the pool and the thing that lay beneath the fall…

Chapter Twenty Five

Too Many Memories

Racing against time and the inevitable collapse of everyone working on it, the railway crossed the last defile in the Kanu hills by means of a viaduct one hundred yards long and thirty feet high. Built entirely of green timber out from the jungle, and held together by pieces of wire without the aid of a single nail, this viaduct was a masterpiece of that creative impulse which is so particularly Nipponese: the ability to make something worthwhile out of nothing.

Straddling the rocks beneath, the viaduct reared itself into the air and, when the first trainload of sleepers and rails crossed breathlessly over, it swayed and groaned like a woman in travail. Yet it held together and allowed the railway to push on to Kinsai, Pramsaki, and Namajon. And that was all the Nips desired of it.

At Kinsai, Sasuki was cracking the whip in a ceaseless urging that flayed the broken hunks of men who had long ceased to respond even to the driving stimulus of fear. To him it was becoming apparent that there was no longer an inexhaustible reserve of manpower for the railway – and the job was not yet finished. Too many lives had been expended recklessly – and needlessly – and now there was no influx of fit men to take the place of the thousands who had died, and the other thousands who were dying.

That did not worry Sasuki a lot. He still had his quota of slaves, even if half of them could count their tomorrows on the fingers of one hand. While they lived he was determined to exact the last ounce of their endurance. Time enough to let them rest when they were dead – or when the railway was finished…

Appealing on behalf of the sick, the officers of Kinsai begged compassion from Sasuki. But the fat Nip could not give that which he did not possess, and his reply was terse and to the point.

Emphasising his determination to let no scruple of conscience stand in the way of the railway's completion, he said:

'If every prisoner and 50% of the Nippon soldier were to die, the railway will be finished...'

That was Sasuki. He had a job to do, and he would do it no matter what the cost in human life. In that, the man was admirable if only for his sheer animalism and the inability to realise that the railway was still dependent for its fulfilment on the ability to endure of some fragment of the demoralised and shattered battalions who had left Changi full of hope and confidence in the future...

Allying itself to our discomfort, the monsoon slashed in a deluge of rain that overflowed the earth and bowed the jungle beneath it. From out of a clear sky it came at unexpected moments to extinguish fires and take the colour out of the vegetable water that was still grandiloquently styled jungle stew. Starting as a muffled drum beat in the far distance, the rain came racing across the roof of the jungle, nearer and nearer, like the pounding hoofs of a ghostly cavalry, to crash in a smothering roar of water that sent thousands of tons of excavated earth avalanching back on to the railway to further imperil the meagre trickle of food coming from Kanburi and Nong Pladuk.

Swollen and arrogant as the Nips, the river swept down in turbulent flood, tearing gargantuan mouthfuls out of the jungle, which it spat at the barges hanging almost motionless in the grip of its pushing might. When the railway was "out" the barges were the only means of bringing food to the working camps, and when they were too long delayed hunger, hanging like a suspended sentence of death, tightened the more, and many died...

Contrary to the generally accepted theory that a man will cling to life no matter how insuperable it may become, many of the sick died *deliberately*. Whatever the idealists may say to the contrary, it was the only sensible thing to do. It was such an obvious and simple get-out from an intolerable position that its inevitability was inescapable even when, on occasions, someone tried to convince himself that a glimmer of hope still shone in the barren waste of our existence.

To die deliberately and without fuss was to remove oneself from the ambit of Sasuki's influence. It was a decisive cutting of an anachronistic convention that bound one's body to an aching weariness that was not lessened by the dividing line between day and night, for day and night were no longer divisible even though the sun went down behind the hills, and the moon rose beautiful over the jungle. Time was measured only by the face of the clock, and by the snatched moments of rest that not even the Nips could entirely eliminate.

No longer did admittance to hospital give an assurance of immunity from the Nips' ceaseless demands. Always insistent on having a full complement of men on every working party, they now stormed through the hospital slashing out with their bamboos in an indiscriminate urging whenever a party was below strength. When, owing to the physical inability of the sick to respond to its caress, the bamboo was unable to fill the gaps, the required number of patients were carried out of the hospital and dumped on the job, to be beaten for their inability to work, and to die before the day's end. Many, of course, did not take the sensible way out – convention still bound them to a hope that was not there anymore. Crawling back to camp on all fours, they died from sheer heartbreak in the lonely darkness, or lived to know the meaning of a useless tomorrow.

Always a commonplace on the railway, death now became almost unnoticed. One day a man was there, and the next day he was not. These days, when the railway was surging to its triumphant conclusion, death came easy and many took advantage of it, for it was no longer a fearful adventure: it was a walk in the park on a Sunday afternoon, or a half somnolent excursion into a world of apple blossom and the song of birds... and many grasped avidly at that lost memory and went out on the first tide of morning or in the evening as the sun went down...

Somewhere in the jungle between Namajon and Tomajo, Little Flower died.

Since Black Joe's death I had seen her but once, though Nai Soon came often at night time to talk in the darkness of the hut or in the moonlight when the rain was on holiday. Those hours with Nat were something I found I could not do without. Dispelling the numbness of helpless impotency that clouded my insensibilities by day, making me susceptible to the tidak apa philosophy of the Malay coolies, they provided a stabilising influence without which it would have been difficult, if not impossible to fight off the insidious suggestiveness that reaffirmed too frequently the undesirability of continued existence.

Nai Soon's quiet assertion stimulated and kept alive the ideals that had been fostered at Changi, and in which John had figured largely. By insinuating John into my thoughts, Nai Soon made me realise that the death of Black Joe had not wiped clean the slate on which the tally of John's debt against the Nips had been set down.

'It is easy to die, Mick,' he said, in answer to a question on the relative values of life and death in such a circumstance as ours. 'Many of your friends had already discovered that though, perhaps, it was forced upon them. Many of the coolies, too, have discovered it with gladness, though for them, it is not so much a joy as a melancholic acceptance of a fate that suggests nothing but the inevitability of death...

'But you, Mick,' he said, formulating a question which I knew he did not expect me to answer, 'You would not accept the fallacy that death is inevitable because life is not all we might wish for it and, accepting that, though you know it to be untrue, escape through the back door, when we have not yet tried the front?'

'The front door,' I said, evading a direct reply, for he had got too close to my thoughts for comfort. 'The front door is slammed shut, Nat. It is fastened tight as though it were nailed to the framework, and neither you nor I can open it...'

'Not now, Mick, but perhaps tomorrow. There is always tomorrow, though sometimes you are inclined to disagree,' he added slyly. 'When the railway is finished we shall have our tomorrow, Mick. I have not forgotten your hopes and aspirations – neither have I forgotten Ah Tek my brother... Remember how we first met, Mick?' he said, going off at a tangent.' The spirit of Ah Tek brought us together, and it still watches over our destiny... We will not die, Mick. We will live, you and me, to laugh in the faces of the Nippons who are going to conquer the world because they have built a railway and killed so many of your friends. We will live, Mick...'

'Yes, Nat,' I said quietly, stirred by his earnest sincerity. 'We will live, to laugh... or to cry, as Ah Tek wills it...'

Then Little Flower died.

Precarious as was our position, the coolies were, if anything, in more desperate plight. Without even the semblance of a medical organisation to give them a sporting chance against disease, their insanitary way of life, plus a serious cholera epidemic, was creating havoc among them.

Places of indescribable squalor and nauseous stinks, the coolie camps bred disease as prolifically as a female rabbit produces young. Dead organisms over which the germs of disease crawled like rats sporting about a rotten corpse, they had about them the staleness of death and the harrowing desolation of a tomb.

An anachronism in such a nightmare world, the frail loveliness of Little Flower belonged more to a memoried past than to the grim reality of a burdensome present. A butterfly lending a touch of grandeur to a dunghill, she spent most of her time in the jungle when the days were fine, instead of in the cook-house where ostensibly she was supposed to serve.

It is doubtful if Little Flower ever did any work, either for the Nips or for the coolies with whom she was included. On the day Terry Reynolds completed his dream picture, I saw her for the last time, and her hands were as delicately beautiful as on the day I met her for the first time in the courtyard at the back of the house in Sarangoon Road. Since that day she had witnessed much cruelty and endured a good deal of hardship, but her wistful appeal and her charming simplicity had not been dulled. And though the portrait was not an unqualified success, owing mainly to the unsuitability of Ashimoto's canvas, Terry had captured the abiding spirit of that ethereal quality that made her beauty so virginal and so unspoilt.

Sitting on a rock with the gay sarong that had lured Black Joe to his death pulled up to show her little feet hesitating by the pool's edge, and with one hand feeling at the trickle of water cascading down the face of the stone, Little Flower smiled with a secret enjoyment of something only she understood, and in her smile was the deep content of a woman well loved.

As I had surmised, Terry did not find in his achievement the joy he had anticipated. There were too many in the hut with the unappreciative mentality of the unfortunate Jackson, who had died soon after he killed his incentive to live. Though none of them was aware of Little Flower's existence, they could see only a subject for bawdy suggestiveness in Terry's creative ability, not knowing that every stupid quip was a pain and a cause for mortification. Rather than subject his idealism to the stupid wantonness of an undisciplined intellect, he rolled up the canvas and hid it in a bamboo beneath his bed.

In Little Flower, Terry knew an abiding joy – a joy that did the same for him as Nai Soon's quiet, unemotional reasoning did for me, but in his joy was the spice of sharp unease that would not remain stilled and let him rest when opportunity afforded. Often at the meshi break he disappeared into the jungle, and sometimes during the night he would leave the hut and walk off into the moonlight, to return hours later, tired and with no time for sleep.

Always at the back of his mind was the fear of cholera – not for himself but for Little Flower. The frequency of death among the coolies was, I think, more of a horror to him than death close to hand. Had he been physically capable, he would, in all likelihood, have taken Little Flower by the hand and walked away from the railway and all its evil portent. But he could not do that: he was beyond it. His vitality was a day to day affair dependent on the ability of Little Flower to sustain it.

On a day when weariness tugged at him like an aching tooth, he hurried into the jungle at the *meshi* break, and she was not there.

And the next day was the same. That night, though the monsoon was lashing the jungle in spiteful reproof, he left the hut naked but for a pair of shorts and returned two hours later, shivering but not feeling the cold.

'Little Flower is ill, Mick' he said pathetically. 'Have you got any quinine?'

It was idle to rant at him and to call him a bloody fool. I had tried that, and we had had a quarrel – a bitter and useless quarrel that produced nothing but the suggestive inference that he was living on his nerves. Now the inevitable had happened, and my fears, and his, were realised. But, thank goodness, it was nothing worse than malaria; she would get over that in a week or so.

'Are you sure it is malaria, Terry?' I asked, looking at him in the watery down, and knowing from the experience of a too frequent repetition, that I should be helping to carry him back to the camp at the end of the day, and knowing also that one day not too far distant it would be for the last time... But I shied away from that thought! It was too blatantly naked, and I did not like what it disclosed.

'She has been ill two days, Mick,' he said, with an unexpected helplessness emphasising his unease. 'And they have no quinine. Nai Soon had some, but he gave it all to those damned coolies – as if they needed it!' he added, ungenerously. 'I wish I had kept some of mine... I will do so in future –'

'Don't be a damned fool!' I said harshly, forgetting a determination to offer nothing but a sympathetic understanding. 'You know the quinine you can get is not sufficient for your own needs. Saving it for Say Leen is as futile as – as buggering off into the jungle in the monsoon. By tonight you will be on your back again, then who will go to Little Flower? You know I cannot walk that far on this blasted leg.'

'Don't let us quarrel, Mick,' he pleaded. 'I know I am wrong, but I cannot rest. And now she is ill, I need your help –'

'It is yours, Terry. It always has been yours and Little Flower's, and Nai Soon's. All I ask in return is that you will consider yourself a little. As things are now, every hour's rest means a day added to your expectation of life – one more day in which Little Flower will have the protection of your regard. Think of it that way, Terry, and you must realise you are not being fair to Little Flower – nor to me.'

It took him two minutes to see it my way, and by that time the water had soaked out of the sky and another day was with us – a day of portent and the cancellation of so many things which might have had a beautiful ending...

'If I can get the quinine,' Terry said, 'I shall know that Little Flower will be all right. Until then I cannot agree to anything. Nai Soon is coming tonight with some tobacco. Do you think-?

'Tobacco will produce almost anything, Terry. When Nat arrives the quinine will be ready, though I doubt if you will be in a fit state to give it to him.'

'He will come to you in any case, Mick,' he said, with a suggestion of regret in his voice. 'I'm afraid I do not mean a lot to Nai Soon. I think, somehow, he consents to my friendship with Little Flower only because of his regard for you...'

There was nothing much I could say to that because, in a way, it was true, though it had not always been so. Without being aware of it, John had found a deeper niche in Nai Soon's affection than ever Terry would inhabit, while between John and Say Leen there had been an attachment I could only guess at. Had John lived, and had Terry remained at Nong Pladuk, Nai Soon would have experienced no regret, for in John's obvious admiration for Little Flower, Nai Soon had found pleasure. Though he made no mention of it, I knew that was so and intuitively, I supposed, Terry knew it too. But he wanted me to deny it. He wanted, unaccountably, to share in Nai Soon's affection – to be accepted for himself alone, as John and I had been accepted, and not because Little Flower had picked him out. That, unfortunately, was an assurance I could not give. It was something he would have to do without – something that was not necessary to him as it was to me. Knowing how close John and I had been, Nai Soon was filling the gap left by his death in a quiet and unassuming manner that brought satisfaction to us both, and which demanded, for him, no other contacts. It would have to remain like that.

'Nai Soon is very conservative in his friendships, Terry. In a lifetime he will have one, perhaps two intimates. I, too, am like hat. John Sommers was to me what I am to Nai Soon, though latterly our dependence on each other has become evened up. You do not feel any sense of isolation because you know, or ought to know, that you can never completely take John's place, Terry?'

'No. Of court not,' he said instantly. 'You and John were more than just friends, Mick. You were more like brothers.'

'And the same is true if you put Nai Soon in John's place. You see you have no justification for believing that Nat does not approve of you simply because he may not give you his complete confidence.'

'No, I suppose not, if you put it that way. But it has bothered me for quite a while, though goodness knows why. Nai Soon is friendly enough, and I have Little Flower –'

'And that is a lot more than anyone else has on the railway, Terry. Count your blessings and leave the sour grapes alone. When Nat comes tonight the three of us will have a talk about the future for the railway will be finished in a month or so. Then, perhaps, we shall have time to think and to plan for the days ahead.'

But we did not have that talk that night, nor did we have it ever...

Two hours in the monsoon-lashed jungle had not done Terry Reynolds any good. Before the sun was well up in the sky, a particularly violent attack of malaria had him staggering around like a drunkard. Yet he would not be sensible and take the obvious way out. Ignoring advice and threats alike, he made his body stand upright when it wanted to lie down and forget about everything. Knowing from experience that when he did eventually go under, he would be out for at least twelve hours, he was determined to hang on until the evening and Nai Soon's coming. He would not be content to let me relay and information Nai Soon might bring. If Little Flower's condition had worsened, he knew I would prevaricate – and he did not want that. He wanted the truth.

Unable to see clearly, he hammered ineffectually at the spikes that fastened the rails to the sleepers, often missing and often crashing his hammer on to the rail. Twice he was assaulted by a dispassionate Nip who could recognise illness only when a man was unconscious or dead, and each time the bamboo fell I winced as though I had been struck. But he did not seem to mind: he was beyond mere physical pain, and there was nothing I could do other than to alternate between compassion for his helpless state and rage at his futile obstinacy.

Watching him, not knowing how to kick out the prop that kept him upright, I saw his hammer come down in a mistimed blow that shattered the haft and brought the Nip shouting and gesticulating with his bamboo. Then my chance came. As Terry bent down, fuddled and but vaguely conscious of what he was looking for, I gave him a push that sent him forward on his face in the mud and he lay still.

'*Byouki!*' I bellowed at the Nip, who was not sure whom to slash. '*Taxan* malaria! No bloody good!' and all the usual patois that was so much gibberish, yet which was indispensable to an understanding between us and the Nips.

'*Bageru!*' he shouted, pointing at the broken hammer. '*Dame, dame!*' The bamboo brought stars, but I had seen them all before; such astral phenomena were not rare and were not dependent on the use of a high-powered telescope to give them brilliance...

When the sun no longer glared like an inflamed eye, we carried him back to camp – not dead and not over-much alive.

Later, when the stars had retreated before the moon, which seemed bent on making up for the night before, Nai Soon came.

The fire had burned low, and most of the men were asleep, too weary and unconcerned with beauty to find any distaste in the squalid gloom of the hut where the mosquitoes buzzed in shrill acclaim.

Among the bamboos was the sigh of a breeze that ruffled the shadows, causing them to dance like marionettes guided by an unskilled hand... Fireflies gleamed like little eyes, kindly and reminiscent of childhood... Far away was the snort and shriek of a train picking its way over the bones of the dead, and not seeing the ghosts that slid, homeless and lonely, through the jungle clearings, or sat pensive on the hillside... Beauty walked hand in hand with dark uncertainty... Memories came, tarried a moment and went back to where they belonged... The Train came nearer and the silence fled... It came back and Nai Soon was with it...

But he had not come for quinine.

'Mick,' he said. 'Say Leen is dead!'

Round the corner of the hill the train shrieked again, and the marionettes danced madly among the bamboos, flinging themselves about in an abandon of grief in time to a mad refrain: 'Say Leen is dead... Say Leen is dead... Say Leen is dead...'

Distance closed round the last shriek of the train, rumbling on over the little bones, so perfect, so pathetically small, and now so useless... The marionettes' frenzied ecstasy quietened to a more formal metre, and Nai Soon spoke again, sharp and decisive:

'Say Leen is dead, Mick. Do you hear me? Say Leen is dead!'

I heard dimly, but very consciously. What could I say? Nothing. Words would not bring her back. The petals had fallen and there was nothing I could do... Little Flower – but it was futile to reminisce. Her beauty and charm, her whimsical little-girl-ness were now nothing. Gone also was the inspiration she had given to someone who could not go on without it... Soon there would be another empty place in which nothing lived but a memory...

'I do not know what to say, Nat,' was all I could manage. It sounded very shabby, but I could do no better, 'Terry said it was malaria. Surely –'

'We thought that, Mick,' he said, accepting my reticence. 'She died at midday. It was cholera...'

My thoughts were beginning to come into perspective.

'This is a sad blow for us all, Nat. She was very dear to me, your little sister who was a woman – my Little Flower. The tragedy of this hateful life we are forced to live is now more grim and terrifying... In me there is a great hurt

313

that was not there before you came… Nothing I may say can adequately express my sorrow, and I am thankful that is not necessary. We understand each other, Nat, and that is sufficient… You are alone now and soon, I, too, shall be alone, for my friend Terry will die… and how can I tell him?'

'It is all right, Mick,' said a quiet, controlled voice, and he stepped out of the shadows at the end of the hut, where the moon and the dulled radiance from the fire did not reach. 'It is all right,' he said again unemotionally, but his voice was dead, flattened as though it had been trodden on. 'I heard everything, Mick… Little Flower is dead… I heard Nai Soon say it…'

He came near to the fire. His face was white and calm like the face of a nun, but his eyes had a queer incandescence about them that made them seem luminous and dilated. When I took hold of his bare arm the flesh was cold, and there was no sign of the burning fever that had been rioting through him an hour earlier. He was a ghost with blood in its veins and I was partly afraid and partly undecided what to do.

Nai Soon, too, was dismayed. But I think he understood better than I what was behind the unnatural façade of Terry's self-control. He said quietly and with an unexpected sympathy:

'I am sorry for you, Terry. You have lost so much –'

'I heard everything, he repeated in the same flat, unemotional tone that was worse than hysteria. Looking at him I realised that shock had done unimagined things to him as he stood in the shadows listening. It must have been awful, hearing it like that, and I had thought him still unconscious in the hospital hut two hundred yards away.

'The fire is dying,' he said, in the same flat voice, kicking at the coals with a bare foot. Then, as though he had discovered something that required repetition, he added, 'Dying… Dying… Dying… Little Flower is dying, Mick, and you stand there doing nothing… Nai Soon said she was dying. Didn't you, Nai Soon?'

'Say Leen is dead!' Nat said incisively and, I thought, cruelly. But he knew what he was doing. It was as effective as a blow – and as unexpected. I could feel the heat coming back into Terry's arm and see the flush of fever mounting into his face. Reason and emotion came back together and he shouted hysterically, as though he had not already spoken the words:

'Little Flower is dead, Mick. I heard everything you said. She is dead!'

I was thinking, holding on to his arm: 'This is going to be awful!' when a querulous shout came from the hut:

'Not so much bloody row out there!'

314

Chapter Twenty Five

Terry heard it and it calmed him. It calmed me, too, making me feel grateful.

'I'm sorry, Mick,' he whispered in a little boy's voice. 'Something happened to me when I heard you and Nai Soon... I feel torn apart. Nothing matters now...'

In the torpid night I could hear him making little plaintive baby noises that were more clamorous than a shout. Unlike the sleep noises made by the other men – moans, shouts, hysterical laughter, disconnected gibberish that mirrored the awful injustice of life and the railway – they simulated the whimper of a frightened child and suggested a maternal commiseration I could not give.

Attracted by the fever sweat that soaked the old shirt we kept for the purpose, the mosquitoes circled and dive bombed in a mass attack that could not be beaten off. Excited, but crafty, they gorged themselves on his blood, to fly off, heavy and sluggish like overladen bombers staggering across an uneven tarmac.

The whole night was uneasy with a spice of despair that lingered like an aged prostitute, tired but still hopeful, at the corner of the street...

I began to think of Little Flower then decided not to... The house went by and the stillness was portentous with sound. There were too many ghosts about. I could hear the slither of their feet as they stole in one end of the hut and went out the other. I imagined them gathered in an admiring circle in the moonlight about the dancing marionettes. Perhaps they, too, danced and were jolly while I was sad... The bamboos squeaked and rustled, and in the hills the echo of a storm shouted with a loud voice... The moon grew weary and went to bed, prematurely and just in time... Overhead the *atap* fluttered with a windy rustle, then the rain came and the ghosts fled: it was morning...

For a week the jungle steamed like a noxious stew and the hills spewed great gouts of water as though they were being squeezed by a giant hand. On the railway there was no let-up; the rain did not matter. Cholera, black water fever, and all their attendant devils crowded closer. Death snatched with greedy and never empty hands. Sometimes finicky and fastidious it chose only the comparatively fit, whose fitness must have been but an outward veneer hiding an inward corruption that had rotted their bodies without their knowing it. At other times it gathered in a great armful of those who had waited too long and were not bothered anymore whether they went or stayed...

Since Little Flower's death Terry Reynolds had not been caring, yet unaccountably death passed him by. He was too anxious for it and it kept him waiting. Apathetic, and with a fierce, unexpected strength, he swung his hammer on the railway as though he were beating out a new destiny on the anvil of time.

Without the tonic of hate to maintain him, for he had never known the fierce joy to be had in its possession, Terry burned up the last inch of the candle of a ruined life, cleaving a way through the wreckage that came between him and yesterday. Desperately ill, in spite of his momentary strength, wanting no respite and getting none, he went to the railway each day as though it were a joy to work in the rain, and to come back stumbling through the darkness to the old hut where nothing remained but a period of waiting for another day's toil.

For him there was no longer any joy in the violin of Gus, the Dutchman, whose playing could bridge the gap between then and now. When Gus played, which was seldom for he was usually too tired, the old hut became metamorphosed, and for a moment our lives were equally changed. Noise and disputation ceased while the smoky, home-made oil lamps distilled a soft radiance that conjured up the tapestry of a rekindled memory. Back came the best from out of the past. Squalor, hunger and despair were stayed. The jungle and the railway faded, and everything we had lost, and many things we never possessed, came to take their place...

Outside the drumming of the rain dulled and receded, while the violin whispered and promised, and sometimes pleaded as Gus, the inimitable maestro, took us on the round tour that embraced hell, heaven, and a return trip to earth.

Open-mouthed, as though sucking in the sound, many of the men leant forward dull-eyed and sleepy looking, hypnotised by a too potent recollection that, when it faded, would bring a starker reality. Others sat smiling to themselves, living again as they had always wanted to live, and making all the old promises so few of them would keep.

Terry Reynolds had always been avid for the visions Gus could bring to life, and long after the last note had escaped out through the *atap* roof, he would sit with his dreams. But not now. As on the railway, he tried to escape from himself whenever Gus began to play. Simulating sleep, he lay on the bamboo platform or, when the night was fine, left the hut until reality came back to put an end to make-believe.

Then suddenly Terry was himself again. That inherent love of music and everything beautiful that had so severely handicapped him on the railway, making his dependence on Little Flower never in doubt, reasserted itself as a final salute to lost hope. For the last time he unrolled the portrait that had not been taken from the bamboo since Little Flower's death, then, unaccountably,

316

he burned it.

Seeing him do that was like witnessing an act of sacrilege, but there was nothing I could do. Indeed, I had no thought to do anything; neither could I understand fully why he destroyed his one tangible link with the past. And when I did arrive at an understanding of something which, at the time, was inexplicable, there was no profit in the knowledge it brought. Terry was dead, and there was nothing I could do about that either...

It was raining again and the railway was a morass of mud in which the Nips bawled incessantly, uneasy lest we falter in the face of the monsoon's displeasure.

On the last day we went out from the camp together; two sad mortals trudging through a world of woe. Unutterably weary and with the flush of a new fever dyeing the pallor of his face, Terry dragged his bare feet through the mud, showing no vestige of the unexpected strength that had possessed him in the days immediately following Little Flower's death. Going down the hill he stumbled and went to his knees. On his feet again, he said with an attempt at gaiety, 'This is divine, Mick. Here am I dying on my feet, going off into the rain to do a day's work! Isn't it absolutely silly...?'

Yes, it was silly – bloody silly, and pathetic, too. My thoughts must have registered on my face. Before I could put them into words, though not necessarily in their original state, he added, 'How pathetic you look! Poor old Mick! I have not been good company since Little Flower died, and now I am dying... we are all dying...!' On that his voice went up an octave and I no longer felt pathetic.

'Don't be a bloody fool!' I said harshly, and the gaiety that was too near hysteria went out of him. 'This is no time to think about dying. Soon the railway will be finished. Then anything may happen.'

'Yes, Mick,' he agreed. But I knew it was no use. The time, short as it was, was too long and besides, he did not care. My friendship was not strong enough to fill the place Little Flower had left empty. He did not mind if I was alone... Perhaps he realised I should not really be alone for there still remained Nai Soon and the memory of John whom Terry could never replace.

Poor Terry!

That night he died, quietly, pleasantly, and with no regrets, as only the very old or the very young can die. Surrounded by memories summoned by the magic of Gus' playing, his body relaxed and all the tiredness and the bitter heartbreak went out from it. Weariness fled, and the hunger and thirst, and the bitter taste of sorrow. No longer did the Nips shout for their voices were stilled...

Outside the old sack that covered him, one hand lay passive – a long, thin hand so like Nai Soon's; a hand that was not fashioned to be sacrificed by toil; a hand that was meant to produce beautiful things, and to give delight, as Gus, the Dutchman gave it. Watching that long hand, so symbolic of the man who was dying, I could still see a beauty in it – a beauty disfigured by the railway's vandalism as the last year of his life had been disfigured. It was a hand that had fashioned pleasant things, tentatively and hesitatingly, for it had not been sure of itself. Now it would soon be stilled forever, and not know the complete joy of full achievement.

It was a pity, that…

The fingers closed slowly and as slowly unclenched as the life went out of them and from his face that was dreaming and glad.

Gus' shadow was immense against the wall of the hut. The music poured out from him in an unnamed and unforgettable melody. It was a paean of ecstatic liberation falling to a whisper, poignant and unbelievably sad.

It was the end…

Chapter Twenty Six

Tomorrow Is Never

The symbolic gold spikes – in this case they were brass – were on the way up from Nong Pladuk where our regimented technicians had fashioned them with a loving care. In Bangkok the dancing girls were laying out their finery, and the Thai officials, paid to forget their illusory independence, were memorising their speeches of congratulation – speeches in which there would be no mention of the unseen multitude watching in the background when the final spike was driven into the last sleeper. In the working camps there was the anticipation of a protracted *yasumi* and a good long sleep. For the Nips everything was rosy, and they had no regrets.

Triumphant, in spite of the monsoon and the other trivialities that had beset it, the railway was surging to its close and the poor neglected ghosts were gathering to witness the culmination of the project that had given them their spectral status. John would be there in the forefront when the great day came, with a pensive Terry Reynolds and a wispy Say Leen. Laverton and Smithy might be there too, but I hoped not, for I wish to have something left...

Unchallenged in their ability to make the impossible become reality, the Nips were knowing the glow of a successful conquest and the deep satisfaction of a well-deserved achievement – an achievement made possible by a ruthless determination personified by the pig, Sasuki, and the putrescent offal that was Black Joe. Without their brutishness the railway would not have become a reality, nor would so many have died to gratify their lust for achievement. Now on the face of the jungle they had made a long straggling mark that would represent, when it was finished, the acme of ambition. The back door to Burma was standing ajar, waiting for the first through rain to push it open.

Banzai!

Remote and comparatively secure in the rear, our statisticians had got their figures to agree with the number of sleepers on the yet unfinished railway: for

319

every sleeper a life, and for every life a sleeper. A simple and not too ambiguous computation that would lend an aura of martyrdom when, and if, they returned home. As usual they would be the heroes, for they would have most to say, and in their loquacity would be the germ of a great tribulation. Like the Thai speeches, however, their loquacity would make reference to John and the other lonely ones only in so far as it was necessary to lend a cloak of reality to a threadbare imagination.

These compilers of woe were not concerned for the men who had died any more than the Nips were concerned. What shocked and gratified them was the numerical suggestiveness of death those thousands had left behind as a legacy. It stamped them with the seal of the martyrised, and in that they found a secret satisfaction…

But there was no gainsaying the fact that many had died, for the railway had been a greedy mistress. Ten thousand? Twenty thousand? I did not know; neither had I counted the sleepers, not even those I had carried, and some of them had been very heavy, suggesting perhaps the presence of a dead man sitting on either end: dead and laughing at my futile mortality.

But what of them, those dead ones? What, after all, were they when compared with their achievement? Nothing, when all is said, if one closes one's mind to the weeping and the wailing of their women folk, who had cried when Singapore discovered its stark vulnerability to the world, and who now would have to cry again. Sooner or later they would have died anyway. Later, in all probability, and in a more congenial fashion doubtless, though not necessarily to such an advantage.

By dying in such an obscure fashion they had attainted to greatness – momentarily, maybe, but to greatness just the same. With no dependence on imagination to give it depth, their greatness was the real thing. Built on experience and personal suffering, it warranted a better appreciation than probably it would ever receive. In building the Railway of Death – horrible excrescence on a people's suffering – the dead had achieved something it is not given to every man to achieve. They had built themselves a monument and a tomb – a monument that would last long after they were dust. Longer even than that. The railway would still be there when its antecedents were forgotten, or perhaps conveniently overlooked, which latter eventuality would not take an inordinately long time – not many years in fact.

Poor railroad builders! How fleeting, after all, is fame…

Re-discovering their lost humanism, or maybe finding it for the first time, the Nips were being kind now that kindness did not really matter. Purely

Nippon, their kindness was not too obvious and unless one realised the sincerity behind it – for, strangely, they could be sincere – one was apt to be confused by its ambiguity.

Now that there would be no further use for them on the railway, all those with a priority in physical decay were being evacuated to Kanburi and Nong Pladuk, and to the camps that had come into being since I crossed the Mae Khlong on the heels of Laverton, now a doubtful entity in an equally doubtful tomorrow.

With one page yet to be written in the second chapter of our lives as prisoners under the Nips, many of the men were concerned only with now. Beyond that they dared not look. Anxiously and possessively they re-examined their frailties, looking for a reprieve from the constant fear of death in the out of the way places to which the railway had brought them. Pathetically eager, they returned to the base camps from which they had been too long away. Still chasing hope and the promise of better times that had inspired them to leave Changi, they turned away from the railway and, excited and tremulous, with some of the horror already forgotten, they left by barge and train to begin another phase of enervating inanition and doleful frustration.

Some escaped this phase on the way down. For them release from the railway came too late or, maybe, they chose not to face the unknownness of what awaited them beyond the Mae Khlong, now lusty and overfull of life, but helpless against the Nip's contriving.

Recognising our usefulness in making the railway a reality, the Nips made a speech, a piece of typical Nip ingenuity that, coming from anyone else, would have stank of deliberate deception and cross purpose.

'Thank you very much,' they said, 'for realising the importance of the railway to Nippon… We are sorry some of your friends have died, but it is the duty of a soldier to die when necessary. Soon the railway will be finished, and soon you will be going back to Nong Pladuk and Kanburi. Continue to be good soldiers… Take care of your health, so that when the peace comes you may return to your own dear country, to your dear wives and children, and to all your dear friends…'

With the speech went a presento, equally ingenuous – two ounces of caustic soap and ten Thai cigarettes for every man in the camp. An expression of heavenly appreciation, to the Nips on the spot this presento was an impressive gesture of Imperial magnanimity. In it was the suggestion that the Son of Heaven had a detached and not altogether mercenary interest in our wellbeing. In honouring us with even a thought, Hirohito, the divine Emperor, had closed

Everything that I had hoped for has come to nothing. John is dead, and very likely my other friends... It seems that ill-fate and mischance have conspired to defeat our purpose. Tomorrow, when it comes, can bring little satisfaction, though, heaven knows, I am grateful that you are left to me. Without you there could be no hope...'

'There is always hope, Mick.' He said earnestly, watching the smoke curling from the last of Hirohito's cigarettes. He put it to his lips, but spat it out as though it gave him a dirty taste in the mouth. 'That cigarette,' he said,' typifies the Nippon: it contains very little that is good... Are we, too, like that, Mick, or are we more sincere? Are we to abandon our ideals because fate has not been kind to us, or are we to find new strength in the memory of John and the others? Say Leen is dead, remember, and Ah Tek... I do not forget easily... In me is still the urge to laugh in the face of the Nippon... Also, I promised that you should have your tomorrow, and you shall...'

It was a promise, and it gave me strength. It took the weariness out of me and made me buoyant, light-headed almost. Nai Soon was a potent spirit. His sincerity and his faith stirred me profoundly, making me feel slightly ashamed and regretful.

Since Terry's death, and since the railway had sprinted ahead leaving my behind, not helpless but nearly so, an enervating lassitude and a don't-care-a-damn fatalism had beset me. I felt shut in, helpless as a toad in the mouth of a fish and, strangely, I was not perturbed. I was eager almost to be swallowed so that I might forget about everything – myself included.

My indifference to tomorrow, about which Nai Soon was so hopeful, kept crowding me close as if eager to push me over the edge before today was finished. For me the symphony of escape that had harmonised my life had become, for the moment, inconsequential and out of time, for in me there was little left to stimulate it and to keep it alive. I had my life, it is true, but I had no more than that. I felt debilitated and purposeless, missing Terry and Little Flower to an extent I had not believed possible.

It would be relaxing to sleep for an indefinite period, waking only when it was time to go to sleep again. That was the metre of my life: I was just ticking over like a rusty motor, and there was no rhythm in me.

Nai Soon had been absent too long on the railway's business, and I had been too much alone. But now he was back offering me the tomorrow about which I had grown careless, and at his reiteration of an old promise, I could feel the spring coming back to oust winter from my blood.

I was a man again and I began to live.

'I know the hope of escaping has animated you and helped you through the dark places,' he continued, after a satisfying pull at the black cheroot that had taken the place of Hirohito's discarded cigarette. 'It was something for which to live – it and your friends. Now hope is all that remains, and sometimes I think for you it has lost its charm. That is a pity, Mick, for hope is a symphony running like a silent river through every man's life, and eventually deciding whether he will be great or small... It has brought us this far; must we abandon it because you refuse to believe in tomorrow? John would not wish it so, Mick...'

That, at least, was subtle if unnecessary. No, John would not be pleased with my inertia. But then, John was dead. His worries were all behind him while mine were all in front. An ineluctable truth that would bring a frown to the smooth brow of Nai Soon it I mentioned it.

I did not mention it. He was already puzzled at my apparent unresponsiveness, and I did not want to get deeper in his disproof. I could not have him believing that I was unappreciative of all he had done, and all he was preparing to do for me. Our regard for each other was too precious to allow any doubt to remain as to the ability of either to come up to scratch when the necessary arose. If he gave me time that was something I could soon put right for already I was feeling better.

Together we would yet laugh at the Nips as he promised and, I felt sure, in our laughter would be little rancour or malice, in spite of all that had gone before.

'You are disappointed in me, Nat,' I suggested, 'as you were disappointed in Hirohito's fags...'

'No, Mick. Not disappointed. Just slightly perplexed. A great deal of the fire seems to have gone out of you since you stopped working on the railway.'

'And why, do you think?'

'That you will have to tell me,' and he smiled warily. 'I should like to know.'

'Have you ever wondered why the British prisoners sing when it is raining and there is no apparent cause for joy?'

'Yes. I have wondered about that often. Why is it?'

'Frankly, I don't know, Nat. It is a racial characteristic – the racial characteristic, in fact, that makes us great. The blacker the outlook, the louder we sing...'

'But I don't see –'

'You shall. Instead of being gratified at finishing with the railway, when the railway could so easily have finished me, I am indifferent and self-sorrowful and inclined to lose sight of what is round the corner.'

'I think I understand,' he said, doubtfully. 'When it rains you sing, and when the sun shines you get the sulks. Is that it?'

I could have laughed at that; he was so much in earnest, grappling with a problem that had mystified the Nips from the day Singapore changed hands.

'You do not quite grasp the importance of our British complexities, Nat, but what you say is near enough to the truth, and I promise not to sulk anymore... Is everything ready for the celebration?'

'Yes, Mick. In two days the railway will be finished; then, perhaps, the Nippons will give everyone a much-needed rest. After that – well, it will be tomorrow, and we shall have much to do. But first, there is your leg. Until that is better we can do nothing, but the rest will do you good, Mick – you look tired...'

When he returned to the railway I sat watching a train struggling up against the current of the hills. Its blatant voice rang and screeched protestingly... It came nearer and its laboured panting ceased. The gradient was behind it and the rhythm of its wheels was a song that was new to the hills. Watching it, I had no feeling of pride, no sense of joy or satisfaction at its achievement. Neither was it concerned with me. I had helped make smooth the way beneath its feet, and it passed me by without recognition or salutation... It went on into the evening, emitting sparks from its gluttonous belly, and when it had pushed itself round the hill it was forgotten.

But the railway was still there and, though I knew it not, it was laughing at me...

Leaving the Nips googly-eyed, the dancing girls gave a final wiggle of their hips, sinuous and suggestive, and returned to Bangkok. With them went the Thai officials, well fed and self-satisfied, and with no wish to be reminded of what they had said and already forgotten.

Burma's back door was open. The railway was complete. The living were temporarily reprieved and the dead were dead – dead and in the main forgotten...

Nai Soon was to bring me a bottle of sake. Together we were going to drink a toast – not to the railway's triumph, but to what was to come after it.

Thinking of the bottle of sake brought back memories – memories in which were a frangipane tree that actually was something else and a laughing John Sommers who was now dust...

I went out to meet Nai Soon, but he never came. Instead, a Nip came hurrying, excited and incoherent.

'All men! All men! Speedo! Speedo…!'

Another derailment.

The railcar was in the siding. With the rescue party I scrambled on to it. There was nothing I could do, but I had to go for there was a voice tearing at me like a blast from a furnace and I was afraid – suffocated almost with dread. Where it had happened twice before, a train had come to grief. Two trucks had broken free to crash down the embankment in hopeless ruin. One, containing 40 gallon petrol drums, similar to those we had doctored with sand at Ashimoto's, was lying in a shattered heap from which came a noise I had heard before – the noise made by a man disembowelled by hot shrapnel.

Soon the noise ceased; then it started again as the petrol drums were rolled clear. A dirge of death from one of Nai Soon's coolies whose feet were crushed as though a steamroller had gone over them.

Quieter were two dead coolies and a Nip whose head was a smear between two petrol drums. Miraculously alive, and with a broken leg, another Nip came out of the wreckage.

Then there was Nai Soon.

It was inevitable, I suppose, and I ought to have known it would happen. We had expected too much from life and had been granted everything and nothing. We had been given an instinctive companionship that was sincere and unblemished by any of the petty complacencies that insinuate themselves between the East and the West. A precious, possession, Nai Soon's companionship had been loaned to me. Now it had been taken away and I had nothing left…

Even the bottle of sake had been denied me. It mocked me from the ruin of the truck. Lying in the blood and grime, it stared at me like an evil eye and I hated it…

Nai Soon was dead. Not devastatingly dead as were the Nip and the two coolies. There was blood on his lips and I wiped a finger across it and put it to my tongue. It tasted like rain – rain and tears without any salt in them…

*****

Crouched by the dying embers of the fire at the end of the hut, I gazed bleakly at the map flimsy I had taken from its hiding place in a piece of bamboo. Yesterday it had been a precious possession; now it was no more than a series of squiggles and quaint names – a shadowland into which now I would never penetrate – yet it was the only viable link I had with John, Nai Soon and the others.

To drop it on the hot ashes as Terry Reynolds had disposed of his final link with reality would be a negation of all we had hoped for, an abject admission of defeat. Nai Soon would not approve…

Making a slit in the piece of bamboo I used as an aid to walking, I folded the flimsy and slid it into its new hiding place.

If Providence willed that I returned to Nong Pladuk where, hopefully, my makeshift briefcase safeguarded in the Japs' search by Laverton's dirty postcard was still hanging on a nail beneath number one hut, the flimsy could rejoin the rest of my contraband.

In the case was an unfinished manuscript, 'Shoddy Heroes', dealing with the Malaya fiasco. It would be an accomplishment to return and finish it as a gesture of defiance to the Japs who had imposed a strict embargo on all writing material.

Thinking on that gave me a small twinge of excitement where before had been room only for despair.

Pulling an old rice sack about me, I stretched out by the embers and lay there waiting…

Standing above the night, the hills were holy temples. On them lay a hush of mellow agedness that had nothing virile or lusty about it. It was the hush of mourning, and it dressed the hills in the crêpe of sadness.

The jungle, too, seemed sad. On it was a serene beauty that lay light as foam on the crest of a wave. Hiding its heart and its thoughts from the world, it professed innocence, showing itself harmless and gentle as a little old lady, yet it was rapacious and savage, and it never slept.

There was too much mystery and too much sadness in the night, and the moon did not help…

In two hours it would be tomorrow, and there was no Nai Soon. He was up there in the temple of the night with John. They had each other and I had no one. Together they stood on the hillside near to the moon and waited…

Slowly, leaning on the bamboo pole, I went up to them, not knowing if I should come down again. But I had to go. There was nothing else I could do… Ascending, I looked back and fires blossomed on the edge of the jungle, showing the figures of men ethereal against the trees. Soon they would be on the way to Kanburi, and they were happy about that – happy and not much concerned for the lonely ones whom they were leaving behind.

I, too, was going to Kanburi, but I did not know whether to go or stay. It would be easier to stay, and more secure. I had to find out about that...

Thinking about it, I went closer to John and Nai Soon, realising that my life was standing at the cross-roads, hesitating, waiting for advice, and not being sure which way to take. As I went up the hill, I could feel it making up its mind to leave me: it was that easy. I put out my hand to pull it back and it stayed with me...

From the silence below, the railway screamed a mockery as a train came rumbling through, throwing sparks at the sky. As it passed the gleam from its fire stabbed spitefully at the hillside, then it was gone and I was alone again...

The night was peopled with thoughts that tugged at me as the river tugged at the jungle. I could see it, a streak of silver slashed across the face of my world – silver with holes in it, jungle flotsam being swept down to Kanburi as the survivors from the railway were being swept down.

At the others, the current of life plucked no more. They had found a quiet bayou and were content. Or were they? I did not know. It would be lonely for them when we had gone. For me, too, it would be lonely... Better to stay with friends I knew than to trust myself among strangers...

They were waiting for me, those friends – I could feel them about me in the silent night – waiting and holding themselves aloof, wanting to be sure.

I, too, wanted to be sure...

Etched by the moonlight, two graves showed themselves on the hillside. I went over, but there were no little crosses on them. They were just two graves and nobody cared...

That was a thought... Nobody cared...

A grave without a cross is like an empty tomb: in is there is not even a memory...

From a tree a shadow jumped. It came closer to sit washing its face with moonlight – a tree rate unconcerned with the silent ones peopling its domain. Watching, I saw it change, and in its place was that blithe spirit that had known my affection at Changi. Reducing the gap between uncertainty and indecision, it gave an assurance of continuity, where I had looked for nothing but extinction as an escape from a loneliness that was no longer oppressive.

I moved towards it, but it did not stay. From a branch it watched me, quizzical and uncertain. Where it had been was a vision of John, laughing as he had laughed at Fishooks jumping out of reach. I was grateful for that...

John's laughter was real – very real and friendly. It gave an added assurance and brought a new faith. The graves were no longer empty. Somebody cared...

I stayed with him for a while. And with Nai Soon...

The gossamer of dawn touched the fringe of the earth as I went down the hill.

The moon came with me and I was not alone...